OXFORD MEDICAL PUBLICATIONS

What is Clinical Psychology?

What is Clinical Psychology?

Third Edition

Edited by

John Marzillier
Consultant Clinical Psychologist

and

John Hall
Department of Clinical Psychology
Warneford Hospital, Oxford

UNIVERSITY PRESS

OXFORD
UNIVERSITY PRESS
Great Clarendon Street, Oxford OX2 6DP

Oxford New York
Athens Auckland Bangkok Bogota Buenos Aires Calcutta
Cape Town Chennai Dar es Salaam Delhi Florence Hong Kong Istanbul
Karachi Kuala Lumpur Madrid Melbourne Mexico City Mumbai
Nairobi Paris São Paolo Singapore Taipei Tokyo Toronto Warsaw
and associated companies in
Berlin Ibadan

Oxford is a trade mark of Oxford University Press

Published in the United States
by Oxford University Press, Inc., New York

© *John Marzillier and John Hall, 1999*

First edition published 1987
Second edition published 1992

All rights reserved. No part of this publication may be reproduced, stored in a retrieval system, or transmitted, in any form or by any means, without the prior permission in writing of Oxford University Press. Within the UK, exceptions are allowed in respect of any fair dealing for the purpose of research or private study, or criticism or review, as permitted under the Copyright, Designs and Patents Act, 1988, or in the case of reprographic reproduction in accordance with the terms of licences issued by the Copyright Licensing Agency. Enquiries concerning reproduction outside those terms and in other countries should be sent to the Rights Department, Oxford University Press, at the address above.

This book is sold subject to the condition that it shall not, by way of trade or otherwise, be lent, re-sold, hired out, or otherwise circulated without the publisher's prior consent in any form of binding or cover other than that in which it is published and without a similar condition including this condition being imposed on the subsequent purchaser.

A catalogue record for this book is available from the British Library

Library of Congress Cataloging in Publication Data
(Data available)

ISBN 0 19 262929 8 (Hbk)
ISBN 0 19 262928 X (Pbk)

Typeset by Hewer Text Limited, Edinburgh
Printed in Great Britain by
Bookcraft Ltd, Midsomer Norton, Avon

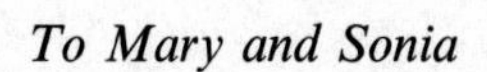

To Mary and Sonia

Preface to the third edition

Many people—friends, patients, professional colleagues—often ask us about our work as clinical psychologists. What exactly is a clinical psychologist? What do you do? How does your work differ from that of a psychiatrist or psychotherapist? It was partly to answer these questions that this book has been written.

We are aware that there are several 'good books' on clinical psychology, and a number of excellent ones. But they do not answer the questions we are asked, for two reasons. First, the vast majority are American. Although there are a number of parallels between the practice of clinical psychology in North America and practice in Europe and elsewhere, there are also significant differences. To take one important example: in Britain most clinical psychologists work in the National Health Service, and are essentially public employees working to meet the health needs of the community. In the United States, most clinical psychologists work in private practice and respond to market demands, which may be mediated by the priorities of health insurance companies. These differences affect how the clinical psychologist works, and what she or he does.

Second, most of the books on clinical psychology are relatively detailed expositions of theory and practice, often concentrating on a particular problem, or on a particular method of treatment. A reader needs to be prepared to take the time and trouble to read through them. We wanted a book that would both be more user-friendly, and above all to describe current practice, so the reader would know what clinical psychologists actually *do*.

The book is written as a number of chapters, describing the work of clinical psychologists in various settings and with different patient or user groups. This seems to be the most sensible division, as it closely accords with present practice, and many readers may have a particular interest in a patient group. There are clinical psychologists who work predominantly with children, others who work with older people, and others who work with people with physical disabilities, for example. We have invited a number of practitioners to provide accounts of their work. The primary attribute they all share is their clinical experience with the group of patients about whom they are writing, alongside their other knowledge and skills. There is inevitably some overlap, although we have minimized needless repetition, and in the final chapter we explore some common themes.

The book does not need to be read from beginning to end, although most readers will find it helpful to start with the first chapter. A glossary of key terms is included at the end of the book to explain the various technical terms used, although we have tried to keep these to a minimum. At the end of each chapter there is a short list of further reading on the material covered by each chapter: these have been chosen to be relatively accessible to the non-specialist reader.

The variety of settings and practice are significant, since they illustrate how much clinical psychology has developed over the thirty years or so that we have both been working as clinical psychologists. Indeed in each successive edition of the book we have had to include new chapters to reflect that growth. We both began our careers working in adult mental health settings, carrying out psychometric assessments on most referred patients, and using a very restricted range of mostly behavioural treatments on some of them. That was then the main role for clinical psychologists. Now the scope of the practice of our colleagues and ourselves has vastly broadened.

In preparing this third edition, we have been even more conscious of the rapid growth in the range of material included since the first edition ten years ago. Clinical psychology continues to be an exciting profession.

We are grateful to all the people who helped us to write this book, especially present and past chapter authors, those who have commented on chapter drafts, and those who have written to us with helpful comments.

Oxford J.S.M.
May 1998 J.N.H.

Contents

Contributors

Professor Ron Blackburn
Professor of Clinical and Forensic Psychological Studies, Department of Clinical Psychology, University of Liverpool, Brownlow Hill, Liverpool

J. F. Brown
Clinical Psychologist, Learning Disabilities Directorate, North Staffordshire Combined Healthcare NHS Trust, Stallington Hall, Stoke-on-Trent

Katherine Carpenter
Consultant Clinical Neuropsychologist, Russell Cairns Unit, Department of Neurological Surgery, The Radcliffe Infirmary, Oxford

Helen Combes
Assistant Psychologist, Learning Disabilities Directorate, North Staffordshire Combined Healthcare NHS Trust, Stallington Hall, Stoke-on-Trent

Professor Chris Cullen
Professor of Psychology of Learning Disabilities, Learning Disabilities Directorate, North Staffordshire Combined Healthcare NHS Trust and Keele University, Stallington Hall, Stoke-on-Trent

Professor Dorothy Fielding
Head of Psychological Services, Department of Clinical and Health Psychology, St James University Hospital, Leeds

Dr Jeff Garland
Consultant Clinical Psychologist, Fulbrook Centre, Churchill Hospital, Oxford

Dr John Hall
Professional Adviser in Clinical Psychology and Honorary Senior Clinical Lecturer in Clinical Psychology, Warneford Hospital, Oxford

Steve Hendy
Clinical Psychologist, Learning Disabilities Directorate, North Staffordshire Combined Healthcare NHS Trust, Stallington Hall, Stoke-on-Trent

Professor Ray Hodgson
Director, Cardiff Addictions Research Unit, Centre for Applied and Public Health Medicine, University of Wales College of Medicine, Lansdowne Hospital, Cardiff

Dr Paul Kennedy
Consultant Clinical Psychologist, National Spinal Injuries Centre, Stoke Mandeville and Senior Academic Tutor, Oxford Regional Training Course in Clinical Psychology, Warneford Hospital, Oxford

Dr Gary Latchford
Consultant Clinical Psychologist, Department of Clinical and Health Psychology, St James University Hospital, Leeds

Dr John Marzillier
Clinical Psychologist and Psychotherapist; formerly Course Director, Oxford Regional Training Course in Clinical Psychology, Warneford Hospital, Oxford

Dr James McGuire
Senior Lecturer in Clinical Psychology, Department of Clinical Psychology, University of Liverpool, Brownlow Hill, Liverpool

Dr Irene Sclare
Consultant Clinical Psychologist, The Bloomfield Centre, Guys Hospital, London

Dr Andy Tyerman
Consultant Clinical Psychologist, Community Head Injury Service, Bedgrove Health Centre, Aylesbury

1

What is clinical psychology?

John Hall and John Marzillier

Clinical psychologists are health-care professionals who work in the fields of mental and physical health. Among their main activities are: (a) *psychological assessment,* that is the use of psychological methods and principles to gain better understanding of psychological attributes and problems. The assessment of cognitive function (memory, intelligence, spatial abilities) following head injury, is one well-established example of psychological assessment. (b) *Psychological treatment,* that is the use of psychological procedures and principles to help others to bring about change. There are many forms of psychological treatment, ranging from brief, practical procedures for overcoming specific fears to lengthy and complex treatments such as some forms of psychoanalysis. (c) *Psychological evaluation,* that is the use of psychological principles to evaluate the effectiveness of treatments or other forms of intervention. Clinical psychologists have been particularly involved in developing methods of evaluating psychotherapies and to a lesser extent physical forms of therapy.

Although these are the main activities of clinical psychologists, there are also others. Training of other professional staff, involvement in administration and advice, involvement in health service policies, and collaborative research are all activities that some clinical psychologists engage in as part of their work. This diversity is well illustrated in the subsequent chapters of this book.

WHAT IS PSYCHOLOGY?

The term psychology is derived from two Greek words: *psyche,* which means 'spirit' or 'mind', and *logos,* which means 'study'. 'The study of the mind' is therefore the literal, though not now the customary, meaning of psychology. Up to the end of the nineteenth century, psychology did not exist as a separate academic discipline but was part of philosophy. Philosophers such as Locke, Descartes, Hume, and

Berkeley addressed themselves to understanding mental processes via philosophical discourse and analysis. Descartes' famous dictum *Cogito, ergo sum* ('I think, therefore I am'), Locke's conception of the mind as a *tabula rasa* (blank slate), and Hume's careful elucidation of the principles of causation via mental association are all examples of a philosophical approach to understanding human behaviour. Psychology departed from philosophy in two fundamental ways. The first was the development of a *scientific* approach rather than a philosophical one. In 1879, Wilhelm Wundt opened the first psychological laboratory in Leipzig, Germany. There began a period of experimental study in which Wundt and his students sought to gain a scientific understanding of conscious experience by a systematic and carefully documented examination of their experiences and sensations when specific stimuli were presented, such as certain colours and sounds. This method of inquiry was known as introspectionism.

Although introspectionism proved a short-lived approach in psychology, mainly because of its reliance on idiosyncratic, personal accounts of experience, it embodied the experimental scientific tradition that has predominated in contemporary twentieth-century psychology.

The second departure of psychology from philosophy came in the extension of the subject matter beyond mental processes. In 1913, J.B. Watson, an American psychologist, had a profound effect on twentieth-century psychology with his call for psychology to be concerned not with internal mental processes, which he regarded as unverifiable and hence unscientific, but with observable behaviour. Behaviourism became the dominant creed of early twentieth-century psychology. Strongly emphasized was the need to place the science of psychology firmly on the bedrock of observed behaviour; experimental studies were conducted upon the behaviour of pigeons, rats, and other animals in the laboratory setting. B.F. Skinner pioneered the use of the famous Skinner box, in which rats pressed levers or pigeons pecked discs in response to various conditions of reward and punishment. These and many other laboratory experiments upon animal behaviour provided the basic psychology of conditioning and learning.

Psychology, therefore, had in the twentieth century moved from being a section of philosophy to becoming a scientific discipline in its own right. It had ceased to be the reasoned study of mental processes and become the experimental analysis of behaviour, animal and human. By this change psychology established links with other sciences such as biology, physiology, and biochemistry. The interrelationship between psychology and these sciences could now be studied by examining the link between observed behaviour on the one hand and its biological basis on the other as, for example, in the relationship between brain waves and sleeping, or cardiovascular systems and emotions such as anxiety. Modern psychology is still rooted in this behavioural–biological tradition.

Academic psychology at the end of the twentieth century is no longer so strongly wedded to a behavioural–biological tradition. Cognitive psychology—the study of basic psychological processes such as perception, learning, memory, language, thought, and emotion—has become the dominant area of interest. Psychological study seeks to describe and understand these processes—for example how memory processes work or in what ways people construct and organize their perceived world. The experimental method remains an important part of the psychological approach, although it is not the only method of inquiry. There has been a resurgence of interest in qualitative methods of inquiry which look closely at naturally occurring processes, often within a narrative paradigm. Developmental and social aspects of human behaviour are also vital features of modern psychology. Understanding human behaviour necessitates the study of its development and change from early infancy to old age. Developmental psychologists study, amongst many things, how children acquire and use language, the effects of early attachment and separation from parents, the processes and functions of play, and the effect of ageing on basic processes such as memory and thinking. Social psychologists study behaviour in its social context, which can be done experimentally in artificially created social encounters in the laboratory or naturally by observation and analysis of the individual in society. Finally, psychology merges into other academic disciplines, biological sciences (such as biology and physiology) on the one hand, and social sciences (such as sociology and anthropology) on the other.

In the example below the psychological approach is illustrated in the example of *pain,* which has an obvious biological and physiological basis in its relationship to tissue damage and the transmission of pain signals in certain nerve fibres to the brain. But it is not enough to describe pain in biological terms. Psychological factors play a significant part in our experience and expression of pain. The contribution that psychology has made in furthering our understanding of pain has led to one of the most influential theories of how pain is processed, the 'gate control' theory of Melzack and Wall (1988). Further, it has led to the development of new and promising treatments for chronic pain as well as effective methods of preparing individuals for necessary painful experiences such as surgery. It is the combination of basic research and theory and applied methods of assessment and treatment that characterizes the branch of psychology that is the subject of this book, clinical psychology.

THE PSYCHOLOGY OF PAIN

As we can all testify, pain is a response to injury or hurt. The more we are hurt the more likely we are to experience pain. Despite its unpleasantness, pain has obvious survival value; it has the vital function of protecting us from serious injury. Thus a child's first contact with a hot stove will cause distress and pain but will rapidly lead to adaptive learning. Pain also sets limits on activity when a part of the body is injured. We learn to rest damaged ankles and knees rather than to continue to exercise them and injure them more.

Yet there are some intriguing facts about pain that cannot be explained solely in biological terms. Severe tissue damage, such as that produced by a deep wound, will in some people not produce any immediate pain despite the severity of the wound. Chronic and unremitting pain can occur in certain people long after the initial injuries have healed, the most dramatic example of which is 'phantom limb pain', pain localized in the place of an amputated arm or leg. The capacity for some people to undergo extremely painful experiences, such as major surgery, while hypnotized and not to report or show any signs of pain has been well documented. The psychology of pain is concerned with understanding and influencing the psychological aspects of the experience of pain.

Psychological experimentation

Psychologists have contributed to our knowledge of pain in several ways. Firstly, by means of scientific experimentation they have clearly shown how psychological factors can affect when people will report pain (their pain threshold) and how much pain they will bear (their pain tolerance). The 'cold pressor test' is a laboratory test involving the immersion of a hand in ice-cold water. The use of this test has shown, for example, that people can learn to tolerate pain for longer periods of time by adopting deliberate strategies such as distraction. Other experimental studies have shown that if people believe they have control over the amount of painful stimulation they are receiving (for example painful electric shock), they can tolerate more pain (even if their perception of control is illusory).

Secondly, reliable measurements of the experience of pain have been developed. One of the best developed is the McGill–Melzack questionnaire (see Fig. 1.1), which presents a series of adjectives to describe the different sensations of pain experience. The adjectives can be categorized into three groups, namely those describing the sensory qualities of experience, those describing the affective qualities (for example tension, fear), and those that evaluate the intensity of the total pain experience. Studies of different types of pain using this questionnaire have indicated characteristic adjectives for different syndromes. For example toothache tends to be described as throbbing, boring, and sharp, whereas menstrual pain is described as cramping and aching. Not only is a questionnaire such as this useful in gaining a better description of what painful experience consists of, it also helps in classifying different sorts of pain.

Thirdly, theoretical models of pain experience have been proposed, the best known of which is the 'gate control' theory. The theory proposes the existence of a neural mechanism, located in the dorsal horns of the spinal cord, which acts like a gate, modulating the flow of nerve impulses from peripheral fibres to the central nervous system. The 'gate' is also influenced by descending influences from the brain, representing the influence on pain of such psychological factors as attention, memory, and emotional states.

Finally, psychologists have developed a variety of treatment strategies for acute and chronic pain. Relaxation, distraction, hypnosis, biofeedback, and planned behavioural programmes have shown promise in helping people cope more effectively with painful experiences.

WHAT IS A CLINICAL PSYCHOLOGIST?

One of the commonest questions put to psychologists both by patients and professional staff is 'What is a clinical psychologist?' or 'In what way is a clinical psychologist different from a psychiatrist, a psychotherapist, or a social worker?'. In Table 1.1 we have listed some of the health-care professionals whose work may in some way overlap with or touch upon that of a clinical psychologist as they relate to each other in Britain.

The main differences between clinical psychologists and other

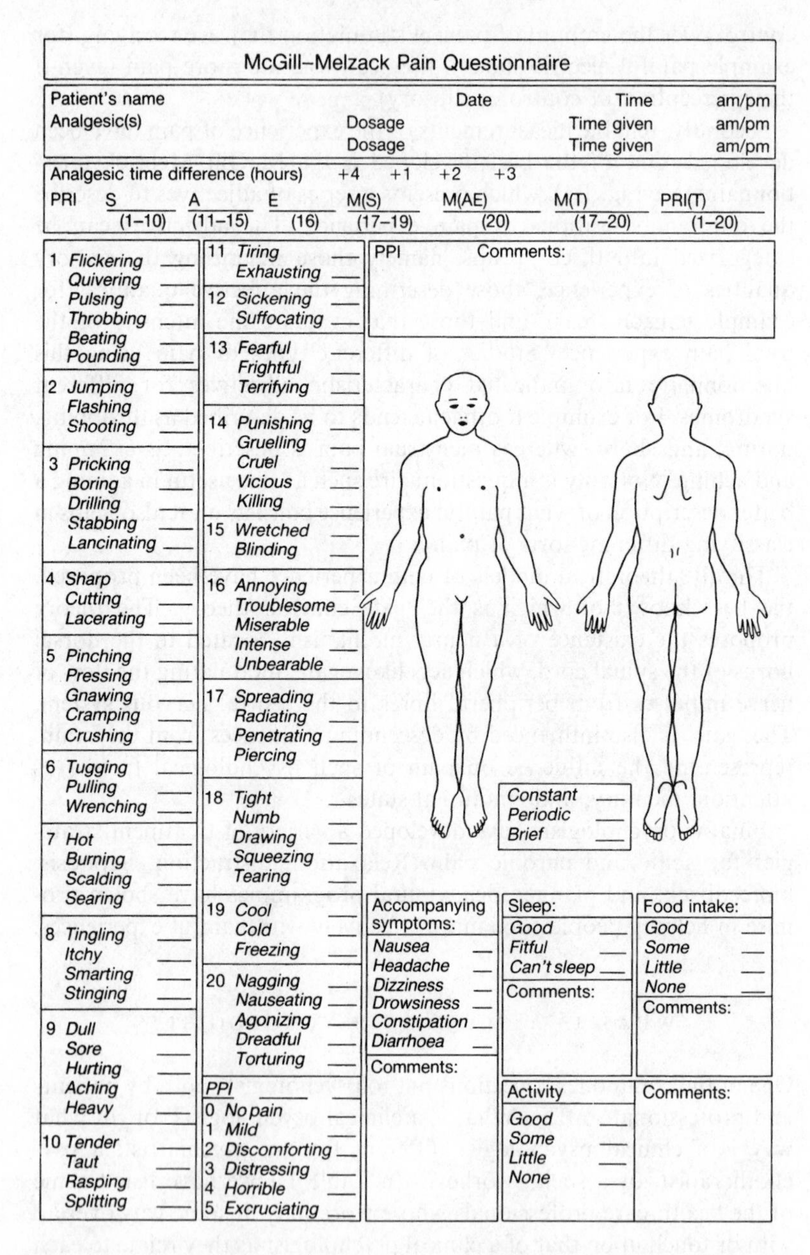

McGill–Melzack Pain Questionnaire

Patient's name Date Time am/pm
Analgesic(s) Dosage Time given am/pm
Dosage Time given am/pm

Analgesic time difference (hours) +4 +1 +2 +3
PRI S (1–10) A (11–15) E (16) M(S) (17–19) M(AE) (20) M(T) (17–20) PRI(T) (1–20)

1 *Flickering*
Quivering
Pulsing
Throbbing
Beating
Pounding

2 *Jumping*
Flashing
Shooting

3 *Pricking*
Boring
Drilling
Stabbing
Lancinating

4 *Sharp*
Cutting
Lacerating

5 *Pinching*
Pressing
Gnawing
Cramping
Crushing

6 *Tugging*
Pulling
Wrenching

7 *Hot*
Burning
Scalding
Searing

8 *Tingling*
Itchy
Smarting
Stinging

9 *Dull*
Sore
Hurting
Aching
Heavy

10 *Tender*
Taut
Rasping
Splitting

11 *Tiring*
Exhausting

12 *Sickening*
Suffocating

13 *Fearful*
Frightful
Terrifying

14 *Punishing*
Gruelling
Cruel
Vicious
Killing

15 *Wretched*
Blinding

16 *Annoying*
Troublesome
Miserable
Intense
Unbearable

17 *Spreading*
Radiating
Penetrating
Piercing

18 *Tight*
Numb
Drawing
Squeezing
Tearing

19 *Cool*
Cold
Freezing

20 *Nagging*
Nauseating
Agonizing
Dreadful
Torturing

PPI
0 *No pain*
1 *Mild*
2 *Discomforting*
3 *Distressing*
4 *Horrible*
5 *Excruciating*

PPI Comments:

Constant
Periodic
Brief

Accompanying symptoms:
Nausea
Headache
Dizziness
Drowsiness
Constipation
Diarrhoea
Comments:

Sleep:
Good
Fitful
Can't sleep
Comments:

Food intake:
Good
Some
Little
None
Comments:

Activity
Good
Some
Little
None
Comments:

Fig. 1.1 The McGill–Melzack pain questionnaire. (Reprinted, with permission, from Melzack and Wall 1988.)

Table 1.1 Training and work of health-care professionals

Profession	Training	Type of work
Clinical psychologist	First degree in psychology plus 3 years postgraduate training to doctoral level	Psychological assessment and treatment Specialist in cognitive–behavioural therapy Research and evaluation
Psychiatrist	First degree in medicine plus 3 years postgraduate specialization in psychiatry	Psychiatric diagnosis, pharmacological and physical forms of treatment Research Statutory duties e.g. sectioning
Social worker	2-year professional training, which may follow a first degree in sociology, social administration	Social casework, understanding and provision of social welfare benefits, housing etc. Acting as a care manager or key worker
Nurse	3-year professional training often to degree level	Direct nursing care of patients, both in hospital and community settings, including physical care and social support
Occupational therapist	3-year professional training to degree level	Provision of varied range of day activities, emphasizing rehabilitation and creative activities
Psychotherapist	Variety of specialist courses of varying lengths from few months to several years	Psychotherapy—type will depend on training and experience
Counsellor	1 to 2-year full-time courses Variety of part-time course	Psychotherapy/counselling for less disturbed individuals Specialist forms e.g. careers

professionals occur (a) in training and (b) in the formal structure of their work. Psychiatrists, for example, receive their initial training in general medicine, which provides a solid basis of biological, anatomical, and physiological knowledge of human functioning. By virtue of this training they have a particular expertise in physical and pharmacological treatments. Of all the professionals listed in Table 1.1, psychiatrists are the only ones with the right to practise medicine, that is prescribe psychotropic drugs or carry out surgical or physical treatments such as ECT. This right is protected in most countries by formal statute or registration.

Clinical psychology training involves specialized knowledge of psychological functioning and psychological methods, which provides particular expertise in carrying out psychological assessments such as psychometric tests, formulating problems psychologically, psychological treatments, and psychological methods of research and evaluation. In some countries the right to practise psychology is embodied into statute, usually by registering the title of 'psychologist'. In 1991, the implementation of Directive 89/48/EEC, under article 27 of the Treaty of Rome, requires all member states of the European Community to harmonize their training standards, to permit free movement of professions within the Community. This process of harmonization will undoubtedly lead to greater uniformity of practice between member states and probably to greater similarities in the protection of titles such as 'psychologist'.

The confusion between clinical psychologists and other professions arises, in part, because of a real overlap between their respective activities. This is most evident in the case of psychotherapeutic skills, which are in some form part of the activities of all the professions listed in Table 1.1. In their basic training, clinical psychologists specialize in particular types of psychotherapy, notably behavioural and cognitive therapies (see Chapter 2 for a description of these approaches). Following qualification, some clinical psychologists go on to train in other forms of therapy such as psychoanalysis or family therapy. Postqualification training is also undertaken by a variety of professionals and so a family therapist, for example, could be a psychologist, social worker, nurse, psychiatrist, or occasionally a specialist without a professional background! To the unsuspecting public this can be confusing. In the United Kingdom, there are two bodies—the United Kingdom Council for Psychotherapy and the British Confederation of Psychotherapists—which publish registers of accredited psychotherapists. This can help employers and patients to judge whether a person is appropriately qualified. The British Psychological Society publishes a list of Chartered Psychologists and is in the process of developing a register of those psychologists who have specialist psychotherapeutic skills. Useful as this information is, it can be difficult to know exactly what skills a particular health-care professional has.

Towards a definition

Clinical psychologists tend to define their profession in terms of (a) the basic science of psychology and (b) its application to the understanding and resolution of human problems. The clinical psychologist is first and foremost an 'applied scientist' or 'scientist-practitioner' who seeks to use scientific knowledge to a beneficial end. Thus, in practising psychotherapy, clinical psychologists are concerned to base their practices on what is scientifically known about problems such as depression, anxiety, schizophrenia, etc. and to use psychological principles that have been well established in experimental studies. They are also particularly concerned to develop and use only those psychological treatment methods that either have been shown to be effective or are in the process of validation. Clinical psychologists are also practitioners who, in common with other health-care professionals, provide services to people, organizations, and communities as part of an established health-care system. Their professional status entails ethical responsibilities which are enshrined in a Code of Conduct that governs the behaviour of members of the profession. In summary, clinical psychologists are *psychologist-practitioners* applying *scientific knowledge and principles* in a *professional role* to the *alleviation of human suffering* and the *improvement of the quality of life*.

An example of clinical psychology in practice

Karen is a 32-year-old computer scientist who 8 months ago was involved in a road accident. She was driving home from work one evening when a car coming in the opposite direction veered out of control and smashed straight into her. She suffered a fracture of the right leg, multiple bruises, and injuries to her mouth and face where she hit the steering wheel of her car. For a few seconds she lost consciousness. The driver of the other vehicle was killed outright. She was taken by ambulance to the emergency department of the nearest hospital where she was assessed and admitted. Because she had lost consciousness she was not given a general anaesthetic and her recollection of her admission to hospital, although hazy, was of considerable anxiety and pain. In the subsequent weeks she underwent two operations on her leg, had considerable dental work on damaged teeth, and began a course of remedial physiotherapy. She was off work for 3 months. During this time she was referred to the local neurology department where, as part of her assessment, she was seen by a clinical neuropsychologist. The neuropsychologist gave Karen a variety of tests of cognitive abilities including tests of memory, concentration, spatial abilities, new word learning, reading, and intelligence. She also asked Karen to fill in the Impact of Events Scale, a self-report questionnaire which assesses the degree of post-traumatic stress, and two measures of general mood. Although Karen showed some impairment of memory and concentration on the formal tests, these were not marked enough to suggest that she had sustained any damage to her brain as a result of the accident; they were more likely to be the psychological consequences of the trauma. On the self-report measures she showed severe levels of both anxiety and depression; on the Impact of Events Scale she was significantly disturbed by intrusive memories of the accident with an overall score that was indicative of post-traumatic stress disorder (PTSD). She was referred on to the clinical psychologists in the adult mental health department for treatment of the psychological consequences of the accident.

Research has shown that survivors of road accidents can suffer significant and enduring psychiatric and psychological disorders. About 20 per cent of all survivors suffer an acute stress reaction in the immediate aftermath of the accident which includes symptoms of agitation, disturbed mood, intrusive memories of the accident, emotional numbing, and occasionally denial of any emotional problems. These symptoms persist for up to 3 months after the accident. In some people, psychological problems persist for longer periods. About 20 to 30 per cent of road accident survivors show marked levels of phobic anxiety about travelling, particularly driving or being driven. About 10 per cent of survivors of major accidents are sufficiently disturbed to be diagnosed as suffering from PTSD. Other common problems that follow road accidents are depression, relationship problems, anger, and excess alcohol consumption (Mayou 1997).

When Karen was seen 8 months after the accident, she showed characteristic signs of PTSD. These included disturbed sleep with nightmares of the accident, daily intrusive recollections of both the accident and hospital treatment, occasional vivid and disturbing flashbacks, a heightened general state of arousal, avoidance of things that might remind her of the accident such as TV programmes showing car crashes, and a general state of negativity about herself and her future. Because she had to drive to work, she had resumed driving, but found the journeys exhausting; she often became extremely angry at way others drove and on several occasions had to stop the car because she was so agitated and upset. Her relationship with her partner had worsened—she admitted that she was often irritable and intolerant. She was also underperforming at work, finding it difficult to concentrate, and was easily brought to tears by trivial problems.

The clinical psychologist proposed that Karen undertake a course of therapy for her PTSD. Herman (1992) has outlined a three-stage process of treatment for trauma victims. The first stage entails building a relationship of trust in which the person feels safe to deal with the legacy of the trauma. The second stage entails an active process of remembering and retelling of the story of the trauma. This is sometimes called 'reliving' or 'exposure'. In the safety of therapy and with the support of the therapist Karen recounted the events and experiences surrounding the trauma including the periods of hospitalization. While at times she became very distressed, her therapist encouraged her to continue with the story and not to avoid the expression of feelings. The retelling of the story was taped and Karen was encouraged to listen to the tape in between sessions. After some weeks of therapy, it became easier for Karen to recount the story and her symptoms of PTSD had significantly lessened. The third and final stage is one of reconnecting with her life and looking to the future. Practical issues such as her difficulties at work were discussed. She and her partner had some joint sessions with the therapist which focused on the difficulties they had been experiencing in their relationship. Eventually Karen learned to put the car accident in perspective. While acknowledging that it had resulted in significant changes for herself and others around her, she felt she could now move on and in a sense reclaim her normal life.

The development of clinical psychology

Clinical psychology emerged as a recognizable profession at different times in different countries. In Britain, clinical psychology was not formally recognized until after the Second World War and it then took until 1966 before a Division of Clinical Psychology was formed in the British Psychological Society. The British Psychological Society (BPS) is the main professional and academic body for all psychologists in the Britain. Most other developed countries have a similar body, such as the American Psychological Association (APA) in the United States and the Berufsverband Deutscher Psychologen in Germany. In the United States and the United Kingdom, a significant impetus to the development of clinical psychology came from the two world wars. The need to recruit and select suitably qualified service personnel led to the development and use of psychological tests and other assessments. Psychologists were confronted with real-life problems and were thereby required to apply their knowledge and skills. In the United States, the psychological trauma caused by battle and injury resulted in psychologists becoming involved in treatment as well as assessment, and the wartime emergency hospitals in Britain became interested in similar problems.

The formation of the National Health Service in 1948 is an important landmark in the development of clinical psychology in Britain. The few clinical psychologists then working in hospitals, mainly in London, were brought under the NHS umbrella; the vast majority working in psychiatric hospitals. In the United States, clinical psychologists found fertile ground in the Veterans Administration Hospitals that were formed after the end of the Second World War.

The role for clinical psychologists in Britain from 1948 until the early 1960s was predominantly that of a laboratory scientist, carrying out psychometric and other types of tests. There was little direct therapeutic practice. The evolution of *behaviour therapy*—methods of treatment founded upon psychological principles and procedures—gave clinical psychology the entrée into therapy. By the end of the 1960s, clinical psychologists had established themselves as clinical practitioners rather than laboratory scientists and had pioneered many successful new psychological treatments.

In Britain, the profession grew rapidly in proportional terms through the 1970s and 1980s, to become an independent profession with therapeutic functions and skills. A government report in 1977 encouraged the formation of larger departments of clinical psychology, rather than having one or two psychologists based in individual hospitals. Since then, clinical psychologists have contributed to a growing range of clinical services outside the traditional areas of mental health and learning difficulties, such as the care of older people, substance abuse, and work with HIV/AIDS. During the 1980s and 1990s, the demand for clinical psychologists in Britain outstripped the supply of newly qualified clinical psychologists, a position that still exists today. In 1988, the British government commissioned a special review of the function of clinical psychologists, leading in 1990 to the publication of two significant reports, the MAS review, and the MPAG report. Taken together, these reports signal a way ahead via a consultancy model, involving clinical psychologists in working with others to enhance and support their psychological knowledge and skills (see Chapter 13).

Elsewhere in Europe, similar developments have taken place. In most Northern European countries, clinical psychology is both the largest field of specialization of psychology students—80 per cent in Germany—and the largest area of professional psychological practice, for example over 60 per cent in the Nordic countries. The Netherlands are training too many clinical psychologists for their own needs, and a number of Dutch psychologists have come to work in Britain. In the United States too, PhDs in the health-service provider subfields of clinical, counselling, and school psychology now constitute 53 per cent of all new doctorates in psychology.

TRAINING AND QUALIFICATIONS

Professional training in clinical psychology falls into two stages. The first stage consists of the basic science, that is the academic study of psychology in the form of an undergraduate degree. In many countries, this is a 3- or 4-year course of study resulting in the award of a Bachelor of Science (BSc) or a Bachelor of Arts (BA) degree. The second stage consists of professional training in clinical psychology. The first degree is not a vocational or professional training in itself, although it may include a number of vocational courses or specialties. Training in clinical psychology varies from country to country. In some countries, such as the Netherlands, Norway, and Germany, clinical training is not separated from the first degree in psychology but embedded within it; students specialize in the subject after the initial 2 or 3 years of introductory psychology. This results in a greater number of clinical psychologists being trained than in countries which require a post-graduate training such as the United Kingdom and the United States.

Generally, clinical psychology training involves combining academic knowledge with practical experience in the form of supervised clinical work in a variety of health-care settings. In some countries, the United States in particular, the academic programme is separate from and precedes the clinical one. Students spend the first 2 to 3 years in full-time, post-graduate study with only occasional short *practicums*, that is a few weeks experience in a hospital or similar setting. Once they have completed the academic programme they move on to full-time *internships* lasting 1 year. In other countries such as the United Kingdom, academic and practical training is integrated from the start. Students spend 2 days per week in lectures, seminars, and personal study and 3 days a week on placement over a period of 3 years. Each method has advantages and disadvantages. The separation of academic and clinical training allows students to devote their whole time to the different forms of learning but also results in an artificial division between theory and practice. Integrated training is a good exemplar of the applied scientific approach but is very demanding of the student.

Another important area of variation is the range of clinical experience required during professional training. In the United States, where practice is dominated by private practice, a student may elect to gain a restricted range of experience in, say, clinical neuropsychology alone. In Europe, where employment by a publicly funded agency is more common, more emphasis is given to gaining experience with a range of client groups and settings.

There is thus considerable variation in the amount and content of clinical psychology training from country to country. This has meant that, as with other professions, clinical psychologists who wish to practise in countries other than those in which they received training need to obtain the relevant qualifications for the country in which they wish to practise. In the United States and Canada, this usually entails formal examinations for the licence to practise as a psychologist. In Britain, there are procedures whereby foreign clinical psychologists may take the British Psychological Society's Diploma in Clinical Psychology or, depending upon the individual case, receive exemption from parts of it.

Professional training in Britain

Until the mid 1990s, post-graduate training in clinical psychology in the United Kingdom varied in length (2 or 3 years) and in qualification offered (MSc, MPhil, Diploma, or Doctorate). However, from 1995 this changed. All the training courses now entail 3 years post-graduate study and all lead to the award of a Doctorate in Clinical Psychology although the exact title varies. Clinical psychology graduates are eligible for Chartered Psychologist status within the British Psychological Society and to apply for posts within the National Health Service.

All training courses combine further academic study of clinical psychology, supervised experience and training in clinical work, and training in applied research. In Table 1.2 the curriculum of one doctorate course is illustrated.

Table 1.2 Academic curriculum for Oxford doctorate course in clinical psychology

Year 1	Term I	Cognitive–behavioural therapy for adult mental health problems Introduction to race, culture, and gender Introduction to lifespan Research in clinical settings 1 Professional issues course 1
	Term II	Cognitive–behavioural therapy (contd—5 weeks) Ethical issues seminars Introduction to systems (5 weeks) Psychodynamic psychotherapy (5 weeks) Research in clinical settings 1 (contd—5 weeks)
	Term III	Working with children 1 Working with people with learning disabilities 1 Clinical seminars
Year 2	Term I	Clinical seminars Research in clinical settings 2 Working with children 2 Working with people with learning disabilities 2 Professional issues course 2 Bereavement course
	Term II	Clinical seminars Health psychology Professional issues course 2 (contd)
	Term III	Clinical seminars Working with older adults Clinical neuropsychology
Year 3	Term I	Research seminars Addictions Psychology and the law
	Term II	Clinical seminars Group work skills Evidence based interventions
	Term III	Research study time

Professional training is achieved through a combination of supervised clinical work on placements in hospitals, clinics, or departments and clinical skills training by means of workshops and courses. The British Psychological Society has specified that all trainees must have supervised experience of adult psychiatric patients (both chronic and acute), adults and children with learning disabilities, children and adolescents with psychological problems, older people, and at least one specialist group (for example neuropsychology or delinquency). Placements vary from 3 to 6 months in duration and in most courses academic study is concurrent with clinical practice. In addition to academic study and clinical training, trainees are required to carry out two or more applied research projects, one of which is written up and examined in the form of a major doctoral dissertation. The acquisition of research skills is seen as a significant feature of clinical psychology training. Assessment of trainees is by a combination of academic course work, written examinations, ratings of clinical performance on placements, case reports of clinical work, and formal examination of the research dissertation.

A qualified clinical psychologist is expected to have acquired the necessary academic knowledge and professional skills to work as a clinical psychologist in the National Health Service, a position for which the award of the Doctorate makes him or her eligible. However, it is recognized that further specialized experience and training is a necessary post-qualification requirement, particularly if a position entails working with a specialized population (for example the neuropsychologically impaired) or acquiring specialized skills (for example family therapy, psychosexual counselling). While the BPS does not approve post-qualification courses, they are few and far between and as yet there is no formal structure for such training; but the need for such training and experience has been recognized.

WHAT DO CLINICAL PSYCHOLOGISTS DO?

Clinical psychologists are asked to assess and intervene in a wide range of problems where they are believed to have special expertise. The range of problems where psychologists probably have a distinctive and prime contribution cover psychological conditions such as phobias, obsessional and compulsive disorders, problems of disturbed and disruptive behaviour, deficits in everyday skills such as dressing and communicating with other people, discrepancies between ability and attainment, and disorders of mental processes such as memory. In all these cases the psychologist is trying to understand or change an essentially psychological problem of an individual, family, or group.

Secondly, a psychologist may be asked to help with the secondary consequences of a medical or physical problem, such as the sexual difficulties which may follow a spinal injury, when either a medical or other approach is appropriate for the primary problem. For some people, little may be possible for the primary problem, but the individual still has a major and perhaps progressive handicap, as with some of the problems of old age.

Thirdly, a psychologist may be involved with an issue which does not primarily relate to identified patients, but affects the health-care system as a whole. For example many of the women who may potentially benefit most from advice on caring for their new-born baby find it difficult to understand some of the relatively sophisticated literature put out both by commercial firms and Government agencies. How can health literature be designed to maximize recall of its contents and application of the recommended procedures? Many hospital staff may have to deal with extremely aggressive people from time to time, even though most of the time their work is routine and even dull. How can non-clinical staff, such as porters and secretaries, be given some guidance or training in how to cope with this sort of infrequent event? In this third category of task, the psychologist is understanding and trying to change aspects of the health-care system itself, or the way in which care is delivered, independent of the needs of individual patients.

A psychologist may respond to this array of problems in a number of ways. Firstly, by attempting to understand, clarify, and define the problem as much as possible, perhaps making use of standardized psychological measures. Secondly, by intervening in the problem, with the specific intention of changing the problem in some specified ways. Thirdly, by evaluating what has been done to change the problem—has it worked? Most of what clinical psychologists do is covered by these three categories of assessment, intervention, and evaluation. There are a number of other functions a psychologist may carry out; one of these major functions is to train or supervise others in the understanding and use of psychological methods, and this is covered in particular in Chapter 13, concerning work with other professions.

Assessing and understanding people

Probably one of the most common stereotypes of the psychologist is as 'tester'. Ever since Binet became interested in the attainments of

Parisian schoolchildren before the First World War, formal psychometric testing of general ability, specific abilities, and of educational and occupational attainments has been viewed as one of the central professional tasks of a psychologist. Yet this attempt to assess the *maximum* performance of individuals, on apparently rather artificial tasks, is only one aspect of the modern psychologist's contribution to assessment.

Testing is an important type of assessment. Educational tests for children have come to be widely used both to see if there are any discrepancies between ability and educational attainment, and to predict the probable level of attainment of a child. Most ability or attainments tests for children and adults consist of a number of subtests, with all items carefully selected, arranged in order of successively greater difficulty, and with information painstakingly obtained on many hundreds of subjects for comparison. The word test can also properly be used to describe the wide range of neuropsychological or cognitive assessment measures, which similarly use a series of carefully selected and scaled items to test specific cognitive functions, such as verbal and visual memory, and symbol recognition.

Another important group of assessment procedures are those known as personality tests, not so widely used clinically as before, which fall into two main subgroups. The first subgroup are the 'objective' personality measures, which take the form of questionnaires completed by the patient. These questionnaires may contain up to several hundred items covering different areas of functioning, such as getting on with other people or the tendency to dominate or be submissive to others. Some of the major work on these questionnaires has been done by personality theorists such as Cattell and Eysenck, who have thus given their names to some personality inventories. The Myers–Briggs Type Indicator is another example, widely used in organizational settings. Some other related measures are not strictly personality tests, but give a clearer idea of how an individual views himself. The personality theory of George Kelly, for example, has given rise to the 'Repertory Grid', a method of exploring an individual's view of his own world that can be represented graphically. The second subgroup of personality measures are the 'projective' techniques. These all rest on the assumption that when an individual makes a response to a stimulus that is essentially ambiguous or unstructured, the detail and structure elicited tell us something about the individual's inner structure, or personality. These tests have continued to have a place in the hands of skilled practitioners; an example of such measures is the set of Object Relations Technique (ORT) cards.

With ability and cognitive tests and personality tests, the psychologist's job is to administer the test on a one-to-one or group basis, carefully following the standard procedure. Many tests have 'norms' available, so that the performance of any individual can be compared with others. By contrast, some assessments are not 'norm-referenced' at all, but assess individuals against an explicit criterion of everyday performance. Criterion-referenced assessments of this type are very helpful in gauging the progress of the individual, when knowledge about other people is irrelevant. An example is given in section 2 of Table 1.3; a person's ability to organize his or her own daily routine can be assessed without reference to anyone else.

Apart from questionnaires used to assess personality in a global sense, many specific questionnaires are available, looking at specific tendencies such as conservatism, and at psychiatric or psychopathological dimensions such as depression. A wide range of checklists and rating scales exists, again mostly related to specific conditions or problems, and which may also be completed by someone who knows the patient well, such as a family member. For example there are several rating scales for use with people with learning difficulties which are completed by a care worker in the home where the person lives. These typically have carefully graded items, so that an action such as 'doing up buttons' itself consists of several stages, such as 'opposes buttonhole to button' and 'inserts button into hole'. A psychologist will often be involved in training and supervising nurses and others in the use of this type of scale.

Another last category of assessment instruments consists of behavioural methods. These make use of direct observation of behaviour, often in a 'natural' setting, without the necessity of patients even being aware that they are being assessed. They yield measures of the exact frequency or length of time of a piece of behaviour, such as an outburst of aggression, and may require the observer to be physically present for several hours. Physiological measures are not strictly behavioural measures, but have the same characteristic of producing a numerical index of functioning, relating to such physiological parameters as heart rate, blood flow, or skin resistance. Small hand-held electronic recorders now make this type of recording easier, and enable more categories of information to be reliably collected.

Table 1.3 provides a categorization of the assessment methods that have just been outlined. The methods can be applied to a number of areas of content, including the conventional general measures of ability and personality, and the more specific measures of opinion, self-report,

Table 1.3 Major categories of psychological assessment

1. Self-description. Refers to those measures where the subject describes his own current feelings and behaviour, either in an open-ended way (as in interviews) or in a forced-choice way (as in personality questionnaires).

Example: personality questionnaire items:

Do you sometimes feel lonely?	Yes	No	Unsure
Are you easily upset when people criticize you?	Yes	No	Unsure

2. Ratings or judgements by others. Where a person other than the subject describes the subject's current emotions or behaviour, again either in an open-ended way or in a structured way (as in a standardized rating scale or checklist).

Example: a checklist item prepared for checking the early morning routine in a hostel, and requiring the observer to tick each item if that act has been performed:

wakes up when alarm rings
washes unprompted before breakfast
chooses appropriate clothes unaided
dresses unaided
goes to kitchen unprompted

3. Life-history. Refers to the recording of *past* factual information about the subject, from whatever source, such as details of education, and of occupation.

4. Simulated real-life measurement. The subject is asked to demonstrate, or rehearse in practice, what is requested, in as real a way as possible.

Example: assessing social skills by role-play

5. Direct observation. Real-time recording of specific events or components of behaviour as they occur naturally.

Example: counting incidents of violence per day

6. Physiological. Refers to measures directly monitoring physiological functions of the subject's body, such as heart rate or rate of sweating, by electronic sensors attached directly to the skin surface.

Example: EMG (electromyogram)

7. Performance tests. This category includes the classic concept of the 'test', and includes all assessment methods where the subject is asked to complete intellectual tasks by use of standard questions.

Example: cognitive or ability test items:

Pick out the word in the list below that does not go with the others

Brig Ketch Steamer Schooner

Write in the next two numbers in this series

3 6 14 27 45 ... ...

and behaviour already mentioned that are more directly related to the patient's clinical problems and to their care and management. A comprehensive series of chapters on different aspects of assessment theory and practice is included in Peck and Shapiro (1990).

All psychological assessment instruments need to fulfil several different requirements. Most important of all, they should contribute unique information which will be helpful to the people intimately concerned with the care and treatment of patients, and which will improve the quality of clinical decisions. They need to be acceptable to the people who use them: not too complex in administration and scoring for the test user, not too threatening or demanding for the subject.

Additionally, they should be psychometrically sound. This means that they should conform to technical standards of validity, reliability, and sensitivity to change. The validity of a measure is the extent to which it measures what it says it measures. This means that the content of, for example, a reading test should be made up of words that are a reasonable sample of the sort of words that children of a particular country or locality use in practice. Validity is also evaluated by examining the relationship between the measure in question and another measure of the attribute. Thus, one index of the validity of a measure of depression would be the relative proportion of high scorers who present for treatment of depression, compared to the proportion of high scorers who do *not* present.

Reliability is the extent to which a measure gives similar results under differing conditions of use. The administrator of a test or checklist may give it in slightly different ways, or pay attention to different characteristics of the patient's behaviour, so that different testers or raters give slightly different results. The similarity of results across two different sets of raters then gives an index of inter-rater reliability. The other important form of reliability is test–retest, or repeat reliability, indicating the similarity of results across two different occasions. The sensitivity to change of a measure is the extent to which a score changes when there is there is other evidence that the attribute being assessed has altered. An example would be looking at the change in a measure of self-help skills when a patient has left hospital and is looking after themselves again after a stroke.

Intervening in peoples' lives

The role of psychologist as therapist has developed rapidly over the last thirty years. A range of psychological therapeutic methods have been introduced; many have been refined to such an extent that they have become the treatment of choice for some conditions (see Chapter 2).

Quite apart from those therapeutic techniques derived from psychodynamic, cognitive, or other theories, most encounters with patients involve the use of general therapeutic skills. These enable the patient to feel relaxed, to have confidence in her or his therapist, and to be able to recount events, experiences, and relationships which may normally make them feel embarrassed or stigmatized. Psychologists have examined the major attributes of the 'good' counsellor or therapist in constructing this basic therapeutic relationship, and drawn attention to the three key attributes of: 'positive regard'—valuing the patient as an individual; 'accurate empathy'—understanding the reality of the patient's experiences; and 'genuineness'.

Those clinical psychologists who spend most of their time in psychotherapeutic work will probably enter advanced training with one of the established psychotherapy organizations, such as the Institute of Group Analysis, and may register as psychotherapists with, for example, the United Kingdom Council for Psychotherapy already mentioned earlier in the chapter. Their clinical work may then be defined more by the nature of their therapeutic training and interests than by their initial training as a clinical psychologist. Psychotherapeutic approaches derive from the seminal work of Sigmund Freud, from the modifications to his theories of his early associates and later defectors such as Jung, and from later and contemporary workers such as Melanie Klein and Freud's own daughter, Anna Freud.

The therapeutic procedures which are currently most characteristic of clinical psychologists are those generally known as cognitive–behavioural methods. Depending on the client group and the problems with which individual clinical psychologists are presented, these approaches combine features of behaviour therapy, cognitive therapy, and often elements of group therapy and family therapy. Many clinical psychologists would describe their overall approach as eclectic, combining individual techniques as appropriate to the needs of the individual, rather than holding to one specified treatment approach. However, it is worth understanding the main features of both the behavioural and the cognitive approaches.

Behavioural methods of treatment require a psychologist first to engage in a behavioural analysis of the problem. A behavioural analysis, or 'functional analysis of behaviour', involves looking at the central problem or *Behaviour* in the light of its *Antecedents*—those prior events or determinants such as time of day or place in the room where the behaviour occurs—and in the light of the *Consequences*—those events following the occurrence of the behaviour in the actual environment.

Cognitive methods of treatment are based on the supposition that psychological problems may be seen in terms of a linkage between behavioural, cognitive, and physiological response systems. These systems do not necessarily change together or at the same time, but the acceptance of these three systems paved the way to go beyond a simple unitary behavioural perspective, and to consider how patients evaluated their own problems. Bandura's work on observational learning drew attention to the way in which behaviour change was mediated by people's perception of how they performed. This in turn led to the development of self-instructional training—probably the first wholly cognitive approach to treatment. Probably the best example of cognitive approaches to treatment is the application to depression, where negative thinking about the past, about the self, and about the future, are so obvious.

Apart from behavioural and cognitive methods of treatment, there are a number of other treatment methods that are based on psychological concepts. Some treatment methods have been based on theories of family functioning, seeing the whole family as a social unit, with the behaviour, emotions, and expectations of each family member having a potential influence on all other members of the family. Other treatments are based on theories of memory, as described in Chapter 7. It is quite common to have to integrate elements of treatment from a number of different approaches, as shown by the case of Alan, whose neuropsychological rehabilitation programme, described below, shows inclusion of several approaches over a considerable period of time.

Psychological approaches to an individual patient

Alan was a 13-year-old boy, previously in good health, and in the top stream of his local school, who was knocked of his bicycle on his way home. He incurred a severe head injury with a compound depressed fracture of the left side of his skull which resulted in a right hemiplegia (paralysis). He was in hospital for 10 days in the neurosurgical ward, and then for a further 7 days in a postoperative ward. Follow-up CT scans showed damage to the left parietal (upper central) region of the brain. He returned to school 2 months after the accident, and initially seemed to be coping well, except for outbursts of aggression. However, later on when getting near his GCSE exams (British national school examinations taken at the age of 15 or 16) he stopped attending school and only carried on studying three subjects (when he should have taken eight in all). With the help of a home tutor he passed one English and the Engineering exams, but failed the third. He stayed on at school, and then passed a further seven GCSEs. He started A level courses (advance preUniversity examinations) in electronics and technology but struggled to cope, with periods off school linked to bouts of both aggression and depression. Four years after his head injury he was referred to the community head injury service.

Assessment and treatment

On initial assessment, Alan showed a wide range of physical, cognitive, emotional, behavioural, and social problems, and the main concerns were aggressive outbursts, depression, and difficulties at school. Formal psychometric assessment confirmed a high level of intellectual ability and preserved memory and learning, but there was also evidence of a reduction in auditory attention, working memory, verbal fluency, and speed of information processing. Parallel occupational therapy and physiotherapy assessments confirmed reduced motor skills, poor gait, and a reduced range of movement of his right leg, ankle, and hip. At the end of the summer he decided not to return to the second year of his A level course, due to mood swings and poor concentration. He then joined a specialist vocational rehabilitation project, and the main problems observed there were variable concentration associated with his mood swings, lack of awareness of risks to his own health and safety, frustration and annoyance at his own restrictions, and loss of self-confidence and self-belief. It was felt that he had the skills to cope with training or employment, but that his emotional and behavioural volatility cast considerable doubt on his ability to cope with the training.

The neuropsychological and resultant social difficulties of Alan can be conceptualized within the framework provided by the International Classification of Impairments, Disabilities, and Handicaps of the World Health Organization (1980):

- impairment—any loss or abnormality of psychological, physiological or anatomical structure or function;
- disability—any restriction or lack, resulting from an impairment, of ability to perform an activity in the manner or within the range considered normal for a human being;
- handicap—a disadvantage for a given individual, resulting from an impairment or a disability, that limits or prevents the fulfilment of a role that is normal (depending on age, sex, social and cultural factors) for that individual.

The impairments following the head injury included physical, cognitive, emotional, and behavioural changes, as shown in Fig. 1.2.

Physical disabilities (restricted range of movements, right sided weakness, and poor gait and balance) were a direct result of his right hemiplegia. However, both his cognitive (reduced concentration, speed, and inflexibility) and his emotional/ behavioural difficulties (lack of confidence, depression, and aggression) reflected a complex interaction of underlying cognitive and personality changes arising from the head injury together with secondary psychological difficulties in adjusting to residual disability and associated restrictions. The difficulties in adjustment were considered to reflect, in part, a lack of previous neuropsychological assessment or rehabilitation. In terms of handicap, his mobility reflected his physical disability alone; his educational and vocational restrictions reflected mainly the interaction of his cognitive and emotional/ behavioural difficulties (plus some specific physical restrictions); his relationship difficulties were primarily a function of his emotional/ behavioural difficulties, mediated to some extent by his inflexibility.

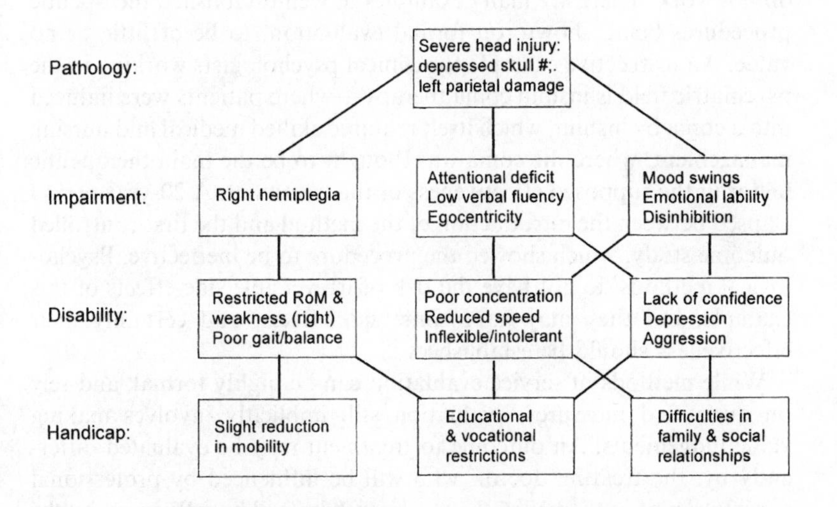

Fig. 1.2 Example of a case formulation.

Initially psychological therapy focused on providing a neuropsychological framework which would help him to make sense of, and manage, his cognitive difficulties at school, and his emotional volatility and aggressive outbursts at home. His parents attended a fortnightly group for relatives of those with head injury, which gave them both support and guidance. After completing a period of vocational rehabilitation and a voluntary work trial he obtained a position as an electrical maintenance assistant in the works department of a local hospital. However, he required a great deal of support to go through with the application and interview, which highlighted both his reduced vocational potential (having previously intended to go to University) and lack of confidence. He continued to require monthly psychological therapy, which dealt with management of his aggressive outbursts, and increasingly his concern about social relationships. After two more years he was more settled at work and was living with his girlfriend. However, he was struggling to manage his emotional and behavioural volatility within the relationship, and he is currently being seen together with his girlfriend to help them cope better with this.

How to evaluate psychological practice

There is no point in using psychological methods of treatment if they do not work. There are many examples of well-established therapeutic procedures being shown, on formal evaluation, to be of little or no value. An instructive example for clinical psychologists working in the psychiatric field is insulin coma therapy—where patients were induced into a coma by insulin, which itself required skilled medical and nursing management, where the coma was thought to be the main therapeutic factor in the supposed effectiveness of the treatment. A 20-year period elapsed between the introduction of the method and the first controlled outcome study, which showed the procedure to be ineffective. Psychological methods do not have the risk of irreversible side-effects of this example, but they may have some side-effects, and certainly their effectiveness should be established.

While methods of service evaluation can be highly formal, and rely on quantified measures, evaluation still implicitly involves making value judgements. An outcome to treatment may be evaluated differently by: the treating doctor, who will be influenced by professional expectation of outcome; by the manager, who will be influenced by the resources required for that treatment; and by the person treated, who will be influenced mainly by the impact on their own quality of life or, for example, freedom from pain. To whose opinion do we pay most attention?

A common first step in evaluation is to show that the treatment under question is better than the routine treatment available as an alternative, or at least better than doing nothing. After that, evaluation usually takes the form of 'unpacking' the several components of the treatment programme, and looking at the effectiveness of each component. For example one behavioural approach to the care of patients with severe mental illness involves a 'token economy', when the patient is given a token immediately after performing some desired act. However, observation of the moment when the token is given indicates that other things are going on at the same time. The patient may be praised verbally ('well done') and perhaps affirmed physically by appropriate touching (a hand on the shoulder), informational feedback may be given ('you have got the token because . . .'), and the patient in any case has an individual social encounter in the midst of an otherwise solitary day. Which of these events is the key therapeutic ingredient?

An evaluation usually focuses on the outcome of individuals or groups who have completed a treatment. However, there are other outcome criteria that can be used to evaluate the effectiveness of a treatment, such as the impact of the patients problems upon those who care for them—the so-called burden or impact of care. Another way of looking at outcome is to examine the amount of resources that have to be devoted to a patient to achieve a given outcome. For example if treatment A produced a given level of therapeutic response after 10 hours of professional time, then it would be more efficient than treatment B, if the latter required 20 hours of professional time for the same level of response.

Attention can be paid to the *process* of treatment, comparing the proposed objectives and activities of a programme with the objectives and activities that are actually implemented and accomplished: it presupposes an operational plan of a programme, and makes it possible to pick up flaws in a programme before it has been completed. Outcome evaluation, on the other hand, is more difficult to perform than process evaluation because, as discussed, there are often different levels of outcome, such as the patient's use of a treatment, or the impact of change in the patient upon the caring family. The particular contribution of psychologists to health-care evaluation is twofold: firstly, by translating overall service objectives into operational objectives; and secondly, by devising measures that may need to be used by relatively unsophisticated staff.

KEY PROFESSIONAL ISSUES

Clinical psychology has had to find its own niche amidst the array of doctors, nurses, remedial therapists, social workers, and other workers helping people with medical and personal problems. Different countries have imposed different constraints upon the development of the profession, so that the precise range of activities carried out by clinical psychologists differs from country to country. One example would be the role of medical doctors with respect to the profession—until recently in France only doctors could practise psychotherapy and in Britain patients seen by psychologists in the NHS normally have to be referred by a family doctor or other medical practitioner. Other professions are understandably concerned to know how clinical psychology fits into the health-care system, and what assumptions they may make about this new professional group. There are three main issues which probably require some explanation at the outset.

Professional independence

Most health-care professions have emerged and developed largely as the consequence of doctors identifying a practical task which needs to be performed, but which does not require a medical training to perform it. Bit by bit, these professions have become more independent of medical supervision, as indicated in Britain, for example, by doctors no longer acting as examiners of professional competence for nurses. Nonetheless, there may still remain an argument that doctors possess an encompassing knowledge of other professions. By contrast, some of the newer health-care professions owe their development to scientific disciplines which cannot be said to be encompassed by medicine—speech and language therapy being a good example. Like clinical psychology, they may owe part of their original development to pressure and interest from medical colleagues, but those colleagues cannot now claim an encompassing knowledge of the procedures used.

Another criterion of professional independence is the existence of a standard of training and clinical competence which permits independence of action. For most European countries the period of clinical experience and level of academic competence required for qualification as a clinical psychologist is comparable to the clinical experience required for qualification as a medical doctor, and similarly follows a degree-level, preclinical qualification, suggesting that individuals entering clinical psychology are as likely to be able to practise independently as medically qualified people.

The expressed aspiration of a profession to achieve independence may not, of course, be consistent with the wishes of other colleagues, who far from wanting autonomy and independence, want close co-operation. In some forms of clinical practice, most notably perhaps child psychiatry, teamwork has been highly valued, so that team members value loyalty and commitment to their teams above commitment to members of their own professions. Co-operation with other colleagues is an essential part of the professional commitment of clinical psychologists, although the exact way in which this is worked out locally and in particular circumstances may need close examination; this is discussed further in Chapter 13.

Responsibility of clinical psychologists

In many health-care professions, responsibility is closely bound up with the legal registration of the profession. In many countries, the major health care professions have some form of registration procedure, which essentially prescribes minimum standards of training and competence, which may protect titles or functions of that profession and which ultimately may lead to members of the profession being 'struck off' if they fail to meet standards of professional competence. Most European countries now have some form of registration procedure for clinical psychologists, though these take different forms—in some cases psychologists are registered along with other health professions, and in some cases along with other areas of activity—in Austria by the ministry which is also responsible for sport (McPherson 1998)!

Apart from this form of legal responsibility, practitioners also owe a legal duty of care towards the patients they see. Quite apart from the specific implications of any registration procedure, an aggrieved patient may have recourse through the courts of law to correct alleged negligence or harm resulting from bad treatment. Professional bodies may also impose their own standards upon practitioners, independent of the standards imposed by courts.

It is consistent with a model of an independent profession to say that the psychologist's first responsibility is to his patient. The patient's needs and wishes should, from this point of view, dictate the psychologist's actions. On the other hand, when a psychologist is employed by a public agency there is no doubt that the policies of that agency may affect how a clinical service is delivered. The question of who is paying—whether patient or employer—alters basic assumptions about responsibility, and indeed in some schools of thought is believed to be an important component of the therapeutic relationship.

There is some ambivalence among British clinical psychologists about the advantages of registration. Sensible of the evidence that professionalization may benefit a profession more than their clients, psychologists hesitated before pursuing this path. In Britain, this hesitation has been supported by the fact that the major professional body for psychologists, the British Psychological Society, was originally a learned society. It still functions as a learned society, so that views of academic psychologists, and of applied psychologists who do not work in health care, have equal weight with those of clinical psychologists. Nevertheless, the British Psychological Society established a process whereby psychologists can become 'chartered' in 1988, and is now seeking Parliamentary time for a Psychologists Act, so further protecting the public.

The role of clinical psychology in the health-care system

Most developed countries attempt some overall planning of health care. In most countries, the relevant government department will have overall strategic health priorities, and will fund public health services to achieve those objectives. Health-care systems differ considerably in the extent to which there is central planning and funding of resources, the degree of choice available to the public, and the proportion of care provided by private or voluntary agencies. For example in the Republic of Ireland services to people with learning disabilities are predominantly provided by religious orders, but are Government funded. The increase of 'socialized medicine' has had an important consequence, in that it has encouraged the planning of health-care services on a population basis. If the size, age distribution, and morbidity of a population is known, then health facilities can be planned on some sort of rational plan and analysis of need. If, however, private practice develops in an unco-ordinated way and forms a major component of the overall service, it is difficult to plan in this way. Within these dimensions, the proportion of psychologists who practice privately as opposed to those who work within publicly funded services, and the proportion of those working closely with primary care services as opposed to those who work with specialized secondary or tertiary services, will affect the type of problem psychologists see.

As preventive medicine has been effective, and as antibiotics, corrective surgery in children, and better care of the aged have developed, so the health problems presented in the population have changed. As health care moves to a more preventive role, so issues of compliance with advice, and personal 'health-care routines'—essentially psychological issues—will become more important. As populations age and contain more people with chronic handicaps which no longer respond to medical intervention, so the emphasis of health care has changed to emphasize coping with disability. It seems that further improvement in the health of a population will rely as much on change of lifestyle as on the ministrations of high technology medicine.

The role of clinical psychology in a health-care system is thus determined by a number of factors. The capacity of clinical psychologists to contribute independently and responsibly is one major factor. The availability of psychological knowledge along the 'primary care–specialist' dimension further influences the number and nature of the problems seen, and by implication the demand for psychologists. The capacity of a health-care system to identify need and to plan provision also implies planning the type and numbers of staff to make that provision. At present, there are growing expectations of clinical psychologists that they will be able to contribute to several points of the system. This book describes both what they are doing at present, and what developments lie ahead.

References

Herman, J. (1992). *Trauma and recovery*. HarperCollins, New York.

Mayou, R. (1997). The psychiatry of road traffic accidents. In *The aftermath of road accidents: psychological, social and legal consequences of everyday trauma* (ed. M. Mitchell). Routledge, London.

McPherson, F. (1998). Thirty years of regulating clinical psychology in Europe. *Clinical Psychology Forum*, **113**, 13–15.

Melzack, D. C. and Wall, P. (1988). *The challenge of pain* (revised edn). Penguin, Harmondsworth.

Peck, D. F. and Shapiro, C. M. (1990). *Measuring human problems*. Wiley, Chichester.

World Health Organization (1980). *International classification of impairment, disability, and handicap*. World Health Organization, Geneva.

Further reading

Butler, G. and McManus, F. (1998). *Psychology: a very short introduction*. Oxford University Press, Oxford. (Just what it says: a very short introduction for readers who have no background in general psychology.)

Frude, N. (1998). *Understanding abnormal psychology*. Blackwell, Oxford.

Power, M. and Brewin, C. (1997). *Transformation of meaning in the psychological therapies: reconciling theory and practice*. Wiley, Chichester.

2

The psychological treatment of adults

John Marzillier

All clinical psychologists work to some extent with adults. Some provide a direct service to adult patients in the form of psychological assessment and treatment. Others work indirectly with adults; so, for example, those who work with children will also work closely with parents, teachers, and other professional staff. This chapter describes the therapeutic work of clinical psychologists, concentrating on the treatment services that they provide to adults in mental health settings. Elsewhere in the book can be found accounts of psychological treatment with specific populations and within specialist services. For example the role of clinical psychologists in the treatment of the severely mentally ill is described in Chapter 3, specialist psychological interventions for those with learning disabilities in Chapter 5, the treatment of alcohol and drug misusers in Chapter 10, and the therapeutic role of those working in general medical settings can be found in Chapter 11.

Psychological treatments take many forms and are characterized by various labels (for example psychotherapy, behaviour therapy, psychoanalysis, cognitive therapy, etc.). There are many 'schools' of psychotherapy, and practitioners can differ in their allegiance to a particular theory as well as in their methods of treatment. Clinical psychologists have, on the whole, practised the briefer and more pragmatic types of treatment such as the cognitive and behavioural therapies. All clinical psychology training courses provide a basic training in this approach (see Chapter 1). In addition, many clinical psychologists go on to receive specialist training in other forms of psychotherapy, such as psychodynamic psychotherapy, family therapy, psychoanalysis, cognitive–analytic therapy, and humanistic therapy amongst others. It would therefore be wrong to equate clinical psychology with one school of psychotherapy even if the cognitive–behaviour therapy school tends to predominate. Surveys have shown that most clinical psychologists, like other psychotherapists, tend to call themselves 'eclectic' and to draw upon therapeutic procedures from a variety of schools. Therefore, a range of psychological therapies is illustrated in this chapter. Is there anything distinctive about clinical psychologists which separates them from other psychotherapists? Two characteristics stand out. On the whole, clinical psychologists are concerned to base their practice on *psychological theory* and are therefore open to new developments as theories develop and change. Secondly, the scientist–practitioner model places great emphasis on the use of *effective therapies*, that is, ones supported by empirical research. A discussion of the effectiveness of psychotherapy is provided at the end of the chapter.

THE SETTING

Clinical psychologists will most commonly see patients for treatment in some form of clinic or centre. The site of the clinic will vary depending on the nature of the service as a whole. In Britain, for example, where clinical psychology has had a close historical association with psychiatry, many clinics are attached to psychiatric hospitals. But clinics may be set up elsewhere, for example in University psychology departments, general practices, community mental health centres, or even over shop fronts in city centres. Where a private health service flourishes, as in the United States, psychologists will set up their clinics alongside those of other professions, and indeed compete for customers.

The word 'clinic' is used to describe the service, although its medical connotations sometimes make it an unpopular term. But in practice most clinical psychologists act like their medical colleagues. Patients are referred by others, most commonly the family doctor or a psychiatrist, are sent appointments, attend at a centre with a receptionist and a waiting area, and are usually given a fixed series of appointments until the 'treatment' has been completed. While the 'clinic' approach is still the commonest way of working, it has been criticized as inefficient and poorly responsive to the needs of the community. Psychologists often find themselves operating long waiting lists, with the result that it is difficult to respond quickly to crises, and both patients and referrers turn elsewhere for help. Situated in a clinic at a hospital or other specialist centre, psychological treatment services can be isolated from other forms of help or care. A service that is based in the community, working closely with voluntary agencies and other professions, has been suggested as a more viable alternative. Community mental health teams, which were first formed in the United States in the 1960s, are now increasingly to be found in the United Kingdom. Clinical psychologists have become part of community mental health teams that operate within a locality or sector and thereby seek to provide a more accessible and flexible service to the community. The value of this development is discussed in more detail in Chapter 12.

COMMON PSYCHOLOGICAL PROBLEMS

Table 2.1 lists some of the commonest problems referred to adult mental health psychologists. This list is not based upon an established system of psychological classification, since none exists, but simply a means of identifying and labelling common psychological problems. There is inevitably overlap between categories. For example a person with a psychosexual problem may also be depressed and experiencing marital difficulties. An alcoholic may behave aggressively towards his family and friends. The labels used in Table 2.1 are simply convenient means for the patient or the referring professional to identify the major problem for which help is sought. It is part of the job of the clinical psychologist to assess the case in greater depth to establish the nature of the problem and whether treatment can be provided.

Two formal diagnostic classification systems exist within psychiatry—the American system, DSM-IV and the European system, ICD-11. These are sometimes used by clinical psychologists to categorize psychological problems. There are advantages and disadvantages in using a psychiatric diagnostic system. On the one hand, there are benefits from working within a scientific system of classification that is used and understood by the international community; this is most obvious when conducting scientific research. On the other hand, the system is an explicitly medical one and many psychologists feel uncomfortable with the assumptions underpinning it. For example is it correct to call emotional experiences, such as depression or anxiety, illnesses when these seem to be common if not ubiquitous reactions to life events? Is there not a risk of pathologizing essentially normal responses? Values are embedded within the psychiatric diagnostic system about what is and is not acceptable behaviour in society. Mental health professionals have been criticized for supporting a system that labels others as 'ill' and thereby deviant. In practice, there is a need to categorize psychological problems in some way in order to share information as well as to draw upon the findings of empirical research. For this reason, psychiatric classification has had an increasing influence on the way psychologists discuss psychological problems. For example a recent book by two British clinical psychologists summarizing the research evidence on the effectiveness of various psychological treatments draws explicitly upon DSM-IV as a way of categorizing psychological problems (Roth and Fonagy 1996).

Table 2.1 Common psychological problems seen by clinical psychologists for psychological treatment

I. *Emotional problems*
1. Fears and phobias
2. Generalized anxiety
3. Obsessions and compulsions
4. Depression
5. Other emotional disturbance, e.g. anger, guilt

II. *Addictions and habit problems*
1. Alcoholism and problem drinking
2. Drug addiction
3. Eating problems, e.g. anorexia, bulimia, obesity
4. Miscellaneous, e.g. smoking, stuttering, gambling, ties

III. *Psychosexual problems*
1. Sexual dysfunction, e.g. impotence, vaginismus
2. Problems of sexual orientation
3. Problems arising out of sexual abuse

IV. *Social and interpersonal problems*
1. Loneliness, shyness, and social isolation
2. Aggressive and antisocial behaviour
3. Marital conflict
4. Relationship problems

V. *Psychosomatic and medical*
1. 'Psychosomatic disorders', e.g. asthma, headache
2. Cardiovascular disorders, e.g. hypertension, coronary heart disease
3. Pain
4. Chronic physical illness

Clinical psychologists vary in the problems they treat and the types of treatments they provide. This variation arises partly from the differing theoretical orientation and experience of the psychologists, and partly from the different demands placed upon them in different settings. Another factor in determining what forms of psychological treatment clinical psychologists offer is *cost effectiveness*. Any therapeutic service, particularly one that is publicly funded, needs to show that the treatments it uses are both of proven value and economically efficient.

BASIC PRINCIPLES OF PSYCHOLOGICAL ASSESSMENT AND TREATMENT

An example of how clinical psychologists practise psychological treatment is given in the case of Jessica and David. In this first case the process of assessment and treatment has been deliberately simplified in order to highlight the basic procedures and principles.

The treatment of a married couple with sexual problems

Jessica and David are a married couple in their early 3Os with two children of school age. David approached his local GP complaining of impotence and lack of sexual satisfaction in his marriage. The GP suggested that he might benefit from seeing a specialist in the treatment of sexual problems and referred him to a psychosexual clinic run in a local clinical psychology department. As is the normal practice of the clinic, both David and Jessica were invited to attend the clinic for an initial assessment interview with a view to beginning a course of treatment.

In the initial interview the couple are seen together in the first instance. The problem that they present is one of impotence on David's part with the consequent breakdown of their sexual relationship. The first part of the interview is taken up with an account of the sexual problem, its origin, its nature, and how it affects their relationship. Some background information is also sought concerning their work, way of life, children, social activities, etc. Then Jessica and David are seen separately for a detailed interview of their sexual histories and to explore their attitudes and feelings about the marriage. Each also fills in a questionnaire on their marital and sexual relationship. Finally, the couple are seen together again for a further discussion which focuses on possible treatments and their expectations concerning therapy. An agreement is reached that they will go away and talk together about the problem and the possibilities for treatment. A brief hand-out concerning psychosexual problems and their treatment is given to them to take away and read. Advice is given to refrain from sexual relations for the time being. Another appointment is made in a week's time, at which time a final decision on treatment will be made.

The next appointment begins with a general discussion arising out of their reactions to the first interview, the information in the hand-out, and the talk they had between interviews. Jessica and David are eager to go ahead with treatment and the psychologist spends some time describing what would be involved both in terms of specific treatment procedures and the general requirements of therapy. It is explained that the treatment is based upon the work of the American researchers Masters and Johnston and in essence entails the relearning of their sexual relationship with the help of specific psychological procedures (see Hawton 1985). The possibility that David's impotence is caused by performance anxiety is raised and it is suggested that a gradual and undemanding programme of resuming sexual activity is a way of overcoming anxiety, allowing potency to return. The first of a series of practical exercises is presented to them and they are asked to implement the exercise at home. Appointments are made on a weekly basis, with the possibility of telephone contact between sessions if necessary. At first treatment progresses reasonably smoothly and Jessica and David gradually increase the intimacy of their sexual contact. However, David still has difficulty in maintaining potency and, after further discussions, is given some training in relaxation and advised not to be concerned with potency or sexual arousal, but to concentrate on remaining relaxed and on enjoying the intimacy of sexual contact. This results in successful sexual intercourse—the first time for many months—and leads to increased optimism and confidence on their part. Further satisfactory progress is made over the next few treatment sessions until treatment is formally ended after 12 weekly sessions. Jessica and David are seen for a final assessment and given a follow-up appointment in 3 months time.

The case of Jessica and David is hypothetical and is used to illustrate how psychological treatment can operate in an uncomplicated fashion. Few cases are perhaps as straightforward as this, but the basic principles are the same. Treatment is always preceded by a period of assessment whose prime purpose is to gather information concerning the nature of the problem so that the psychologist may arrive at an informed decision about treatment. The initial assessment also allows the patients and the psychologist to get to know each other and establish a relationship of mutual trust and confidence without which treatment is unlikely to succeed. The decision on treatment should be a mutual one, and therefore the patients must be informed about what the treatment involves and its likelihood of success. The active involvement of the patient in therapy is also something of importance, as treatment is regarded as a co-operative venture in which therapist and patient work together to achieve change. Treatment takes place over regular weekly outpatient sessions, although this will vary according to the type of problem treated. Some cases need to be seen intensively at first and others require a period of inpatient treatment. In some cases, patients may be seen in groups and in others the psychologist works closely with other professionals, for example doctors, nurses, health visitors, and social workers. Finally, the effects of treatment are monitored by regular assessments and a final evaluation of the extent of improvement. Patients are often given one or more follow-up appointments to assess whether improvement is maintained.

Psychological treatment is not always as straightforward as this example suggests. For example it is not always possible to define psychological problems simply or to use well-established treatment methods. An important part of psychological treatment is working with the patient to establish what exactly the problem is and working out an individually tailored way of treating it. In the hypothetical example, David's impotence could have been an expression of more fundamental marital difficulties and, if that were the case, the psychologist would need to shift his or her attention to that problem and consider whether he or she could provide help to resolve it. Psychologists differ too in how they conceptualize psychological problems, and this affects what treatment is offered. To some psychologists impotence may suggest unconscious conflicts about one's own sexuality, and treatment will be concerned with exploring such conflict in an attempt to make it conscious and resolve it.

COGNITIVE–BEHAVIOUR THERAPY

The case of Jessica and David can be seen as an example of behaviour therapy. This is a school of therapy which developed in the 1960s out of experimental studies of psychological principles in the laboratory, principles of learning in particular. The basic tenet of behaviour therapy is that emotional and other problems are learned and that by applying learning principles to their problems patients can learn to resolve them. It is now more common to describe this treatment approach as *cognitive–behaviour therapy* (CBT) to underline the importance of focusing on thoughts, images, beliefs, and other cognitions as well as behaviour.

Cognitive–behavioural treatments tend to be brief—a few weeks or months at the most—and can in some instances be as short as four to six sessions. Their aim is to help the patient change his or her problem behaviour directly. Although a good therapeutic relationship can be important in cognitive–behaviour therapy it is not regarded as the main vehicle of change. The approach is best described as an educational and problem-solving one, with the therapist using his or her specialist knowledge to guide the patient towards a solution to his or her problems. Another characteristic of the cognitive–behavioural approach is the emphasis on the systematic assessment of change using scientifically derived assessment measures and carefully evaluated techniques (Hawton *et al.* 1989).

Cognitive–behaviour therapy for anxiety and panic

Cognitive–behavioural treatments have proved to be particularly successful in helping people for whom anxiety is a major problem. Anxiety is commonly defined by subjective feelings of distress, often persistent and intense, in which there is a dread or apprehension about some unpleasant and uncertain future occurrence. There is little doubt that anxiety is, in itself, a normal experience which all of us encounter from time to time. The prospect of difficult examinations, a visit to the dentist, the vicissitudes of a difficult personal relationship, having to make a speech at a formal reception, are all examples where the experience of anxiety would be quite expected. In clinical practice, anxious patients seek help if their feelings of anxiety are so persistent and intense that they interfere with their daily lives or if they experience the sensations of anxiety without fully understanding what they are or why they occur.

The cognitive–behavioural treatment of an agoraphobic woman with panic attacks

Jean is a 33-year-old married woman with a young son of 7 years old. She is neatly dressed, pleasant-mannered, and articulate, but rather reticent and soft-spoken. She complains of a fear of leaving her home on her own and of crowded places such as supermarkets in particular. Even at home on her own she experiences panic attacks and has to ring her husband frequently for support and help. She has very few friends and very little social life except for her mother, whom she tends to see most days. She can recall having experienced her fear and panic for several years, and has sought help now because she worries that her son may be experiencing similar anxieties; he has reported feeling nervous at school and on occasions has been reluctant to go.

Jean has a problem that is commonly called 'agoraphobia', which literally means (from the Greek) 'a fear of the market place'. The main characteristics of agoraphobia are: (1) fear about leaving home or any place of safety on one's own; (2) a fear of crowded places; (3) a fear of 'fear' itself; and (4) avoidance of confined places, where escape is difficult. In this instance cognitive–behavioural treatment consists of (a) a systematic programme of increasing exposure to the situations that provoke fear and anxiety; and (b) teaching Jean to become more confident in her ability to manage difficult situations on her own—that is restoring her confidence in herself.

In the first two sessions, Jean and her therapist drew up a list of the most anxiety-provoking situations and worked out a graded programme of 25 steps ranging from: (1) opening the door of her house and standing alone on the doorstep for 30 seconds to (25) travelling by bus to the centre of town on a Saturday afternoon and visiting a supermarket. Jean was also taught progressive muscular relaxation and given a rationale to the effect that her fear of going out had been acquired as a result of the panic that she had first experienced and was now being maintained mainly by her 'fear of fear', that is of the panic recurring. Successful treatment entailed her regaining confidence in her ability to be out on her own and to cope with symptoms of anxiety and panic.

There are two possible strategies that the therapist and Jean could have adopted at this point. The first is the graduated approach whereby the easiest situation in the hierarchy is tackled first until Jean can master it without undue anxiety. This may be done first in imagination and then in reality. Once Jean is confident in this situation, she progresses to the next, each time using relaxation to combat her feelings of anxiety. And so on until each situation in the hierarchy is successfully tackled. This method is known as 'systematic desensitization'.

The other method, known as 'flooding' or 'prolonged exposure', entails tackling the most difficult situation first and persisting in it until Jean's anxiety decreases, a procedure which may take several hours. In Jean's case this meant visiting a crowded supermarket on a Saturday afternoon and spending the whole afternoon in the supermarket, resisting the urge to escape even if anxiety became intense. Although this is often a distressing procedure, it can have a rapid and dramatic beneficial effect. In Jean's case, she realized that none of the awful things she feared actually happened, and her anxiety feelings eventually diminished so much that she was able to do her weekly shopping. The therapist and Jean repeated the treatment a couple of times, and each time it proved much easier for Jean. She was encouraged to tackle less difficult situations on her own, and thereby began the process of successfully counteracting her agoraphobia.

Jean's success in the behavioural programme helped to counteract her worries about possible catastrophe, since she could see how her panicky symptoms were due to anxiety and that she could manage them herself. In addition, on the advice of the therapist, she joined an assertiveness training group, in which she and other patients discussed and practised ways of being more assertive, that is standing up for themselves and taking an independent line. The group boosted Jean's confidence further and enabled her to deal more effectively with the demands of her family—her mother in particular. At the end of her treatment, she had not only become confident enough to go out alone but had also become a more outspoken and confident person who, as she put it, had learned that she was not there 'just to make up the numbers'.

Jean's case illustrates the way in which behavioural principles can be used in a practical and effective way to reduce anxiety and restore confidence. Many agoraphobic patients have been helped by cognitive–behaviour therapy, and research studies have confirmed the value of this approach (Mathews *et al.* 1981). This is not to ignore the fact that agoraphobia can be a complex condition in which factors other than anxiety on leaving home may play a part. Issues of dependency and lack of assertiveness may be evident, as they were in Jean's case. Marital and family relations can be disturbed. The more chronic cases do not respond well to treatment. However, the value of a pragmatic cognitive–behavioural approach for many patients has been established.

Cognitive–behaviour therapy for panic attacks

Recent research in both the United States and Europe has shown that cognitive–behaviour therapy can be successfully applied to panic attacks whether or not they are accompanied by agoraphobia. A panic attack is the sudden onset of intense fear and the accompanying sensations of breathlessness, dizziness, increased heart rate, feelings of choking or suffocation, and chest pain. The experience, although physically harmless, can be very frightening. Agoraphobic patients with panic tend to be able to identify when and where such attacks are likely to occur and try to avoid them. But in some patients these attacks come out of the blue and in such cases the panic attack is the major focus of therapy. From a cognitive–behaviour therapy perspective, a major component in panic attacks is a cognitive distortion which takes the form of patients tending to misinterpret the bodily sensations accompanying anxiety and panic as more dangerous than they are, for example as a sign of a heart attack or of going mad. This catastrophic misinterpretation will in turn create more panic as well as sensitizing the patient to any sign of distress however slight. Caught in a vicious circle of fear and worry, patients are unable to escape the spiralling effects of panic. Cognitive–behavioural treatment involves, amongst other things, patients learning to recognize and counteract catastrophic misinterpretations and so interrupt the spiral of fear and worry. Empirical research has shown that between 74 and 94 per cent of patients were panic free following treatment by this form of cognitive–behaviour therapy (Clark 1997).

The cognitive–behavioural treatment of obsessional–compulsive disorders

Obsessional–compulsive disorders are characterized by the dual components of obsessions and compulsions. Obsessions are recurring, repetitive thoughts, images, or impulses which are experienced by the patient as intrusive, unwanted, and often abhorrent and senseless. They are often thoughts or images about doing harm, or harm being done to other people. One woman, for example, was beset with the image of stabbing her daughter through the heart with a knife. Occasionally, meaningless, repetitive, phrases are experienced (for example 'Put jam on it'). The intrusiveness and the unpleasant content of the obsessions cause considerable distress and anxiety.

Compulsions are stereotyped, repetitive behaviours, often ritualistic, evoked by a strong, subjective urge which the patient finds hard to resist. Quite often the behaviour is designed to forestall possible harm (for example washing hands thoroughly to avoid contamination) and its performance tends to lead to feelings of relief and the reduction of tension. Obsessions tend to lead to compulsions, although not in all cases. The commonest obsessions are repetitive thoughts of violence, contamination, and doubt (for example wondering whether the house is securely locked). Compulsions include repeated hand-washing, counting, and checking.

Obsessional disorders can be tackled on three fronts. Firstly, the emotional component of the problem is directly tackled by means of anxiety-reduction methods. For example a patient with obsessional anxieties about contamination by dirt may have his or her environment totally contaminated by the therapist in order to expose that person fully to obsessional stimuli and produce habituation of anxiety. Secondly, the behavioural components of the obsessional disorder, often expressed in terms of ritualistic behaviour designed to avoid or ward off anxiety, are directly tackled by a procedure known as 'response prevention'. As the name implies, the patient is encouraged not to carry out ritualistic behaviour in order that full exposure to the anxiety cues is achieved. Finally, patients are taught to distract themselves from upsetting thoughts and ruminations and, if possible, to dismiss them as irrational and unwanted.

The treatment of obsessional patients by these procedures is not easy to carry out, and is often facilitated by either admitting the patient to hospital and carrying out the treatment intensively with the help of other professional staff, as may be the case with the more severe disorders, or carrying out the treatment in the patient's home environment, again on an intensive basis. Serotonergic antidepressant medication has been shown to be helpful especially when there is a strong depressive component. Empirical research has provided strong support for the effectiveness of a comprehensive behavioural approach of this sort. Rachman and Hodgson (1980) report a success rate of between 70 and 80 per cent for obsessional patients treated by this method and followed-up for up to 2 years after the end of treatment (see also Roth and Fonagy 1996).

Cognitive–behavioural treatments have been successfully used for many types of psychological problems, for example addictive behaviours such as smoking and excessive drinking, psychosexual problems, relationship difficulties, eating disorders, and problems such as insomnia and excessive anger. The simplicity and directness of the approach are amongst its main assets, as is the research underpinning the approach.

COGNITIVE THERAPY

Cognitive therapy consists of methods of treatment which are specifically directed at the patient's cognitive or thinking processes. It is held that the emotional problems experienced by patients can be directly attributed to distortions in their thinking. These can take the form of the predominance of negative thoughts, thinking errors (for example over-generalization, polarized thinking), and irrational or maladaptive ideas and beliefs. In cognitive therapy, patients are taught to recognize and counter their cognitive distortions and thereby reduce or manage their emotional distress. Like cognitive–behaviour therapy, cognitive therapy is a practical, problem-solving form of treatment which has been particularly used in the treatment of depression and anxiety. The therapist takes an educational approach, although the value of developing a good therapeutic relationship is also stressed. In reality, cognitive–behaviour therapy and cognitive therapy merge into each other and distinctions between the two approaches are becoming less significant.

Cognitive therapy for depression

Depression is characterized by persistent and pervasive feelings of hopelessness and low mood, often accompanied by a number of somatic symptoms such as disturbed sleep, loss of energy, poor appetite, and psychomotor agitation or retardation. Depressed patients lose interest in normally pleasurable activities, find it difficult to concentrate or make decisions, and may experience intense feelings of guilt and self-reproach. Thoughts of death and suicide may be prominent. The experience of depression in mild or moderate forms is something many people have. Severe depression is experienced by a substantial number of people, perhaps as many as one in eight of the population.

Until recently, antidepressant medication was the clear treatment of choice for depressed patients. Both tricyclic drugs and the more recently developed SSRIs, such as Prozac, have been shown to elevate mood and produce symptomatic improvement in a large proportion of depressed patients. For most doctors they remain the first choice in treatment. Medication, however, has several limitations. Not only can drugs produce toxic- and side-effects, but they can undermine the depressed patients' capacity to recover on their own. Any improvement may be attributed to medication rather than the patients' own resources. In this way medication can reinforce a patient's belief that he or she is hopeless and inhibit attempts to cope.

Cognitive therapy aims to help depressed patients marshal their own resources to elevate mood, counteract depressive thinking, and produce positive changes in their behaviour and environment. It is practical and problem solving, with the central aim of identifying and correcting the major distortions in thinking that are characteristic of depression. Mrs Harris, for example, was severely depressed when referred for psychological help. She spent many hours of the day in bed, and had great difficulty in getting simple tasks around the house done. She was frequently tearful, and reproached herself for her inadequacy as a mother, housewife, offspring, and spouse. The first stage of therapy entailed asking her to keep a detailed record of her activities, and from this selecting the tasks that could be most easily mastered. She was seen twice a week at first and gradually, by means of structured planning and support, built up her activities. At the same time, she learned to attend to, monitor, and eventually challenge negative thinking. For example she frequently had the thought 'I am hopeless. I cannot do anything right'. In therapy the accuracy of this thought was questioned; she was asked to find and list things that she in fact had done correctly. The thought was seen as an example of depressive thinking rather than a realistic appraisal of herself. She was helped to find a way of countering the thought, firstly by distraction and then by direct challenge. She learned that she could in fact achieve many tasks provided they were specific and small scale. When Mrs Harris questioned the value of such achievement ('Anyone could do them. They are trivial'), therapy turned to a discussion of some of her basic assumptions and beliefs. It emerged that she had adopted a very rigid and perfectionist set of standards, which had been instilled into her from early childhood. Until her treatment, Mrs Harris had not articulated these standards and she was quite surprised at how extreme and rigid they were. It became clear to her that much of her depression was directly caused by her standards, which, because of their extreme nature, made it very difficult for her to succeed at anything. As therapy progressed she began to experiment with alternative ways of seeing herself and the world. Her depressed mood began rapidly to lift.

There is an increasing body of evidence to suggest that cognitive therapy is an effective method of treatment for depression. For example in a controlled evaluation of cognitive therapy for depressed patients referred by general practitioners, Teasdale and colleagues (1984) found that cognitive therapy resulted in a clinically and statistically significant improved rate of recovery compared to the customary treatment from their GPs. Roth and Fonagy (1996) summarized the results of the increasingly large pool of research studies into the effectiveness of cognitive therapy and other psychological treatments for depression. A number of brief, structured treatments were shown to be effective with cognitive–behaviour therapy emerging as 'a powerful and useful method for treating the acute symptoms of depression'. However, those with severe depression have a generally poor prognosis and the longer-term effects of all treatments apart from pharmacological therapy remain uncertain. Attention is now being paid to factors that might prevent relapse as well as examining diagnostic and other differences in response to therapy.

PSYCHODYNAMIC PSYCHOTHERAPY

In all therapies, including behaviour and cognitive therapy, the relationship between therapist and patient is important, since without a good relationship where there is an element of trust and respect there is unlikely to be the basis for meaningful change. In psychodynamic psychotherapy the therapist–patient relationship is the central core of the therapy and the main vehicle of change. The term 'psychodynamic' refers to the theoretical origins of this approach, in particular the ideas and practices of the psychoanalytic school. The focus in psychodynamic psychotherapy is not on producing symptomatic and behaviour change directly, but on establishing a therapeutic relationship in which the patient feels safe enough to reveal and explore emotionally charged and often upsetting material. This is a process of uncovering and of 'working through', with the therapist applying analytical skills to enable the patient to explore his intrapsychic world in an effective and productive way. There are many different 'schools' of psychodynamic psychotherapy, which reflect theoretical differences and divisions in the psychoanalytic movement. However, it has been suggested that the common factors in psychodynamic psychotherapy probably outweigh the differences between schools. An example of a psychotherapy case is given to illustrate this approach.

Treatment by psychodynamic psychotherapy

Jack is a 38-year-old teacher, married with three children. He was referred to a clinical psychologist who specialized in psychodynamic psychotherapy by his GP because of frequent bouts of depression. Jack was ill at ease when he arrived, and initially quite reticent and defensive. He began by saying, 'I didn't really want to come here, you know. It was Sheila's idea . . . I don't want to waste your time'. He did not believe he had a 'problem' as such—just sometimes he got very unhappy. He did not know why. He was happily married in a great job with 'three lovely children'. As the interview progressed Jack relaxed and began to talk more freely about himself. He recounted some of the experiences of his childhood, which had been quite harsh at times. His family had been poor. His father had been frequently ill and off work, and there had been very little money around. He and his elder brother, Jim, had both done well at school; but, while Jim had gone on to University and eventually a successful job in engineering, Jack had left school at 16 against his parents' wishes. At first he had 'bummed around', taking various jobs before deciding upon teaching as a career. He entered a teaching training school, where he met Sheila. Shortly after he had qualified, they got married, and, after a couple of years in one school, he had got a job at his present school, where he had been for the past 14 years.

Jack said that there had been times during his childhood when he had felt very unhappy; but once he began on his career as a teacher, he had felt fine, very happy. It was only in the last year or so that he had felt very depressed, and he could not see why. He reiterated his statements about being really very happy with his family and in his work, but in a rather quiet and depressed tone of voice, so that the therapist gained a strong feeling of deep unhappiness and misery. The assessment interview continued, with the therapist asking Jack more about himself, his family, and his current life. Jack's unhappiness became more obvious; and at the end of the interview the therapist asked Jack whether he wished to embark on a course of psychodynamic psychotherapy, explaining that this entailed weekly therapy sessions of 50 minutes lasting for up to a year. She said that she felt that Jack was indeed very unhappy, and that psychotherapy was a way of exploring what the unhappiness was about; and that sometimes this could be a painful and difficult process, but in the end it could be of benefit. After a moment's hesitation, Jack agreed to 'give it a try'.

In an assessment interview such as this the therapist seeks to establish some form of psychological contact which will serve as the basis of the psychotherapeutic relationship. She or he also seeks to understand what it is that is troubling the patient, and perhaps already has some ideas about how to proceed. Jack's present unhappiness may well have an important relationship to his upbringing and the expectations of a bright young boy from a deprived background. But these are only tentative ideas. More will undoubtedly emerge as the therapy progresses. Jack too will have formed an impression of the therapist and have some thoughts about what therapy could offer. Sometimes these are unrealistic expectations and hopes, which are modified during treatment. Like any other relationship, a psychotherapeutic relationship entails a process of mutual adjustment and understanding.

It is not possible here to describe in detail the vicissitudes of Jack's therapy. Briefly, after a 'honeymoon period' of regular attendance, Jack became morose and withdrawn. He began missing sessions and arriving late. The therapist sought to explore what was happening in their relationship, thereby provoking considerable feelings of anger and hostility on Jack's part. A crisis point was reached when Jack might easily have terminated treatment. But the therapist worked hard to get through to Jack, accepting his anger without rebuff or recrimination and pushing Jack to examine why he should feel this way. Out of this emerged a picture of a younger brother who had felt neglected by his family and had harboured a deep resentment of his parents' apparent indifference to him in contrast to his elder brother. He had rebelled and left school and had eventually thrown himself into teaching partly perhaps as a way to provide others with the care and guidance he felt he had lacked. He had married a warm and openly affectionate woman who gave him the support and succour he felt he needed. He had immersed himself in bringing up his own family. However, lately, when his depression had returned, he had a powerful conviction that he had really achieved nothing worthwhile in his life and that he was a charlatan, someone who did not deserve the attention and interest of other. In therapy he had become withdrawn and angry at the therapist's constant attention, particularly as he had begun to develop warm and positive feelings towards her. His defence against such feelings was to withdraw; but when the therapist did not let him, he experienced powerful feelings of anger and hostility.

The experience of strong feelings towards the therapist, or 'transference', as it is known in psychodynamic terms, is regarded as many as a vital part of the therapeutic process. Jack's feeling towards the therapist can be seen as reflection of feelings experienced at other times and towards others, parents perhaps. It is the therapist's job to recognize these feelings and, with the patient, to 'work through' them in therapy. The patient may then begin to learn something about himself and how his current feelings are expressions of other thoughts and experiences of which he may have been unconscious. In Jack's case the therapist's acceptance of his anger and the open way she talked about their relationship proved a turning point. He began to examine his past experiences, his childhood in particular, from a different perspective. He felt valued, almost for the first time, as a person in his own right. He saw how much he had striven hard either to meet the aspirations of his parents or to reject them. He ended therapy feeling an upsurge of morale and confidence and with the conviction that he had the capability to do well both at work and in his family.

A brief description such as this can only touch upon complexities of a psychotherapeutic relationship. Patients vary, as do the problems they present and the ways in which they respond to treatment. Therapists too have different styles and theoretical orientations. The essential features that distinguish this approach from the behavioural and cognitive therapies described earlier lie in the focus on the therapist–patient relationship and on the analytic skills of the therapist in understanding and interpreting the feelings and problems of the patient. The practice of psychotherapy demands considerable personal skills from the therapist and the capacity to maintain a positive relationship with patients, sometimes under difficult and trying conditions. Not all clinical psychologists feel equipped to offer this form of treatment, and some are frankly antagonistic to it. Some schools of thought argue that those who practice psychotherapy should themselves have been in psychotherapy as an integral part of their training. Not all agree with this point of view. But certainly it is desirable that a psychotherapist receive regular supervision from another experienced therapist.

THE ECLECTIC APPROACH

The differences between psychodynamic psychotherapy on the one hand and the cognitive–behavioural therapies on the other are not as definitive as might appear from the accounts of therapy given so far. Certainly there are real differences in theory; but theoretical differences relate only loosely to therapeutic practice. And some of the most obvious difference in practice can disappear as therapists of all persuasions converge towards an essentially similar pattern of treatment. One example is the trend towards brief psychodynamic psychotherapy which can be shorter in time than some of the cognitive–behavioural therapies. Although the psychodynamic approach is still essentially interpretative, with an emphasis on the therapist–patient relationship, the treatment is problem focused and time limited. A patient receiving brief psychodynamic psychotherapy will be encouraged to select a specific problem in therapy to work on just as he or she would be in cognitive–behavioural therapies. Another example of a convergence between the two schools of therapy is the way cognitive–behavioural therapies have taken up the significance of the therapist–patient relationship. This is particularly seen in the treatment of more severe problems such as personality disorders in which the therapeutic relationship may be threatened by the patient's extreme behaviour. Cognitive–behaviour therapy for personality disorders is often lengthy, taking 1 or 2 years, and the therapist has to work hard to counteract what psychodynamic therapists call 'acting out'. Schema-focused cognitive therapy, in which the underlying and often unconscious beliefs of the patient are addressed, parallels many aspects of psychodynamic psychotherapy (Young 1994).

Many clinical psychologists describe their therapeutic approach as 'eclectic'. By that they generally mean that they do not rigidly adhere to one treatment model, but are prepared to use a variety of models and techniques in helping a patient, that is they tailor the therapy very much to individual needs. Susan's treatment is a good example of this form of 'eclecticism'.

The treatment of a student with an eating disorder

Susan was a 21-year-old student in the final year of a history degree. She had become obsessed with food to such an extent that she found it impossible to concentrate on anything else. Her work had 'gone' and she had stopped seeing most of her friends. The GP who referred her for psychological treatment diagnosed her problem as *bulimia nervosa,* an eating disorder characterized by episodes of binge-eating and self-induced vomiting or purgative abuse, a constant preoccupation with food and eating, and a morbid fear of fatness. Susan was not markedly underweight, but appeared pale and drawn. She admitted that she binged two or three times a week, eating huge quantities of food and then deliberately vomiting. At other times she ate very little, and only a selection of carefully chosen 'good' foods which she believed were not fattening. Her mood was low and she felt unable to exercise any control over this part of her life.

A cognitive–behavioural treatment for *bulimia nervosa* has been described and evaluated (Fairburn 1985). It has three stages. Firstly, an intensive and supportive phase designed to disrupt the pattern of habitual overeating and vomiting. Susan was asked to keep detailed records of her food consumption and to identify meals in which she felt that she was in control and those in which she was not. She was advised to restrict her eating to three planned meals a day regardless of hunger. No attempt was made at this stage to check her vomiting or modify the type of food she was eating. The therapist gave Susan as much support as possible, seeing her initially two or three times a week, and provided her with corrective information about food, weight, and diet. As a result Susan gradually brought her eating more under control, and the episodes of bingeing and vomiting were markedly reduced. Her mood lifted and she began to take up her work again.

In the second phase Susan was seen on a weekly basis, and the focus shifted to the problems and stresses that had provoked the eating disorder. The therapist encouraged Susan to relax her rigid restrictions and try 'banned foods', as an experiment designed to demonstrate that this would not lead to a massive loss of control nor immediate weight gain. At this point Susan began to talk more generally about herself and in particular about her parents. The psychologist detected ambivalent feelings in Susan about her family. She described her father in highly idealized terms, yet it also appeared that he was rarely at home, and when he was he would shut himself away to work. Susan was often rather contemptuous about her mother's contribution to the family ('cook and housewife'). Yet it appeared that she was emotionally quite close to her. Susan also mentioned casually, in passing, an exboyfriend whom she had been very close to for most of her student life. These messages alerted the therapist to the role played by disturbed relationships in Susan's problems. Since the worst part of the eating disorder had been brought under reasonable control, the treatment focus could be shifted towards exploring Susan's feeling in relation to her family and her exboyfriend.

The final phase of Fairburn's approach focuses on the maintenance of change and preparation for possible relapse. In Susan's case, less emphasis was given to food as she regularly saw the psychologist over the next few months. As her trust for the therapist increased, she was able to admit for the first time how resentful and angry she felt towards her parents, her father in particular. The psychologist for her part was able to get Susan to see that such feelings were not abnormal and that Susan's worth as a person was not dependent on the approval of her parents or others. Susan's self-image had been narrowly restricted to her appearance; hence her excessive concern with food and eating. The treatment allowed her to see how other aspects of herself were valuable and important.

Susan's treatment illustrates how a practical cognitive–behavioural treatment can be successfully combined with a more psychodynamic approach. There was a clear need in the early stages of treatment for the therapist to provide practical help and emotional support. After that a variety of possibilities arise. A more specifically cognitive approach can be adopted, in which the patient's beliefs and attitudes about food and eating are directly tackled. This could be very much a part of Fairburn's approach; and for some patients this direct attack on their cognitions is of benefit. Alternatively, the patient's family could have been brought into treatment in the form of family therapy. The choice of strategy will depend very much on the type of patient and the nature of his or her problems, as well as on the particular experience and expertise of the therapist.

Research evidence supports the effectiveness of cognitive–behaviour therapy in the treatment of bulimia with about two-thirds of patients benefiting from this approach (Roth and Fonagy 1996). Other psychotherapies have been less well researched but, where the studies have been done, comparable results have been found. In one treatment study, cognitive–behaviour therapy proved most successful at the end of the treatment compared to interpersonal therapy (IPT), a psychodynamic approach. However, at 12-months follow-up, those receiving IPT had continued to improve and showed as good or better rate of recovery to those receiving cognitive–behaviour therapy (Fairburn *et al.* 1991). Given the complexity of eating disorders, an eclectic approach may well be necessary if all aspects of the problem are to be addressed.

COGNITIVE–ANALYTIC THERAPY

A few therapeutic approaches deliberately combine elements of different schools of therapy to create a new form of therapy. Cognitive–analytic therapy (CAT) is one such approach. It is a form of brief psychotherapy in which the pragmatics of the cognitive–behavioural therapies are combined with the insights and interpretations of the psychodynamic school. In cognitive–analytic therapy patients are encouraged to keep a diary and monitor their progress by means of rating scales; the approach is time limited (usually 16 sessions) and problem focused. These practical procedures are combined with a written psychodynamic formulation and interpretations of the transference issues that arise in the therapeutic relationship. Research has begun to show that cognitive–analytic therapy can be a cost-effective and helpful method of therapy (Ryle 1997).

MARITAL OR COUPLES THERAPY

Most of the cases described so far have been examples of individual treatment where the therapeutic contact is between two individuals, patient and therapist. But, as the example of Jessica and David illustrated, sometimes patients can be seen in couples. In psychosexual counselling it is generally desirable to see both partners, where that is possible, since the problem is expressed in terms of sexual relationship. Moreover, the practical procedures that are part of sex therapy are obviously much more applicable to a couple than to a single individual.

Marital or couples therapy is another example where both partners are almost always seen, for the same reasons as in sex therapy. The relationship is the crucial factor, and it is very difficult to work productively on a relationship when only one partner is present. In marital therapy, the psychologist's role is that of both facilitator and teacher. As a neutral outsider she or he can enable the couple to perceive and understand more clearly what the nature of their problem is, and by skilful guidance can hopefully help the couple resolve their difficulties and adopt a more productive way of relating to each other. Not all clinical psychologists will practise marital therapy, some preferring to refer patients to specialist organizations such as RELATE in the United Kingdom. On the other hand, there has been a particular interest in applying behavioural and social learning theory to marital therapy, and several practical psychological strategies have been devised. For example where partners have a particular difficulty in communicating with each other, the psychologist can directly teach communication skills. This is done in relation to a practical problem in the marriage, and can be expanded to include problem-solving skills in general. Another approach is to examine the ways in which the couple seek to influence each other's behaviour. In some instances couples may be encouraged to make explicit contracts with each other which are written down, specifying the behaviours that they would like to see and what contingencies would follow (contingency contracting). By making the rules specific and explicit, the couple can learn the important skills of reciprocity and positive reinforcement.

FAMILY THERAPY

Another approach that differs from one-to-one treatment methods is family therapy. As the name implies, psychological problems are seen not so much as deficits or psychopathology within the individual, but rather as a product of the family and family relationships. Family therapy consists of bringing the whole family (or as many of the family as possible) into therapy and working with them in order to produce changes in the family structure and relations. This is sometimes generically known as a *systemic* way of working, underlining the need to look at a problem in relation to the system as a whole and not in isolation. This approach first began in relation to psychological problems in children and adolescents, where it clearly makes sense to see the child's problem in its context. For example a child with nocturnal enuresis (bedwetting) might be providing a focus away from the parents' marital difficulties which are too difficult for the family to deal with directly, or an adolescent's anorexia is a response to implicit family demands to succeed at academic work at all costs by being too ill to work effectively.

A number of psychologists have begun to use family therapy approaches with adult patients. Members of the immediate family are invited to attend for therapy, and the family structure is explored. This is commonly done by means of a *genogram,* which is in effect the drawing up of a family tree, in the process of which family patterns, myths, and structures begin to emerge, and the problem, initially defined as the referred patient's, becomes more of a family one. Family therapists tend to work in a different style and format from most individual therapists. For example it is common for therapists to work as a team, perhaps of three or four people, one of whom is the recognized therapist and the others advisers. The advisers watch the therapist and family working, perhaps from behind a one-way screen, and may interrupt the therapy to provide advice or suggest therapeutic strategies. The therapist will seek 'time out' from time to time to discuss progress (or the lack of it) with her advisers. Generally, family therapy is not a lengthy affair; it may be as short as three or four sessions, and can be spread out over a longer time period (meetings every 3 weeks, for example). Most importantly, the systemic approach stresses the capacity of the family system to find and implement change itself; the therapists' role is to enable change by focusing on the family's strengths and allowing the family to gain a new perspective on its problems. Family therapy for adults is still in an early stage of development. However, the systemic approach has a broad application and can be used in individual, couples, and group therapy.

GROUP THERAPIES

Some people's psychological problems may best be dealt with in groups. This can be true when people share a common problem which requires a common treatment strategy. Agoraphobic patients, for example, with a fear of leaving the safety of their homes can be helped by means of a planned behavioural programme carried out in small groups of five to eight patients. The psychologist may set up a week's intensive treatment in which the group meets every day at the clinic and each day carries out a part of the behavioural programme, at first with the supervision of the psychologist and then on their own. Alternatively the group may meet weekly for a period of 6 weeks, with homework tasks set in between. Behavioural groups such as these can be very effective, particularly when the group is cohesive and mutually supportive. It is easier for some patients to take risks when others are in the same boat.

For some patients a group is part of the problem. People who are shy, unassertive, nervous of others or who lack 'social skills' may benefit from a group treatment since it allows them to learn how to overcome their difficulties and interact more effectively with others. Social skills training groups, for example, are ones in which people are directly taught various social skills, such as those used in holding conversations, making requests, forming friendships, or dealing with people in authority. Another related approach is assertiveness training, in which anxious and inhibited patients are taught how to stand up for themselves more effectively and to be more open and expressive in their feelings towards others.

Social skills and assertiveness training groups vary in size from as little as four patients to as large as ten or twelve, and often have two therapists. In most instances the period of training is deliberately circumscribed and a highly structured programme is followed. The content of the training varies from focusing on small and specific aspects of social interaction, for example, eye contact in talking to other people or the use of gesture in conversation, to generalized and quite complex aspects of interpersonal relationships, for example, responding to criticism from other people, or breaking into a social group at a party. Training consists usually of modelling or demonstration by the therapist or others of appropriate social behaviour, repeated practice in the form of role play in the group or individually with the therapist, feedback on how successful the practice was, further repeated practice, and homework assignments for the patients to carry out outside the treatment.

Some forms of group therapy are much less didactic. Group psychotherapy, for example, can involve two therapists and eight or more patients meeting weekly for as long as 18 months. The focus of the group is on interpersonal learning, but by means of shared experiences rather than specific teaching. Typically, the therapists do not 'lead' the group, but seek to guide it forwards, creating a constructive and helping atmosphere in which personal problems can be freely discussed. The group itself becomes an important and valued entity, and is seen as the main vehicle of change. It may be that elements of both the skills training and the interpersonal learning groups can be combined to good effect. Practical role-playing exercises, for example, can often be a part of group psychotherapy, although their use is less for acquiring skills than for providing personal feedback.

HOW EFFECTIVE ARE PSYCHOLOGICAL TREATMENTS?

This question is not an easy one to answer. Firstly, there are many forms of psychological treatment, so that a general statement about their effectiveness is hard to make. In some quarters there is a widely held belief that all forms of psychotherapy are 'modestly effective', and no one treatment strategy is really superior to any other. But, optimistic as this verdict may be, it is undiscriminating and not very helpful. If all treatments are of equal validity, how does one decide which treatment to use? And is it plausible to maintain that any form of psychological treatment is of benefit? Surely some approaches are better than others. In the United Kingdom, the Department of Health set up a Task Force to summarize the evidence on the effectiveness of the various psychotherapies so that the results could be disseminated to service providers and purchasers (Department of Health 1996). A detailed study of therapeutic outcome was commissioned and the results published in a book (Roth and Fonagy 1996). It is clear from this review that many psychotherapies have achieved impressive results, particularly in the short and medium term. There is stronger evidence in favour of the shorter, more prescriptive therapies, such as cognitive–behaviour therapy. But there are many areas where empirical knowledge is lacking. This is partly due to the absence of good outcome studies. Psychoanalysis, for example, the oldest form of psychological treatment, has had very little empirical research carried out into its effectiveness. One reason for this is the enormous complexity of the task. It is exceedingly difficult to translate the sophisticated theoretical terminology of psychoanalysis into practical data that can be scientifically measured and studied. The greater concreteness of behavioural and cognitive treatments has certainly helped researchers in designing and carrying out sound empirical research. It is easier to show that agoraphobic patients are able to go out more on their own after treatment than it is to show that their unconscious conflicts have been successfully resolved.

One should not underestimate the complexity of showing that a form of psychotherapy 'works'. For example while people may show considerable improvement during treatment, it is often difficult to distinguish the various factors that account for that improvement. The personality of the therapist, the personality of the client, the particular setting, the patient's desire to please the therapist, the reactivity of the measures used, the influence of extraneous variables, the passage of time, are all factors that can produce change. Research designs are becoming more sophisticated in the attempt to control for various factors, but it remains difficult to carry out complex outcome research successfully. Therefore many forms of psychological treatment remain of uncertain value. This does not mean that most treatments are ineffective; merely that there is insufficient knowledge to conclude definitely that a particular treatment works—a state of affairs that is not uncommon in other fields of clinical practice.

Clinical psychologists have shown a particular interest in treatment research, and have often been in the forefront of designing and carrying out outcome studies. A recent development has been to look more closely at the *process* of change. We need to know not only that a psychological treatment is of benefit, but how such treatments work, which patients respond well and which badly, what therapists actually do that helps their patients, and many other important points. Process research uses a different strategy from outcome research. There is a closer look at specific therapeutic processes often in the form of a qualitative analysis. For example audiotape segments of therapist–patient interactions may be closely analysed to develop and test theories about the way crucial changes occur in sessions. The advantage of this approach is that it is very close to the reality of clinical work. A disadvantage is that it can be difficult to generalize the results obtained.

SUMMARY

Clinical psychologists are specialists in psychological treatment and, in particular, have developed expertise in the short-term, pragmatic cognitive and behavioural methods. These methods have been described and illustrated with reference to anxiety and depressive disorders. Some clinical psychologists go on to acquire further specialist training, which can take the form of a particular type of therapy (for example, sex therapy, marital therapy) or a particular theoretical orientation and practical skills. The psychodynamic approach has been described and illustrated with reference to a therapy case. Recently there has been a convergence of different schools of therapy, and many clinical psychologists describe themselves as 'eclectic', preferring to use a variety of methods and tailor these to the individual case. Finally, the effectiveness of psychological treatments has been examined in various research studies. There is now a strong body of evidence supporting the effectiveness of various forms of psychotherapy, particularly cognitive–behavioural therapies. More research is needed particularly into the process of therapy and therapist–patient interactions.

References

Clark, D. M. (1997). Panic and social phobia. In *Science and practice of cognitive behaviour therapy* (eds D. M. Clark and C. G. Fairburn). Oxford University Press, Oxford.

Department of Health (1996). *NHS psychotherapy services in England. Review of strategic policy*. Department of Health, London.

Fairburn, C. G. (1985). Cognitive behavioural treatment for bulimia. In *Handbook of psychotherapy for anorexia nervosa and bulimia* (eds D. M. Garner and P. E. Garfinkel). Guilford Press, New York.

Fairburn, C. G., Jones, R., Peveler, R., and Carr, S. (1991). Three psychological treatments for bulimia nervosa: A comparative trial. *Archiv. Gen. Psychiat.*, **48**, 463–9.

Hawton, K. (1985). *Sex therapy. A practical guide*. Oxford University Press, Oxford.

Hawton, K., Salkovskis, P., Kirk, J., and Clark, D. (1989). *Cognitive behaviour therapy for psychiatric problems*. Oxford University Press, Oxford.

Mathews, A., Gelder, M. G., and Johnston, D. W. (1981). *Agoraphobia. Nature and treatment*. Tavistock, London.

Rachman, S. and Hodgson, R. J. (1980). *Obsessions and compulsions*. Prentice-Hall, Englewood Cliffs, NJ.

Roth, A. and Fonagy, P. (1996). *What works for whom? A critical review of psychotherapy research*. Guilford Press, New York.

Ryle, A. (ed.) (1997). *Cognitive-analytic therapy. Developments in theory and practice*. Wiley, Chichester.

Teasdale, J. D., Fennell, M. J. V., Hibbert, G. A., and Amies, P. L. (1984). Cognitive therapy for major depressive disorder in primary care. *Brit. J. Psychiat.*, **144**, 400–6.

Young, J. E. (1994). *Cognitive therapy for personality disorders: a schema-focussed approach*. Professional Resource Press, Sarasota, Florida.

Further reading

Bloch, S. (ed.) (1996). *An introduction to the psychotherapies*. Oxford University Press, Oxford.

Butler, G. and Hope, T. (1997). *Managing your mind. The mental fitness guide*. Oxford University Press, Oxford.

Gurman, A. S. and Messer, S. B. (eds) (1995). *Essential psychotherapies: theory and practice*. Guilford Press, New York.

Hammen, C. (1997). *Depression*. Psychology Press, Hove.

Yalom, I. D. (1995). *The theory and practice of group psychotherapy* (4th edn). Basic Books, New York.

3

Working with people who are severely mentally ill

John Hall

Most adults with psychological problems, such as those described in the previous chapter, are not permanently handicapped by their difficulties. They can continue to lead some sort of normal life, and can make most decisions relating to day-to-day living. A small but significant proportion of those in contact with mental health services are seriously handicapped by psychological and psychiatric difficulties, and some may not be able to continue living in their own homes. Another group of people, while also seriously handicapped by mental health problems, are not in contact with specialist mental health services but may be homeless, living in hostels, or in intermittent contact with the probation service or the police. This chapter describes how psychologists help members of both of these groups: that is people with major and seriously handicapping psychological difficulties in a range of settings—now often described as the severely mentally ill.

For many professional health-care staff, the care of acutely ill people offers more professional reward than the care of people with more long-term conditions. With the less severely ill it is certainly easier to see the relationship between the use of particular treatments and specific benefit; and, usually, acute patients tend to be more articulate and verbal, so they are often seen as more rewarding to help. However, many psychologists enjoy working with people with more long-term conditions for a number of reasons. First of all, perhaps simply because they are the most handicapped and disturbed, and hence deserving of special care. Often work with them—and with their families—extends over a number of years, affording an opportunity to understand individuals and their needs in an unusually deep way. Third, perhaps because working with them is intrinsically interesting because of the complex interaction of the range of factors that have to be considered. A fourth possible factor is the reward of the close teamwork that is often involved. A final factor which has emerged in the past few years is the promise of a new range of psychological treatments for individual symptoms.

THE IDEA OF SEVERE MENTAL ILLNESS

Until about the mid-1970s, most accommodation for adults with chronic psychiatric conditions was provided in large psychiatric hospitals, most of which were built during the late nineteenth century. The initial enthusiasm for asylum care in the early nineteenth century was generated by genuinely humanitarian reasons, and the very title asylum implied the recognition of the need for a safe place to protect the incapacitated. Most of these hospitals had a number of chronic or long-stay wards, where up to one hundred patients might live, the majority of whom had at some time received a diagnosis of schizophrenia. The 'chronic schizophrenic' was then the stereotypical long-stay patient.

Surveys suggested that the specifically psychiatric nature of their handicaps was often unclear in a substantial minority of the most chronic cases, although the application of modern diagnostic criteria retrospectively to these patients is admittedly fraught with theoretical difficulties. The run-down of large psychiatric hospitals that started in most European countries and in North America in the mid-1950s usually meant that the least disabled patients were discharged first. As the 'old' chronic patients left hospital, there was a growing awareness that a small proportion of newly-admitted adults with diagnoses such as schizophrenia were still going on to become severely psychiatrically disabled. The continuing accumulation of 'new chronic' or 'new long-stay' patients suggested that even with the most vigorous pharmacological and social care, a small proportion of patients could not be satisfactorily left unsupported (Murphy 1991).

With more assertive community treatment, and the acknowledgement that some disabled patients did not want to enter hospital, community mental health services now support a number of people with chronic conditions living in the community. While a substantial proportion have had more than one psychotic episode, it was recognized that diagnostically these people formed a very mixed group. They were characterized not so much by a single diagnosis, but more by their level of handicap and by their high use of services, especially as inpatients, when many have been compulsorily detained under the 1983 Mental Health Act.

Services to people with severe mental illness often include, in addition to those with a formal psychiatric diagnosis, several other groups of people, such as young adults with serious head injury, adults with a moderate degree of learning disability and with behaviour problems, and people with some progressive physical conditions, such as Huntington's chorea. These groups are very small in number in any locality but they pose real demands upon their families, and the local community may show limited tolerance to them. The ability of a family to cope with these difficulties is strained by the constant vigilance required, so that people who are strictly speaking not psychiatrically ill may be cared for on a long-term basis in a setting primarily intended for those with a severe mental illness. The term 'vulnerable adults' is sometimes used to describe these groups.

All of the above groups have some common characteristics. Most of them either have in the past or now display patterns of thinking and behaviour which have led them to be diagnosed with a serious psychiatric disorder. They may be living in a range of settings, but typically may be living on their own, in some sort of hostel, or may be homeless—certainly in conditions which most of us would not choose for ourselves. They probably are out of work, and probably have few close relationships. They are usually in high contact with specialized mental health services. They are 'severely mentally ill'.

THE PROBLEMS AND NEEDS TO BE IDENTIFIED

A major concern in this chapter is to look at psychologically disabled people in the setting where they live and spend their waking life. A psychological analysis of their problems and needs should therefore take account both of the problems posed by the person and their needs, and of the problems posed by the environment.

An important contribution of psychologists to the care of adults with severe mental illness has been the notion of need assessment. The idea of 'problems' begs the question about who perceives the problem to exist. Häfner (1985), writing from his experience in Germany, has suggested that the old asylums met a number of needs: accommodation, social, recreational, occupational, and treatment. A complementary alternative approach has been to formulate needs in a number of areas of functioning, such as categories of symptoms and behaviour problems, and categories of personal and social skills—such as personal cleanliness and management of money. For each area of functioning the exposure of a patient to a relevant intervention can be assessed, so that for each category of functioning the need status could be ascertained as either no need, met need, or unmet need. This approach also leads to the interesting concept of over-provision, or over-met need, where an intervention has continued even though the patient is functioning well. A recent instrument implementing this approach—the Cardinal Needs Schedule (Marshall, *et al.* 1995)—has been developed which is short and hence applicable in clinical settings, and takes into account the views of patients and their carers. This reflects the increasing realization that the great majority of people with severe mental illness are well able to express their own wishes, so that psychologists now take trouble to elicit user's views into greater account, both in planning services and in work with individual patients.

Problems and needs of severely mentally ill people

Psychologically, the problems of these people are not defined primarily by their diagnosis. It is true that the majority of such patients are likely to have been diagnosed as having some form of schizophrenic disorder at some time. It is significant that with increasing lengths of stay in hospital the proportion of patients who are so diagnosed increases to well above 50 per cent. Chronic schizophrenia thus forms the most serious psychiatric condition to continue to be found in psychiatric settings. However, a significant proportion may have a severe mood or affective disorder—chronic depression or mania—or have been diagnosed as having a personality disorder (a widely used but unsatisfactory term, often describing, in fact, major behaviour disorders, including arson and lack of self-control resulting in aggressive behaviour). In addition to the primary problems arising from their psychiatric condition, people with severe mental illness may have disabilities with other causes. They frequently have other premorbid handicaps, such as lower intellectual ability or poorer work records, before they ever became ill. They may also have secondary handicaps arising from the way in which other people, including their families, view and respond to them. Most people who have lived continuously for any length of time—say 1 year or more—in a psychiatric institution will have had access to psychotherapy, social case-work skills, and other treatments, as well as carefully considered medication, and so sometimes are seen as the 'failures' of acute psychiatric and psychological help.

Psychologically, most severely mentally ill patients have some common attributes. Many are slow, in speech, in thinking, and in the speed at which they do every-day activities, such as washing and moving about. Many may lack concentration, so they are relatively easily distracted from what they are doing. The most handicapped may have very low levels of motivation, as indicated by their poor response to the normal encouragements of praise, and little interest in actively doing those recreational activities enjoyed by most people.

From the point of view of a clinical psychologist, the most obvious problems are their lack of skills of every-day living and of social behaviour. Some of these skills are self-help skills, such as attention to their own personal hygiene. A lack of social skills may be illustrated by an unwillingness to initiate conversation with others, a lack of persistence in games or other social activities, or a lack of eye-contact with others.

From a psychiatric point of view, contrasted with these 'negative symptoms' are psychiatric 'positive symptoms', most commonly delusional ideas and hallucinatory ('hearing voices') experiences, which can give a profoundly unreal experience to conversing with some of these people. Positive symptomatic behaviour has a particular capacity to confuse and antagonize families and neighbours, although an important recent insight into the subjective experience of hearing voices suggests that for a number of patients their 'voices' are friendly and they do not wish to lose that experience. These patients may also display other odd behaviour, such as bizarre patterns of hand movement and gesticulation, or the abnormally large amounts of fluid that a few of them drink. A very small proportion of these patients may be episodically aggressive (see Chapter 9 on working with offenders), but some patients may be classified as 'potentially violent' even though they are cared for and managed so that years may have passed without a single violent episode. These positive, or deviant, patterns of behaviour are more idiosyncratic or individualistic than the negative deficits.

Last of all, it is important to acknowledge the need for medical care for many of these patients. First, many of them will be receiving maintenance medication, either of oral drugs or of depot injections of neuroleptic drugs, which ensure that medication can be reliably administered without the individual patient's needing to remember a complex tablet-taking regime. Correct medication may be very important in preventing relapse. Second, people with severe mental illness may need medical attention for ordinary physical ailments, especially since some of them may have high pain thresholds, and thus physical problems may be well advanced before they are detected. This is particularly true for those severely mentally ill people who are homeless, and who thus may suffer from all the additional health risks of living in cold, damp circumstances. As these people become older, they are likely to have physical problems; and even among younger patients physical needs should not be overlooked, as they may not self-present for health screening programmes. Providing physical aids and prostheses, such as dentures and spectacles, can overcome some problems, but only if patients understand their value and are trained to make use of them.

Problems of psychiatric institutions and settings

As already discussed, the most common living environment for people with severe mental illness used to be a large psychiatric hospital or institution. These hospitals were remote both from the neighbouring community, so reducing the opportunity of patients using local shops and libraries, and from the community of origin of the patients, so that relatives faced a time-consuming and expensive journey when and if they visited. A formal definition of such an institution is a living place where there are separate groups of staff and inmates or residents, and where the living conditions of the resident group are primarily determined by the staff group. Western European societies have traditionally provided a number of such institutions, most notably prisons, hospitals, and accommodation for the poor and 'needy'. Irrespective of the precise nature of the inmate group, sociologists, followed by social psychiatrists and psychologists, proposed that all such institutions have a similar, essentially negative, impact on the resident group. The consequences of long-term exposure to institutional life, especially if the individual began their institutional 'career' in childhood, are known as institutionalization or institutional neurosis.

Erving Goffman (1961) is probably the best-known critic of institutional care. He coined the phrase 'total institution', which he defined as 'a place of residence and work where a large number of like-situated individuals, cut off from the wider society for an appreciable period of time, together lead an enclosed formally administered round of life'. Goffman considered that *the* central feature of institutional life is a breakdown of barriers between three spheres of life: sleep, work, and play. This definition emphasizes a number of characteristics of the total institution, such as one organizational system embracing all aspects of the resident life and the homogeneity of the population of residents of any one institution. The total institution is at one end of a continuum, the other end of which is 'normal' self-determined life in domestic surroundings, with work and leisure carried out in different places.

Goffman's definition included reference to places of work: ordinary people usually go to work at a place other than their home, and those who work at home typically enjoy more autonomy in their pattern of work than those who are employed outside their home. A characteristic of many of the old psychiatric institutions was that day activities were provided on the same site as the living facilities, and that the same group of staff supervised the residents in both settings, so the range of social relationships in which they are engaged was thereby narrowed. Providing the range of services to meet the needs identified earlier by Häfner on different sites, away from residential facilities, then broadens the range of social relationships, quite apart from the extra social contact that results.

What this definition makes clear is that institutional care is defined by a pattern of life, as much as by other physical features of the institution. Thus many people with severe psychological difficulties live in group homes run by charitable bodies, in hostels provided by public social welfare or social services departments, and in sheltered housing with resident workers. Whatever the name given to these institutions, some of the practices encountered in Goffman's total institutions *may* be encountered there. Awareness of the continuing risk of institutionalization in *any* long-stay residential setting is one contribution a psychologist can make, and of course the ability to take steps to counteract those risks.

A psychologist should, of course, be asking 'Why institutions anyway?' Why not accommodate everyone with severe mental illness in ordinary housing? There may be some positive reasons for providing special environments for these groups of people. They have historically often been exploited, and may benefit from protection. Some of the most handicapped people may benefit from a specially structured environment to enable them to acquire and maintain the skills they lack. A few may be seen as constituting some risk to the general public, so that some degree of security is needed. This does not suggest they require institutional care, in the passive meaning of that word; but perhaps they *do* require a special place for living that cannot readily be provided in ordinary, unstaffed domestic housing.

Adopting this approach has led to a new type of residential provision, called hospital-hostels, for longer-term patients which minimize institutional factors and increase as far as possible individual programmes tailored to the needs of residents (Garety and Morris 1984). A major factor of these units is the presence of a psychologist who has the task of designing individual programmes for residents, within the overall regime of the unit. We are currently in a novel situation where the case for any specialized setting for the provision of care has to be argued anew. Psychologically, any special residential provision should be as need-specific as possible, permit links with the outside community, maximize independence, and keep to a minimum the rules imposed by others.

Over the past 25 years in Britain, most of the older larger hospitals have been replaced by networks of accommodation in ordinary housing, group homes, hostels, and new, small purpose built units. This process has been paralleled in most European countries and in North America, though at different rates. These units are of two broad types—purpose-built new units or hostels, either on a general hospital campus or in an ordinary street—and adapted larger houses. Whatever the type of housing, the buildings should be acceptable and accessible to the families and friends of residents. The internal physical arrangements of the buildings should allow privacy for individual residents, and opportunities for personalizing their room or bed area.

As the deinstitutionalization movement has progressed both in the United States and Europe, there has been major concern that the level of reprovision has not matched the numbers of those discharged, leading to people with serious psychiatric illness who are homeless, or who have been placed within the penal system rather than the hospital. Night shelters may exist for some of the homeless, or in Britain they may be supported by local authorities in what is usually a poor standard of bed-and-breakfast accommodation. These settings have not been specifically set up to cope with people with long-term psychiatric problems, and often offer little or no special facilities for these people; hence the risk of relapse in such settings is high. It is a grim paradox that the lack of adequate provision for people with serious handicaps has been one of the greatest spurs to rethinking the whole issue of the best way to help and care for them.

Care practices in psychiatric settings

The quality of care in any institutions arises from two sources; staff practices, and the rules of the institution. Psychological studies of nurse–patient interaction suggest that in most psychiatric settings the least well-trained staff spend more time interacting with residents than the more well-trained and senior staff, at least in part because of the administrative duties which have to be done by the latter group. This means that in many settings for people with severe mental illness the staff with the greatest capacity to change the residents behaviour, psychologically speaking, are the least skilled to do so. This is not to deny the very real interest in residents shown by less-trained staff, but to acknowledge their need for practical skill-based training and guidance, which takes into account their attitudes and implicit philosophies of care. It is not unusual for longer-stay units both in hospital and in the community to be seen as less interesting than 'acute' settings, so they may be prone to poorer levels of staffing and low morale. The psychologist's role in this setting then becomes one of staff facilitation, empowerment, and support, as well as the more public one of technical treatment expert.

The formal and informal 'rules' of institutions form the other social determinant of the institutional environment. These rules effectively structure the degree of independence and self-determination open to residents. One categorization of environments is to divide them into either 'block' or 'individualized' regimes, depending on the amount of choice allowed to individual residents. Another categorization is to classify the level of 'restrictiveness' of a unit, noting the amount of restriction on, for example, use of tobacco, access of visitors, and the time when lights have to be out, compared with a normal home. Hospitals, according to this model, are the most restrictive type of environment because they cater for peoples' total needs over a 24-hour period: even seriously disabled people do not necessarily need total care in all areas of their life for 24 hours. Some of these regulations are purely local to an individual hospital or indeed to a single ward or unit within the hospital, some may be imposed by government regulations, and some may have their origins in the practices of individual professions. A psychologist can contribute to the social functioning of a unit by joining in regular reviews of ward procedures, so that regimes are as individualized and as minimally restrictive as possible, consistent with the safety of residents and staff.

THE WORK OF THE CLINICAL PSYCHOLOGIST WITH PEOPLE WITH SEVERE MENTAL ILLNESS

The task of the clinical psychologist with this client group will vary considerably, primarily depending on the level of disability of patients and the range of settings in which they live.The most handicapped group of patients may lack basic self-care skills, may be heavily dependent on care staff, and will most probably continue to spend most of their lives in a highly sheltered environment. Such a patient might be a 67-year-old obese woman, Susan, who has been in hospital continuously for the past 23 years. Admitted after her parents died, she never married or carried out a full-time job, and is now unable to dress herself without help and has difficulty climbing stairs. She finds it difficult to concentrate on games or other recreational activities, and her conversation with other residents or staff is virtually incoherent, except to the two or three staff who know her well. She is now diabetic, is likely to become more physically dependent, and needs careful medical attention.

An intermediate group of less disabled patients may not need to be in hospital continuously, although both to them, and perhaps more especially their families, the knowledge that they can return easily to hospital if needed is a support to them. They can use community facilities, such as local shops and pubs, and can often use a wider range of facilities with suitable help. Bernie is only 26, but he has already had four admissions to his local hospital. He attends a local day centre three times a week, and his parents are strongly involved with the local branch of the National Schizophrenia Fellowship (a British charity primarily for the support of relatives).

The least disabled group of 'high contact' patients may still be in close contact with their families and may be seeking work, even though they have intermittent episodes of acute symptoms. An example of such a patient would be a 41-year-old man, Jack, who failed to complete a college course of higher education when he was younger, and who then drifted into casual hotel work. He still keeps a job, even if part-time, for most of the year, and nearly always when demand for such work is high over the summer, but has periodic psychotic episodes. He is then off work, but his landlord helps him to maintain contact with the general practitioner and community nurse, and he may go to stay with his older married sister who lives 50 miles away.

Thinking about therapeutic aims and goals

The generic phrase 'rehabilitation' has often been used as a catch-all title to describe the range of activities undertaken to care for and treat people with severe mental illness. This implies a return to earlier levels of performance and hence ignores the possibility that the skills learned by the patient are totally new for them, so habilitation might then be a better term. Another term used is continuing care, which tends to imply a passive rather than an assertive approach. While no one term is really adequate to describe the range of procedures that have to be carried out, rehabilitation continues to be one of the most widely used names.

Bridges, Huxley, and Oliver (1994) have emphasized the need to define the concept of rehabilitation, to clarify aims, and hence to determine the form of interventions which may be needed. They point out that talking only of treatment suggests the removal of symptomatology, while rehabilitation implies the restoration of functional skills. They take account of the highly variable course which long-term psychiatric disorders, and the highly complex interactions which can occur between the person and his or her social environment. They therefore suggest that rehabilitation has a number of aims, which include:

- preventing or reducing impairments and social disabilities;
- restoring potential abilities to perform social roles;
- strengthening latent abilities and assets;
- facilitating adaptation to unchangeable impairments;
- enabling optimal levels of self-determination and independence;
- improving the sense of well being;
- minimizing burden upon primary supporters and staff.

Within this or a similar framework, it is important to define goals of work with chronic patients, and for everyone involved to adjust to longer time scales and slower rates of expected improvement. A number of factors interact dynamically when considering how to intervene to achieve these aims, as shown in Fig. 3.1.

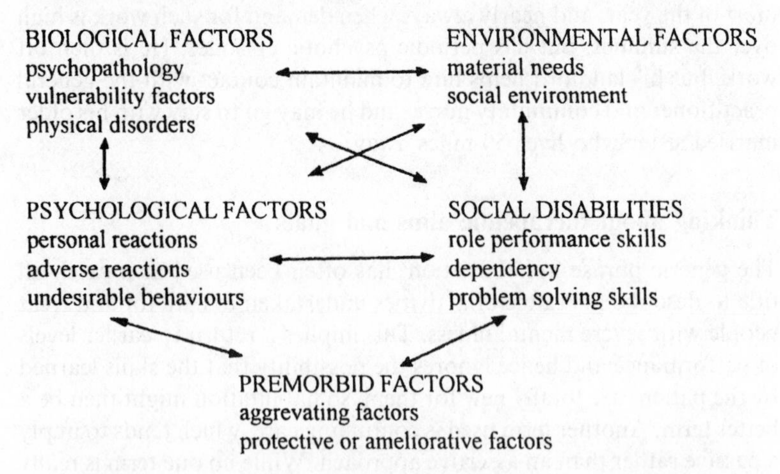

Fig. 3.1 Interaction of factors in psychiatric rehabilitation.

A psychological contribution to this field has been the development of overall goals of services to psychologically handicapped people, which can be integrated into the care plans of individuals. Perhaps the concept of 'normalization', now reconceptualized as 'social role valorization', applied particularly with respect to people with learning disability and discussed in Chapter 5, is the best example. This initially simple idea has been developed so that it carries with it the notion of availability of choice in different areas of living, the use of socially valued means of help with problems to counteract stigma, and the corollary of having to face reasonable risks.

Other overall or superordinate objectives of services have already been mentioned. One concept already hinted at is that of the 'least restrictive environment': a goal for services would then be that they should seek to provide the least restrictive environment possible for an individual, based on an assessment of his continuing abilities and disabilities, and offering the 'minimum therapeutic dose' of assistance needed for each area of disability. A similar notion is that of the 'least segregated environment'. Segregation implies reduced contact with the neighbouring community, whether family, friends, or facilities such as shops and pubs. Segregation would then be reduced not only by the siting of a unit near main centres of population, but also by ensuring, in detail, that a unit was near a post office and a bus stop, and that members of the outside community could come into the environment.

A rather different objective is that of 'personalization'. The concept of institutional neurosis views loss of personal events and personal possessions as one of seven contributory factors to this type of neurosis. The appropriate corrective action would accordingly be to ensure attention to personal events such as birthdays, and to provide space for personal possessions, such as little trinkets and photographs next to where the person sleeps.

These overall objectives can be an important contribution by clinical psychologists to care plans. They can be very helpful as a way of bringing cohesion to what could otherwise be a rag-bag of low-level subordinate goals, such as 'encouraging conversation' or 'going to the shops more', and can be directly applied to goal-planning meetings, as described in the section on individual therapeutic programmes.

Assessing and understanding the individual

By definition, patients with severe mental illness will already have had some prior contact with specialist services, so some information about them will normally be available when a psychologist working in this field meets them for the first time. For patients with very long experience of hospital life, there may sadly be relatively little information about their past in their case notes. For patients who have only recently become more disabled, there is now likely to be an indication of the current problems of the patient, and how much he or she has changed over recent weeks or months. A detailed knowledge of the history of a patient can give an idea of past interests—to be hopefully reawakened—and of the level of contact with relatives, and possibly of those circumstances that the patient has found particularly stressful in the past, which may give some ideas about what precipitates a worsening in their condition.

A special issue with this group of patients is that of creating an open and constructive therapeutic relationship, which requires a rather different approach than that described in Chapter 2. Perkins and Dilks (1992) describe the impact of severe mental illness upon the individual, pointing out the impact of disturbed perceptions—such as thinking that others are talking about them—and of confused thinking, so that they believe thoughts are being 'inserted' into their heads. They describe very sensitively how to respond to these disturbances, as by framing questions in an unambiguous way, by limiting the duration of sessions to take account of short attention span, and by flexibly adjusting the amount and type of input to take account of variations in mood and concentration. An ethical difficulty in working with chronic patients is their reticence in expressing their own wishes in a way that is consistent. Often such patients may have difficulty in understanding questions, may be inarticulate in their replies, or may be easily influenced in their answers, so it is difficult to have confidence that you really have found out what they want. This can lead to problems when there is no relative or next-of-kin to whom you can turn when difficult decisions have to be made. Clinical psychologists working with such patients often need to spend time with them, maybe only 10 or 20 minutes at a time, to enable the patient to become used to them but not to be stressed by the demands of too much time with someone who is initially a total stranger to them.

The focus of most assessment methods is the behaviour of the patient, both past or present, and looking at the remaining assets of the patient, as well as the deficits (or negative symptoms or handicaps) and deviations from normal (or positive symptoms or bizarre behaviour). Consistent with the analysis of the impact of different factors on the patient, it may also be helpful to assess formally the physical environment of the patient, the social environment created by staff or relatives, and indeed the burden or impact of care upon both the family and care staff. Accordingly, useful assessment instruments should be able to be used in both hospital and community settings.

The main areas of psychological concern about patients will normally revolve about their day-to-day social functioning and self-help skills. It is also important to understand the precise nature of their presenting symptoms. While delusions and hallucinations are the most common focal symptoms, and these may be the focus of specific psychological interventions, as explained later in the chapter, a patient may be intermittently anxious or depressed, and they may then benefit from treatment aimed at these secondary problems. It is also common practice for some form of risk assessment —of harm to others or to self—to be carried out. Although the great majority of patients are never violent, such an assessment is good practice for the protection of the patients, for other residents, and for staff. For those patients on medication, some assessment of side-effects of that medication will be important to medical colleagues.

As well as the assessment of individual patients, one practical task for the psychologist working with severely mentally ill people may be to contribute to an understanding of the range of needs that a local 'rehabilitation' service may try to meet. This can lead to a distinctive type of assessment procedure, a large-scale survey of all of the clients in contact with a service, which has few parallels in work with more acute patients.

Examples of assessment procedures

The two most frequently used types of assessment with this group of patients are ratings—based either on observation of day-to-day behaviour in a day or residential setting or on the observations and responses gathered during an interview—or behavioural assessment procedures. Ratings require observers to record, in a standard way, their *opinion* of the relative strength of a particular attribute. Ratings of day-to-day behaviour are usually completed by nurses or hostel staff, often on the basis of a few days' observation, and typically are high on general relevance. Conversely, ratings of interview behaviour may be more reliable, but may not be closely related to what the patient does outside the interview. Self-completion questionnaires may be difficult to use with more disabled patients. Given a renewed interest in the neuropsychology of psychotic disorders, there is a role for formal psychometric assessment, especially those tests illuminating attention and abstract thinking.

An example of a day-to-day behaviour rating scale is the REHAB scale, which has been used for a number of years and was recently reviewed by Baker and Hall (1994). The content of the items was chosen from research studies, to include items of problem behaviour that occurred most frequently, and to cover the full range of disability that can be shown with this client group. The basic period of observation is 1 week. Deficits of behaviour are assessed using a linear-graphic type of item, as shown below:

'How well did the patient get on with others on the ward or unit?'

Very poor relationship with other patients Solitary and withdrawn	Got on with some patients	Got on well with other patients

Positively deviant or bizarre behaviour is typically infrequent and unpredictable, such as shouting. This requires a different sort of item, mainly assessing the frequency with which such behaviour occurs.

With the development of psychological treatment of individual symptoms, a new family of psychological assessment instruments has been developed. An example is the Characteristic of Delusions Rating Scale of Garety and Hemsley (1987), which assesses 11 subjective attributes of an individual's beliefs, such as conviction about the belief, absurdity of the belief, and the amount of reassurance seeking undertaken by the patient. In addition there is an assessment of the level of distress caused by the delusional belief. Key dimensions of the scale in considering recovery, in addition to distress, are conviction and preoccupation.

Behavioural assessment procedures usually involve some timing or counting of events immediately as they happen, or the use of a simple coding system to categorize events. 'Time-sampling' is a frequently used behavioural assessment procedure in group 'staff–patient interaction' or 'engagement' studies. Time-sampling involves selecting a suitable schedule for observing each patient in turn, so for example, every 20 seconds a patient would be observed for 5 seconds exactly, and at the end of that 5-second period the patient's behaviour would be coded, using a set of behavioural categories. Adequate time must always be allowed for the appropriate category or categories to be selected and recorded, so the observer can then pick out the next patient in plenty of time, without being hurried. Although there can be a problem of 'reactivity', which is the way in which a patient behaves differently because he knows he is being observed, an observer can be passive and non-responsive to patients, thus minimizing this problem. The advent of relatively cheap hand-held electronic event-recorders means that this type of assessment can now be carried out unobtrusively and can yield very accurate results.

Psychological assessment has often been seen as the exclusive preserve of the psychologist. In long-term care settings, by contrast, the psychologist is very much concerned to work with other groups so that the assessments which *they* necessarily must make can be better understood and used. The psychologist then becomes an assessment resource and support to other colleagues, helping them to construct rating charts and checklists for individual patients.

Planning individual therapeutic programmes

Overall objectives for each patient, negotiated with and accepted by all staff concerned, are essential to develop a detailed programme of targets and a set of evaluation measures which are mutually consistent, and which can then provide an overall framework of treatment for staff and residents alike. Most units for people with severe mental illness have regular case conferences, often weekly, when all the residents are discussed in turn by all the clinical team. Good practice in this sort of setting is to review one patient in detail each week, as otherwise the quieter patients may slip from view with the more disturbed patients tending to take more time at the meetings. At these meetings, major changes in the care plans of a patient can be set, and all the staff present can agree on the priorities for each patient.

There is evidence that identifying specific therapeutic goals precisely, and communicating these goals clearly to both direct-care staff and to the patients themselves, is therapeutic. Only a limited number of goals should be set at one time, so that staff and patients alike are not overwhelmed by too many goals. These may cover any general area of functioning, such as the patient's ability to care for his own personal needs, or may cover more specific skills within this category such as washing, dressing, shaving, sanitary care, cleaning teeth, toileting, feeding, etc. Abilities may need to be defined at several different levels of handicap, so some sort of rating technique may be required to produce a change-sensitive measure of each individual skill.

Just as important as the initial specification of the goal is the regular checking or monitoring of the target that has been set, to see if change has indeed occurred. All assessment methods should be capable of being repeated from time to time to review patients. This is particularly important given the difficulty of maintaining staff behaviour consistently over the very long periods of time inevitably involved with this group of patients, and the possibility of complex cause-and-effect relationships developing between staff and residents. Psychologists often help to design attainable long-term recording systems, so that patients can be tracked over months or years to check their progress on key targets.

There have been exciting recent developments in the range of individual therapeutic procedures psychologists can use with this group of people. Most have been derived from cognitively-inspired research, analysing the problems of severely mentally ill people. Among these procedures are what have come to be known as 'psychoeducational programmes', and the direct psychological treatment of residual psychotic symptoms. These procedures can be offered to severely mentally ill patients both in institutional settings and to those living in their own homes, and will be considered in turn.

Psychoeducational interventions developed from the concept of 'expressed emotion', a measure of social environments characterized by high levels of hostility and critical comments, which was found to be highly predictive of relapse in psychotic patients. In turn it was found that levels of expressed emotion could be modified by providing information to families of patients about the nature of psychotic illness, by teaching them problem-solving skills, and by directly modifying their levels of hostility and criticism. A psychologist—or colleague—using these approaches will accordingly meet the family to assess the level of expressed emotion, and will gather other information from the family about their understanding of the identified patient's behaviour. Maintenance medication is important for many of these patients, and the information given both to the patients and to their families about the nature of drugs and their effectiveness can increase compliance with medication.

While different groups of researchers in this field have given differential attention to the components of psychoeducational treatment, there is good agreement on what those components are (Barrowclough and Tarrier 1992). The main elements are: education about the illness; stress management techniques, including problem solving; and goal setting for individual patients. This may involve, for example, the psychologist in meeting the family, identifying the problems they are currently encountering, and working with them to generate solutions to those problems. Many relatives have in the past been told little about the nature of their relative's condition, and hence may have had no constructive framework within which to view the odd behaviour of the relative. Psychologists can then offer information through running relative groups, through workshops, and via video and audio tapes. Often families misattribute some of the causes of the patients behaviour, so improved information can reduce blaming and scapegoating of the patient. Stress management approaches emphasize a detailed analysis of the situational factors leading to stress, especially those factors which are most consistently apparent, and the use of role play to rehearse alternative strategies. Goal setting approaches are similar to those already identified, and usually involve family members together working out what needs are common to both the family and the patient. It is important that there is a regular review of progress, since the rate of improvement may be slow, and family members may need support to persist with the programme.

Cognitive–behavioural approaches to psychosis employ the same basic cognitive–behavioural methods as used with depression and anxiety states (see Chapter 2). They aim at reducing the distress and interference in functioning caused by persistent psychotic symptoms, at trying to engage the patient in self-monitoring their own symptoms so that among other things they can detect incipient relapse, and at reducing feelings of hopelessness and negative self-image. In addition patients may be taught coping strategies, so that they can manage the occurrence of psychotic symptoms better.

Cognitive approaches to treating delusions partly follow on from the assessment of the nature of the delusions, as discussed earlier in the chapter. The psychologist will explore alternative explanations of their belief. For instance, if the patient believes that a relative is persecuting them through words that the patient hears on the TV, then the psychologist will elicit specific examples of what the patient believes the relative has done, and in language that the patient can understand will look at all the factors which affect what is said in a TV programme. An exploration of the events that appear to precede the onset of the delusional thoughts may unearth the cognitions that preceded the delusional idea. Cognitive distortions will then mediate the extent to which the thoughts which are identified are seen as self-referent. Direct confrontation of delusional beliefs should usually be avoided.

Perhaps surprisingly, hallucinations are not uncommon but the discovery that about 10 to 15 per cent of the general population report experiencing hallucinations indicates that they are not necessarily seen as distressing. It is therefore not the existence of hallucinations by themselves that justifies treatment, but the distress caused by the hallucination, and the associated level of any other symptoms. Intense anxiety frequently accompanies hallucinatory experiences, and there is some evidence that anxiety management training is helpful, so the psychologist could give some simple relaxation training. It is also possible that there is some suggestibility effect, so providing opportunities for reality testing may be helpful. Kuipers (1996) offers an excellent brief review of these approaches.

Group therapeutic programmes

Historically, the treatment of chronic patients in the older institutions was dominated by so-called 'social' models of treatment and work-related approaches to treatment, which essentially involved groups of patients. The wide-spread nature of these programmes also reflected the very low staffing levels at many of the old psychiatric hospitals, so that individual work was in any case simply impossible. Going back to Pinel and Tuke in the eighteenth and nineteenth centuries, 'moral' treatment approaches were the most influential, and indeed represented an often heroic attempt to combat exploitation and devaluing of the chronic patient. The Second World War, and the battle-stress problems which became apparent, led to the development of more structured ideas of social treatment, particularly associated with the Therapeutic Community movement. Therapeutic communities, whether hospital-wide or simply involving one ward, became quite common. The next major innovation, led by clinical psychologists, was the introduction of group behavioural programmes—the so-called 'token economy' programmes, based on an operant conditioning model, with psychologists also instrumental in developing social skills training regimes.

Psychologists may thus be involved in three main approaches to group programmes—the milieu, behavioural, and social skills approaches. All three will be outlined, but they should not be thought of as mutually exclusive. Elements of each approach can be combined, as long as they meet the needs of the group concerned, and of course as long as the underlying rationale of the programme is coherent and can be understood by all the staff involved. In addition, the place of work in rehabilitation programmes will be considered.

All therapeutic settings necessarily have some sort of milieu or atmosphere, but it may not be specifically recognized as a major tool in rehabilitation. A therapeutic community is a specific type of therapeutic milieu. The therapeutic community concept has been further subdivided into the general therapeutic community approach, and the therapeutic community 'proper'. This provides an essentially hierarchical classification but an examination of therapeutic communities highlights some of the main features of this approach.

A fundamental feature of the milieu approach is its treatment of authority, so that authority on a ward is not exercised hierarchically, but diffused through the staff. Authority is often invested, at least partially, in regular unit meetings, often daily, which focus on immediate events and identify publicly the contribution of individual community members to those events. Responsibility is seen as being passed back to the patient for most areas of his life, including caring for himself and his immediate personal space. Reality confrontation may be an important part of small groups within the ward, and the detailed analysis of events that then occurs makes it difficult for conventional barriers of confidentiality to be maintained. The psychologist working in a therapeutic community would then be a member of the daily meeting, and is often a key leader of small groups.

Group behavioural approaches, based on operant conditioning models, were introduced by clinical psychologists in the early 1970s, replacing the essentially casual reward systems used in many long-stay wards. Cigarettes, for example, have for years been doled out by nurses and ward domestic staff, without any attempt to analyse the effectiveness of this practice, and unrelated to the main presenting problems of the patient. Group behavioural programmes, by contrast, introduced the use of systematic reinforcement programmes as a consequence of the patient attaining a previously stated clinically relevant target. Such programmes were called token economies when the achievement by the patient of an identified target behaviour meant that they were given a 'token', usually a coloured plastic disc or punched or marked card, which they could then exchange for some goods or facilities which they chose. The psychologist contributes to these programmes by careful design of the overall regime, calculating the probable average token earnings for each patient, and assigning an appropriate proportion of the total tokens to each target area.

Token economies were widely used in the 1970s and 1980s, and undoubtedly contributed both to the atmosphere of realistic optimism about the degree of resettlement that could be achieved, and also contributed significantly to the clinical psychology scientific literature on long-term psychiatric disorder. However, a number of careful research studies showed that use of a physical token was *not* central to the improvement found in token economies. The use of ward-wide token economies has now been superseded by the use of individualized behavioural programmes as components in an overall care plan. The central psychological factors at work, including the creation of individualized graded therapeutic targets for each resident, contingent informational feedback and social reinforcement, and the encouragement of a degree of choice, remain applicable to many patients.

A third treatment approach is that known generically as Social Skills Training (SST). The main features of this approach are the use of modelling (the demonstration of the relevant skills), rehearsal (repeated practice by the patient in a 'safe' setting), and feedback (detailed comment and criticism both by the therapist and by the use of audio- and videotape recordings). This approach lends itself to group work, as it is usually fairly easy to find groups of patients with similar deficits in the area of social functioning. The psychologist's contribution to such a programme would involve a number of different components. The psychologist and others would have to contribute to the initial modelling of the relevant skills, so a certain degree of acting talent, and willingness to make a bit of a fool of yourself, might then be desirable professional qualities! One of the distinctive features of SST is the amount of therapeutic training that may take place actually in the supermarket, or at the bus-stop, or at the bar of the local coffee-shop.

The contribution of psychologists to group programmes will have some similarities to the contribution of members of other professions, for a proportion of the time. All will be asked to contribute to group meetings, and perhaps to lead staff feedback groups after main group meetings. The specific professional skills of the psychologist are likely to be called on to select patients, to identify common goals, and to train and prepare nurses and occupational therapists, and other staff, for the tasks involved in the programme. As in all rehabilitative treatments, steps need to be taken to ensure that the results of the treatment generalize, or spread, to other novel situations. Involvement in this sort of regime may offer an opportunity to contribute other psychological skills, such as evaluating the effectiveness of the ward.

Work as a form of therapy has become less common, with widespread unemployment severely reducing the availability of work to those suffering from major psychiatric handicaps. At the same time, the role of work in offering a range of structured social relationships, in offering a meaningful daytime activity, and in requiring the individual to meet a range of expectations in the areas of skill, work rate, and time keeping, has become apparent. Unless work is to be merely the performance of simple repetitious tasks, patients should be offered tasks which are within their competence and interest, but which also stretch them. A number of charities offer imaginative day work programmes, often involving craft work, gardening, and provision of services (such as sandwich making), and have set up retail outlets and workshops where patients can be involved in a complete process of production and selling, and where patients can be fitted into the right slot for them. A number of countries have sheltered workshops, which may offer an off-site day activity for people who still have homes in hospital. The system of hospital reward payments and social security benefits in Britain and other countries is so complicated that considerable attention needs to be paid to working out how there can be effective incentives for work. The role of the psychologist in contributing to the design of such work regimes is then more akin to an occupational, rather than a clinical, psychologist.

Ways of delivering services

More so than in so-called 'acute' settings, psychologists working with this group need to co-ordinate their work with that of others, both in residential and community settings. This co-ordination can be viewed systemically, requiring psychological contributions to assessment and monitoring (the psychologist as psychometrician), promotion of group working among both staff and patients (the psychologist as group facilitator and therapist), fitting both staff and patients to the activities to which they are best suited (the psychologist as occupational adviser), and the design of individual therapeutic programmes (the psychologist as expert therapist). The literature on the psychologist's role as a 'change agent' will alert her or him to the need to promote group cohesion and group commitment to change amongst all involved.

In addition, there has been concern about how to co-ordinate the work of different carers and agencies working together with the same patient in the community. A number of ways of ensuring that patients do not 'slip through the net' have been devised, of which case management is probably the best known. This involves assigning a limited number of patients to community staff, who are then given the responsibility of regularly maintaining contact with their clients, and who become the 'key worker' for that client. A number of variants of this approach have been developed, such as the Programme for Assertive Community Treatment (PACT), which focuses on the most seriously handicapped clients within a service and, as the name implies, requires the key worker to keep assertively in contact with the client. A variant of this approach, called the Care Programme Approach, has been introduced compulsorily in Britain, but the effectiveness of the process in achieving its stated objective is uncertain. All of these variants have a positive motivation to provide care for the most needy, but may also have a less positive aim of keeping people in the community, arguably when some of them may benefit from specialized residential care. The effectiveness of these programmes, from a research point of view, is still unclear

Apart from the concerns of professional staff and families to ensure that the most seriously disabled patients are helped as much as possible, there are also political and public pressures to ensure that priority is given to this group. This is partly because of the considerable media attention paid to those tragic but in fact rare incidents where a member of the public is seriously assaulted by a person who has had a history of mental illness. This presents the same dilemma as discussed in Chapter 9, which is the issue of balancing the risk to the public of harm against the civil liberty concerns of those who then face the possibility of life-long incarceration, when if they had been sentenced normally they would have been discharged from prison. Again, a special semistatutory procedure called the Supervision Register has been introduced in Britain for those patients in the community deemed to be at most risk of self-harm, harm to others, or of self-neglect. Similar statutory procedures such as these are used in other countries, such as the involuntary hospitalization procedures used in the different states of the United States.

SUMMARY

Psychologists have a number of specific contributions to make to the care of people with severe mental illness. The difficulties of such poeple can be conceptualized in psychological ways that help to frame treatment objectives. Those difficulties need to be understood specifically and individually, and carefully chosen and applied psychological instruments can add to that understanding. Some of those difficulties can be moderated and overcome by a range of psychological interventions, if only partly and slowly.

A major area of concern is the relative lack of evaluation of the effectiveness of all elements of the treatment available in different settings. Specific psychological and pharmacological treatments have been evaluated, but the same attention has not been paid to the overall functioning of the packages of care, or of group programmes within institutions. For example there has been relatively little examination of the effectiveness of the major discharge policy adopted in Britain and most other European countries.

There is little factual evidence to support a complete abolition of institutional care. This does not mean that large, isolated, minimally resourced institutions should continue. It does mean that some small, accessible, adequately resourced residential provision will continue to be needed, alongside good quality community care, and that a wealth of psychological, sociological, and psychiatric guidance now exists to give no excuse for not providing co-ordinated, appropriate, and caring residential regimes (Shepherd 1990).

People with severe mental illness often do not engage well with specialized services. This may be seen as their right. Equally, as a group they are at risk from exploitation by others, and at risk of clinical deterioration if they are not regularly in contact with a key worker. A significant professional issue is how to design services so that they are seen as attractive to those who use them.

References

Baker, R. D. and Hall, J. N. (1994). A review of the applications of the REHAB assessment system. *Behavioural and Cognitive Psychotherapy*, **22**, 211–231.

Barrowclough, C. and Tarrier, N. (1992). Interventions with families. In *Innovations in the psychological management of schizophrenia* (ed. Birchwood, M. and Tarrier, N.), pp. 79–101. Wiley, Chichester.

Bridges, K., Huxley, P. and Oliver, J. (1994). Psychiatric rehabilitation: redefined for the 1990s. *The International Journal of Social Psychiatry*, **40**, 1–16.

Garety, P. and Hemsley, D. (1987). Characteristics of delusional experience. *European Archives of Psychiatry and Neurological Science*, **236**, 294–298.

Garety, P. and Morris, I. (1984). A new unit for long-stay psychiatric patients: organisation, attitudes and quality of care. *Psychological Medicine*, **14**, 183–192.

Goffman, E. (1961). *Asylums: essays on the social situations of mental patients and other inmates.* Anchor Books, New York.

Häfner, H. (1985). Changing patterns of mental health care. *Acta Psychiatrica Scandinavica*, **71** (suppl. 319), 151–164.

Kuipers, E. (1996). The management of difficult to treat patients with schizophrenia, using non-drug therapies. *British Journal of Psychiatry*, **169** (suppl. 13), 41–51.

Marshall, M., Hogg, L.I., Gath, D.H. and Lockwood, A. (1995). The Cardinal Needs Schedule—a modified version of the MRC Needs for Care Assessment Schedule. *Psychological Medicine*, **25**, 605–617.

Murphy, E. (1991). *After the asylums*. Faber and Faber, London.

Perkins, R. and Dilks, S. (1992). Worlds apart: working with severely socially disabled people. *Journal of Mental Health*, **1**, 3–17.

Shepherd, G. (1990). Foreword: psychiatric rehabilitation for the 1990s. In *Theory and practice of psychiatric rehabilitation* (2nd edn), (eds F. N. Watts *et al.*), pp. xiii–xlviii. Wiley, Chichester.

Further reading

Birchwood, M. and Tarrier, N. (1992). *Innovations in the psychological management of schizophrenia*. Wiley, Chichester.

Kingdon, D. G. and Turkington, D. (1994). *Cognitive behavioral therapy of schizophrenia*. Erlbaum, Hove.

Torrey, E. F. (1995). Surviving schizophrenia: a manual for families, consumers and providers (3rd edn). HarperPerennial, New York.

Watts, F. N., Bennett, D. H. and Shepherd, G. (eds) (1990). *Theory and practice of psychiatric rehabilitation* (2nd edn). Wiley, Chichester.

4

Working with children and young people

Irene Sclare

INTRODUCTION

All clinical psychologists undertake some work with children and young people during clinical psychology training. Approximately 350 qualified clinical psychologists in Britain have chosen to specialize in this area of work within the health service and, increasingly, in social services and education agencies. They carry out a range of types of work with troubled or troubling children, including assessment, treatment, consultation, research, and training. Clinical child psychologists work with parents, other family members, and other involved professionals as well as with the child, so that they need to draw on knowledge and experience of adult as well as child psychology and the psychology of organizations. Clinical child psychologists work with the most complex and serious childhood problems and disorders as well as those which are less troubling or which have only recently emerged for the child or family. In order to help reduce the likelihood of problems emerging, many child psychologists carry out preventive work with vulnerable children and parents to build their resilience to stress.

PSYCHOLOGICAL PROBLEMS IN CHILDHOOD AND ADOLESCENCE

There has been a rise in the number of children and young people being referred to clinical psychologists and other staff such as child psychiatrists and child psychotherapists in recent years, perhaps reflecting an increased awareness of children's psychological needs and the range of interventions that are available to help them. Typically referrals are made by general practitioners, social workers, health visitors, and paediatricians, all of whom have regular contact with distressed or troubled children and parents. Most psychology services have to operate waiting lists for all but the most urgent cases because of the high demand. Although, generally, services are designed for children and families from birth to 16 years of age, many psychologists specialize in research and clinical work with children at a particular stage of development, such as adolescence, or with specific types of problems, such as hyperactivity or the psychological problems associated with closed head injury.

Because of children's dependence on adults, children under 16 years of age are unlikely to go directly for psychological help themselves if they are troubled or if their behaviour is causing problems for others. They usually rely on adults such as parents or teachers to recognize the problems and identify a course of action, such as talking to the general practitioner or a social worker who may then refer them on for psychological advice. Those children whose parents do seek psychological or psychiatric help have been found to have parents who are more anxious about the problems and perceive them as more worrying than parents whose children have similar problems but who do not seek help, suggesting that parent characteristics rather than child characteristics determine whether a troubled child is referred. It has been estimated that only a very small proportion of children with psychological problems get referred to psychologists and other child mental health staff such as child psychiatrists or child psychotherapists. Most services acknowledge the need to make their work more accessible to a broad range of vulnerable and troubled children and parents so that psychologists and others can be involved with more representative groups of children and young people in the communities which they serve.

Prevalence of children's psychological problems

Many children and young people experience difficulties in behaviour, feelings, or relationships which cause worry at home or at school at some stage of their lives. In addition, some children are slow to acquire certain abilities such as bladder control or learning to read and this can cause stress and upset. Some children's problems resolve without needing help from professionals whereas others persist, impacting on the child's adaptation and well being and on family life. Recent studies from a number of different countries have shown that around 20 per cent of children and young people may have problems or difficulties which are sufficiently complex or severe to be classified as *child mental health disorders* (Costello 1989). This term refers to patterns of behaviour, emotions, or relationships that cause concern to the child, parents, carers, or teachers and which are judged to be severe, either because of the negative effect on the child and others, or because the problem is intense, hard to manage, has lasted a long time, or is not appropriate for the child's age. Children frequently have more than one disorder (Offord, *et al.* 1987). The prevalence figures for child mental health disorders are greater in socially deprived areas and in groups or communities affected by traumatic or stressful events. Some childhood disorders persist into adulthood affecting the adult's adaptation and ability to cope. In fact, some adult psychological problems have their origins in childhood or adolescence, emphasizing the need for help and intervention to be made available as early as possible in a troubled or vulnerable child's life.

Children who have physical disabilities such as spina bifida or cerebral palsy or chronic physical conditions such as asthma or diabetes have been found to be at high risk of developing psychological problems. Eiser (1990) describes the negative effects of illness and disability on children's self-esteem and emotional adjustment, including the siblings. In addition, parents of disabled or sick children have been found to experience high levels of stress and anxiety which reduce their ability to cope with the extra demands they face in caring for the child. While some of the stress derives from socioeconomic or illness-related factors, Eiser suggests that by improving the way in which aspects of chronic illness are managed by doctors and nurses, child and family levels of stress can be reduced; for example by ensuring that medical procedures do not cause excess pain or distress. In addition, treatment compliance can improve if doctors and nurses improve their communication with parents and sick children. There are obvious roles for psychologists in teaching these skills to medical and nursing staff, including the use of pain management techniques and setting up parent support groups in hospital. Other aspects of psychologists' work with sick children will be discussed later in this chapter.

The nature of child mental health problems

Children's psychological problems can be categorized as primarily behavioural, emotional, or developmental, although in reality troubled children may have problems which cover all three areas. The most frequent problem to be referred for help is disruptive behaviour, and generally more boys have these patterns of troubled and troubling behaviour than girls. Severe behaviour problems such as disobedience, temper tantrums, and aggression towards peers can be present at the age of 3 years, and are typically associated with specific patterns of interaction between parent and child. If left untreated the problems can persist into adolescence and even adulthood, with major effects on the child or young person's friendships, family relationships, and school achievements.

James

James is a 12-year-old boy who has had a series of problems and difficulties at home and at school. He was an active and demanding toddler whose behaviour was hard to manage. At nursery he was often aggressive towards other children, particularly if they tried to share his toys. He found it hard to settle into school at the age of 5, and needed close supervision from teaching staff in the playground to prevent him from fighting with other children. He enjoyed football and did well in the school team but tended to react poorly to being told off in class. He got restless during lessons, often interrupting other children's work, and was slow to learn to read and write. Inexperienced teachers found his behaviour challenging although if he was motivated he could be helpful and enthusiastic. His parents were unable to handle him when he was angry and defiant and tended to give in to him. James moved to secondary school without having acquired age-appropriate reading skills and needed extra help from a specialist teacher to catch up with his classmates. He took to truanting from school whenever he found himself in conflict with teachers and began to hang around with older boys who encouraged him to join their gang. This greatly alarmed James' parents who felt that he was likely to get into trouble with the police.

Troubled feelings and unhappiness or anxiety are less easily recognized by parents or teachers, but are important and worrying. Children may withdraw, become clingy, or be perceived as good because they make few demands on adults who are preoccupied with other stresses. Children and young people can experience depression and severe anxiety disorders, either of which can have marked effects, including attempted suicide. There are links between these problems and the nature of parent–child relationships such as the quality of the attachment with the child and threats, real or perceived, to family stability.

The troubled, sad, or anxious feelings and difficulties in relationships with significant others may continue into adulthood, affecting adult adaptation unless help can be provided for the child and family. Intense fears and panic attacks, which are more easily identified by parents because of the marked effects on behaviour, can form part of these emotional disorders and may also occur independently.

Jane

Jane was a well behaved and highly motivated child who enjoyed school and loved ballet and swimming, which were the centre of her life. Her mother was a professional dancer and Jane was encouraged to follow in her footsteps. She had one close friend at home who went to the same school and who also participated in ballet classes with her. Jane was keen to do well in all of her work and took pride in her achievements. She was close to her grandmother who had been involved in her care since Jane's parents had separated when Jane was 3 and her older brother was 6. Jane saw her father regularly but her parents continued to argue about this contact after the divorce. Jane believed that she was responsible for the rows between her parents, which intensified after her father met a new partner and remarried. At the age of 14, Jane became noticeably withdrawn and sad after her grandmother died following a short illness. This coincided with Jane's best friend's departure to live in the United States with her family. Jane's school performance deteriorated and she lost interest in her appearance. She failed a ballet examination and felt that she had let her parents down. She felt hopeless about her future and very isolated. She began to experience intense panic attacks in public after a visit to her father's house and became reluctant to leave home in the mornings unless accompanied by the family dog.

Post traumatic stress disorder (PTSD) has now been recognized as present in some children and young people who have witnessed or experienced traumatic or life threatening events or situations. Children with post traumatic stress experience intrusive thoughts about the disaster or accident, and they are likely to have difficulties concentrating on schoolwork. In addition, they are likely to have emotional problems, for example mood changes, heightened fearfulness, and sleep disturbance. These effects can continue unabated, especially if additional support is not made available.

Anorexia is a severe and life-threatening disorder which is known to occur in adolescence as well as adulthood and has rightly received greater attention in recent years. The disorder derives from a complex interaction of psychological difficulties, probably originating in early childhood. Treatment is likely to involve hospital doctors because of the risk to life and needs to be co-ordinated between paediatricians and specialist child mental health staff, and should involve both the young person and his or her parents. Parents and professional such as teachers and general practitioners need to be aware of the early signs of these and other serious mental health problems so that very troubled young people can access specialist help at an early stage in the formation of the problem.

Developmental disorders with poor outcomes in adult life are autism and attention deficit with hyperactivity disorder (ADHD), both of which can be diagnosed under the age of 5 years. These disorders can involve marked difficulties in social relationships with peers, learning difficulties in school, and high levels of family stress. Psychologists have had some success in helping modify and shape social responsiveness and attention to tasks amongst children with ADHD and autism using cognitive–behavioural therapies. Additionally, psychologists help improve parents' and teachers' capacity to cope with the child's developmental problems themselves by teaching them relevant techniques based on cognitive-behavioural principles.

How do problems emerge?

It appears that certain groups of children are particularly vulnerable to developing severe and persistent psychological problems while others are more resilient. The reasons appear to be partly to do with genetic factors and are partly psychological in nature. From temperament studies it has been shown that some children are more difficult to manage and are less rewarding for their parents from a very early age. Children with physical disabilities, chronic childhood illness, or brain damage (including epilepsy, autism, and ADHD), all of which are constitutionally determined, are at greater risk of developing psychological problems at school and at home, partly because of physical or neurological influences on behaviour, and partly because of the effects of the illness or disability on relationships.

Certain other risk factors increase the likelihood that a child will develop severe problems. The quality of parenting they receive is a key influence. Parents who have other mental health problems of their own such as depression are less effective in addressing their children's needs. Parenting styles such as harsh or inconsistent styles of discipline, poor anger management skills, and troubled marital relationships also influence the development of child mental health disorders. Divorce interrupts stable patterns within the family and can cause children to become unhappy or difficult to manage, particularly if the parents continue to row and argue after separation. Children vary in their resilience to stress, trauma, or loss. They are more likely to remain free of long-term psychological disorder after undergoing stress or change if they are brought up by stable and well supported parents who can protect their children from the negative effects of any stress and prevent children from blaming themselves when problems occur. Parents with low self-esteem and who lack skills and confidence are generally less able to supervise their children and give them a sense of being valued and respected. The school can act as a support for vulnerable children and families by offering individual support and advice. It can also exert a negative influence on their psychological well being. For example children can perform below their potential or become victims of bullying by peers, if teachers fail to provide well organized and structured frameworks for learning.

Why work with parents?

From the above it is obvious that help for children and young people with behavioural or emotional problems must involve their parents and, where possible, the school, both of whom play key roles in setting values and standards for acceptable behaviour and providing emotional support. Parents are responsible for providing adequate emotional care and supervision and for ensuring that a child feels valued and safe. Parents and children form stable patterns of response to one another, shaping each other's behaviour, and these may maintain problem behaviours despite the input of outside professionals. Adults rather than children have the power to change many of these patterns, and the situations in which problems generally occur. Parents will be more likely to try out new ways of responding to their children and find solutions to children's difficulties if they feel supported and empowered by professionals rather than blamed for the child's problems. Parents who themselves suffered abuse or rejection in their own childhood and who are experiencing difficulties with their children usually require outside assistance to draw on different models and principles of parenting and develop new patterns of behaviour and responses to their children.

The changing shape of the family

Family life has undergone substantial changes in recent years, and some of these changes have increased family stress and heightened the need for professional advice. Greater social mobility, for example, reduces contact with the extended family and diminishes family support networks. More women have joined the workforce, albeit often still in less well paid work than men. Yet the majority of women continue to bear the bulk of responsibility for childcare. Divorce is more common, and there has been a rise in the number of remarriages to form stepfamilies, complicating professional thinking about the role of parents in therapeutic work. Very real inequalities of opportunity and income exist within urban populations and across Britain, especially for black children and young people. Lone mothers head the household in a large proportion of families in inner cities, some of whom have little or no contact with, or support from, the father or from the extended family. Psychological services need to fit these realities of family life rather than impose an idealized version on parents and children which ignores cultural and social change.

The influence of development on child problems

Working with children involves thinking about the links between their developmental progress and their problems. Rapid change takes place during the normal course of childhood and adolescence. Emotional and social factors have an influence on the course of a child's development and it is difficult in practice to separate the influences of heredity and environment on development. Changes can be charted in a child's physical growth, the development of their thinking and reasoning, communication skills, the capacity to relate to peers, and the amount of independence from caregivers. Typical patterns of behaviour and abilities specific to different ages and stages are described in most child care textbooks with each stage seen as having key developmental tasks which require different parenting skills. However, in practice children develop at different rates so that there is great variation amongst children of the same age or stage as well as similarities. Some children are generally slow in their development and may need extra help to acquire new skills and to generalize these. For some, certain areas of development lag compared to other areas of their development or may never develop, causing a child to have specific disabilities, such as reading and writing difficulties, attention problems, hearing impairment, or restricted mobility.

Developmental psychologists have identified key stages in children acquiring cognitive skills and the way in which these link with emotional and social developmental pathways. These have, for example, shed light on the nature of the constitutionally determined impairments seen in autistic children. Children usually develop the awareness of other peoples' perspectives or 'theory of mind' by aged 5 or 6 years. Autistic children lack this ability, which causes them to have difficulty 'reading' the feelings and intentions of other people.

Children's development can be directly affected by their experiences. Obvious physical harm can be caused to a child's developing abilities as a result of an accident or illness, especially if the brain is assaulted. If the child was deliberately harmed by the parent, there are likely to be additional emotional effects and these can be manifested in slow acquisition of skills, poor concentration, or impulsivity. A few children who are traumatized lose their communication skills and may be unable to learn. Certain rare neurological conditions can mimic psychological problems. Consequently, a child seen as distractible, naughty, or unhappy could in fact have an underlying progressive disease which is affecting their development and abilities.

The effects of deprivation on children's development

Adverse environmental conditions have a marked negative effect on young children's emotional and cognitive development. Classically, these effects are in evidence in institutions in which there is an absence of individualized emotional and social care including opportunities for play and learning. Residential care is now used less frequently for disabled or young children because of their vulnerability to long-term effects. Severely dysfunctional family contexts can have similar effects on children's social and cognitive development, particularly if the parents are unpredictable and inconsistent in their approach and use extreme forms of punishment, emphasizing the links between the provision of secure attachment relationships between parents and children and children's resilience to stress. Developmental recovery may take place if warm, loving, and consistent care can be provided instead.

How does information about the course of a child's development help the clinical child psychologist?

Epidemiological studies have helped to show that certain problem behaviours occur commonly at particular ages across the child population, because of normal developmental processes, and usually resolve as the child matures. When a child is referred with a problem, it is important to determine whether or not the problem is 'normal' for that child's age and fits the overall developmental stage they have reached. On this basis, a boy who is wetting the bed at age 8 years who is otherwise developing normally is judged to be more likely to need intervention than a child of 3 years. In addition, parents may have less tolerance of age-inappropriate behaviour and therefore experience stress if the boy's bedwetting persists beyond what is 'normal'. He will be more vulnerable to feelings of failure or embarrassment about bedwetting, because of his awareness of others' viewpoints and values.

An 8-year-old may also be able to understand the effects of his problem on others, and can be motivated to overcome the problem with psychological input. He will respond to therapeutic work which allows him to play an active part. Praise and reward from parents for success will be powerful techniques to encourage new patterns of behaviour and at this age he can also use imaginary techniques and metaphors to 'fight' his problem with his parent's help.

During assessment sessions with children, it is essential to bear in mind the ways in which young children's cognitive development will limit the way they can make sense of a traumatic or frightening event or understand the implications. Some issues may need to be explored through play. Even the way we ask questions needs to bear in mind developmental factors, such as whether young children can describe their thoughts and the intentions of others. Young children do not recall information as easily as older children and need cues to help them recall events. They are more suggestible than adolescents so that interviewing them in front of their parents is likely to influence their responses. Parents exert a powerful influence on children's ideas about right and wrong. This is problematic when parents are behaving abusively towards a young child and silencing the child with threats. Parents and other adults may have fixed perceptions of how their child should behave at a given age and may request psychological help to change behaviour which may not fit the child's actual developmental capacities. A 7-year-old child referred by teachers, for example, because she is viewed by them as excessively shy and will not communicate, could in fact have an underlying specific language delay or disorder which is constitutionally determined, limiting her speech and language development, and her confidence.

Finally, it is important to remember that children have rights that need to be protected with regard to giving their consent to assessment and treatment. Obviously in order to give their consent, children need explanations about what a psychologist does and why they are meeting to talk together, at a level suited for their age and stage.

The family context

The family has been the focus of considerable attention within the field of child psychology and child mental health. The family can be viewed as a resource or as a negative influence on children's development. The family 'environment', that is the quality and nature of relationships, family beliefs, and the experiences that are provided for children by parents, is seen as contributing to children and young people's perceptions of themselves, their self-esteem, and their capacity to make relationships with peers. Specific hostile and inconsistent styles of parenting and family patterns have harmful effects on children, emotionally as well as developmentally, particularly if they are subject to violence or the threat of harm. The parents in such families typically have a long history of difficulties, and little or no positive influences on their ability to raise children. If professional help cannot bring about change in severely dysfunctional parenting, children and young people may be removed from parents' care by the courts if there is evidence that their needs cannot be met within the family. Assessing whether or not the child is at risk of abuse needs a thorough appraisal of parent–child relationships, past and present, and the influences affecting the parents' behaviour.

Reder and Lucey (1995) set out frameworks for assessing abusive parenting and parents' capacity to change harmful or neglectful patterns of behaviour towards a child. This involves assessing the family relationships in context, the parents' own relationship, their views of the child's problems, the parents' own mental health, and the child's strengths and difficulties and integrating clinical views with psychological and developmental theories concerning children's well being. Children's wishes and feelings about their parents and their preferences about being looked after may be taken into account, although this has to be balanced with the risk to their safety. These complex assessments are usually carried out by two or three professionals working together over a number of sessions with a family. Psychologists involved in this distressing area of work draw on knowledge and experience of childhood disorders, a child's developmental needs, family functioning, parenting skills, and adults' capacity to change patterns of behaviour towards children and helpers.

Fostered and adopted children and young people may remain troubled and difficult to manage despite the positive influences of new carers and the change of context. The impact of a major change of carers can affect the child's identity or self-esteem. In order for the child to make sense of the changes, information needs to be available about the reasons for being removed from parents, in ways which fit the child's cognitive abilities. Obviously this is a very skilled task which needs to be adapted to the individual child. Substitute carers will benefit from psychological support and advice to help manage any challenging behaviour and help children to settle in to the family and form attachments to them. Very disturbed children who are removed from dysfunctional families and placed in foster care have a tendency to test adults' endurance and to find it hard to trust others. If major problems occur that cannot be managed by foster or adoptive parents, the placement may break down, causing the child to experience further rejection and loss. Some psychology departments work closely with social workers from adoption and fostering agencies and with foster parents and offer advice and training to help prevent the onset of overwhelming problems as well as providing individual or family-based help for specific problems.

SETTINGS IN WHICH PSYCHOLOGISTS WORK

National surveys of clinical child psychologists in Britain have shown that there is great variation in the sorts of organizational structures in which psychologists are working. Some psychology services are based within multidisciplinary mental health services whereas others form part of community child health services. Some psychologists are employed directly by hospital trusts which provide acute medical care and have no formal links with traditional child or adult mental health frameworks. A few psychologists are specifically employed by community-based services (for example general practitioner surgeries), within the voluntary sector, or directly in Social Services departments. Child psychology services are diversifying, and many psychologists now specialize in work with particular client groups within their catchment area, for example children with disabilities, children who have been abused or traumatized, or children undergoing medical and surgical treatments. This trend matches the development of the work of clinical psychologists with adult populations, many of whom specialize in one problem group or setting. Psychologists who offer very specialized services for children or young people with complex or unusual problems usually do so with team colleagues in centres of excellence, very often simultaneously conducting systematic research into underlying processes of a problem and the effects of treatments. For example innovative interventions with children with autism, young depressed mothers, young male abusers, and young people with early-onset anorexia have evolved from research programmes. The results of projects in these and many other areas act as standards of good practice for others in the field.

Multidisciplinary teamwork

Psychologists frequently work as members of specialist multidisciplinary child mental health teams where work is collaborative across the disciplines, and with social workers seconded from the local authority to the team. Treatment is usually on an outpatient basis. Team members usually liaise closely with referrers and will, for example, visit referred children's schools to support and advise teaching staff about a child whom they referred for help. Consultation and staff support will be offered to professionals who work with very troubled children in other settings such as Local Authority residential children's homes who may be reluctant to attend a child mental health centre. A few clinical psychologists work in specialist inpatient units which are mainly staffed by nurses and child psychiatrists who provide 24-hour care for children and teenagers who have serious mental health problems such as depression or psychosis. Working in multidisciplinary teams can be rewarding and supportive, and allows for shared approaches and perspectives when dealing with complex and long-standing child and family difficulties. It also provides for in-service training and a forum for new ideas. However, there can be associated problems in teamworking, usually connected to unresolved conflicts about leadership and dominant models of treatment.

A second model is for clinical psychologists to work autonomously from a clinical psychology base with other clinical child psychologists, seeing children and parents referred to them. In this way of working, when a child is referred, a partnership is set up with key adults who are involved, for example schoolteacher, parent, and school nurse, to create specific ways to solve that child's problem in the home setting and in class, rather than the clinic. While this way of working is responsive to families and referrers, it can sometimes be difficult for staff to draw in other more specialist services if these are needed unless good links exist. Some clinical child psychology services find that multidisciplinary services overlap with theirs and referrers can become confused about which service to involve.

A third way of working is for the clinical psychologist to be attached on a part time or full time basis to a service for children in which no other child mental health staff are working. This allows psychologists to reach children and parents who have significant psychological needs but who may not access specialist child mental health services. There are clinical psychologists working, for example, in general paediatric services, child development centres, general practitioner surgeries, hospices for dying children, social services offices, centres for offenders and schools, or a social services team for children being fostered or adopted. Often clinical psychologists have split duties with a base in two or more teams or types of child services. These newer arrangements will usually be formalized through service level agreements which specify the aims and objectives of the psychology work and evaluate the effects of the service on child and family difficulties. A drawback can be that a psychologist employed in this way can become isolated from psychology colleagues unless supervision and support is made available.

Organizing psychology services to respond to different levels of need

There have been important changes in recent years to the ways that health services for children and young people are delivered and more change is planned (see Williams and Richardson (1995) *Together we stand* for a fuller description). The aim of these changes is to ensure that psychologists and others offer services which have been shown to be effective and relevant to the needs of children within the local community. Parents' and children's expectations of psychological treatment and responses to it are being considered more carefully by child mental health services, using questionnaires and verbal feedback from families regarding satisfaction with services offered. This is an important development when considering ways of meeting the needs of children and parents from culturally diverse backgrounds. The amount of help required by a child or family will vary according to the severity of problems. Ideally, services should match or fit the level of need created by the problem or problems, so that the most complex and severe problems receive the most specialist treatments. Some children may have only one mild problem or difficulty, such as a fear of needles and injections, or a single behaviour problem which could be resolved with a relatively straightforward psychological input, probably by a health visitor or general practitioner who has had some psychological training. A child with a single or mild problem could be seen as having a lower level of need for a child mental health service than children with several problems, such as a child with sleep difficulties, fear of travel and panic attacks whose parent is mentally ill, or a single severe problem such as obsessive compulsive disorder, both of which require more intensive psychological help, possibly from more than one child mental health professional over a longer period of time.

The Parent Adviser Scheme in Bermondsey in South London (Davis *et al.* 1996) is a carefully evaluated child psychology service offering early intervention to parents of young children with child mental health problems in the community. Parent Advisers are not qualified psychologists but are trained in parent counselling and problem solving skills by clinical child psychology staff who then offer regular supervision of this work. The scheme has been shown to be effective in resolving a significant proportion of referred problems without the need for more specialist help.

Children and parents with more severe disorders should be seen and helped in services which are designed to offer longer-term psychological treatments, possibly involving two or more staff. The rationale of organizing services according to level of child and family needs is that more children's psychological needs can be addressed in a coherent way, with better access to earlier intervention, with specialized services being reserved for those most in need. Clinical child psychologists can be involved in work at each level or 'tier' of child mental health provision, including the interface with other child health services, such as paediatrics, and with social services departments.

THE NATURE OF WORK UNDERTAKEN BY CLINICAL CHILD PSYCHOLOGISTS

Psychologists use a range of models or theories to explain how problems arise and to guide their thinking about intervention or treatment. In this next section, examples will be given of the different sorts of activities which psychologists undertake to help referred children and their families. When working with children and families, the psychologist needs to decide who to involve in assessment and treatment, for example the child, parents, brothers or sisters, or other key professionals. The process is time consuming given the range of variables and the different perspectives to be considered. It may lead to the setting up of training or consultation work with staff as well as, or instead of, direct clinical work.

The assessment process

Clinical psychologists used to have, primarily, an assessment role, helping with diagnostic procedures when child psychiatrists or paediatricians wished advice about children's intellectual abilities in relation to other presenting problems which they themselves were assessing and treating. Assessments of children's cognitive skills relied on applying a limited range of standardized psychometric tests of general intelligence and educational attainments. In recent years, new tests have been devised which enable psychologists to assess other aspects of cognitive functioning such as attention and distraction. Tests of general intelligence are useful for ascertaining whether specific patterns of strengths and difficulties are present and can aid in the diagnosis of developmental disorders such as ADHD. However, psychometric assessment is no longer seen as the focus of psychological assessment work. Clinical psychology assessments of problems have broadened to include a detailed appraisal of the nature of a problem, the effects on the child and family, the nature of family relationships, developmental factors, and the meaning the problem has for a child and family. Clinical psychology assessments appraise the child's problem in the social context, which involves evaluating family relationships, school factors and peer group relationships, and their contribution to the problems being experienced. This is achieved by discussion, observation, questionnaires, and reading reports. The aim is to collect information about the problem and the relationship with other aspects of the child's life, in order to chart the problem severity and the sorts of work needed to change the situation. Most parents want to know why a problem is occurring as well as what to do to change it. Similarly, the psychologist needs to determine what has helped create the problem or triggered it and what problem solving capacities exist to dissolve it, within the child, the family, and the broader network.

Stages in the assessment process

There are a number of tasks involved in the process of assessment. Firstly, a detailed description is taken of the problem, as it exists at the present time, where and when it occurs, and how long it has been in existence. Parents or teachers usually give a label to a problem they are concerned about, for example, 'aggressive and violent' or 'has a communication problem with her sister'. At this early stage in the assessment process it is helpful to get a set of behavioural descriptions for the problems, so that there is clarity about what actually occurs. The effects of the problem on the child are carefully noted, both the negatives and any positives. Any other characteristics of the child relevant to the problem would be noted, such as their likes and dislikes. Also, the child's general progress in other areas of their development needs to be determined.

It is important to establish whether the problem occurs in all contexts or whether it is restricted to a situation, so that an idea is formed as to how severe it is. In addition, the assessment needs to focus on links between the problem and the behaviour and responses of others, and how the problem is influenced by other environmental factors. Is the problem being shaped by parental or sibling responses which are reinforcing the problem behaviour, such as attention? Is the child modelling others around him? Does the problem get triggered by an event or other stimulus? Is the physical environment not suited for a child with these needs?

The next step is to explore how the problem is perceived by everyone involved. This could include the parents, brothers and sisters, as well as the child giving their views about the nature of the problem and its severity. Family members can have differing perceptions of the behaviour that is causing concern and the reasons for it, some perhaps blaming one family member, or attributing the problem to an event which occurred in the past. The referrer may have a different view from the parents as to what the problem is, and therefore what needs to change. There may be a general perception about the child as a 'bad lot' or 'an angel', which may prevent them noticing adaptive or helpful aspects of the child. The child himself may also feel worthless and perceive the situation as being beyond his control.

At a broader level of assessment, it is important to gauge the family member's feelings about the child and the problem, for example whether the problem is creating intense anxiety or despair. In addition, family relationships need to be appraised such as the quality of attachments in the family, family styles of communication and discipline, and whether the parents are in opposition to one another or able to problem solve together without conflict. This may be obvious from the interview or may need colleagues to assist, for example by observing family interactions through a one way screen. The psychologist will also wish to ascertain if the parents are supported by friends or family and if there are other stresses currently which affect coping, including the parents' own mental health, financial pressures, or harassment from neighbours. Some of this information can be obtained from checklists or self-report questionnaires. Historical information about past traumas or losses, changes in family circumstances, and how the parents and child have dealt with difficulties in the past is also needed. Information gathering can take two or three sessions and may require individual sessions as well as family interviews.

At the end of this assessment process the psychologist should be ready to make a formulation about the problems and the salient factors associated with it. The formulation will provide an explanation of the difficulties, what needs to happen to bring about change and the approach to intervention. Together the psychologist, parent, and child then need to agree the goals for change, the approach to solving the problem, and how changes will be monitored over time.

What sorts of treatment are carried out?

Advances in clinical practice, research, and training have widened the scope of the interventions which clinical child psychologists now use. Differences in the way they conceptualize problems influences the way they approach assessment and treatment. Many psychologists specialize in one approach, for example family therapy or psychoanalytic psychotherapy, and after qualifying may undertake further specialized training. Not all treatment approaches have been evaluated in depth to determine which approach is most effective and for which problems. Target and Fonagy (1996) carried out a systematic review of treatment efficacy for childhood problems. They note that there have been many more systematic studies of behavioural and cognitive behavioural treatments, which tend to be symptom focused, than of family therapy and individual psychoanalytic psychotherapy, which aim to treat associated difficulties within the family or child. Target and Fonagy concluded that both behavioural and non-behavioural approaches can be effective and have contributions to make. In practice, many psychologists integrate ideas and techniques from several theoretical approaches, as in the following case. A behavioural approach was used in assessment and intervention work with a mother and young child, although attention was also given to parents' feelings, attitudes, and current family interactions.

Example of assessment and treatment of a 3-year-old girl

Barbara is the younger of two daughters and is a lively 3-year-old who eats very little food and has great difficulty sitting at table to eat her meals. Her mother, Christine, is desperate to change the mealtime problems as she is going back to work soon. Mealtimes are fraught and the parents disagree about how best to get Barbara to sit and eat. Barbara's father feels that Christine is too lenient and that she has given in to Barbara. Christine finds it wrong to chastise children as she herself was given harsh discipline by her parents when she was a child. She cannot break the pattern of feeding Barbara on the floor while she plays because of her worry about Barbara's low food intake. Barbara was born prematurely and there were medical concerns about her growth and development in her first year of life.

Outline of assessment and treatment approach

The psychologist met Barbara and Christine at the office and Christine described the problems in detail. The psychologist sought to create a relationship of respect and trust with both Barbara and her mother and at all times tried to validate Christine as worthy and resourceful. Christine was asked for some information about the family and any other stresses currently and she described their worries about financial matters, and her dread of returning to work. The psychologist checked details of Barbara's general development at present and learned that there were no medical concerns but that Christine still felt watchful and protective. She also asked about the child's relationships with other adults and children and about her general temperament, for example whether Barbara was usually easy or difficult to manage, happy or unhappy. She observed Barbara with Christine during the session, noting the close and affectionate way in which they communicated and played together in the room yet that Barbara would not put the toys away despite being asked repeatedly. With the parents' agreement the psychologist then went to observe a mealtime at the family home, noting the context in which the meal took place and the patterns of behaviour and responses between the mother and the two children.

She began to collect further information to assess the problem in a wider context. In order to determine what Barbara's diet actually comprised, Christine agreed to record everything that Barbara ate over a period of 7 days in the form of a daily inventory of her food intake, including snacks such as sweets and crisps. She was encouraged to visit the health visitor at the local baby clinic to have Barbara's weight and height measured and compared with other children of her age. Christine completed a standardized questionnaire to elicit measures of the level of stress and anxiety she experienced as a parent. The scores from the questionnaire showed that Christine had very high levels of anxiety and felt stressed in her role as a parent. The diary showed that the little girl was eating small snacks during the day but rarely ate what her mother gave her at mealtimes. Despite Christine's worries, Barbara's height and weight were within normal limits for her age.

The psychologist shared her hypothesis about Barbara's eating problems with Christine. The psychologist suggested that Barbara had learnt that it was worthwhile screaming as her mother then let her eat on the floor while playing. She suggested that Christine gave in to Barbara when she would not eat because she believed that it was of prime importance that she should not be a harsh parent because of her own past experiences and should be especially protective towards Barbara because of her early developmental problems. They discussed the report from the health visitor about Barbara's weight and the evidence that Barbara had grown in health and strength since babyhood and was now more resilient. In addition they discussed ways of being firm and fair without being harsh or cruel. The psychologist described the approach she thought might help to set new conditions using rewards to shape sitting at table. She suggested that Christine should decide what Barbara needed to eat at table before being allowed to play. If she ate, Christine would praise her and let her play with a favourite toy. If she screamed, Christine would not cajole her but instead would ignore her and eat her own meal quietly. She was also encouraged to cut out snacks so that Barbara had an appetite at mealtimes. Christine was asked to set up the dining area differently so that the toys were less accessible. Christine agreed to try the approach. She and the psychologist drew up a programme describing what actions were to be taken and how Barbara would be rewarded. They arranged that Barbara's father would be briefed about the new plan and asked to offer support along the lines set out. Christine was given a diary to record whether the child sat and ate or ran to play, and whether the mother resorted to feeding her and playing away from the table or managed to ignore her.

They agreed to remain in touch by telephone during the next week and to meet the following week for a review. Christine returned to the health visitor so that Barbara's weight could be monitored under the new mealtime regime. As progress was maintained, a review was held a fortnight later, during which time they discussed Christine's feelings about the changes and her desire to continue to set limits and not let her daughter determine the routines at home, while remaining a loving parent. As well as diary reports of Barbara's increased food intake, evidence of change came from the scores in the parenting stress measure. When repeated at the end of treatment, the scores indicated that Christine felt less stressed and perceived herself as more able to cope. This was backed up in further discussion about the return to work and the effects on both children, and her relationship with Barbara's father.

Types of treatment approaches used with children and families

This example involved assessing and changing 'here and now' patterns of behaviour and the responses of a mother to her child, with associated factors being tackled indirectly. Few problems can be defined clearly or solved without addressing other aspects of the child and family situation and the home environment, especially if there are chronic problems associated with the referred problem such as overcrowding or maternal depression. If these obstacles are present, the psychological work would need to shift to other aspects which are open to change, and which can facilitate change in the child's behaviour. In practice, most psychologists tackle referred problems eclectically, addressing the child and his or her social context at several levels. The choice of treatment approach will be influenced by the resources that are available to the psychologist, and the level of their expertise. Barbara's problem could be addressed in a number of ways depending on the conceptual framework applied to the situation, including behaviour modification, cognitive behaviour therapy, family systems therapy, and psychoanalytic psychotherapy. Some health visitors carry out psychological treatment with parents and young children with feeding problems using behavioural or counselling approaches in the home or clinic.

Behaviour modification or behaviour therapy was developed by applying social learning theories and principles to children's problems. This form of therapy aims to reduce undesirable behaviour and teach parents to build on and extend positive sequences of behaviour which fit the child's age and stage. Parents are taught new ways of responding to their child's behaviour and of shaping new and more appropriate behaviours by altering the reinforcement used and thus altering the problem patterns of interaction. The aim is also to change the context in which problems occur. It is a particularly useful approach for resolving problem behaviours where parents are motivated to change their responses to their child and reward children systematically.

Cognitive therapy focuses on tracking and changing perceptions and beliefs about self and others in order to alter feelings and behaviour. It is based on a theory that an individual's problems derive from specific habitual errors in thinking and interpreting events under stress. Cognitive techniques involve identifying and testing out perceptions of reality. The model was developed for adults and has been adapted for use with young people, especially with anxious and depressed adolescents. It is less suited for younger children who are not as sophisticated at challenging their own thinking about themselves and others because of cognitive–developmental factors.

Many psychologists use a cognitive–behavioural approach (CBT) in work with children and families. This is a problem solving approach which integrates both cognitive and behavioural techniques and aims to develop new strategies to deal with problems (see Chapter 2). It acknowledges the importance of linking children's thoughts with problem feelings and behaviour and emphasizes the role of parents and peers in problem solving. The therapist may work directly with the child acting as 'coach' or may draw the parents in to help the child to carry out assignments. Kendall (1991) outlines the basis of this approach and describes relevant clinical programmes for a range of childhood problems. CBT is used, for example, in the treatment of hyperactive children, oppositional behaviour, and with children who have post traumatic stress disorder. CBT can be carried out directly with the referred child, individually, or in groups, for example teaching fearful children to face rather than avoid frightening situations and to use cognitive strategies to solve problems and adapt.

In the mid 1980s new ideas from family therapy influenced most multidisciplinary teams working with children. The family was conceptualized as a system of mutually influencing relationships which maintained the connection between individual problems and other family members' behaviour and perceptions. Change in one relationship would affect other relationships. Many psychologists became involved in systemic family therapy which gave a framework for changing the way family relationships and patterns of interaction are structured and how individuals are viewed by family members. The approach is used with families of children and young people with a range of problems with the aim of providing parents with new ways to think about children's problems and bring forward new solutions. Some systemic techniques used by family therapists are similar to behavioural or cognitive strategies, but there is less emphasis on giving advice directly. Systemic ideas have also been applied to understanding more about the referral network or system of professional helping agencies who become involved with a family when a child is seen as having a problem.

Some psychologists have applied psychoanalytic models to work with individual children and to groupwork, and incorporate play and art therapy techniques to allow a safe place for a child to explore strong feelings which are in conflict or confused. Parents may receive individual therapeutic help in their own right when their child is referred with a problem. This may be because there are past or present personal factors which affect the parent's mental health and therefore the capacity to cope with parenting, for example severe depression or marital violence. The idea is that improving parents' well being will improve their parenting. Community services such as Newpin pioneered group interventions based on psychoanalytical principles with isolated and depressed young mothers in inner city areas with the aim of improving their mental health. Mothers who completed a set of therapy sessions were trained to befriend other mothers who were new to the service thus increasing social support within the local community. The service was shown to be very effective, although evaluation studies failed to demonstrate an influence on the mothers' behaviour towards their children.

Webster Stratton and Herbert (1993) put forward the case for an integrated treatment approach for children with severe behavioural problems, including disruptive and defiant behaviour. They describe the approach as behavioural family therapy. The treatment programme has been carefully evaluated and has been found to be effective with children aged 3 to 8 years. Although it is intended as parent training, it is collaborative in its approach. The package of intervention begins after careful assessment and interviews. It aims to address current patterns of behaviour between parent and child, beliefs about the problem, family interactions, and advice about the child's developmental needs. It incorporates skills teaching, collaborative problem solving, work with the parents' marital relationships, and the organization of family relationships. It also offers parents support and advice. The parents are the focus of the therapy, rather than the child, and they are seen in groups in community settings. Psychologists who have been trained in this approach work with cotherapists and generate discussion amongst the group on specific topics such as rewards and punishments. Alternative behaviours are modelled by the therapist or by watching specially prepared videos.

Consultation work

Few psychologists spend all of their time working directly with referred children. As well as undertaking activities such as training and research, most psychologists are involved with other professionals who themselves care for or work with children, consulting to them about problems they experience and helping them devise new ways of responding to the needs of children or their parents. The primary aim of this consultative work is to help deliver psychological care to children or young people who might not access help directly. Psychological ideas can be passed on and developed by staff who are involved with vulnerable children, to enhance their skills and confidence and to reduce the likelihood that outside help will be needed in future. The input can take the form of discussion of difficult cases, training in specific skills such as communication, or setting objectives and/or supervision of their psychological work with children or families. Consultation sessions can focus on aspects of work with children that causes staff stress and anxiety and helps them to recognize emotional strains and conflicts inherent in work with troubled children. Research studies have demonstrated that organizational factors such as the nature of shift work and the degree of autonomy in decision making influence the way that staff interact with children in residential care, especially the amount of communication and play they initiate. Staff support therefore needs to be carefully negotiated with staff managers to ensure that the organization does not undermine any psychological input and is willing to consider new ways to address work stresses.

Psychologists build up consultation links in two major ways. Firstly they will involve staff who work with children who are known to be at risk of developing psychological problems due to family circumstance, social factors, or their special developmental problems, or a combination of all three. Obvious workplaces therefore are nurseries, hospital wards, and residential care facilities. Secondly, consultation and training may evolve as a result of clinical involvement with a particular agency or staff group who refer children with problems to the psychologist and who might instead wish to change their work practices to prevent the problems occurring.

Example of consultation to physiotherapists

A group of physiotherapists worked together in a community child health service in an inner city catchment area. Their main tasks were to provide home-based treatments of disabled young children and to ensure good communication with other professionals involved with the families. The physiotherapists were members of the local Child Development Team for children with physical and learning disabilities, as was the clinical child psychologist, a speech therapist, two community paediatricians, and an occupational therapist. The psychologist received referrals from all team members to assess and treat disabled children who had emotional or behaviour problems and their families. After receiving four consecutive referrals from the physiotherapy staff of children with muscular dystrophy with problems dealing with the impact of this degenerative neuromuscular condition on their quality of life, the psychologist offered to meet the physiotherapists to discuss alternative ways of helping the staff to help these children and their families. It emerged that the physiotherapists were unsure about whether or not to discuss emotional aspects of the disease and as a result tended to avoid talking about feelings. If a parent of a child with muscular dystrophy seemed distressed, or if a child seemed lethargic, they would refer the family to the psychologist for help. One of the physiotherapists had in fact tried to counsel a mother and child with muscular dystrophy at home. The mother became very distressed once she talked about her feelings, and the physiotherapist felt she had done more harm than good. Careful discussion with the physiotherapy group revealed that the majority wanted to communicate with parents and children about their feelings and felt that it would be beneficial to integrate their practical work with a psychological approach. However, they felt wary of changing their role and wanted to discuss and practice basic counselling skills as a group. The psychologist agreed to provide some teaching on communicating with distressed parents and children and then met the staff on a regular basis to consult about effective ways of working with specific families. This arrangement was ratified by the senior physiotherapist on behalf of her staff, with a review session built in after 3 months. As the group sessions continued, the staff shared some of their own distressed feelings about working with disabled and dying children and being helpless to change their condition radically. The sessions allowed staff to set more realistic yet meaningful objectives for their work with the children and improved the quality of the emotional support provided.

The physiotherapy group reviewed their caseloads and planned to devote more time for home-based sessions specifically with children with deteriorating physical conditions and their parents, to ensure that they discuss emotional issues with the family, and offer additional support. The psychologist agreed to help run a group for parents of the sick children who sought more support to discuss the stresses they faced and ways in which they could support one another.

SUMMARY

This chapter has described some of the contributions that clinical psychologists are currently making to the psychological well being of children and young people and the families who care for them. It has outlined three major aspects of clinical child psychology work—the problems children experience, the ways that services are structured to meet their needs, and the sorts of work that clinical child psychologists undertake. Children's problems arise and are maintained in the context of relationships with significant others, primarily their parents, who are themselves influenced by social and environmental factors. This means that psychological assessment and intervention needs to be wide ranging in order to be useful. There is some variation in the way that problems are conceptualized by psychologists and an outline has been given of the types of treatment approaches that can be taken; continued efforts are needed to evaluate their effectiveness and appropriateness. Psychologists working with children and young people usually work with parents as well as directly with children and families and the approaches adopted need to respect parents and support their endeavours to respond to their children. Finally, consultation and staff support are also important ways of improving children's care and examples have been outlined here of the effectiveness of group consultation in developing new ways of working and different responses to their needs.

References

Costello, E.J. (1989). Developments in child psychiatric epidemiology. *Journal of the American Academy of Child and Adolescent Psychiatry*, **28**, 836–841.

Davis, H., Spurr, P., Cox, A., Lynch, M., Von Roenne, A., and Hahn, K. (1997). A *description and evaluation of a community child mental health service. Clinical child psychology and psychiatry*. Vol. 2 no. 2 pp 221–238, Sage Publications, London.

Eiser, C. (1990). *Chronic childhood disease. An introduction to psychological theory and research*. Cambridge University Press.

Kendall, P.C. (ed.) (1991). *Child and adolescent therapy cognitive-behavioral procedures*. Guilford Press, New York.

Offord, D., Boyle, M., Szatmari, P., Rae-Grant, N., Links, P., Cadman, D., Byles, J., Crawford, J., Blum, H., Byrne, C., Thomas, H., and Woodward, C. (1987). Ontario Child Health Study. II: Six month prevalence of disorder and rates of service utilisation. *Archives of General Psychiatry*, **44**, 832–836.

Reder, P. and Lucey, C. (eds.) (1995). *Assessment of parenting; psychiatric and psychological contributions*. Routledge Press, London.

Target, M. and Fonagy, P. (1996). The psychological treatment of child and adolescent disorders. In *What works for whom? A critical review of psychotherapy research* (Roth, A. and Fonagy, P. eds). Guilford Press, London.

Webster Stratton, C. and Herbert, M. (1993). *Troubled families: problem children*. Wiley Press, Chichester.

Williams, R. and Richardson, G. (1995). *Together we stand. The commissioning, role and management of child and adolescent mental health services*. HMSO Publications, London.

Further reading

Copley, B. and Farryman, B. (1987). *Therapeutic work with children and young people*. Robert Royce, London.

Dowling, E. and Osborne, E. (1994). *The family and the school. A joint systems approach to problems with children* (2nd edn). Routledge, London.

Edwards, M. and Davis, H. (1997). *Counselling children with chronic medical conditions*. BPS Books, Leicester.

Frude, N. (1990). *Understanding family problems. A psychological approach*, Wiley Press, Chichester.

Happé, F. (1994). *Autism: an introduction to psychological theory*. UCL Press, University College, London.

Herbert, M. (1991). *Clinical child psychology social learning, development and behaviour*, Wiley Press, Chichester.

Jones, E. (1993). *Family systems therapy. Developments in the milan-systemic therapies*. Wiley Press, Chichester.

Meadows, S. (1993). *The child as thinker. The development and acquisition of cognition in childhood*. Routledge Press, London.

Trowell, J. and Bower, M. (1995). *The emotional needs of children and their families. Using psychoanalytic ideas in the community*. Routledge, London.

5

Working with people who have intellectual impairments

Chris Cullen, J. Fredrik Brown, Helen Combes, and Steve Hendy

WHAT IS A LEARNING DISABILITY?

First, a note on terminology, we will use the terms 'learning disability' and 'intellectual impairment' instead of other terms such as 'mental retardation' and 'learning difficulties'. We have done this not because we believe that labels in themselves have major effects (although there is some debate on this), but because we wish to acknowledge some important distinctions and relations between impairment, disability, and handicap. The World Health Organization suggests that impairments bring about a person's disability. For example it is known that taking the drug thalidomide during pregnancy has led to children being born with physical impairments, such as improperly formed limbs. Such impairments often result in disabilities, which are sometimes severe. For example having no arms makes it difficult to do certain things for yourself. The extent to which the disability becomes a handicap is dependent partly on societal reactions. If special aids—prostheses—are provided, the person with impairment may be able to do much for themselves, and the handicap may be slight. However, if peers and those with whom they come into contact react to the disability by shunning the person, the social handicap would be severe. Similarly, learning disabilities, which may be brought about by different impairments, sometimes originating in early damage within the brain, can become a handicap unless special help is provided. We suggest in this chapter that clinical psychologists are one of the groups of people who can provide that help.

People with intellectual impairment have difficulty in learning from early in their lives. This simple statement requires some elaboration before we get a clear picture of the situation. Most of us have some difficulty in learning some things; but a person with an intellectual impairment finds it difficult or even impossible to acquire some basic and important skills. These might include self-care skills such as washing, dressing, or feeding oneself. If this were the case, then the people affected might be described as having profound or severe learning disability, especially if they could not communicate at all with those around them or if they had very little awareness of their environment. People with less severe intellectual impairments can be expected to learn to care for themselves in many respects, but may have problems with more advanced skills, such as handling money, using public transport and other local amenities, reading, writing, socializing, and so on.

It is relevant to consider why a person has difficulty in learning. A very young child cannot handle money and would have difficulty learning to do so before other relevant skills are acquired. Such a child would not, though, be said to have a learning disability. So there must be some reference to the person's having failed to learn to do things that others of his or her own age can do. Some people fail to demonstrate normal behaviour because they have suffered an injury that prevents them from doing so. Here the issues become contentious, and it is more difficult to be certain. If perfectly normal people have road traffic accidents that leave them incapable of speech, incontinent, and immobile, should they fall into our group? Probably not, although methods of helping them might well include those used with people with intellectual impairments. If a child is born with cerebral palsy, a disorder of the central nervous system, that may make it very difficult to acquire some basic skills such as walking or self-feeding—should that child be in our group? No, because he or she is almost certainly failing only because of a physical impairment. In fact, it is now realized that there are many people who have been labelled as learning disabled in the past who actually have physical impairments which have prevented them from acquiring normal behaviour. Deafness is a good example. It has been estimated that there are significant numbers of people cared for in learning disability services whose main problem has been that they did not develop normally because they were deaf or hard of hearing.

No mention has been made so far of intelligence. Learning disabilities are associated with low intelligence, but we need to be careful. Intelligence is a complex concept, although the term is often used to summarize a person's overall level of functioning. What is more important is what the person actually does. For example there are some people who score poorly on intelligence tests, but who are totally independent and would not need support from specialist services. There are those who score within the normal range on intelligence tests, yet their level of functioning is such that they may benefit from using learning disability services. However, it is a 'rule of thumb' that the lower a person's score on an IQ test, the more difficulties they are likely to have adapting to the demands of everyday life.

Finally, it is important to clarify what we mean by the word 'behaviour' since it will be used regularly in this chapter. The basic unit in psychological science is the relationship between the individual and the world they live in. This relationship is what we mean by 'behaviour'. Clearly, a small and unique part of the world is inside every one of us and consequently inner or private events (that is emotions and physiological processes) play an important role in behaviour analysis. Defined as a person–environment relation, behaviour does not refer solely to skeletal movements, but to everything a person does in relation to both internal and external events. Thinking is something a person does in relation to their internal and external world and is therefore technically behaviour. Due to their private nature only the person having them observes their own thoughts. This, however, does not exclude them from a scientific analysis; it simply demands a different methodology. Recent developments in behaviour analysis have highlighted the need for clinicians, in learning disability services, to consider the role of 'cognition' in their work. Some of this research will be covered in more detail later in the chapter.

Interactional challenges

A significant part of the profession's clinical work with people with severe intellectual impairment relates to the management of challenging behaviours. Many of the referrals made to our department request help with the assessment or management of a difficult behaviour, and unfortunately this can result in an inordinate amount of time being devoted to proactive, at the expense of preventative, work.

Much of this chapter will focus on the major issue facing clinical psychologists working with people with severe intellectual impairments who also have problem behaviour. Before we proceed, we should explain what this means. The term 'challenging behaviour' is commonly used throughout learning disability services. Challenging behaviours are often defined by their relative intensity, frequency, and duration and the likelihood of them leading to harm or exclusion from services. It is important to remember that challenging behaviours, like other behaviours, are often a function of the person's environment. In this sense, challenging behaviour is one behaviour within a repertoire of behaviours brought about by the same contingencies. For example a challenging behaviour may lead to social contact from staff or parents. The challenging behaviour may not be the only behaviour capable of eliciting this reinforcing consequence. The reason challenging behaviour may occur at a higher intensity, duration, or frequency is that they are relatively more efficient at eliciting reinforcement than the other behaviours in the repertoire. Therefore, rather than using the term *challenging behaviour* (which risks being misinterpreted as a person-centred problem) we prefer the term *interactional challenges*, which makes the point that the behaviour is the result of the individual interacting with their environment. This is a social process in which social values and attitudes influence how we label and categorize behaviour. When behaviour is labelled as 'challenging' it adds little to our understanding of how that behaviour functions in allowing the person to adapt to their world. Referring to an interactional challenge alerts us to the necessity of looking beyond the person, often to others in their immediate environment.

SERVICE OPTIONS

People with an intellectual impairment need the same range of services, including general health care, as any other sector of the population. Beyond this, some may need specialist care. From a psychological perspective the major special needs are for:

- help with behaviour change;
- a range of facilities, such as residential and day-care settings, which will encourage as valued a life as possible.

People will have varying requirements for facilities and teaching at different stages in their lives. A severe intellectual impairment is often identified at birth or in the first few years of life. It is possible to recognize certain impairments as the unborn child develops in the womb, but these account for only a small proportion of cases; more often specific causes of learning disability remain unknown. The identification of a disability is the point at which psychological needs can first be addressed for the individuals and, importantly, for their parents and other family members. Families adjusting to this situation will require counselling and support in dealing with their own emotional reactions. They will later need advice and guidance in child management in relation to the learning disability; and such support and specialist advice should continue at some level throughout the child's preschool period.

Educational facilities for children with special needs, while imperfect, have progressed considerably in recent years. Special schools are often able to admit children at a very early age, and good schools have strong links with the families they serve. Self-care, communication, and preacademic skills are likely to be central to the educational and social care planning undertaken in the schools and within the community. The focus then is upon applying specialist knowledge of teaching methods to helping both child and family.

Since the introduction of the 1981 Education Act, the goal of integration (called 'mainstreaming' in the United States) of children with intellectual impairment into ordinary schools has been pursued with varying degrees of commitment within the United Kingdom. Both moral imperatives and educational assumptions underlie this. The moral imperatives are best described by a quote from the Warnock Report which paved the way for the 1981 Act: 'handicapped people should share the opportunities for self-fulfilment enjoyed by other people.'

The educational assumptions are that integrated education should lead to: a demise of pejorative labelling; increases in social benefits for children with learning disabilities; improvements in the partnership between parents and schools; more effective education; and benefits to peers who do not have learning disabilities. Unfortunately, there is not yet strong empirical evidence which allows us to believe that all the educational assumptions are justified (Danby and Cullen 1988). There is still a need for more research into these issues so that educational practices can be adjusted to meet the goals of the moral imperative—that children with intellectual impairment have the right to be educated with other children and for their education to be effective and beneficial.

When a child is clearly benefiting from being at school, education in Britain is often extended to the age of 19. Further specialized day training may then be offered within day centres managed by local authorities, and some people with intellectual impairments have opportunities to attend courses at colleges of further education. However, the quality of day services in Britain varies considerably through the country, a point made as long ago as 1985 in the House of Commons Social Services Committee Report on Community Care, and again a few years later by the Department of Health Social Services Inspectorate. Some areas have a reasonable network of day facilities, including special-care units for people with profound disabilities, sheltered workshops, and recreational facilities supported by Community Learning Disability Teams. There is an increase in work opportunities for some people, where they might, for example, produce plants for sale at commercial rates. Other areas, unfortunately, still have poor and inadequate services.

The other kind of facility that might be required for people with intellectual impairments and their families is residential care. In the early years, the emotional and practical demands upon a family can be great, and a child with a disability requires a disproportionate amount of parental time and effort. Families may require a respite-care facility to give them a chance to relax or give time to other members of the family. This kind of support may be offered in a number of ways, including the use of foster families, hostels, or small-group homes. Many professionals feel that it is particularly important that families are encouraged to use these facilities as the child grows older, both for the immediate relief they offer and because they afford an opportunity for parents to view their growing child in a normal way. Most non-disabled children leave home at some time and live away from their parents, and the use of short-term care not only provides relief but also enables families to prepare for the eventual separation of parent and child at the point at which this seems natural. This objective requires appropriate facilities such as group homes and supported living arrangements, and this is an area in which an immediate growth in community resources must take place.

In summary, the developmental needs of a person with learning disabilities are similar to those of other individuals. However, they differ in both time scale (they change more slowly) and the extent of independence (they may require a more elaborate supporting environment than the average person). From the psychologist's point of view the individual and their families are susceptible to the same range of needs as any family. In addition they may require special help, counselling, or guidance in relation to the learning difficulties experienced by the person with an intellectual impairment and in relation to emotional pressures which may result directly or indirectly from the impairment. In practical terms, the points at which a clinical psychologist may help depend upon the nature of local services, and may range from a direct role in the teaching of a person with intellectual impairment to a role in the planning and management of facilities.

THE ROLE OF THE CLINICAL PSYCHOLOGIST

The work of a clinical psychologist with people who have severe intellectual impairment is varied. Clinical psychologists often work directly with the referred person, or with a staff system to support the needs of the client. This work can take place in a variety of settings such as a person's home, residential unit, day centre, or school, and with a diverse group of people, including family and professionals. Some time will inevitably involve training and supporting other staff involved in direct service delivery and in developing the overall service structure. For example if a gap in the service is identified, a clinical psychologist may put together a proposal for additional service funding. As the clinical psychologist becomes more experienced they are increasingly likely to contribute to the development of the profession, for example by becoming involved in and organizing special interest groups or developing professional guidelines. Also, clinical psychologists have a role to play in informing national policy and legislation on people with intellectual impairment, by, for example, being involved in debates on delivering community care to people with learning disabilities following the closure of the large, residential institutions.

A clinical psychologist working in a service for people with learning disabilities is almost always working in an actively multidisciplinary setting. This may involve professionals such as teachers, social workers, direct-care staff; doctors, nurses, health visitors, administrators and planners; speech and language therapists, physiotherapists and occupational therapists, and, importantly, parents. Each group has its own definable contribution, although there may be a good degree of overlap in the activity of the contact-oriented groups such as social workers, nurses, and some clinical psychologists. This is particularly so in the area of general counselling, and recently in the teaching of behaviour-change procedures. The exact contribution of each professional tends to be determined by a combination of professional training, some statutory responsibilities, and local need.

There are two related but separate aspects of the psychologist's role. The first is research related. This could be the implementation of a particular procedure, such as functional communication training (see below) or it might be an investigation into an aspect of service delivery. For example the move to community care has come about partly as a result of research showing that large institutions tend to be places that result in clear disadvantages for people with intellectual impairment.

Clinical psychologists have been prominent in bringing this information to the attention of service planners (c.f. Cullen *et al.* 1995).

The second aspect of the psychologist's role is the application to everyday clinical practice of a systematic scientific approach (c.f. Dallos and Cullen 1990) using a framework which helps in the formulation and treatment of problems. This psychological analysis has the following characteristics:

1. assessment—the process of gathering information about a person;
2. interpretation—relating the observations to a broader theoretical framework;
3. intervention—putting into practice a treatment plan which follows from the interpretation;
4. evaluation—monitoring change and, where necessary, reformulating the initial interpretation.

Assessment and interpretation

Initially we must find out enough about the person to enable an individual plan to be drawn up. It is essential that the assessment should lead to some action—it is not sensible to initiate the assessment process without having good reason (Cullen and Dickens 1990). The purpose of an assessment may simply be to say whether or not a person has an intellectual impairment. This is essentially a screening function, and here it might be appropriate to use a test that compares the person with others of his or her own age. Such tests are called norm-referenced tests, and include the familiar intelligence and personality tests. While these procedures have a wide acceptance in society, their use by clinical psychologists working in learning disability services has decreased steadily during the past two decades. The main reason (although there are others) is that the results do not help much in determining a plan of action. It is of little practical use to know that a person has an IQ of 57 or a Developmental Age of 2½ years. The habit of some of our senior judges in asking the mental age of a person with an intellectual impairment before them in Court, rests on an unfortunate but common misunderstanding. The (il)logic of the argument is that a woman with a mental age of 7 is 'really' like a 7-year-old girl regardless of the fact that she might have a chronological age of 30 and many of the emotional needs and aspirations of any other adult woman.

The alternative to norm-referenced assessments is to measure how much of a skill someone has. This allows a training procedure related to that measure to be devised. Much of the assessment now carried out in a learning disability service is of this sort. There is a wide range of such assessments available, and some of them are related to norm-referenced tests, since they allow a computation of developmental age so that a comparison with other learning-disabled (and non-disabled) people can be made. Some of the most popular functional assessments in current use are the Progressive Assessment Charts, the PIP Development Charts, the Adapative Behaviour Scale, the Behaviour Assessment Battery, the Vineland Adaptive Behaviour Scale, and the Everyday Living Skills Inventory.

All these allow the assessment of important skills. The items are usually ordered in increasingly difficulty. The same broad skill areas are covered in each (for example self-care, communication, educational achievement, and socialization). Sometimes the items are linked together, forming a chain leading to a final goal. For example 'visual fixation' precedes 'visual tracking' in the Behaviour Assessment Battery. Some of the assessments allow a measure of how much help a person must have —what type of prompt—before they can complete a task. This kind of information is very useful in designing treatment plans, since it helps to know what the minimum help has to be in order to get the person to succeed at the task. (More details on these and other assessment devices will be found in Cullen and Dickens 1990.)

Intervention and evaluation: the functional paradigm

We have argued above that behaviour is largely a function of a person's environment. In order to understand behaviour, therefore, we should carry out a functional analysis. There are two distinct conceptual paradigms in contemporary psychology, the structural and the functional. The basic assumption underpinning the functional position is that all behaviour is meaningful in that it serves a useful function. Although knowing the topography (or structure) is important, knowing why something happens is more useful to a clinician who wishes to bring about change. The relationship between the structure of behaviour and its function is not always straightforward. People may shout because they are happy, angry, or scared and simply describing the behaviour does not tell us why.

The process of identifying the meaning of behaviour involves a functional analysis. For example a person with intellectual impairment may shout to initiate social contact with a member of staff. Due to other variables influencing staff behaviour, it may be that only every tenth vocalization on average is followed by staff interaction. This may not seem particularly efficient, but the person might not have any other way of communicating. If, however, another behaviour becomes more effective at initiating social contact (such as aggression or self-injury), the person may come to emit that behaviour instead. Clearly, a functional analysis enables us to understand how behaviours change over time and across situations.

There are a variety of methods for assessing behavioural function. Common methods include interviews and questionnaires for direct care staff (e.g. the Motivational Assessment Scale), direct observation of the antecedents and consequences of the target behaviour, or experimental analogues. Experimental analogues are an increasingly popular technology that assess the function of behaviour. In contrast to naturalistic observations, they systematically programme antecedents and consequences for defined behaviours. If a particular behaviour increases when social contact is programmed to follow it, but not when tangible reinforcement is offered, then it is possible to hypothesize that it has a social function. Analogue assessments are relatively complex to undertake. They are, however a powerful tool for clinical psychologists trying to uncover the functions of behaviour.

For a complete assessment it is important not only to have a picture of what the person can do —referred to as assets—but also what excess behaviours they have. Consider the following situation. A child with a learning disability giggles and runs away whenever she is asked a question. This may not be noted on a typical assessment scale, but could be important in understanding the child and subsequently helping her. Someone in regular contact with the child, perhaps the mother, would be asked to keep a careful record of the following:

1. Antecedents—under what circumstances does the child run away? From which people? What locations? What kinds of questions?
2. Behaviours—exactly what form does the behaviour have? Does she run far away, or does she just run out of reach? Does she look to see what reaction she is getting?
3. Consequences—what happens when she runs away? Does anyone chase her or remonstrate with her? Does it result in questions being asked again?
4. Alternative—what would have been more socially appropriate and valued behaviour under the circumstances?

After a few days of collecting observations the following picture emerges. She runs away when she is not familiar with the person asking the question or when she is unlikely to know the answer. In fact, she often cannot answer questions. The usual effect is that she receives attention by being followed. In fact, she does not go far and seems to be waiting to be followed. She also manages to avoid answering the question, since it is usually not asked again. This kind of exercise involves an assessment of the situation and interpretation of the possible causes or functions of her behaviour. In this case it is reasonable to hypothesize that running away is partly an avoidance response—it serves the function of avoiding a situation in which she would fail. It also receives attention, and is quite effective at getting people to interact with her. This analysis leads to a programme which concentrates on the child's deficits,that is things she cannot (or does not) do. For example she should be taught to say 'I don't know' if she cannot answer a question; she needs to learn ways of getting to know people with whom she is unfamiliar; and she needs to be taught to ask questions herself. To summarize, an assessment should tell us about:

1. assets—those skills or patterns of behaviour in an individual's repertoire which are acceptable or useful and strong;
2. deficits—those skills or patterns of behaviour which are absent or weak and thought to be desirable or necessary;
3. excesses—those patterns of behaviour which are strong and unacceptable or disadvantageous to an individual.

There is a subtlety in this that may not be apparent. These ways of describing behaviour are culturally relative: what may be acceptable in one setting and can be described as an asset may not be in another setting, and may be though of as an excess. Take, for example, the occasion when a case conference was called to discuss the public disrobing of a young woman. She had the habit of dashing out of the house and stripping in the road. For many months she had been attending a self-help skills teaching programme where we were trying to teach her to undress before going to bed.

Another subtlety is that what may at first be considered an excess can be turned into an asset. Fleming (1984) reports the case of a man with a learning disability who had a history of ejecting clothes through a ward window and hiding them behind lockers. These were not his clothes but those other residents had left lying around. Rather than simply dealing with this as a problem to be removed, Fleming construed the situation in a different way. The man had a useful skill; he could recognize unattached and disordered items of clothing, collect them, and transport them, with the effect of tidying the environment. The intervention, which depended on an imaginative assessment and interpretation of the situation, was to ask the man to collect loose items of clothing and take them to a large cupboard. This took place six times each day and he received praise from staff for completing the task. There was a decline in the number of items of clothing which were ejected through the window. Six weeks after the intervention ended, when staff were no longer asking him to take items to the cupboard, the man was reported to be independently collecting items and taking them to the cupboard. This is a good example of the approach we are advocating in this chapter—a constructional approach.

THE CONSTRUCTIONAL MODEL

In a seminal paper, Goldiamond (1974) outlined the application of the functional paradigm to clinical and social problems. Goldiamond differentiated between a pathological and constructional model of human behaviour. Goldiamond argued that the pathological model is based on negative reinforcement and punishment and results in the elimination of an underlying pathology. It is used pervasively within our society and focuses on avoiding aversive situations and eliminating particular repertoires. In contrast, the constructional model aims to increase an individual's competence and construct alternative repertoires. It conceptualizes all behaviour as functional and tries to develop an alternative, socially desirable set of behaviours that can usefully replace the challenging behaviour. Goldiamond describes the constructional model as being in apposition to the pathological model. If the constructional approach is successful, the level of undesirable behaviours should reduce.

When faced with interactional challenges, there is often a pressing need to remove or reduce them. Carers find the behaviour aversive and it is clearly not beneficial for the person. However, there are ethical and practical problems associated with using eliminative interventions to reduce certain behaviours. Let us take the ethical question first. A functional approach holds that behaviour is purposeful. Can we always justify the elimination of such interactions? Consider a young man whose spitting functions to initiate social contact with those around him (i.e. people rush to stop him). His behaviour indicates that he wants social contact (as indeed this is important to most of us) and to ignore it is to deny his needs. The pathological model is not particularly effective because, as in the above example, it is most likely that the young man will find another way of initiating social contact. This may be referred to as 'symptom substitution', but it really reflects the use of another behaviour to achieve the ends that a previous behaviour achieved. Although we may be able to eliminate this behaviour by ignoring it, are we meeting his needs by doing so? The constructional model would advocate teaching an alternative repertoire that acknowledges and meets the needs of the client.

Assessment and interpretation, therefore, is not a mechanical exercise. It requires clinical judgement and experience. It is important to consider the purposes being served, which might include:

- helping in the formulation of objectives for care plans;
- producing data which would allow progress to be evaluated;
- discovering the critical functional relationships between key behaviours and the environment—the causes of behaviour.

These often require different methods. As noted above, formalized rating scales may help the clinician to describe current skills, and should lead to an outline plan for further investigation. However, more detailed observation and recording of activity will usually be required prior to the instigation of a training procedure in order to clarify the nature of the skills to be taught and to provide a baseline against which progress may be measured. This latter point is particularly important for people with intellectual impairments since change is often slow.

Functional communication training

Functional Communication Training (FCT) is an approach based on the constructional model and provides a useful example of an intervention. In the words of two of the pioneers of FCT,

> . . . the key notion underlying the effectiveness of communication training is that of functional equivalence. Specifically, although two behaviours may differ in form (e.g., aggression versus the phrase, 'Am I doing good work?'), they may nonetheless be identical in function (i.e. both aggression and the verbal request produce attention). The communication training strategy capitalises on this equivalence by strengthening a socially desirable form (i.e. a verbal request) that serves the same presumptive function as

> the socially undesirable form (i.e. aggression) thereby weakening or eliminating the latter.
>
> (Carr and Durand 1985, p. 125)

FCT has proved to be a positive and effective approach to supporting people with intellectual impairments. In using the metaphor of communication to understand interactional challenges we can think of them as communicating something to us about a person's life. For example, Kemp and Carr (1995) found that a man with a severe intellectual impairment frequently became aggressive when working in a greenhouse. A functional assessment suggested that the man's aggressive behaviour enabled him to stop work and leave the greenhouse. Using the communication metaphor, the man's behaviour can be conceptualized as 'I want to stop this and do something else'. The ability to say this is something most of us take for granted. Imagine yourself in a similar situation when you want to stop doing something, but are unable to say so. What would you do? The constructional alternative to the man's aggression was to point to a picture of broken clock face whenever he wanted a rest.

Horner, Sprague, O'Brien and Heathfield (1990) described a study in which a 14-year-old boy was aggressive in order to escape from demands. Initially they taught him to ask for assistance by typing out 'help please'. They found that there was no drop in the level of aggressive behaviour. When he was taught to press a single key, however, there was a reduction in the aggressive behaviour; that is when the boy was taught a second more efficient, functionally equivalent behaviour. Similarly, Horner and Day (1991) showed that when a young boy had to sign a complete sentence to stop a work assignment ('I want to go, please') there was no reduction in his aggressive behaviour. However, when he had to sign only a single word ('break'), his aggressive behaviour reduced in frequency.

The social context in which communicative behaviour occurs is also an important variable. In particular, it has been recognized that the new response must be both acceptable and recognizable to carers for the intervention to be successful. For example, although hugging or kissing are social behaviours, they are not a conventionally acceptable way to initiate social interaction with staff. Carers must be able to recognize the new replacement behaviour if they are to be able to respond to it. Everyday vocal language is the ideal, but it is often not possible to teach people with severe impairments to talk. Sign language is a good alternative in environments when carers know the language, but obviously there will be problems in generalizing to mainstream society. Finally it is possible to use idiosyncratic gestures and vocalizations for individuals to communicate their needs, but the downside of this is that these responses will have little meaning beyond those directly involved in the intervention.

Other approaches

People with learning disabilities are just as likely as other people to experience emotional problems; in fact they are more likely to have emotional difficulties given the generally devaluing manner in which they are treated in our society. In recent years, the climate has been changing and people are demanding, and increasingly being given, access to the services and environments that other people take for granted. Access to psychotherapy, however defined, is just one of these new options. Cullen (in Waitman and Conboy-Hill 1992) reports that he had some trouble in identifying a psychotherapist to speak at a conference on psychological therapies for people with intellectual impairments. On looking at the literature it became clear that this was a problem that had persisted over the past few decades. While we have concentrated on personal self-care skills, social skills, interactional challenges, and the like, we have rarely attempted to deal with the emotional needs of clients.

Psychotherapy is a broad church. It is not delineated by professional background but by what the therapist actually does in relation to the client: from individual to group therapy; from sexuality to bereavement; from coming to terms with one's identity to the effects of disability on siblings and other family members.

Psychotherapists have generally been at the forefront of 'political' thinking, challenging people to re-examine their values. Not only are we forced to consider the intellectually disabled person as a person, but as someone on the same level and with the same needs and demands as the friend, the family member, and the therapist. For many this is not a comfortable message, but it is an urgent one.

CHANGING SYSTEMS OF CARE

So far we have described aspects of the psychologist's role that involve face-to-face contact with clients. However, there are other considerations that have influenced how psychologists work. One of these is that there are too few psychologists to carry out all the one-to-one teaching required, and much of the work could be carried out by appropriately trained direct-care staff or parents. This has led, in recent years, to a burgeoning of staff-training workshops and home-teaching systems. Essentially psychologists are operating through others, the people who are in most contact with the person with an intellectual impairment.

Staff training has been the subject of evaluative research, unfortunately the outcome is not always encouraging. Most authors who review the field of staff training have found that, while it is possible to achieve short-term changes in staff skills and attitudes, they are rarely found to last and staff do not usually change their practices when back in the workplace. Hence their clients may not benefit from the new procedures which the staff have learnt. Of in-service training for staff—usually conducted by psychologists—Ziarnik and Bernstein write:

> It is our contention that the effectiveness of staff training has yet to be demonstrated because it is often incorrectly applied. That is, the assumption underlying the decision to provide staff training is that staff cannot perform the needed skills. That assumption is not always correct. Poor performance may be related to a variety of factors, only one of which is skill deficiency.
>
> (Ziarnik and Bernstein 1982, p. 111)

This is an interesting comment because it indicates that the failure of staff training to result in lasting changes in staff behaviour may be due to factors other than the training (c.f. Cullen 1992). It is a consideration of these factors which has led to some psychologists' moving away from face-to-face client teaching and from staff training. Often it is the very setting in which a person lives which is the main cause of the problem.

Consider the following case. A middle-aged woman was referred to the Psychology Department. She had spent much of her life in institutions, was active, and relatively able in self-care. Care staff requested help with persistent interactional challenges, the most evident of which was a tendency to take off her clothes. As part of an assessment of the situation, interactions between the woman and the care staff were observed. This was done by watching the woman for short periods of time during the day, choosing time-samples so that a representative picture of the day would be formed. Table 5.1 shows the proportion of sample observations for each of the three interaction categories.

Table 5.1 Percentage of different types of interaction

Type of interaction	Percentage of total observations
Unattended	63.4
Engaged with staff in connection with problem behaviour	33.3
Engaged with staff in connection with acceptable behaviour	3.3

An intervention was then designed which had two major components:

1. an attempt to increase adaptive behaviour through brief periods of individual teaching, planned to occur on a regular basis, involving direct-care staff as far as their other commitments would allow;
2. a management procedure designed to affect the disrobing problem directly by removing her into her bedroom every time she removed her clothes inappropriately.

Both aspects of the programme were monitored with the support of clinical psychologists. The frequency of the use of disrobing declined from an initial average of 14 incidents per day to approximately one per day after 45 days. However, while the number of teaching sessions initially increased, a gradual decline took place between days 25 and 45. The frequency of sessions appeared to follow the frequency of problem behaviours. After day 45, both frequency of problem behaviours and that of teaching sessions rose again.

It seems as though pressures on staff in some way contributed to this phenomenon. Initially the woman may have been seen as extremely difficult and time-consuming for staff. A consequence of the intervention was a reduction in problem behaviour, and hence less demand on staff time. Relative to others, this woman became less of a problem and less often a subject of discussions between care staff and their senior managers. Other residents became more of a priority. The effect for the woman, as the problem reduced in frequency, was a reduction in the overall level of contact with staff. So the frequency of problem behaviour then increased as she returned to ways of behaving which had been successful in gaining staff attention. It seems likely that, in general terms, managers are most concerned about disruptive behaviours that may cause harm or indignity to others, or damage to property. Consequently, staff work hard to reduce these behaviours and are forced into a pathological orientation which produces cycles of behaviour problems. The task for the clinical psychologist is to reverse the tendency for staff to be most affected by behaviour problems and achieve a switch of emphasis to the maintenance of development gains. In this instance contact between staff and the woman were almost invariably prompted by the behaviour problem. A procedure was designed which could effectively operate on this; but the residential system worked against long-term maintenance.

The societal imperative

If it is the whole system that is at fault, the solution is to change it. Clinical psychologists are currently involved in different ways of trying to achieve this.

Influenced largely by Wolfensberger and his colleagues from the United States in the 1970s and 1980s many psychologists have advocated the principle of *normalization* as a means of solving the problems of people with learning disabilities. The basis of the approach is an assertion that it is largely the way in which society as a whole treats people with intellectual impairments which is at the heart of the matter. The community has refused to accept intellectually impaired people as equal members with equal rights and privileges, and has devalued them by either consigning them to segregated settings or by refusing them access to normal facilities and services. Change all that and many of the problems will disappear. There are those, though, who see normalization as a collection of slogans and statement, some of which are contradictory, and few of which are based on evidence that people with intellectual impairments would benefit from the changes suggested (Mesibov 1990). These criticisms have led Wolfensberger to refine and rename his theory, and in 1981 he proposed that normalization be replaced by *social role valorization* (SRV). This requires 'the support and defense of valued social roles for people who are at risk of social devaluation' (Wolfensberger 1981, p. 234). Proponents of SRV believe that people with intellectual impairments should have a useful and valued role in society. They argue that society has devalued and deskilled them. The argument is not that people with intellectual impairments should become normal (in the sense of suddenly acquiring new repertoires) but that they will become valued members of society and acquire new repertoires in a supportive and conducive environment. The two interrelated and essential elements of SRV are image enhancement and competence enhancement. Both are important, although in this chapter we have emphasized the clinical psychologist's role in competence enhancement. If we wish to influence the way in which people with intellectual impairments are cared for by society, we have to arrange for them to be in environments that are associated with a positive image. Our procedures designed to enhance competence must not be ones that contribute to negative imagery.

FUTURE DIRECTIONS

Cognition

Psychologists working within a behavioural perspective have tended to ignore the analysis of cognition and feelings, but in recent years there has been a burgeoning of research in the area of equivalence which may prove to be of direct relevance to clinicians working with people who are intellectually impaired. Sidman (1995) describes research over more than two decades into the defining features of language. Initially he used the match-to-sample paradigm to teach an intellectually impaired man to read. First he was taught to select a printed word (B) in the presence of the spoken word (A). He was then taught to select the picture of the object (C) in the presence of its printed word (B). After this teaching procedure, other responses emerged without direct training. The man was able to match the printed word in the presence of the picture and to say the name of the word in the presence of the picture and the printed word (see Fig. 5.1). Through a novel teaching procedure an intellectually impaired man had been taught to read with understanding. He had also learnt new tasks without any direct training. The emergence of these untrained relations shows that the stimuli are substitutable, through this process people acquire symbolic understanding. These findings show that through words people can adapt within an environment without having had contact with it. Sidman believes that equivalence is 'given'. He argues that equivalence will only be demonstrated if the teaching procedure brings responding under appropriate contextual or stimulus control. This kind of research investigates cognitive abilities, but equivalence also has relevance to other areas.

Adults with mild to moderate learning disabilities often experience psychological problems such as low self-esteem. This can lead to aggressive behaviours, depression, and anxiety. An adult with a learning disability may have a history of being told 'you are slow'. Then they are asked to do difficult tasks. There is frequent pairing of the word

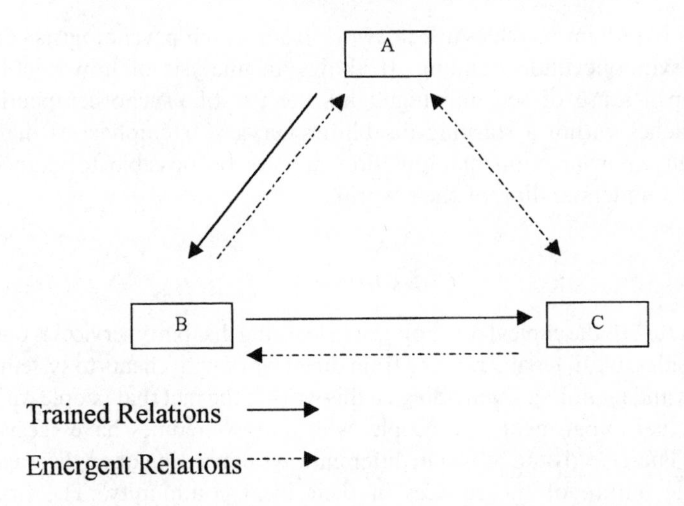

If A is equivalent to B and B is equivalent to C then:
C is equivalent to B
B is equivalent to A and
C is equivalent to A
A is equivalent to C

Fig. 5.1 An equivalence relation. Participants are taught to match A—B and B—C (solid line). Other novel stimulus relations then emerge (dotted lines).

'slow' with an aversive event, and pairing of the aversive event with negative feelings and emotions. This leads to adults with learning disabilities believing they are slow, thus contributing to the poor image identified as so crucial by Wolfensberger (see above). Pairing the word 'slow' with other events, such as feelings of worthlessness, may create a network of aversive thoughts and feelings. Adults with learning disabilities may come to believe they are worthless. They may then avoid learning new skills. Within a therapeutic setting the psychologists role should be to build up alternative repertoires and to strengthen other equivalence relations. If we want clients to understand the relation between events, words, and feelings it is essential that we explore appropriate teaching procedures. This needs innovative practice, perhaps through a precise manipulation of the environment. This manipulation may help people with learning disabilities to understand the situations in which they can achieve and those in which they cannot.

This paradigm provides a framework from which psychologists can study symbolic understanding. It allows an analysis of how people develop a sense of self and highlights the use of psychotherapeutic approaches within a learning disabilities service. It emphasizes that, through environmental manipulation, it may be possible to change people's understanding of their world.

CONCLUSION

The picture of the clinical psychologist in learning disability services is one of considerable diversity, ranging from direct work with clients to systems change and planning. Over-riding all this work is the fact that people with intellectual impairments are people, who may sometimes have special needs. These needs can be met in different ways depending upon their age and the nature of the services in their local community. The first characteristic of a psychological contribution is an analysis of the whole situation. This is accomplished by a variety of means, but leads to an intervention which is an experiment in the sense of being susceptible to continual modification in the light of changes for the disabled person. The interventions may be simple or complex, but they should be flexible.

In an attempt to help wider groups of clients, many psychologists have moved to work at a macro-level, designing, and influencing systems. The knowledge base is not so secure here, and some activities—such as staff training—are yielding disappointing results. But as long as psychologists work at the macro level with the same experimental rigour as they do at the micro level, there is cause for optimism. It should be the central concern of psychologists that whatever is done for people with learning disabilities has good reason. The history of services shows that there is rarely a shortage of good intentions. One of the roles for the psychologist should be to provide evidence to show which of the available options are likely to lead to the most benefit for clients. This should apply as much to service systems as to individual therapy.

References

Carr, E. G. and Durand, V. M. (1985). Reducing behavior problems through functional communication training. *Journal of Applied Behavior Analysis*, **18**, 111–127.

Cullen, C. (1992). Staff training and management for intellectual disability services. In *International Review of Research in Mental Retardation* (Vol. 18), (ed. N. W. Bray). Academic Press, New York.

Cullen, C. and Dickens, P. (1990). People with mental handicaps. In *Measuring human problems* (ed. D. F. Peck and C. M. Shapiro), pp. 303–16. Wiley, London.

Cullen, C., Whoriskey, M., Mackenzie, K., Mitchell, W., Ralston, K., Shreeve, S., and Stanley, A. (1995). The effects of deinstitutionalization on adults with learning disabilities. *Journal of Intellectual Disability Research,* **39**, 484–494.

Dallos, R. and Cullen, C. (1990). Clinical Psychology. In *Introduction to psychology* (Vol 2), (ed. I. Roth), pp 724–70. Lawrence Erlbaum Associates (in association with the Open University), Hove.

Danby, J. and Cullen, C. (1988). Integration and mainstreaming: A review of the efficacy of mainstreaming and integration for mentally handicapped people. *Educational Psychology*, **8**, 177–95.

Fleming, I. (1984). The constructional approach to 'problem behaviour' in an institutionalised setting. *Behavioral Psychotherapy*, **12**, 249–355.

Goldiamond, I. (1974). Toward a constructional approach to social problems. *Behaviorism,* **2**, 1–84.

Horner, R. H. and Day, H. M. (1991). The effects of response efficiency on functionally equivalent competing behaviors. *Journal of Applied Behavior Analysis,* **24**, 605–804.

Horner, R. H., Sprague, J. R., O'Brien, M., and Heathfield, L. T. (1990). The role of response efficiency in the reduction of problem behaviors through functional equivalence training: A case study. *Journal for the Association for Persons with Severe Handicaps,* **15**, 91–97.

Kemp, D. C. and Carr, E. G. (1995). Reduction of severe problem behavior in community employment using a hypothesis driven multicomponent intervention approach. *Journal for the Association for Persons with Severe Handicaps,* **20**, 229–247.

Mesibov, G. R. (1990). Normalisation and its relevance today. *Journal of Autism and Developmental Disorders,* **20**, 79–90.

Sidman, M. (1995). *Equivalence relations and behavior: a research story.* Authors Cooperative, MA.

Waitman, A. and Conboy-Hill, S. (1992). *Psychotherapy and mental handicap.* Sage Publications, London.

Wolfensberger, W. (1981). Social role valorization: A proposed new term for the principle of normalisation. *Mental Retardation,* **21**, 234–239.

Ziarnik, J. P. and Bernstein, G. S. (1982). A critical examination of the effects of in-service training of staff performance. *Mental Retardation,* **20**, 109–44.

Additional reading

Brown, H. and Smith, H. (1992). *Normalisation a reader for the nineties.* Routledge, London.

Jacobson, J. W. and Mulick, J. A. (1996). *Manual of diagnosis and professional practice in mental retardation.* American Psychological Association, Washington.

6

Working with physically disabled people

Paul Kennedy

> I deliberately avoid the phrase 'I am a quadriplegic' as I am not. I am the same person I was before the injury, except that I now have some very different needs for physical support. My intellect is not impaired, I still have the same desires as anyone else to live, love, work and play. I am me.
>
> Ernie Lightpole (1991) (pseudonym)

INTRODUCTION

The prevalence of disability increases with age and as people live longer, many more people will experience a longer period of their life in a state of limited physical functioning. Historically, the contribution of clinical psychologists to people with physical disabilities was to assess psychopathology, but now clinical psychologists contribute not only to the management of mood and adjustment disorders, but contribute to rehabilitation planning, assist with the amelioration of psychophysiological aspects, and have taken the lead in developing a variety of self-management techniques. Before discussing this contribution further, it would be helpful to describe the terms most commonly used, summarize the main causes, and outline the incidence and prevalence of the major conditions.

Definitions

The World Health Organization (WHO 1980) proposes a model of disability that distinguishes between impairment, disability, and handicap. Impairment refers to the loss of functioning in the body organ or system (for example muscular weakness). Disability is defined as a restriction in the ability to perform normal activity (for example walking), and handicap is defined as a disadvantage resulting from the impairment or disability and prevents the individual fulfilling a social role (for example inability to work). This is a widely used model of disability which has served as a framework to understand and identify the physical, psychological, and social impact of disease, acquired injury, and congenital disorders. Johnston (1996) reformulated the WHO model to incorporate social, cognitive, and behavioural factors to enable a more comprehensive understanding of the experience of disability.

Prevalence of physical disability

The Office of Population Census and Surveys (OPCS 1988) estimates that there are over 6 million adults with one or more disabilities in Great Britain (out of a population of 58 million). In view of the wide variation in type and cause of disability, it is difficult to summarize the lifecycle experiences. For example spina bifida is a congenital condition which affects the individual throughout their lifespan, whereas the age of onset of asthma tends to be by the age of 8 to 12. In conditions such as osteoarthritis, rheumatoid arthritis, and multiple sclerosis, increasing age is positively associated with greater physical disability. Disability can also result from accidents such as in spinal cord injury and traumatic amputations, and may also result from degenerative neurological disease and cerebral vascular accidents. Whilst there are many people born with disability or acquire their disability in adolescence or young adulthood, the prevalence of severe disability within the United Kingdom population remains stable until the age of 60, from then there is a considerable increase in the prevalence, severity, and range. In general, there are four broad conditions that account for most of the physical disabilities in the United Kingdom. These are illustrated in Table 6.1.

Not surprisingly, the conditions listed in Table 6.1 create a range of functional problems that impair general, physical, psychological, and social functioning. These conditions can cause problems related to movement, reaching, and dexterity; others include problems with vision, hearing, and communication and other people can experience distressing problems associated with continence, behavioural disorders, and impaired consciousness. The extent of functional loss will depend on the severity of the condition and chronicity.

The clinical context

Before describing the role of the clinical psychologist with people who have physical disabilities, it is important to highlight the general

Table 6.1 Major conditions causing physical disability

Condition	UK prevalence	Causes
Neurological	1.5 million people	Stroke, epilepsy, Parkinsons disease, multiple sclerosis, motor neurone disease, muscular dystrophy, cerebral palsy, spinal cord injury
Musculoskeletal	3 million people	Osteoarthritis, rheumatoid arthritis, systemic lupus erythematosus, juvenile arthritis, osteoporosis, fractures and injuries
Sensory	1 million have significant sight loss	Congenital, glaucoma, diabetes, retinopathy, otitis media, presbycusis, meningitis
Chronic respiratory	5% of population	Cystic fibrosis, asthma, emphysema, chronic bronchitis

rehabilitative context within which these services are provided. Rehabilitation is defined as a process of active change by which a person who has become disabled acquires the knowledge and skills needed for optimum physical, psychological, and social functioning. Physical rehabilitation also refers to the application of all measures aimed at reducing the impact of disabling and handicapping conditions and enabling disabled and handicapped people to achieve maximal social integration. The disability movement in Britain prefers not to use the term 'people with impairment', or 'handicapped people' and prefers the use of the generic term 'disabled people'. It is important for rehabilitation services to be user- and community-centred with the emphasis on the rights of individuals to make choices and take control of their own lives from a range of options.

Over the past 5 years there has been a growing demand for clinical psychology services in clinical health and rehabilitation services. Most organized physical rehabilitation teams have clinical psychologists as part of their team or have access to clinical psychology resources. Many of these teams are based in the community and are funded by community health services and general practitioners. Clinical psychologists are also employed in specialist centres, for example spinal cord injury rehabilitation centres, specialist centres for people with hearing and visual disabilities, services for people with muscular skeletal disorders, and neurological impairment (see also Chapter 7). Input is provided at all stages of the process and includes specialist services for children, adults with acquired injuries and disabilities, and people living in the community. Clinical psychology services are provided to hospital-based populations, outpatients, community rehabilitation facilities, health centres, general practitioners' surgeries, and in the person's home.

THE PSYCHOLOGICAL PROBLEMS

Emotional aspects

There is a growing body of research evidence that clearly documents the emotional impact of these chronic conditions. Psychological distress, usually in the form of anxiety and depression, has been found to be higher in people with physical disabilities such as multiple sclerosis, rheumatoid arthritis, and spinal cord injury. There is also a significant body of evidence from a variety of conditions that have highlighted that there is little relationship between the extent of the physical disability and degree of psychological well,being (Newman 1997; Kennedy 1997; Dupont 1997).

Depression can emerge in response to perceived losses and anxiety can occur when people perceive that their existing coping strategies are insufficient to meet unknown future demands. These may emanate from the sudden onset, continued chronicity, or ongoing deterioration of the condition. Some people experience considerable guilt in response to their inability to perform roles and tasks such as in intimate relations and vocational responsibilities. Whilst many people understand the organic condition that caused their disability (although this is not always the case) they may feel angry as to why this part of their disability has happened to them and feel frustrated in having to manage the consequences within their particular context.

Adjustment and adaptation

Depending on the onset, severity, and chronicity, the condition will normally require considerable adjustment and adaptation. There are a number of psychological theories which help us understand these complex processes, including the biopsychosocial model (Engel 1980), the Coping with Stress paradigm (Lazarus and Folkman 1984), and the various phase or stage theories for which there is little empirical evidence (Wortman and Silver 1989). Adaptation is a process whereby the individual conceptualizes the nature of their condition, considers the implications, acquires new skills for old goals, relinquishes unattainable goals, and re-establishes previously held life goals. Adjustment is theoretically conceptualized as the end point of the adaptation process. Here the person assimilates the functional limitations associated with the disability and continues to develop in personal, social, and vocational spheres. However, when thinking about adaptation, it is important to distinguish adaptations to disabilities associated with a traumatic event, such as a spinal cord injury, and adaptations that are associated when the onset is gradual and insidious.

In anecdotal and clinical reports, denial is often referred to an important component of the psychosocial adaptation process. It is conceptualized as either a phase in the process or a psychological mechanism to minimize distress. Often it refers to denial of outcome (e.g. 'I will not go blind' or 'I will walk again'), functional limitations, or chronicity. Historically, denial was viewed within the psychoanalytic perspective as an unconscious defence mechanism. However, more recently, denial is conceptualized within an information processing model. Here, it is viewed in the short term as an adaptive strategy to minimize seriousness, prevent the person from being overwhelmed, and facilitate assimilation to the permanency and change. However, there is some evidence that denial in the longer term is associated with increased morbidity and dysfunction.

The disabling environment

When considering the contribution of clinical psychology within this context, it is important to remember that the experience of disability is not solely a condition of the individual. From the perspective of disabled people, the negative experiences of disability, such as architectural and social inaccessibility, are physical or social creations in a society geared by and for able-bodied people. This is not to deny the personal experience of disabling conditions, but to highlight the impact of a world designed for non-disabled living. Therefore, the creation of more enabling physical, psychological and social environments can change the experience of disability. The Professional Affairs Board of the British Psychological Society produced a document entitled *Psychology and Physical Disability in the National Health Service* (Working Party of the British Psychological Society Professional Affairs Board 1989) which criticized the lack of co-ordination, poor communication, and discontinuity of services for people with physical disability. It also drew attention to the limits of using the medical model which puts undue focus on medical treatment and fails to address emotional, personal, and social aspects of disability. This report recommends that clinical psychologists should be available in each health district (now trust or authority) to provide specialist skills in assessment and intervention with people with disabilities, their carers, and other staff. It proposes that psychological expertise should be sought in the analysis of, and the solutions to, health problems of people with disabilities and that services should be provided in the context of active partnership with persons with a disability, the family, and professionals. Recommendations are also made to encourage the development of psychological services, the extension of training for clinical psychologists, and the priorities of psychological research and disability.

The history of physical rehabilitation (and indeed clinical psychology) is relatively short and tied to the major conflicts of the twentieth century. Services in the early part of the twentieth century focused on the level of impairment and the restoration of functional abilities. However, since the Second World War, and in response to the assertions of the Independent Living Movement, rehabilitative services have begun to address personal responses, emotional issues, social factors, and vocational opportunities. Also in the twentieth century, the pattern of physical illness afflicting developed economies has changed considerably. In the early part of this century, acute and infectious diseases were the leading cause of death, which have now largely been controlled by the advances in biomedical science. There is now a growing population of people with chronic illness and disability where psychologists can play an important role in: modifying health related behaviour such as adherence to medical regimens; managing psychological distress; minimizing the negative consequence of disability; using psychological techniques to prevent the exacerbation of certain symptoms (chronic pain management); and promote healthy behaviour and prevent illness (see also Chapter 11). Physical rehabilitation services aim to enable people with disability to live with dignity, to maximize their potential and minimize disabling experiences. Clearly services need to optimize functioning, self-care, and autonomy. Services need to recognize the comprehensive needs of the person with disability which will include requirements for alterations in accommodation, legislation to maximize employment and educational opportunities, acquire necessary illness-related health-care skills, and a wide range of needs to include mobility, assistive technologies, and care management. It is also important to remember that disability occurs within a social context, normally a family, and depending on the extent and onset, may influence the issues associated with roles and responsibilities.

THE ROLE OF THE CLINICAL PSYCHOLOGIST

Clinical psychologists provide a broad range of services to people with disabilities. As mentioned, these services are provided across a range of sites that range from acute treatment centres to an individual's home. Services are provided on a one-to-one basis with individuals, and with couples, families, and groups. Clinical psychologists also make a contribution to service planning, organizational aspects, management, and administration. It is helpful to conceptualize the work of clinical psychologists with physically disabled people in three ways. Firstly, the contribution to assessment and formulation, secondly the contribution to treatment and intervention, and thirdly the wider societal and contextual contribution.

Assessment and formulation

Assessments with this population may serve a variety of purposes. Assessments are generally used as part of determining individual needs, to help in the formulation of intervention techniques, and treatment planning and outcome evaluation.

Needs assessment

Survival is conditional and people must take specific actions to fulfil needs. The onset of disability will trigger a re-examination of need. Clinical psychologists provide standardized and objective assessment of the nature and severity of disability with individuals and patient groups. This can include broad health status, type assessments such as the Sickness Impact Profile, or more specific assessments such as the St George's Respiratory Questionnaire. Other assessments may focus on the assessment of mood disorder such as the Hospital Anxiety and Depression Scale, functional limitations such as the Functional Dependence Measure, and psychosocial impact such as the Psychosocial Adjustment to Illness Scale. Other measures include the Acceptance of Disability Scale, the Ways of Coping Scale, and the Multidimensional Pain Inventory. In addition to these psychometric instruments and rating scales, psychologists can also assess problems by direct observation. Behavioural assessment techniques include a variety of behavioural rating scales, time-sampling techniques, and naturalistic observations such as behavioural mapping.

In adopting a more objective approach to assessment, clinical psychologists can assess the extent of psychological distress within an individual or a patient group. For example between a quarter and one-third of people who are chronically disabled, have clinical levels of depression and anxiety. This can help with the individual treatment planning and the organization of general services. Behavioural observations have been proved to be both reliable and valid and can help with a range of issues which could include the assessment of an individual's capacity for independent living in an independent living unit, and levels of patient activity and engagement in treatment and rehabilitation centres.

Assessment for formulation and interventions

Assessments are carried out to answer questions, and formulation and intervention provide the rationale for these questions. Assessments which help in formulation may include identification of behavioural risk factors, as in the acquisition of pressure sores and the identification of negative assumptions following acquired disability. Questionnaires, self-report, and self-monitoring techniques are helpful in assessing anteceding conditions, responses, and consequences in a traditional cognitive–behavioural therapy (CBT) formulation. The assessment of individual coping responses also helps by identifying propensities to engage in emotional-focused and problem-focused coping strategies. Lazurus and Folkman's (1984) transactional model has had a major impact on the current conceptualization of coping with chronic disability. In this model, the patients' coping responses are determined by their appraisal of the degree of threat posed by an illness and the resources available to help them cope. These assessments can help identify adaptive coping strategies which are useful in many chronic conditions. In general, strategies that include the processes of acceptance, reframing, planning, and utilization of social support have been found to be adaptive, whilst behavioural disengagement, mental disengagement, and alcohol and drug use ideation are associated with increased distress and disability. Many formulations require multifactorial assessments. This is not surprising given the comprehensiveness of the biopsychosocial prospective. These assessment techniques can help in the prediction of problems and in some cases help in the prediction of morbidity and, indeed, mortality. For example a brief self-completed questionnaire assessing instrumental activity of daily living was sent to an elderly sample living in the community, which proved to be a significant predictor of mortality independent of demographic or other social factors over a 4-year period (Reuben *et al.* 1992).

Assessing outcomes

Health-care providers have to take their place in the competition for resources. Clinical psychologists have access to a range of measures that provide evidence of the effects of intervention and progress of patients over time. These can include observer-based assessments such as needs assessment checklists, the Barthel Index, or standardized interviews and questionnaires such as the Sickness Impact Profile, the SF-36 (Short Form 36 Health Survey Questionnaire), and the Nottingham Health Profile. As we move into the 21st century and evidence-based approaches, outcome assessments, and evaluations become more important, clinical psychologists have an important role in ensuring that psychological outcomes are placed on the agenda and that the effects of interventions which most directly address patients concerns are recognized.

Outcomes are the result of interventions. Examples of outcome include employability, performance of activities of daily living, and satisfaction with quality of life. Outcome measures are used to demonstrate that particular goals have not only been identified, but achieved. Historically, professionals working with disabled people have defined independence in terms of physical functioning, whereas clinical psychologists equate independence with social and psychological autonomy.

Assessment of social and vocational issues

Social support serves as a general resistance resource in the management and recovery of illness and disability. It is important not only to assess the numbers of social support, but their perceived quality. An example of an assessment tool that incorporates both is the Social Support Questionnaire (Sarason and Sarason 1983). This tool has a subscale which assesses both quantity and quality. Access to employment is important for those of working age. When Sir Ludwig Guttmann (who set up the first treatment and rehabilitation centre for people with spinal cord injuries) was asked to define rehabilitation, he said it was to make the person ‘a tax payer’. This highlights the importance for clinical psychologists to contribute to the assessment of vocational needs and training. The vocational impact of disability is assessed in many of the subscales assessing quality of life and psychosocial impact. Other tools include vocational preference checklists and attainment scales.

Other assessments

Clinical psychologists also have access to a range of psychometric and psychophysiological techniques for assessing a variety of sensory and somatic aspects of disability. This would include questionnaires assessing pain intensity such as the McGill Pain Questionnaire and various visual analogue scales and psychophysiological measures such as monitoring electromyographic activity and penile plythysmography. Many people with physical disabilities have concurrent cognitive difficulties which will include problems with memory, concentration, and attention. A comprehensive description of assessment techniques is presented in the next chapter and other clinical, health-related assessment tools are described in Chapter 11. Whatever, the assessment tool, clinical psychologists recognized the necessity to select reliable and valid measures when assessing psychological aspects of disabling conditions. There are few sound multidimensional measures but the General Health Questionnaire, Psychosocial Adjustment to Illness Scale, and the Sickness Impact Profile are useful general measures of psychosocial adjustment. Good measures which are specific to disability are rare, but the Arthritis Impact Measurement Scales are an excellent exception.

Approaches to treatment and interventions

Clinical vignette

Martin, a young man aged 22, acquired a traumatic spinal cord injury as a result of a road traffic accident which rendered him paralysed from almost the neck down. He was unconscious for 40 minutes and reported a post traumatic amnesia of 2 days. During the initial acute phase of his treatment, nursing staff reported that he seemed to be coping well. Two weeks after he was mobilized in his wheelchair, he was approached by a trained keyworker who administered the needs assessment to help him conceptualize and prioritize his new needs. Goal planning meetings were arranged in association with the keyworker and the key members of the rehabilitation team. These occurred every 2 weeks, whereby new targets were set and he was provided with feedback on achievement. A month after his rehabilitation he joined the Coping Effectiveness Training Programme which he attended for 4 weeks. During these sessions he was taught the relationship between appraisal and effective coping, and when situations were appraised as being uncontrollable, emotion-focused strategies were encouraged, whilst problem-focused strategies were advocated for controllable aspects of the disability. Other practical management situations were discussed in the group, such as how to manage a bladder accident, and a lot of information and concerns were shared about the consequences of the injury and the impact of disability. Assessment of mood state and coping strategies before and after the programme demonstrated a reduction in anxiety and an increased use of adaptive coping strategies. After Martin had spent his first weekend home as part of his rehabilitation programme, he raised concerns about not having sufficient information concerning sexual aspects of his disability. Both Martin and his partner were seen on three occasions and provided with sexual counselling, which included information on the nature of the changes and specific suggestions were given on how to maintain an erection, change positions, and deal with problems. This was supplemented by giving him the patient information booklet on *Sexuality after Spinal Cord Injury*.

Intervention services can be considered to operate at many levels, and may include the provision of a treatment programme to an individual or family and the organization of rehabilitation planning within a health-care system. Services are provided in a variety of settings. Disabled people are referred to psychology services in primary health-care teams, adult mental health services, community mental health teams, or acute or specialist hospitals. Hospitalization occurs when aspects of the disability can no longer be managed within the home environment and when specialist investigations or treatments are required.

It is important for a clinical psychologist to become familiar with the medical and organic factors of the disability, as well as the psychosocial. When an inpatient is referred, it is good practice to become familiar with the available information on the medical condition on the ward. When a patient is confined to bed, it is important to be careful when entering the patient's space that permission is sought and an attempt is made to sit next to the patient rather than hover above their bed. The clinical psychologist will then explain their role to the patient, and their brief, to assist the patient in managing the stress associated with their disability, hospitalization, and/or other emotional concerns.

A major source of stress in hospital is the investigations and treatment which may involve pain and uncertainty of outcome. However, when the concerns of hospital patients have been examined, many of their worries are unrelated to the hospital environment and often concern family well being and issues irrelevant to personal health. It is important to spend time with the disabled person to understand their needs and concerns. It may also be appropriate for the psychologist to act as an advocate on behalf of the patient with other members of the team, explaining major concerns and sources of misunderstanding. Patients in hospital depend on staff for their care and treatment and there are high levels of dissatisfaction with the amount of treatment they receive. Many patients report having difficulty in understanding their medical condition and the prognosis. There is growing evidence that patients, regardless of the severity, or indeed the terminal nature of their condition, report positive aspects of being fully informed of the physical nature of their condition. In addition to ensuring that accurate and accessible information is provided, clinical psychologists also help the team understand and normalize emotional reactions to disability. Postural, mobility, and illness factors may require that the disabled person is provided with therapy or treatment in a non-traditional environment, such as whilst on bed rest or lying in a prone trolley. It is then even more important to work on maximizing eye contact and posture symmetry. The clinical psychologist may also have to acquire skills in managing some medical problems, for example chest suction for people on ventilation. In emergencies, they may be required to provide assisted breathing, pressure relief, or empty the patient's leg bag. These are just some of the specific issues that clinical psychologists working with disabled people may have to address.

Psychological treatments and interventions are provided to individuals and families, groups, and broadly within the health-care system, as described below.

Individual therapy

CBT is a common intervention for the management of emotional concerns of disabled people. The CBT perspective suggests that there is a reciprocal interdependence of feelings, thoughts, and behaviour. Turk and Meichenbaum (1994) characterized five central assumptions of treatment. First, individuals are active processors of information rather than passive reactors to environmental contingencies. According to the Cognitive Behavioural Model, each person's perspective is based on his/her idiosyncratic attitudes, beliefs, and unique schemas. Behavioural responses are elicited from significant others that can reinforce both adaptive and maladaptive modes of thoughts, feelings, and behaving. In this perspective, anticipating the consequences are as important as actual consequences. The second assumption of their more constructivist perspective is that thoughts can elicit or moderate affect and physiological arousal. The third assumption recognizes the reciprocal relationship between the individual and the environment. The fourth requires that interventions should not focus exclusively on changing thoughts or feelings or behaviours, but that successful interventions should target each, and not one to the exclusion of the others. The final assumption emphasizes the role that the individual has as an active agent of change or maladaptive modes of responding. Patients with chronic disability, no matter how severe and despite common beliefs to the contrary, are not helpless pawns of fate. They can become instrumental in learning and acquiring more effective modes of managing the consequences of their disability within disabling environments.

Clinical vignette

Mary had become progressively more disabled with her rheumatoid arthritis. She had been to see her general practitioner who was concerned about her current mood state and level of depression. She was seen in the health centre by the clinical psychologist who provided her with a treatment plan consisting of eight sessions of cognitive behavioural psychotherapy. The two major initial problems were severe depression and chronic pain. A number of other issues were explored as Mary's two children had recently left home and she had given up employment in a local school because of ill health. Negative thoughts included 'I'm just going through the motions of life', 'nobody needs me anymore', 'my husband and friends will reject me'. Intensive cognitive behaviour therapy challenged these assumptions by exploring the evidence for and against, and examining alternatives. In the first two sessions, Mary was taught relaxation techniques and was encouraged to pace activity to help with the management of pain. It was also important to work at developing distraction techniques and recreation opportunities. Reframing attributions from helplessness and hopelessness to resourcefulness and confidence and altering catastrophic thinking patterns were also important components of the intervention. This restructuring enabled Mary to become more aware of the role of thoughts and emotions in potentiating and maintaining distress and physical symptoms. Therapy aimed to help Mary manage the consequences of the pain rather than the pain per se. During the final sessions, self-monitoring charts were used to reinforce treatment success, and relapse prevention was discussed to help Mary identify potential risk situations and responses that may be necessary for successful coping. Generalization was helped by developing specific plans for specific situations and being able to develop these plans generally. Two months after treatment Mary, who had not been looking forward to her Silver Wedding celebrations because of anticipated problems such as not being able to organize, not being able to dance, etc., had developed a plan to cope by preparing, pacing, and planning.

However, CBT is not a panacea and more powerful and prolonged CBT interventions are required to yield long-term significant change with clients who have severe, chronic conditions. Many of the perceived losses are unchangeable and are not a function of cognitive distortions or irrational beliefs. Here, coping appraisal training is important. The patient is encouraged to develop emotion-focused strategies such as positive reframing and acceptance for those aspects of disability which are unchangeable, and to acquire problem-focused coping strategies to manage those consequences of the disability that are capable of being changed. This intervention technique will be described later in the chapter when discussing group approaches.

CBT procedures have been successfully applied to diverse clinical populations. The two clinical populations that have received most research attention are those suffering from anxiety and depressive disorders (see Chapter 2). A number of randomized control trials have demonstrated the efficacy of this approach for the management of depression, generalized anxiety disorders, and social phobias. Emotional distress in disabled people is formulated using the same CBT treatment conceptualizations as those for able-bodied people. However, it is always important to acquire an understanding of the specific disabilities to help in establishing rapport, preparing individuals for therapy, and engaging them in the treatment process.

Another example of individual theory-based psychotherapy is Rodin *et al.*'s (1991) integrated psychodynamic approach for the treatment of depression in people with chronic medical conditions. They advocated three phases that would begin with facilitation of grief and mourning. Here, people are encouraged to express feelings of loss and bereavement. The next phase explores the individual's understanding and personal meaning of the disability. At this point, the severity of the impairment is linked with the individual's belief system, prior experience, and premorbid personality characteristics. The therapeutic process finishes with the achievement of a sense of mastery over feelings associated with the chronic condition. In general, psychoanalytically based, psychodynamic therapeutic interventions are characterized by assisting the person with an acquired disability or chronic condition to gain insight into the impact of the disability on their present conflicts, anxieties, and vulnerabilities.

In addition to the more theory-based approaches, many clinical psychologists work within humanistic and general counselling frameworks. The goals of these interventions are similar to those previously discussed and often incorporate information giving and emotional support. Typically, these interventions assist in enabling the client to deal with the personal meaning of the disability and explore issues associated with loss, suffering, acceptance, and coping. Disabled people are encouraged to describe their feelings and integrate the meaning and reality of the loss. Whatever the therapeutic approach, clinical psychologists recognize the importance of providing an opportunity to ensure that disabled people are seen in accessible environments and free from disturbance during psychotherapy. Once contact and rapport is established and the therapeutic rationale explained, exploring and influencing can begin. This is often done in a combination of questioning, information giving, and problem solving. This is then monitored and evaluated and the therapeutic process is terminated by mutual consent.

Sexual counselling

Clinical psychologists are often involved in helping individuals and couples explore sexual needs and concerns. Many professional and disabled groups express concern that sexual themes continue to be an area neglected within the health service, often based on the assumption that disabled people do not have sexual needs, wishes, and rights. There is general consensus that the P-LI-SS-IT (Permission-Limited Information-Specific Suggestions-Intensive Therapy) developed by Annon (1974) provides a useful framework for organizing sexual counselling. This model has four levels of intervention, each increasing in sophistication. Permission giving is the first level and relates to the general responsiveness within the therapeutic context to discuss sexual issues and concerns. Limited information is provided depending on the person's ability and level of concern. Patient information booklets are useful and should be available upon request. With the next stage, specific suggestions are offered to the individual and partner, and suggestions include advice on positioning, comfort, and relationship issues. People with more complex sexual difficulties may require more intensive therapy such as sensate focus techniques. In the United Kingdom, a London-based organization called Sexual Problems of Disabled People (SPOD) helps by providing telephone counselling, professional training, and information.

Some disabling conditions may directly affect genital functioning. Secondary complications, such as respiratory failure, spasticity, and pain may also affect a person's ability to engage in sexual activity. In both static and progressive conditions, fatigue, anxiety about causing damage, and the side-effects of medication may also impair sexual function. Clinical psychologists assist in this area by examining the physical, emotional, and relationship issues involved. Many couples require advice in resuming activity, challenging unhelpful attitudes, and exploring alterative methods.

Behaviour modification

Clinical psychologists have used behaviour modification techniques to manage a number of problems within rehabilitation environments. Operant behavioural techniques have been used to increase the frequency of pressure lifting in spinal patients and classical conditioning techniques have been used in the management of hypotension. Reinforcement contingencies have helped in managing problems with treatment adherence and underpin many of those rehabilitation programmes based on goal planning and goal setting.

Biofeedback

Some clinical psychologists use biofeedback to help in the management of mood disorders and, more specifically, to reduce levels of functional impairment. Clinical psychologists have worked with occupational therapists and physiotherapists to use electromyographic biofeedback to manage problems associated with foot drop, shoulder dislocation, and maximizing muscular function in weak muscle groups. Here, the therapist's expertise is combined with the psychologist's awareness of systematic observation and use of operant behavioural techniques.

Skills training

As an adjunct to many of the psychotherapeutic interventions mentioned, clinical psychologists are also involved in relaxation training skills and assertiveness and social skills training. Relaxation training can take the form of traditional Jacobsonean relaxation training, but as this is contraindicated in many disabled people (e.g. people with chronic rheumatoid arthritis, spinal cord injury, and muscular paresis), autogenic relaxation training can be provided which focuses on using imaging techniques. Relaxation training is designed not only to help individuals learn a response that is incompatible with muscular tension, but as an additional coping skill which can be used to strengthen the disabled person's belief in exerting control. It has a value in the reduction of generalized arousal, enhancing control, and reducing the experience of disability.

Assertiveness training is important and may help people re-establish roles and responsibilities and gain control. Assertiveness training can also include the use of role models and behavioural rehearsal to assist people anticipate behaviours and rehearse problem-solving strategies. These are more usefully implemented on a group basis and clinical psychologists have organized such self-management and social skills groups in hospitals and in day centres in the community.

Interventions with families

Families play an essential role in health care across the lifespan. There is growing evidence of the critical role families have in health beliefs, risk behaviours, and adherence issues. There is also evidence that involving family members in health risk intervention trials improves success. Romano (1992) found that solicitious family responses to expressions of pain was positively associated with higher levels of pain and disability. Kerns and Weiss (1994) used a cognitive behavioural model of family functioning to underpin interactions, which aim to increase self-management, improve communication, and promote problem-solving skills for medical needs. Clinicians are also involved in helping families renegotiate roles, encourage independence, and increase family, social, and recreational activities. Psychologists not only recognize the importance of therapy to increase family motivation and involvement, but that many non-disabled family members require support to help with their adjustment issues. Disability occurs within a social context.

Group interventions

Problem-solving skills training and coping effectiveness training are more focused group intervention techniques. Group work, as opposed to individual therapy, not only has advantages in terms of cost effectiveness, but also in increasing the potential for learning and obtaining the support that comes from one's peers. In problem solving training, individuals define their source of stress, or stress reactions, set a range of concrete goals, and consider a wide range of possible alternatives to attain these goals. Turk and Meichenbaum (1994) usefully summarize these problem solving steps through seven specific questions. These are illustrated in Table 6.2.

Coping effectiveness training is a development from Lazurus and Folkman's (1984) transactional model of stress. It utilizes cognitive methods to appraise the stressor and identify the changeable and unchangeable aspects. When these demands are perceived to be amenable to change, a problem-focused strategy is applied whereas in situations where demands are not changeable, individuals utilize emotion-focused strategies. Affective coping involves an accurate appraisal of these demands and fits between threat, risk, and behaviour. These interventions emphasize specific training on problem-solving skills such as planning and active coping, as well as more emotion-focused skills such as acceptance and reframing. The outcome of these interventions is to improve psychological adaptation and encourage changes in self-perception and prevent social devaluation. Social support techniques are often incorporated into the training exercises.

Table 6.2 Problem-solving questions

Problem identification	what is the concern?
Goal selection	what do I want?
Generation of alternatives	what can I do?
Consideration of consequences	what might happen?
Decision making	what is my decision?
Implementation	now do it
Evaluation	did it work?—if not, retry

Adapted from Turk and Salovey (see Nicassio and Smith 1995)

Group interventions are provided in hospital settings and in the community. They generally last between seven and ten sessions, with between four and ten participants. They often include more long-term follow-up. In addition to the psychological framework previously discussed, groups also enable participants to share positive and negative experiences of disability, discuss disability-related problems, and encourage the normalization process. Many community rehabilitation services provide essential opportunities for people to discuss the emotional and practical aspects of being disabled. Many groups utilize shared experience to endorse effective coping, increase confidence, and perceive self-efficacy. In summary, group interventions have been shown to reduce mood disturbance, improve social functioning, and facilitate adaptation.

Contribution to the health-care system

In addition to individual, group and family interventions, clinical psychologists make a significant contribution to organizational and health-care systems. They are often involved in ensuring awareness and recognition of psychological issues in hospital-based ward rounds, community case conferences, and health-care planning groups. However, it needs to be remembered that much of the focus of rehabilitation effort is on changing behaviour. Clinical psychologists recognize the importance of incorporating behavioural change principles in many aspects of health-care provision. Goal planning provides a systematic framework for doing this. This is a 'soft' form of behaviour modification that is applied by clinical psychologists across many rehabilitative settings, both in the community and in hospital.

In understanding behaviour, goal directedness is critical. The common features of goal directed action include those which are generated within the individual, have a significant association with the management of need, and recognize the interplay between physiological, cognitive, and environmental factors. Rehabilitation is a process of active change by which a person who has a disability acquires the knowledge and skills for optimal physical, psychological, and social functioning.

There are many variants in goal planning, but they generally share the following elements. The first principal of goal planning is participant involvement. Practice that is client-centred, rather than therapist-centred, recognizes the need to engage a disabled person throughout the rehabilitation process as an active participant. Secondly, all disabled people have strengths that can be identified and it is the therapist's role to build on these strengths. These strengths not only compensate for loss of function, but enable maximum control and independence. By emphasizing needs rather than disabilities, goal planning identifies difficult areas and explores ways in which these can realistically be tackled. A similar approach is described in working with people with learning disabilities in Chapter 5. The third component indicates that goals need to be set by the disabled person in collaboration with the therapist. The values and choices of the client will dictate the goals to be achieved, as well as the targets or the small steps which will be taken along the way. The time scale for achieving these targets may vary from weeks to months. When setting goals it is important to specify who (i.e. the disabled person or multidisciplinary team member) will be carrying out the activity; what (i.e. specifies the behaviour required); under what conditions and how often the activity should take place. A goal must be about behaviour, it needs to be clear, refer to the disabled person's behaviour where possible, and specify who will do what, under what conditions, and to what degree of success. This approach to task analysis is fundamental to behavioural programming, whereby long-term goals can be broken down into smaller steps or targets which are tailored to the needs of the individual. Social reinforcement provides the essential flux that incorporates meaning to goal planning meetings.

Psychologists often utilize more formal assessments such as Needs Assessment Checklists and behavioural indicators to set standards and monitor progress in rehabilitation. Standards are statements of best practice and provide a benchmark to compare services. These behavioural indicators which express qualitative and quantitative aspects of intervention can also be used for audit purposes.

In view of the wide range of needs which may arise from the many forms of disability, it is clearly beyond the capacity of any one professional to have expertise in all areas. Disabled people need to draw upon the skills, knowledge, and support of the multidisciplinary team or rehabilitation professionals. Most physical rehabilitation teams will be composed of medical doctors, nurses, physiotherapists, and occupational therapists, and can include clinical psychologists, speech therapists, social workers, discharge planning co-ordinators, and care managers. Goal planning alerts each professional to the specific needs with which an individual requires help.

Goal planning is a behavioural process to maximize engagement in rehabilitation. Research has demonstrated that the best predictor of post-discharge behavioural or medical status is engagement in a comprehensive rehabilitation programme. Many goal-planning programmes utilize a keyworker as part of this process to empower and involve the disabled person. The keyworker generally co-ordinates, advocates, and supports the individual within the rehabilitative process. This approach to rehabilitation planning not only provides a safety net for disabled people, but highlights gaps in services and unmet needs. It also supports the rehabilitation team in minimizing role ambiguity and role conflict which can undermine team effort, essentially demonstrating needs and achievements over disability and losses.

In addition to organizing and training in goal planning, psychologists also provide teaching and training in many other related issues. Typically, this would include education about the specific psychological needs of a disabled group, adaptation issues, as well as the provision of basic training on approaches to counselling, social skills, and assertiveness. Training can also be provided to support risk assessment and promote prevention strategies. Clinical psychologists contribute to the teaching and training of other professionals involved in rehabilitation. Many academic and professional courses incorporate teaching on psychological needs in order to underpin practice with general psychological sensitivity and responsiveness.

Legislative context

In promoting the philosophy of care that recognizes the full range of individual needs rather than the functional limitations, clinical psychologists acknowledge the influence of progressive legislation and policy making on the experience of disability. The Swedish Fokus Schemes, Collectivhaus in Denmark, and the Het Dorp in Holland informed policy makers on the need to provide a more community-focused, local, and integrated service for disabled people. In many developed economies, disabled groups have collectivized, such as the British Council of Organisations for Disabled People (BCODP) to influence legislation and ensure accessible transport, prevent discrimination, and promote integrative social change. In the United Kingdom, the 1992 Building (Disabled People) Regulations Act ensures access and facilities for disabled people to all storeys of new, non-domestic buildings, and the Disability Discrimination Act (1995) provides new rights in areas of employment, obtaining goods and services and in buying or renting property. However, many observers have commented on the limitations of these legislative initiatives, for example the Building Act does not address the architectural inaccessibility of many existing British public buildings and the Disability Act fails to address many of the associated resource issues.

Research

As part of the portfolio of skills, clinical psychologists offer significant research skills which can range from pure research endeavours to service evaluation and audit. Researchers have explored elements of theoretical models of impact and coping and helped identify factors such as social support that can buffer against the adverse impact of disability. Service evaluation can help identify procedures and services which are most affective in managing needs. The dissemination of psychological research findings and knowledge through publishing and presentations at scientific and professional meetings is an important professional responsibility.

CONCLUSIONS

In summary, there is an increasing number of clinical psychologists involved in providing services to disabled people. There is also an increasing number of people for whom chronic conditions and physical disabilities are a common experience. This group of people will require an increasing proportion of health-care expenditure. Clinical psychologists contribute to the management of these needs by combining theory and practice in integrated health-care delivery systems. They do this by utilizing objective and standardized approaches to assessment, the implementation of scientifically based clinical intervention strategies, and collaboration with health service users to support informed choices. They participate at many levels ranging from the individual, the family, and health-care systems, providing individual psychotherapy, group work, and developing client-centred care and goal planning. They also contribute by disseminating knowledge to health-care professionals, providers, and the general public. They possess a broad portfolio of skills which also includes education, training, and research. Whilst a lot has been achieved, there is yet more to be done to ensure that the needs of disabled people are recognized and that they become active participants in the rehabilitative process. Clinical psychologists have professional responsibility to ensure the evidence base of their interventions and need to compete effectively for resources for service developments and research.

Many myths have yet to be challenged to ensure that the needs of disabled people are effectively addressed. Psychologists are well placed to respond to these challenges in the next millennium.

References

Annon, J.S. (1974). *The behavioural treatment of sexual problems* (Vol. 1). Enabling Systems Incorporated, Honolula.

Dupont, S. (1997). Medical topics: multiple sclerosis. In *Cambridge handbook of psychology, health and medicine* (eds A. Baum, S. Newman, J. Weinman, R. West, and C. McManus). Cambridge University Press, Cambridge.

Engel, G.L. (1980). The clinical application of the biopsychosocial model. *American Journal of Psychiatry*, **137**, 535–544.

Johnston, M. (1996). Models of disability. *Psychologist*, **9**, 205–211.

Kennedy, P. (1997). Medical topics: spinal cord injury. In *Cambridge handbook of psychology, health and medicine* (eds A. Baum, S. Newman, J. Weinman, R. West, and C. McManus). Cambridge University Press, Cambridge.

Kerns, R.D. and Weiss, L. (1994). Family influences on the cause of chronic illness: a cognitive-behavioural transactional model. *Annals of Behavioural Medicine*, **16**, 116–121.

Lazarus, R.S. and Folkman, S. (1984). *Stress, appraisal and coping*. Springer, New York.

Lightpole. E. (1991) Quadriplegia – what I feel. *Medical Journal of Australia,* **154** 562–563.

Newman, S. (1997) Medical topics: rheumatism and arthritis. In *Cambridge Handbook of Psychology, Health and Medicine* (eds A. Baum, S. Newman, J.

Weinman, R. West, and C. McManus). Cambridge University Press, Cambridge.

OPCS (Office of Population Censuses and Surveys) (1988). *The prevalence of disability among adults*. HMSO.

Reuben, D., Rubenstein, I., Hirsch, S., and Hays, R. (1992). The value of functional status as a predictor of mortality: results of a prospective study. *American Journal of Medicine*, **93**, 633–639.

Rodin, G., Craven, J., and Littlefield, C. (1991). *Depression in the medically ill: an integrated approach*. Brunner/Mazel, New York.

Romano, J.M., Turner, J., Friedman, L., Bulcroft, R. Jensen, M., Hops. H. and Wright, S. (1992) Sequential Analysis of chronic pain behaviours and spouse responses. *Journal of Counselling and Clinical Psychology,* **60**, 777–782.

Sarason, I.G. and Sarason, B.R. (1983). Assessing social support: The social support questionnaire. *Journal of Personality and Social Psychology*, **44**, 127–139.

Turk, D.C. and Meichenbaum, D. (1994). A cognitive-behavioural approach to pain management. In *Textbook of pain* (eds P.D. Wall and R. Malzack). Churchill Livingstone, London.

Working Party of the British Psychological Society Professional Affairs Board (1989). *Psychology and physical disability in the national health service. partnership, participation and power: Report of the working party of the British Psychological Society Professional Affairs Board*. DPS Publications, Leicester.

World Health Organization (1980). *International classification of impairments, disabilities and handicaps: A manual of classification relating to the consequences of disease*. Geneva, Switzerland.

Wortman, C.D. and Silver, R.C. (1989). The myth of coping with loss. *Journal of Consulting and Clinical Psychology*, **57**, 349–357.

Further reading

Davis, H. and Fallowfield, L. (1991). *Counselling and communication in healthcare*. John Wiley and Sons, London.

Livneh, H. and Antonak, R.F. (1987). *Psychosocial adaptation to chronic illness and disability*. Aspen Publications, Maryland.

Nicassio, P.M. and Smith, T. (1995). *Managing chronic illness: a biopsychosocial prospective*. American Psychological Association, Washington DC.

Swain, J., Finkelstein, V., French, S., and Oliver, M. (1993). *Disabling barriers—enabling environments*. Open University, London.

Wright, B.A. (1983). *Physical disability—a psychosocial approach* (2nd edn). Harper and Row, New York.

7

Working in clinical neuropsychology

Katherine Carpenter and Andy Tyerman

INTRODUCTION

Clinical neuropsychology is concerned with people whose thinking, behaviour, or emotions have become disrupted as a result of brain damage. Such neuropsychological changes often have a major effect on lifestyle, occupation, and family relationships.

This specialty is often thought of as dry, difficult, and removed from generic clinical psychology practice. Clinical neuropsychology does indeed have its own specialist knowledge base of neurology, neuroanatomy, and brain–behaviour relations. However, it still involves work with people and their own everyday life events and stresses who experience similar psychological problems (such as anxiety and depression) to those in mental health settings, in addition to their specific neuropsychological changes.

The clinical neuropsychologist needs the expertise to make sense of what can be bizarre and frightening experiences for patients (such as their not being able to remember anything from one day to the next, or not being able to recognize their family by seeing their faces but only on hearing them talk). However, sensitivity and understanding is also required to see patients with these problems as a whole person in a family and life context not just as a dysfunctional brain. During the course of recovery the professional role evolves, often quite naturally, from that of an expert assessor/advisor to a trainer or guide in rehabilitation, to that of a mentor or facilitator in long-term personal, family, and social adjustment.

THE SETTINGS

In the United Kingdom fewer than 200 clinical psychologists have specialized in work with people with acquired brain damage and their carers. They work in a range of settings and at different stages in the pathway of care from acute to community.

Neuropsychologists working with people at their first point of contact with services, either as outpatients or on admission to hospital, are usually in a hospital-based neurosciences centre. These centres bring together specialists such as neurologists (concerned with medical aspects of central nervous system disorders and their treatments) and neurosurgeons (similarly concerned with what surgery can contribute to management). Much of the work carried out in such units involves emergency treatment or investigation of very sick or at risk patients. Many patients will be struggling with serious physical illness or impairments, such as paralysis down one side of their body, and will not have had time to take on board the longer-term cognitive effects of their condition. Neuropsychologists work closely with medical and nursing staff but often need to see patients again as outpatients at a 'post-acute' stage, when many of the acute medical features have settled and cognitive and emotional changes become much more relevant.

Until recently, clinical neuropsychologists working in rehabilitation in the United Kingdom were based primarily within a few specialist regional inpatient neurological rehabilitation centres (catering for people with severe and multiple disability) or in specialist centres in the independent sector for persons with severe behavioural problems. Provision of services outside such centres was very limited with little rehabilitation to assist the person in returning to an independent and productive role in society (Greenwood and McMillan 1993). However, over the last decade, an increasing number of clinical psychologists have taken up posts within generic physical disability/ rehabilitation teams or within specialist community brain injury or stroke rehabilitation services. The last few years has also seen the development of specialist centres for cognitive and vocational rehabilitation.

In illustrating work in this specialist area we shall first consider the acute neurological/ neurosurgical setting and then move on to the rehabilitation and community setting.

The acute neurology/ neurosurgery setting

The patients

Patients present at all ages and a good working knowledge of the developmental context is important for the younger ones. Detailed comprehensive assessment needs to take account of any sensory or perceptual disturbance, any problems with movement or posture, and any episodes of altered awareness (faints, blackouts, funny turns), as well as the more usual areas of premorbid medical/ psychiatric history.

This is important because neurological disorders tend to present with a complex interplay of cognitive, emotional, behavioural, and physical features. These interact with each other and may affect assessment or measurement of any one component. For example if you are testing a patient's verbal memory by reading them a short paragraph and asking them to tell it back to you and they are suffering from tinnitus (ringing in the ear), then this may affect their attention, making the test less valid as a test of verbal memory.

Some common causes of neuropsychological impairment are shown in Table 7.1 An important distinction is made between relatively circumscribed lesions such as those caused by a stroke (where a blockage or constriction of an artery results in loss of blood and oxygen to a particular area) or a penetrating missile injury (such as a bullet wound), and diffuse brain injury caused by a progressive degenerative process (such as Alzheimer's disease) or a subarachnoid haemorrhage (in which an artery ruptures explosively driving blood into the space around the brain causing widespread damage).

Table 7.1 Causes of neuropsychological impairment

Alcoholism
Anoxia (lack of oxygen)
Benign tumours (e.g. meningioma)
Cerebrovascular accidents (e.g. intracerebral haematoma, stroke, subarachnoid haemorrhage)
Dementias (e.g. dementia of Alzheimer's type, multi-infarct dementia)
Degenerative diseases (e.g. multiple sclerosis, Parkinson's disease)
Epilepsy
Head injury
Hydrocephalus (excess fluid in the ventricles of the brain)
Infections (e.g. AIDS, herpes simplex virus encephalitis)
Malignant tumours (e.g. metastatic carcinoma, glioma, astrocytoma)
Poisoning (e.g. carbon monoxide following a suicide attempt)

Medical context

Trainee psychologists are often surprised by what can seem an intimidating 'Casualty' or 'ER' type environment in the acute setting. Neuropsychologists need to be flexible in switching between a medical model, which allows them to communicate rapidly with medical colleagues, and more meaningful and ecologically valid psychological models which may have greater relevance when helping patients and their carers try and make sense of their experiences. Inpatient clinical work is often constrained both by competing demands (such as pressure on beds resulting in a short hospital admission with patients being transferred some distance to a more local district general hospital) and by the general level of 'unwellness' of patients.

Parallel investigations

Clinical neuropsychology at the acute end is best thought of as one of a number of investigations available to the neurologist or neurosurgeon co-ordinating care of the patient. Psychometric test results must be interpreted in the context of overall formulation of the case and in the light of parallel investigations. History taking is 'the cornerstone of neurological diagnosis' (Donaghy 1997), with many disorders being diagnosed on clinical grounds and examination confirming information anticipated by the history. The explosion in scanning techniques over the past 15 years has radically altered the role of neuropsychology in relation to other specialties. Computed tomography (CT) involves X-rays and is particularly good at detecting blood (e.g. a blood clot). Magnetic resonance imaging (MRI) exploits the different radiofrequency signals produced by the protons in tissue molecules which are first lined up by a powerful magnet and then displaced by radio waves. MRI is much more sensitive for imaging the substance of the brain and has replaced CT scanning for routine clinical work (see Fig. 7.1). It is less invasive than CT but very noisy, 'a bit like lying on a building site' said one patient, and can feel claustrophobic. CT and MRI allow us to look at neuroanatomy and pathology in the living brain which means that localization of pathology is no longer so central for psychology. Cerebral blood flow techniques, positron emission tomography (PET), and functional MRI (fMRI) allow us to observe the dynamic metabolism of the working brain. This will be increasingly crucial for our understanding of brain–behaviour relations. For example if a non-brain damaged subject is speaking does the region thought to mediate spoken language output (Broca's area) 'light up' on a PET scan? Similarly if a patient with a significant lesion in Broca's area identified on CT brain scanning can still speak what area 'lights up' when a PET study is done (Ogden 1996)? Neurophysiology, which measures electrical brain activity using electroencephalographs (EEGs) and evoked potentials, is particularly important in the diagnosis of epilepsy.

Other disciplines which impact on neuropsychology are: medicine (e.g. endocrinology and diabetes, neuro-oncology, plastics and craniofacial surgery, ENT, gerontology, psychiatry); physiotherapy; speech and language therapy; and occupational therapy.

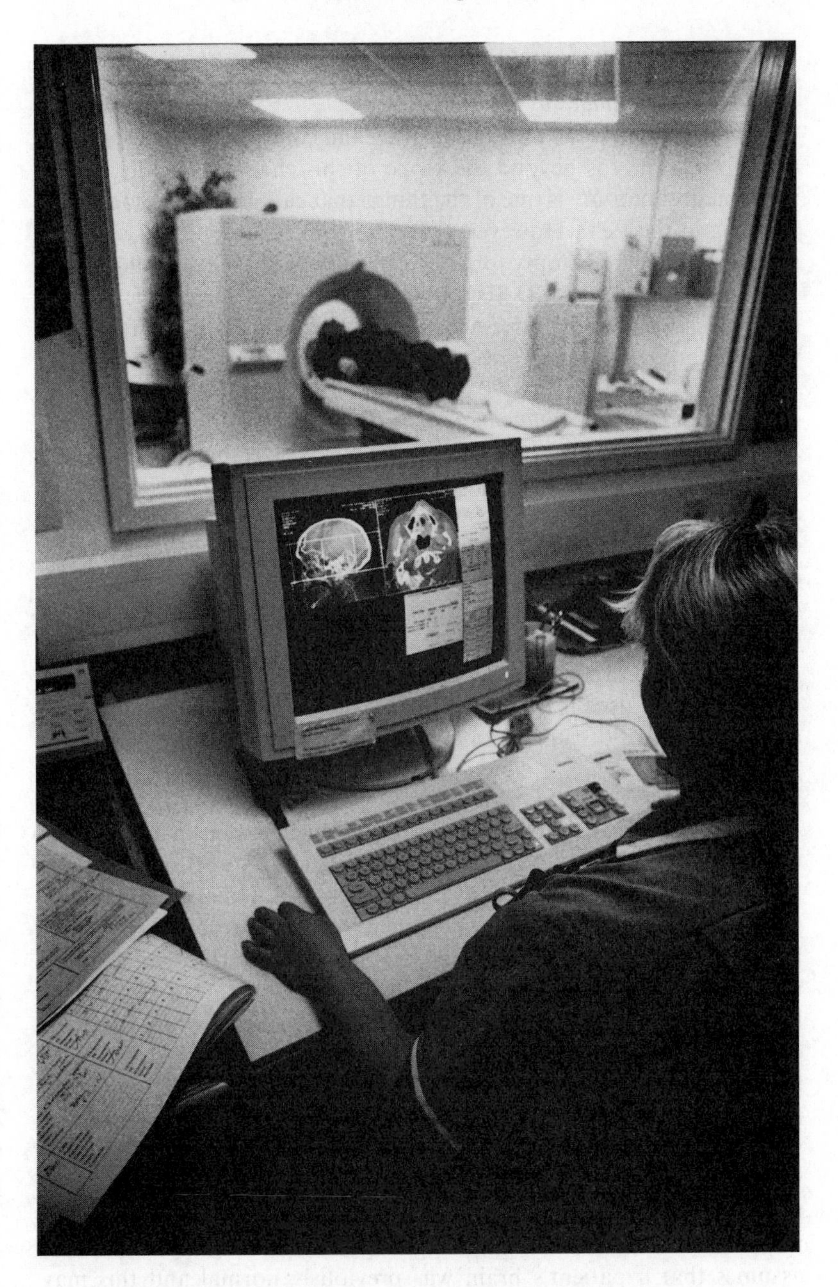

Fig. 7.1 Structural imaging of the brain (MRI).

Neuropsychological context

Functional neuroanatomy

The human brain is the most fascinating and complex biological system and it's anatomy is beyond the scope of this chapter. Feeling woolly about neuroanatomy is one of the things that can put psychologists off working in the field. However, there are some excellent and readable sections on neuroanatomy for neuropsychologists (Walsh 1994; Lezak 1995) and interactive CD ROMs will increasingly be on the market (Coppa and Tancred 1995). A basic knowledge is adequate for many purposes and work in the area necessarily brings increasing familiarity.

Neuropsychological terminology

Similarly, somewhat impenetrable technical terminology for syndromes can be off-putting. Although unnecessary jargon should be avoided where possible, jargon is often a useful shorthand between clinicians for what would otherwise be a complex phenomenon or concept to express. One or two pointers can help. Many terms are derived from the Latin and their meaning can be worked out. Strictly speaking any label with the prefix *a-* denotes loss of a function, as opposed to the prefix *dys-* denoting partial impairment although the two tend to get used interchangeably. So, *amnesia* means memory loss, *dysphasia* means disruption of speech or language.

Underlying concepts and assumptions

It is worth bearing in mind a few key tenets which underpin much of the way neuropsychologists think. Lateralization of function refers to hemispheric specialization or so-called cerebral dominance. In the vast majority of right-handers (>92 per cent) and in a large proportion of left-handers (69 per cent) speech, language, and verbal memory are represented in the left or dominant hemisphere. In contrast, the right hemisphere is predominant for tasks involving stimuli that cannot be easily put into words, such as visual memory, visuospatial function, interpretation of emotional expression, and probably attention. There is a subtle interplay between specialization and functional plasticity, whereby areas of the brain can apparently take over functions for which they are not normally thought to be specialized, at least sometimes following brain damage in childhood. Making inferences about normal brain function from the study of brain-damaged patients assumes that a patient's brain was previously normal and this may not always be the case (e.g. following early insult such as epilepsy). As

Ogden (1996) points out, it also presupposes we know what 'normal' is when there is individual variation and evidence that the same lesion does not always lead to the same impairment.

Neuropsychological assessment

Clinical interview

Neuropsychological assessment usually involves an appointment lasting from 2 to 5 hours. With adults a comprehensive, semistructured interview first reviews a wide range of factors relating to the patient's views (and those of a close relative) on the medical, social, and educational/ occupational background, presenting problem, and current symptomatology. This includes the following:

- previous or concurrent treatment (especially for epilepsy, learning disability, head injury, alcoholism);
- previous psychiatric/ psychological history, medication, significant recent stressors (e.g. bereavement, crime, financial/ work pressure);
- mental health screen (e.g. mood, appetite, sleep, sexual interest, drive, headaches);
- sensory–perceptual screen (i.e. vision, hearing, touch, smell, taste);
- movement–posture screen (i.e. weakness, paralysis, inco-ordination, gait, balance);
- cognitive screen (concentration, orientation, new learning, organization, reasoning).

As with any other interview, the psychologist is constantly developing a hypothesis and looking for disconfirming evidence, as well as making qualitative observations on aspects such as insight, comprehension, speech, mental state, etc.

Psychometric testing

A standard battery of tests can be administered. However, most neuropsychologists adopt a more flexible approach (Lezak 1995; Walsh 1994), often using certain core tests plus other tests sampling specific cognitive domains as and when appropriate. Neuropsychological tests are aimed at sampling behaviour in one or more cognitive domains, such as general intelligence, visuospatial perceptual ability, language, memory and concentration, attention, and higher order skills such as planning and so called 'executive' function. As is common in many standard forms of measurement, the scores obtained by an individual on a test (measurement) of a particular psychological characteristic or process are compared with the average score obtained by a comparable group of individuals, usually the same age and from the same general population. The average of the comparable group is calculated and an individual score is expressed in terms of its departure from the group average. This allows one to take into account, for example, the fact that younger people tend to remember more than older people, and similarly brighter subjects should remember more than those of more limited ability. An estimate is made of the patient's level of *premorbid* ability, both on the basis of education and occupational attainments, and from their performance on more 'crystallized' components of cognitive performance (for example lexical knowledge or knowledge of word meanings which is more robust in the face of neurological and neurosurgical conditions). In addition to quantitative indices, qualitative observations on test performance are also made. Standardized questionnaires may also be included to access general health, quality of life, and mood.

A standard assessment should include a measure of premorbid function (e.g. the National Adult Reading Test); a measure of general intelligence (e.g. the Revised Wechsler Adult Intelligence Scale); orientation (e.g. the Revised Wechsler Memory Scale protocol); verbal memory tests, including *immediate* and *delayed* recall of both narrative material and unrelated words (e.g. the Adult Memory and Information Processing Battery—Story Recall and List Learning); a non-verbal memory test (e.g. the Rey Complex Figure Test and Recognition Trial); attentional and 'executive' tests, as appropriate, (e.g. the Test of Everyday Attention; the Stroop Test; Trails A and B; the Wisconsin Card Sorting Test); and verbal fluency (e.g. letters F,A,S and animals); and additional language tests if appropriate.

Choice of test instruments obviously needs to take into account any sensory, motor, or linguistic constraints on the person. Where English is not the first language, more non-verbal tests of global ability (e.g. Raven's Standard Progressive Matrices) may be helpful, although cultural and ethnic differences still need to be taken into account both in administration and interpretation. Many of the widely-used tests (e.g. the Revised Wechsler Adult Intelligence Scale, Wechsler Memory Scale) have been translated into other languages, but the proviso remains that in general the normative data on which they are based are North American.

Testing is another area that can seem dry to the uninitiated. In fact this is far from the case. Cognitive evaluation involves what is effectively a series of controlled behavioural experiments in which as many variables as possible are controlled. A skilled neuropsychologist needs to be capable of developing and maintaining rapport with a patient while coaxing them through what can be an exacting set of tasks. Imagine being faced with a bright person, perhaps a company director or doctor, in the early stages of an insidious dementing process; extracting the greatest amount of information possible from a minimum of testing, which protects the dignity of the patient, is an undoubted challenge. Quiet, well lit surroundings without any undue distractions or interruptions are preferable to maximize the patient's performance; quite an opposite set of conditions are obviously required if one is assessing a patient's capability of returning to a stressful job in a busy open-plan environment.

Neuropsychological report

A full written report is prepared following assessment and usually comprises sections on the medical background, personal history, clinical presentation, neuropsychological evaluation, and conclusions. Reports vary according to the audience for whom they are written. Internal reports in an acute neurology/ neurosurgery setting tend to be succinct with cross referral to other medical reports. Rehabilitation reports often serve as a contract between the patient, their carers, and the interdisciplinary rehabilitation team and, as such, may use a goal-setting model. A good report should appropriately convey the clinical problem and its context, together with a detailed description of the test results and findings and their interpretation, with a clear distinction between fact and observation and inference and interpretation. Medicolegal reports, usually required for personal injury cases following traumatic brain injury in a road traffic accident, need to be comprehensive and intelligible to a non-specialist and should include an opinion on likely prognosis.

Purpose of assessment

In the acute setting the emphasis is on differential diagnosis, evaluation of outcome of intervention (e.g. drug treatment or operation), monitoring of change, and early identification of cognitive sequelae. All the information is taken together and interpreted in the light of the questions to be answered. These obviously vary from patient to patient but include the following: is there evidence that the patient's cognitive function has been adversely affected from a previously higher premorbid level? Is the pattern of deficits consistent with the known pathology and medical variables? Does the test profile reflect focal pathology or a generalized decline? What are this person's current strengths and weaknesses? Are their deficits likely to progress or improve? What is the likelihood of this person being able to return to their previous employment or academic study? and so on.

Case 1

Mrs Freeman was a 58-year-old former nurse referred by a neurologist, with progressive memory loss over 3 years. On interview she presented well socially and appeared relatively intact, at least in conversation for a short period of time; she also had limited insight and tended to deny any difficulties. When she talked more freely, about her family for example, she had some difficulty in expressing herself. Spending longer with her, the difficulties became more apparent. She was forgetful during the assessment and sometimes lost the thread of what she was saying. Her husband, who accompanied her, gave various instances of her confusion, disorientation, and memory loss at home. He was clearly searching for an alternative explanation for his wife's problems to the possibility of a dementing illness, and spoke of lead in their water pipes and the fact that they had lived abroad for many years. There was no evidence of depression although she appeared mildly anxious.

On testing it became clear that her intellect and memory were severely deteriorated. An estimate of premorbid ability based on her current single word reading (National Adult Reading Test) was 'high average' (110), in line with her nursing background, but Verbal (86) and Performance (74) quotients on the Revised Wechsler Adult Intelligence Scale fell in the 'low average' and 'borderline' ranges respectively. Her range of subtest scores showed a typical pattern often seen in dementia of adequate scores on more 'crystallized' components of intelligence, such as vocabulary and general knowledge, and severely impaired scores on speed of information processing, visuoconstructional ability, and abstract verbal reasoning. She was able to repeat nine digits forwards but only four backwards suggesting a deficit in auditory 'working' memory (confirmed on other tests). She was unable to give the date or say where she was. When read a short story (Adult Memory and Information Processing Battery) she was unable to remember more than a few words from the last sentence immediately afterwards, and half and hour later could remember nothing of the story. Her copy of a complex geometric design (Rey Osterrieth figure) was spatially distorted and incomplete, and after half an hour she was unable even to recall having done the copy and instead drew an elephant! Further testing confirmed diffuse generalized loss of cognitive function including memory.

Dementia is usually due to incurable disorders such as dementia of the Alzheimer's type or multiple cerebral infarctions. An important aim of parallel investigation is to uncover reversible causes. Pseudodementia due to depression can be treated; however such patients usually show more concern and insight into their memory loss in addition to symptoms of depression. Mrs Freeman turned out to have changes on brain imaging consistent with the neuropsychological test profile and suggestive of dementia of Alzheimer's type. Intervention involved sensitive feedback, support, and advice to the family on managing the problems. This straightforward case has been used for clarity, however diagnosing advanced dementia is not difficult whereas diagnosing early dementia can be. In addition, depression and dementia are by no means mutually exclusive since elderly patients often become depressed when they are beginning to lose their mental faculties.

Intracarotid sodium amytal testing (the Wada procedure)

This is a particular form of neuropsychological assessment which is carried out in the context of elective surgery as treatment for drug-resistant, temporal lobe epilepsy. This test involves injection of a barbiturate (sodium amytal) into the internal carotid artery of each hemisphere on consecutive days. The test is designed to anaesthetize part of one hemisphere for a short time while language and memory functions of the other hemisphere can be assessed. The test was originally designed to establish the side of language dominance but was adapted in the early sixties, by the neuropsychologist Brenda Milner, to assess the likely adequacy of everyday memory function following a temporal lobe operation. Since approximately 90 per cent of right-handed temporal lobe patients and 75 per cent of those with left or mixed hand preference have left hemisphere language representation, what one tends to see following left internal carotid artery injection is a hemiplegia on the right side the body lasting about 5 minutes, together with arrest and/or disruption of speech and language comprehension. Immediately following injection, the neuropsychologist administers language and memory tests in order to check the function of the non-injected side. If memory tests are failed when the side of the proposed surgery is inactivated by amytal, this suggests that there may be a pre-existing abnormality in the medial temporal lobe structures in the non-operated temporal lobe in which case surgery may be contra-indicated.

Interventions

Intervention in the acute setting can be tantalizing and frustrating because the turn-over of inpatients is high and because a specialist tertiary neuroscience centre may serve a population of 2 to 3 million, many of whom live some distance away. Specialist services (such as epilepsy surgery) are often supra-regional. Most work is necessarily time-limited, postacute, outpatient follow-up.

Interventions are generally either neuropsychological rehabilitative procedures, or cognitive or behavioural treatments derived from mental health work. Rehabilitation is not as fully developed in *acute* neurology/neurosurgery as it should be; detailed assessment of the problems forms the basis for (limited) goal planning, education, and information-giving, and introduction of palliative coping strategies and techniques (such as a watch with an alarm, sticky-backed notes, a diary, Filofax or personal organizer, routine). Neurological/ neurosurgical patients with emotional or behavioural problems may require a range of techniques, such as cognitive therapy for depression or anxiety (especially post-traumatic stress disorder), anger management, progressive muscle relaxation, sexual and relationship counselling, management of pain, etc. Brain surgery is always a major life event. Sometimes the problems predate the neurological condition but are exacerbated by it or need tackling because they interfere with recovery; sometimes they are a direct result of an underlying neurological/ neurosurgical condition (such as a frontal brain tumour or head injury). Either way they are often best dealt with by a neuropsychologist who is more experienced with the neurological context and the constraints of memory loss, language difficulty, dysexecutive symptoms, sensory and perceptual problems, seizure activity, etc.

Case 2

Michael is a 37-year-old electrical engineer who was admitted as an emergency with raised intracranial pressure. He was found to have a colloid cyst in one of the spaces in the brain containing the cerebrospinal fluid that bathes and cushions the brain in the skull. These tumours are benign but potentially life-threatening in that they can block cerebrospinal fluid flow causing dangerously high intracranial pressure; they are also situated close to structures crucial to memory and either the cyst itself or the necessary operation to remove it can result in memory loss. Preoperative cognitive assessment revealed Michael's general intellectual function remained 'high average' but his memory was already severely affected. He was not aware of this since he was more preoccupied with intense headache, unwellness, and anxiety about what might be wrong. Postoperative assessment 6 weeks later showed that there had been no further drop in memory scores. Follow-up work over 6 to 12 months involved helping Michael implement memory management strategies and ultimately negotiate return to full-time work. He was introduced to an electronic personal organizer as a memory aid and the best methods of using it were discussed with him in relation to his specific needs at work and in the family. Information was given on the structure of memory and memory strategies. Sessions were audiotaped for him to listen to at home and key points and guidelines were given as written hand-outs. He was also encouraged to monitor his own performance, which resulted in positive feedback on rate of recovery and adjustment.

Consultation and team work issues

Neuropsychology cannot be useful clinically without liaison with parallel disciplines in the neurosciences. However it is important not to overestimate others' knowledge about neuropsychological variables; what often seems straight-forward advice to us may be invaluable to the referrer.

Case 3

Tom was a bright sparky 8-year-old boy who was referred to us from the children's neurosurgery ward because the nursing staff felt his parents were having difficulty coping. He had been admitted 6 weeks earlier to have a tumour removed which turned out to be benign. He had a stormy postoperative period with a fluctuating temperature, vomiting, headache, and general unwellness. This was due to inflammation (but not infection) of the meninges, the membranes covering the brain, which is a relatively common condition but unusual in this case in that it lasted longer than 2 to 3 weeks. Tom had improved and was more bright and cheerful since insertion of a drain to reduce the pressure of cerebrospinal fluid on the brain. Intervention involved seeing both Tom and his parents on the ward, as well as nursing staff, to assess the problem and intervene appropriately. Nursing staff felt Tom's parents were excessively anxious and 'difficult', by which they meant they were hostile and made constant and unrealistic demands. The parents had undergone a prolonged period of stress and uncertainty and felt their questions and concerns about Tom were being ignored by staff. Intervention involved daily sessions with the parents on the ward for a week to; offer support, allow ventilation of feelings, provide medical information, problem solve better coping strategies, and mobilize resources for their management of Tom. Work also involved liaison with ward staff to help reframe interaction with the family more positively. On discharge, contact with the family continued. Tumours like Tom's do not normally result in any significant intellectual changes but affect balance and co-ordination, including fine co-ordination such as handwriting, and concentration. Advice needed to be given both to the parents and to Tom's school when he was ready to return, and encouragement to manage him as normally as possible (not easy when a child has been such a source of worry for so long). A full neuropsychological assessment was carried out at 3 months and results on Tom's strengths and weaknesses and the sequelae in terms of attention and co-ordination were discussed with Tom, his family, and teachers.

Research and audit

Research in the acute setting is at the sharp end of clinical practice and, in the current, pressured National Health Service environment, predominantly aimed at evaluating outcome (cognitive status, functional disability, and quality of life). The British Medical Research Council, together with local research and development committees, is concerned to enhance the quality of randomized clinical trials in the neurosciences and the potential future contribution of neuropsychologists in this area is considerable.

The rehabilitation/community setting

In rehabilitation the majority of referrals are of persons with head injury and stroke. In disability teams, referrals will also include persons with multiple sclerosis. Neurologically, the different pathology in these three core client groups results in a contrasting profile and course of disability. Whereas for multiple sclerosis the major symptoms (at least in the early stages) are usually physical, disability after stroke tends to be a mixture of physical and psychological effects, and after head injury the major effects are usually psychological. Whereas head injury and stroke are of sudden onset followed by a period of recovery and adaptation, the onset of multiple sclerosis is typically episodic with a variable and uncertain course (i.e. total remission, relapse/ remission, or progressive decline). This makes contrasting psychological demands on the person and family. Furthermore, onset peaks at different stages in the life cycle: typically, head injury affects the young single adult; multiple sclerosis, the married person with a young family; and stroke, the older adult with grown up children.

The impact on the person and the family is very variable, depending upon the specific pattern of disability, individual coping resources, and family and social circumstances. In outlining the role of the clinical neuropsychologist in rehabilitation we shall review the nature of residual neurological disability, its social and family effects, and the process of rehabilitation. This will be illustrated with a representative case example.

Neurological disability

The nature of long-term neurological disability is extremely varied, encompassing both physical disability (i.e. motor and sensory deficits) and psychological changes (e.g. cognitive impairment, altered emotional responsivity, and loss of behavioural control).

Physical disability

Physical disability after neurological illness/ injury ranges from generalized paralysis affecting all four limbs, control of speech, swallowing etc. (e.g. in advanced stages of multiple sclerosis), through more specific changes such as paralysis down one side of the body (typically after stroke) to a more subtle reduction in strength, co-ordination, and balance (typical after head injury). Many clients are also troubled by headaches and fatigue, and some experience more specific changes such as sleep disturbance and altered sexual response. Many have some sensory deficits with visual disturbances (e.g. reduced field of vision after stroke, double vision after head injury) being the most common, but hearing deficits (where present) are a major restriction on communication. Reduced sensation is common after stroke and multiple sclerosis; loss of taste and smell are common effects of head injury. Some also experience the additional stigma and restrictions of post-traumatic epilepsy and associated anticonvulsant medication. (See Chapter 6 for a detailed general account of working with physical disability).

Cognitive impairment

After generalized brain injury the most common cognitive difficulties are with attention, concentration, memory, and reduced speed of information processing. After more focal damage (such as stroke and tumour) more specific deficits may been seen in motor skills, visual perception, spatial judgement, language function, etc. Disruption of executive function (i.e. higher level reasoning, planning, problem solving, and self-awareness and self-monitoring), which are very common after severe head injury, are of particular importance in rehabilitation as they affect insight, understanding, use of compensatory strategies, and long-term adaptation. The realization of confusing changes in cognitive skills (particularly perceptual skills) that we usually take entirely for granted can be a bewildering and frightening experience. Marked impairment of memory compromises a sense of continuity in our lives, as well as perception of progress in rehabilitation.

Changes in personality

A wide range of emotional and behavioural changes may be experienced, reflecting an interaction of primary neurological damage and secondary psychological reactions to neurological illness/ injury and its effects. Whilst an extensive array of behavioural change is reported, common primary changes (particularly after head injury) are of increased irritability, disinhibition, impulsivity, emotional lability, mood swings, and aggressive outbursts. Equally, a wide range of emotional reactions are experienced such as frustration and anger, fear and anxiety, depression, and loss of confidence/self-esteem. For some this may be an early reaction to the trauma of neurological illness/injury, the loss of skills, roles and control over one's life, the slow pace of progress, and the uncertain extent of future recovery. However, early in rehabilitation many may appear unconcerned about their predicament due to limited insight into the extent of cognitive and emotional/ behavioural changes together with unrealistic expectations of a full recovery. As such, anxiety, depression, and loss of confidence may surface only later when the person has developed greater insight and/or attempted and struggled to resume former family, work, and social roles.

Social/family effects

The complex array of neurological disability often has far-reaching effects upon the person, family, friends, and employers/work colleagues. Whilst recovery and adaptation may continue over several years (particularly after traumatic brain injury) many will be faced with restrictions in independence, work, leisure, social, and family life. These restrictions are often shared by members of the family who may experience great stress in caring for and supporting the person with the injury, often amidst marked changes in family relationships, roles, and functioning.

Independence

Neurological disability often results in a loss of independence—assistance in personal and domestic care for those with severe physical disability, guidance and supervision for those with marked cognitive or personality changes. Others may be independent in their daily care but be unable to travel independently, or need help from the family in making decisions or in managing their financial affairs.

Occupation

Return to education, training, or work represents a major challenge after neurological disability. Reduced cognitive and motor speed, limited concentration, unreliable memory, headaches, and/or fatigue render many uncompetitive. Others face more specific restrictions: physical disability restricts manual work; visual deficits may preclude driving; poor executive skills may exclude more managerial positions;

poor behavioural control is unlikely to be tolerated in the workplace; whilst those with emotional vulnerabilities may not feel able to cope with pressure or responsibility.

Leisure and social lives

Many with neurological disability face restrictions in their leisure: sports, cycling, and walking may be precluded by physical disability or impeded by an inability to drive; less active pursuits (such as photography, model-making) may be less rewarding due to loss of dexterity; cerebral activities such as chess or bridge may be limited by poor memory, concentration, and reasoning; reading will be limited by visual/perceptual deficits. Unable to pursue former activities, persons with neurological disability often lack the imagination, initiative, or confidence to explore alternatives. The person may also feel less inclined to pursue an active social life due to lack of confidence, low mood, intolerance to noise, or difficulty in contributing to conversations. Friends may feel uneasy about physical disability or struggle to cope with: the changes in personality and behaviour; the irritability and aggression; the repetitive nature of their conversation; and the impulsivity, disinhibition, and general loss of refinement in social skills. As such, many friendships fall gradually by the wayside. As this includes boy and girl-friends, there is often a considerable degree of sexual frustration.

Marital relationships

Marital relationships often become strained after neurological illness/injury: physical disability may disrupt household routine and shared activities; cognitive impairment may limit conversation and companionship; personality changes may alter the dynamics of the relationship; behavioural difficulties may cause both embarrassment socially and tension or threat within the relationship; changes in arousal may disrupt sexual relations. Spouses may also find the behaviour of their partner incompatible with that of a sexual partner. Spouses often struggle to cope with competing needs of work, home, partner, and children, feeling trapped in a relationship they no longer find rewarding. Some couples adapt positively, others remain close but with less intimacy and fun in the relationship, but for some the extent of disability is such that the person and/or spouse are unable to cope and the marriage fails.

Family effects

Neurological disability also has a major impact upon the whole family, who are often left to cope with little support, especially where the person is left with subtle changes in cognition and personality which may not be apparent to extended family and friends. Many primary carers are under considerable stress (often with high levels of emotional distress), and many families face changes in relationships and disruption to overall family functioning. As life is tailored to meet the needs of the person, the occupational, leisure, and social lives of other family members often falters.

The consequences of neurological disability can therefore be quite devastating for the person with major restrictions in independence, occupation, leisure, and social life. This is often mirrored by substantial psychological and social impact upon the family, with couples often experiencing marital and sexual difficulties. The challenge for rehabilitation services is to ensure that persons with neurological illness/injury achieve and maintain optimal recovery and to facilitate long-term personal, family, and social adaptation. Clinical psychologists have a vital role to play in the rehabilitation process and are increasingly leading community rehabilitation services.

Assessment

The complex, long-term needs after neurological illness/injury require specialist and detailed assessment to clarify the nature of disability and to plan rehabilitation. Whilst formal testing of cognitive function is undertaken routinely, supplementary assessment of emotional state and behaviour are often required, either on initial assessment or during the course of rehabilitation. The fundamental principles of neuropsychological assessment are described above for the acute setting. In rehabilitation the focus of assessment tends to be more functional, identifying strengths as well as weaknesses and clarifying potential for rehabilitation. In this respect the results of formal neuropsychological testing need to be considered alongside self and family reports, observations of both nursing and rehabilitation staff, and parallel assessments completed by other professionals.

As in acute work, neuropsychological assessment in rehabilitation is seldom completed in isolation but is commonly undertaken as part of an integrated, multidisciplinary assessment process. This will routinely include medical, nursing, occupational therapy, physiotherapy, and speech and language therapy assessments, as well as neuropsychological assessment. In our Community Head Injury Service in Aylesbury, for example, clinical neuropsychology plays a lead role in the initial identification of need in the Head Injury Clinic with subsequent neuropsychological testing a core component both of standard rehabilitation team assessment and also of specialist vocational and driving assessment programmes (see Tyerman 1997).

Feedback of complex test results in a clear and sensitive way to the person (who frequently lacks insight and is quite defensive) and family (who may be understandably protective) is a highly skilled and challenging task. This can be undertaken separately or as part of an integrated feedback of team assessments. The main purpose of feedback is to provide a framework of understanding, to explain the results and their implications, and to engage the person positively in the rehabilitation process.

Interventions

The identified needs require a broad range of psychological interventions including: cognitive rehabilitation; behavioural management; rehabilitation counselling; individual psychological therapy; long-term psychotherapy; and specialist family interventions.

Cognitive rehabilitation

Core interventions are likely to include an explanation of general cognitive function and specific cognitive impairment. This may be followed by provision or supervision of reorientation exercises, reconstruction of lost memories, computer-based rehearsal of core skills, and/or strategies to help compensate for skills deficits (for example through the use of systematic scheduling, programmed prompts, manual or electronic organizers and other external memory aids, etc.). Teaching about cognitive difficulties and general strategies (such as use of diary, note book, and memory boards) can often be undertaken as a group using handouts, etc. In the longer term, the focus often shifts to exploring alternative ways of organizing tasks and limiting demands to cope with long-term difficulties, for example in the work place. Regular reviews and formal reassessments are vital to monitor progress, review rehabilitation strategies and goals, and guide resettlement, especially in managing a return to education or employment when cognitive skills are likely to be put to the test.

Behavioural management

Behavioural management is most commonly required after traumatic brain injury. Early in recovery, persons with brain injury are often restless and agitated and may display disinhibited, sometimes aggressive, behaviour on the ward. Nursing, and later rehabilitation, staff may require advice from the clinical neuropsychologist about the management of difficult behaviour. In some cases a psychiatric opinion and medication may be required on a temporary basis to contain severe behavioural problems. Where major problems persist a formal behaviour modification programme may be required. In extreme cases referral to a centre specializing in the management of severe behavioural problems may be appropriate.

Rehabilitation counselling

The course of recovery after neurological illness/injury is usually both uncertain and protracted. This may provoke a wide range of emotional reactions. Where the person is aware of the nature of their difficulties there may be fear, anxiety, and a profound sense of loss. Where the person lacks insight there may be confusion, frustration, denial, and aggression. Specialist rehabilitation counselling (supportive counselling, information, explanation, negotiation/monitoring of goals, promotion of insight/realistic expectations, and joint resettlement planning) may serve a vital function in guiding and supporting the person through the process of rehabilitation and resettlement. This function may be provided directly by psychologists or by other rehabilitation staff, drawing on psychological expertise as appropriate. Whilst individual rehabilitation counselling, ideally combined with a person-focused discussion/support group, will meet many of the emotional needs of persons with neurological illness/injury, some require individual psychological therapy.

Psychological therapy

A wide range of individual psychological therapy may be required in parallel with cognitive rehabilitation and rehabilitation counselling. This will include anxiety management, anger management, help with depression, post-traumatic stress counselling, pain management, management of obsessional behaviour, and help with alcohol/drug abuse. Whilst such interventions are not specific to neurological rehabilitation, standard techniques are often ineffective in this context and have to be adapted both to compensate for the cognitive constraints of persons with neurological illness/injury and to take into account any loss of emotional and behavioural control.

Long-term psychotherapy

Given the complex nature of neurological illness/injury it is not surprising that some struggle to adapt to long-term disability, particularly where cognitive impairment has reduced the capacity for self-appraisal and problem solving. In the confusion of the present and the uncertainty about the future there is a tendency to cling to the illusory security of the past. Common difficulties in adaptation include: preoccupation with lost skills/roles (with a failure to recognize remaining potential); a striving for 100 per cent recovery (to the detriment of positive adaptation); repeated failure and lost of confidence/self-belief (often arising from lack of insight and/or clinging to prior aspirations and standards that can no longer be met); social withdrawal due to fear of loss of emotional/behavioural control; strained family relationships; and social isolation. Individual psychotherapy, adapted to the neuropsychological context and constraints, offers a structure within which to assist the person forward: in making sense of and in reconciling changes in themselves and their lives; in reviewing strengths and weaknesses; in identifying, clarifying, and prioritizing unresolved issues; and in finding the strength and direction through which to start to rebuild their lives.

Family interventions

It is vital to include the family as fully as possible in the process of rehabilitation. Wherever possible a family member should be included in initial interviews about past history, early recovery, and current problems, particularly where the person struggles with memory and/or lacks insight into current difficulties. It is equally important to include the family in the feedback of test results to check for consistency with performance and behaviour at home, to help the family to understand the nature and implications of difficulties and the rationale for proposed rehabilitation. Thereafter close liaison with the family is essential both to receive feedback about progress at home and to explain ongoing rehabilitation strategies which can then be reinforced at home. However, it is vital not to view family members as therapists and great care is required not to add further to the stress on family members and/or alter further the dynamics of family relationships. The needs of families warrant attention in their own right as family members may themselves be in need of specialist advice and support in coping with the impact both upon themselves and the family as a whole. Our experience in Aylesbury is that relatives value our separate family programme comprising specialist marital/family assessment, individual supportive counselling, a programme of family workshops, and specialist marital/family counselling.

Interventions in rehabilitation and the community are therefore many and varied. For example, the core interventions provided within our Community Head Injury Service in Aylesbury are illustrated in Fig. 7.2. These will be illustrated with a case example.

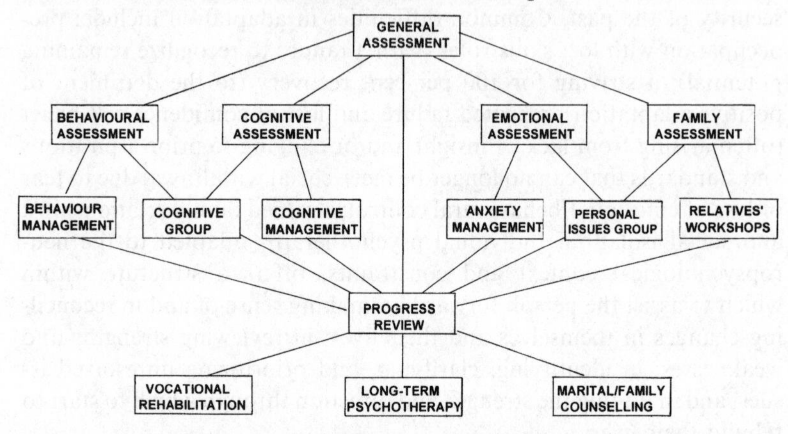

Fig. 7.2 Neuropsychological rehabilitation: a service example.

Case 4

A professional man in his late thirties was living with his wife (who was expecting) and 4-year-old daughter when he incurred a very severe head injury and orthopaedic injuries in a road traffic accident. He was admitted unconscious to his local general hospital where his level of consciousness gradually lifted but he remained in intensive care for 18 days and in hospital for 9 weeks.

Assessment He was seen for initial assessment at 5 weeks postinjury. He had no recall of his accident or of the preceding few weeks, and was only just emerging from a post-traumatic amnesic state. At this early stage he was aware of some of his physical disability (fatigue, slurred speech, reduced vision) and cognitive difficulties (speed, memory, expressive language) and many of his changes in emotion/behaviour (irritability, frustration, aggression, disinhibition, mood swings, and depression). He reported a low self-concept but did not report significant anxiety or depression. His wife identified his major problems as his obsession with returning home, lack of insight, aggression, disinhibition, being overly talkative, and very self-critical. In addition to his self reports, she noted his pain and restricted movement of his right elbow, his poor concentration, poor comprehension at times, word finding difficulties, and his anxiety about the future. A neuropsychological assessment confirmed substantial cognitive impairment of a generalized nature: reduced general intellectual ability; word finding difficulties; visuoperceptual difficulties; markedly reduced speed of information processing; and impaired verbal memory.

General rehabilitation After discussing the assessment results in the Head Injury Clinic he commenced an outpatient rehabilitation programme 2 days per week comprising: psychological therapy; occupational therapy; physiotherapy; and a weekly cognitive rehabilitation group programme (combining educational/coping groups with individual retraining sessions). Our goals were initially to improve right hand/arm function, to improve constructional skills, and to work on word finding and memory strategies. The early individual psychological therapy sessions concentrated on providing general emotional support and understanding of and response to the rehabilitation programme. As he progressed the focus of psychological input shifted to planning/organization skills and improving insight, awareness, and understanding. A neuropsychological reassessment at 7 months confirmed substantial progress with consistent gains in a range of intellectual tasks, object naming, and visual–perceptual tasks, but speed of information processing and psychomotor speed remained below average and marked impairment of verbal memory persisted. At 10 months he felt that he had improved physically, cognitively, and in behaviour but acknowledged that he remained irritable and liable to lose his temper at home. He was by now becoming more aware of the full range of his psychological difficulties, but with his increased insight came a mild degree of anxiety and high level of depression.

Vocational rehabilitation At 9 months he joined our specialist vocational rehabilitation programme, attending a weekly work preparation group, two community rehabilitation activities, individual project work, individual rehabilitation counselling, and a weekly personal issues group. In groups he was noted to be outspoken, dominating, and, at times, insensitive and dismissive of others. However, if criticized or feeling threatened, he tended to opt out of discussions. On individual project work he found it hard to accept guidance from staff and demonstrated marked difficulty with planning. He was more at home on a practical engineering activity, although it was noted that he preferred to work alone and found it hard to accept instructions. By 16 months he reported that he had been 'terminated' from his former job and acknowledged that he was 'bitter' about the lack of contact with former colleagues. In line with progress the emphasis gradually shifted from rehabilitation activities to individual project work, to a desktop publishing course, and voluntary work. At 2 years postinjury he started a voluntary work trial in a local printers—he coped well with technical skills, but had difficulty in planning and creative design work. After 6 months he started a second part-time work trial but this did not develop into a job as he had hoped and ended abruptly after 4 months. At 3 years postinjury he decided that he did not feel able to cope with the pressure of paid employment and expressed a wish to continue with part-time voluntary work. Whilst our view was that he had the skills to return to work in a part-time supported capacity, our impression was that any job with which he could cope would not be acceptable to him at that time. It was agreed that he would continue to work in a voluntary capacity, but that we would keep the door open in case he wished to seek employment in the future.

Marital counselling During rehabilitation his wife was supported regularly by our specialist social worker. At 1 year the family situation was causing great concern. His wife reported that he was preoccupied with his head injury and unable to cope with family life. He was reportedly irritable, frustrated (especially by his inability to drive and loss of independence), unable to discuss family matters without getting irritated, and verbally aggressive if challenged or criticized. He was intolerant of noise and unable to cope with the pressures of a young family—tending to opt out and take refuge on his computer. His relationship with his older daughter was causing concern—not dealing well with discipline and struggling to cope with her demands or join in her play. Specialist scales confirmed major marital difficulties with both partners rating the relationship as having 'very severe problems' with low levels of intellectual, emotional, and sexual intimacy. As such we instituted monthly marital counselling sessions. Over a period of 2 years we sought to guide and support the couple in understanding the family impact of the head injury, in managing his anger, in identifying and resolving (as far as possible) friction in the family, in starting to rebuild his relationship with his older daughter, in facilitating open communication, and in supporting the marital relationship. A major challenge was to use specialist neuropsychological knowledge and skills to help him to compensate for his cognitive difficulties in order to participate productively in marital counselling. (He found it difficult to appreciate others' views—tending to dominate discussions, interrupt frequently, and see issues categorically from his own perspective). Whilst the couple remained somewhat distant with little joint decision-making or sharing at a personal level and no physical intimacy, marital counselling served to contain confrontation and stabilize and support the strained family relationships under extremely difficult circumstances.

Individual psychotherapy As the lack of feelings of emotional and sexual intimacy was a major long-term concern he was offered exploratory sessions of psychotherapy. Unfortunately, the indication from these sessions was that he was not holding back on emotional intimacy or sexual arousal due to anxiety and/or lack of confidence, but rather that he was not experiencing any such feelings as a direct result of his injury. He did not appear ready yet to deal with the more sensitive issues in his marital relationship, remaining preoccupied with the effects of his head injury on himself. (The extent of preoccupation was evident from self-descriptions pre- and postinjury and his insularity illustrated by the choice of constructs and the distance between ratings of himself and significant others on a Repertory Grid). He appeared largely unaware of the impact of his expressed lack of feelings of intimacy upon his wife and further discussions focused on helping him to appreciate the impact of his injury, behaviour, and the current situation on his wife and family, as well as himself.

Follow-up When followed up at 4 years postinjury he had continued with his part-time voluntary work and appeared somewhat more settled and relaxed. This was reported by his wife to have eased slightly the stress and friction within the family, although significant family tension remained and his wife continues to receive support. He was at this stage resigning himself to his residual disability and associated family, vocational, leisure, and social restrictions. The offer of further sessions of psychotherapy to seek to assist him in long-term personal, family, and social adaptation remains open, as and when he feels ready.

The above example illustrates well the wide range of psychological interventions that may be required in rehabilitation, in this case working continuously to promote recovery and adaptation over a 3-year period: individual/group cognitive rehabilitation; individual/group rehabilitation counselling; anger management; vocational rehabilitation; family education and support; marital counselling; and long-term psychotherapy. Such interventions are usually integrated within a interdisciplinary rehabilitation programme. For example all the above groups are run jointly by at least two professions in order both to broaden the perspective and to promote shared understanding and joint working. It is equally important to work in partnership with other health services (i.e. general hospital, specialist neuroscience services, and general practitioners) but also with other agencies: with social services to secure appropriate day care and residential care; with employment services to address vocational assessment/rehabilitation needs; with education services for those wishing to continue with former or alternative studies; with voluntary agencies in distributing information, in providing specialist day care, and in supporting families. Working in partnership we can offer persons with neurological disability and their families the opportunity to optimize recovery and adaptation and, thereby, lay the foundation for a gradual rebuilding of their shattered lives.

CONCLUSIONS

Whilst often thought of as academic and narrow, clinical neuropsychology is a rich blend of specialist neuropsychological expertise and core clinical psychology skills. We hope that we have conveyed a flavour of this fascinating and challenging area including something of the similarities and differences with other specialties. We hope too that we have provided an insight into the complex pathway of care from diagnosis and assessment in the acute setting, through rehabilitation of skills and behaviour, to the promotion of long-term personal, family, and social adjustment in the community.

Whilst operating within a common neuropsychological framework the nature of the work and core skills differ in emphasis across acute, rehabilitation, and community settings. As such, clinical neuropsychologists are a disparate group with different settings attracting practitioners with contrasting interests and skills. A basic grounding in neuropsychology is provided in clinical psychology training but practitioners need to develop their specialist expertise. A number of post-qualification courses are now available with information available from the Special Group in Clinical Neuropsychology of the British Psychological Society. It is envisaged that formal training and a further qualification will be required in the future for practitioner status as a Chartered Clinical Neuropsychologist.

This is an exciting time in the neurosciences with major technical advances in *in vivo* imaging, image-guided neurosurgery, and work on implants and neuronal plasticity. Computer technology also offers major potential benefits for those struggling to cope with neurological disability but the challenge is to make such advances accessible to those with neuropsychological impairment. Advances in technology will hopefully extend the range of medical treatment and rehabilitation options. This will increase the need for specialist neuropsychological expertise.

References

Coppa, G and Tancred, E. (1995). *Brainstorm interactive neuroanatomy*. Harcourt Brace/Mosby, St Louis.

Donaghy, M. (1997). *Neurology: Oxford core texts*. Oxford University Press, Oxford.

Greenwood, R.J. and McMillan, T. M. (1993). Models of rehabilitation programmes for the brain-injured adult. 1. Current provision, efficacy and good practice. *Clinical Rehabilitation*, **7**, 248–255.

Lezak, M.D. (1995). *Neuropsychological assessment*. Oxford University Press, New York.

Ogden, J.A. (1996). *Fractured minds: a case-study approach to clinical neuropsychology*. Oxford University Press, New York.

Tyerman, A. (1997). Head injury: community rehabilitation. In *Rehabilitation of the physically disabled adult* (eds C.J. Goodwill, M.A. Chamberlain, and C. Evans). Stanley Thornes, Cheltenham.

Walsh, K.W. (1994). *Neuropsychology: a clinical approach* (3rd edn). Churchill Livingstone, Edinburgh.

Further reading

Clare, L. and Wilson, B.A. (1997). *Coping with memory problems. A practical guide for people with memory impairments, their relatives, friends and carers*. Thames Valley Test Corporation, Bury St Edmunds.

Cull, C. and Goldstein, L.H. (eds) (1997). *The clinical psychologist's handbook of epilepsy: assessment and management*. Routledge, London and New York.

Damasio, A.R. (1995). *Descartes' error: emotion, reason and the human brain*. Picador, London.

Lishman,W.A. (1997). *Organic Psychiatry: the psychological consequences of cerebral disorder* (3rd edn). Blackwell Scientific Publications, Oxford.

Ponsford, J. (1995). *Traumatic brain injury: rehabilitation for everyday adaptive living*. Psychology Press, Hove.

Rose, F.D. and Johnson, D.A. (1996). *Brain injury and after. Towards improved outcome*. John Wiley and Son, Chichester.

Sacks, O. (1985). *The man who mistook his wife for a hat*. Picador, London.

8

Working with older adults

Jeff Garland

To engage in this specialty is to increase respect for human endurance and appreciate the complexity of lifespan development (life has to be lived forwards, but it can only be understood backwards). There are frequent *memento mori* prompts to the psychologist of the ever-present need to prepare, through personal development, for the anticipated rigours of one's own later life; there is bracing concentration of mind for both client and therapist, aware that the next life-threatening crisis may be painfully near; and at every turn there are openings to encourage the client's self-advocacy in challenging paternalistic care.

However, it must be acknowledged that it is not easy to work with the substantial minority of older adults who have been 'volunteered' by their carers for psychological intervention, but who profess to know little about it and care less. This is particularly true of the disproportionate number of those referred to clinical psychology as so-called 'heartsink' or 'thick casenote' patients, veterans of many encounters with would-be therapists over the decades.

To explore the possibility of working constructively with negation, a recent series of 22 such clients were asked, on referral to me, to give their responses to the topic: 'Why I can't possibly change'. The 10 most frequent reasons were: too old (19); history of failure to change (17); problems too severe or numerous (13); too little time remaining (13); insuperable physical difficulties (12); others—usually family carers—were the real problem and they would not change (10); problems too complicated—'would not know where to start' (eight); unable to define targets of change (six); no incentive to change (five); and prospect of change seen as frightening or otherwise undesirable (five). For 19 of these clients, their individual responses proved a valuable resource in setting up agreed, generally paradoxical, interventions.

It is sometimes suggested that older adults are not well served by being a subject of specialty, with the possible consequences of segregation from the mainstream of clinical psychology. Certainly there is a degree of cognitive dissonance for the clinical psychologist who inveighs against ageism and proclaims conversion to social role valorization, while being required to operate in an age-segregated specialty where, from the client's point of view, to be 65 can spell Lear-like banishment to the badlands of 'old age psychiatry'.

In an ideal world, the psychology of adult health care should extend beyond 65 without a qualm. However, for the foreseeable future, the practitioner may struggle to resolve dissonance with some intellectual contortion by reflecting that perhaps a specialist service at least has its uses in ensuring that concerns affecting older people and their carers are not neglected. PSIGE, the national special interest group for clinical psychology in relation to older adults and their carers, has worked hard to strengthen the specialty since its first conference in Oxford in 1980.

Certainly the specialist never wants for clients. Fifteen per cent of the population of the United Kingdom are over 65, the age usually taken as the start of the later phases of the lifecycle (Victor 1991). Much effort with the most severely impaired older adults, particularly with the growing numbers aged over 85 (sometimes identified as the 'old-old'), needs to be expended on supporting professional and paraprofessional health and social care workers, supplementing volunteers, neighbours, friends, and family drawn from a wide age span.

Preventive care is not to be neglected, and the continued campaigns for 'grey power', rights of retired people, education for the Third Age, and to improve health for 'seniors' (people over 50) offer opportunities to engage applied psychology.

THE RANGE OF CARE PROVISION

Geriatrics

This is a title properly used to define an area of medical specialization with patients usually over 65—geriatric medicine—but is sometimes misused to label patients. Inpatient provision usually includes: acute beds in general hospitals for emergency admission; rehabilitation beds with fast or relatively slower turnover; and continuing care wards. 'Holiday' or short-term care beds are widely used to back up community care. Day attenders are catered for by day hospitals in many localities. Outreach may include outpatient clinics, home visits, and home-based support from geriatricians, geriatric liaison nurses, occupational therapists and physiotherapists, social workers, and psychologists.

It may be difficult to tell if the problems of a given patient are primarily physical, social, or psychological; but there are as yet relatively few areas of the United Kingdom that offer a unified approach, with primary health care, social services, geriatricians, and mental health professionals working together as a matter of course. In many localities, progress has been made in shared assessment procedures and in review panels for joint decision making. In many instances one or more members of a mental health service may be called in for consultation by a geriatrician, either in an *ad hoc* way or as part of an established liaison service organized for crisis prevention.

Psychogeriatrics

This term refers to old-age psychiatry, specializing in patients aged 65 or over, although again it is sometimes inappropriately used to describe the patients themselves. Traditionally, a local service has had some or all of the following types of in-patient provision. Continuing care wards look after long-stay patients, often with a mix of chronic psychiatric patients grown old as 'graduates' of the hospital system, and patients admitted in later life with disorders related to ageing. Acute admission/assessment wards are for patients who, in theory if not always in practice, come for short-stay admission, often to resolve a crisis in care. In general, for administrative reasons, these wards do not segregate 'functional' and 'organic' patients, although the patient whose primary concerns are anxiety or depression may report that these are exacerbated by sharing accommodation with patients suffering from brain failure. It is scarcely surprising that the cognitive and behavioural impairment of 'organic' patients can be misread by some 'functional' patients as sign posting their own future. Occasionally, as in Oxford, a specialized unit will deal with challenging behaviour, such as physical 'aggression', 'wandering', or excess noise-making. In some cases wards may mix continuing care, medium-term care, and assessment. 'Floating beds' on a rota system may be available, so that through planned, periodic admission relief is offered to a number of patients and their supporters; and 'holiday beds' offer short-stay admission responsive to immediate needs. Many such wards also serve a small number of day patients, usually attending for from 1 to 5 days each week; and, more rarely, a few have a limited number of night 'hostel' beds catering for individuals whose management is most problematic at night.

In many areas this pattern is changing, with the closure of large hospitals subject to heavy capital charges, and a move away from the provision of continuing care, to create small-scale, localized services primed to give early community-based support. In Oxford, for example, a support service for carers of middle-aged individuals with an early dementia has been set up, and a teaching nursing home is being developed, in partnership with a charity, to sustain the NHS contribution to continuing care and to offer outreach to private nursing homes.

Many old-age psychiatry services also operate day hospitals, catering for attenders coming from 1 to 5 days each week, and may also support day centres, often run by local branches of national societies concerned with older people. Other psychiatric services are likely to include outpatient clinics, home visits, and home-based support to patients and their families, friends, volunteers, and professional staff. These services tend to rely on a front line of community psychiatric nurses, linked with social workers, psychiatrists, occupational therapists, and psychologists.

Social services

Local authorities make provision for older people apart from that made by health authorities but, unless there is unexpected resolution of current funding difficulties, they can be expected to continue to reduce provision. Home care schemes, also being cut in many areas, enable the client to stay at home with varying degrees of support. Sheltered housing with a warden provides for those becoming frail but still largely able to cope unaided. Old People's Homes are for those deemed to need full-time residential care. In some authorities homes are designated for the elderly mentally frail; in others *de facto* segregation is imposed by reserving part of each home for 'confused' residents; or relative integration may prevail.

General practice

In the United Kingdom, those doctors responsible for health care in the community, the general practitioners, are paid extra for looking after older patients because of anticipated extra demands on time. While intensive screening of this age group does not appear to be cost effective, an increasing number of GPs have special clinics for older patients, employ counsellors to work with patients encountering major life events (which affect many older people), and sometimes involve a clinical psychologist through direct referral.

Community hospitals

These are relatively small units for a local community with beds controlled and serviced by local GPs. They usually have a large proportion of older patients, who are either receiving day care, in-patient rehabilitation, or longer-term care. Such units supplement the geriatric provision of larger hospitals. However, in Oxfordshire, as in other parts of the United Kingdom, such units tend to be criticized as not cost effective, and are becoming open to pressure to rationalize resources by concentrating services in and around district general hospitals.

Voluntary societies

There are a number of national organizations with local groups or initiatives related to local needs of older people. Age Concern, Help the Aged, the Alzheimer's Disease Society, and the Parkinson's Disease Society are examples. Psychologist and colleagues from other disciplines are likely to be found in such settings from time to time, offering consultancy or working with individual clients referred by the agency or self-referred.

Private care

Provision of private residential or nursing home care for older people in the United Kingdom has been growing rapidly, and input by National Health Service staff to such businesses appears to be increasing. State assistance to private enterprise is provided in some cases where, on completion of active treatment and in the absence of a health or social services unit able to accept transfer, the financial resources of a resident from an NHS facility may be 'topped up' to enable that individual to enter private care, and so freeing a bed. Private homes may seek consultancy from psychologists and others on general issues affecting staff training, management of 'difficult' residents, and improving quality of life. Occasionally the more far-seeing of such homes will employ a psychologist to prepare potential customers by working with families in decision making, preparatory to applying for entry into care for an older member.

TYPES OF PSYCHOLOGICAL PROBLEM

Physical, social, and psychological factors interact in older people to produce increased variability in behaviour and a wide range of reactions to ageing processes. Treatable physical causes should be dealt with at an early stage, and social needs should also be met as far as possible, leaving the psychologist free to home in on residual factors; but in practice this rarely happens. Continual awareness that psychological factors cannot be approached in isolation remains necessary.

In listing the major types of psychological problem experienced by older people, we must recognize that many of these can occur in clients from other age groups. While older people do have their characteristic concerns, they are basically just people who happen to have been around longer than the rest of us. There is no widely accepted system of classification of the psychological challenges of late life. The common behavioural distinction between 'deficit' and 'excess' categories, which can be subdivided, offers a starting point. Interview schedules, behaviour rating scales, and other psychological tests have been widely used in large-scale surveys without, as yet, yielding a taxonomy that can be applied readily. This is hardly surprising when we consider the following selection culled from records of a series of 100 new clients over a 6-month period of practice. Three main headings are: primarily physical, relating to physical activity and needs; primarily social, concerning social functioning; and primarily psychological, relating to thoughts and feelings. Some of the problems clearly come under more than one category.

Primarily physical

The following issues relate to physical needs and action, but have social and psychological components, since the behaviour, thoughts, and feelings of the client and others are intimately related.

- Maintenance of the activities of daily living, for example dressing or undressing, or performing domestic tasks, can be disrupted in late life, so that the client requires retraining or other assistance.
- Maintenance of health, together with necessary compliance with medical or other treatment, may by interfered with through inability or unwillingness to act reliably in, for instance, maintaining body temperature by appropriate dress and heating.

- Sleep can be less satisfying in late life, with sleep dissatisfaction tending to increase after 50, sometimes involving exacerbation cycles (worry over lack of sleep, leading to reduced sleep, which leads to further worry).
- Apparent incontinence without a direct physical cause may occur through inability to recognize a toilet, or failure to reach a toilet in time because of reduced mobility, or for many other reasons.

Primarily social

The social network of an impaired older person may be put under severe strain in attempting to cope with the major personality changes which Stuart-Hamilton (1994) describes. Needs for information, re-assurance, access to services, and specific counselling and advice on the understanding and management of behaviour, offer an unfolding series of challenges.

- Loneliness, under-reported by older people who understandably may be reluctant to admit what can be seen as social failure, can be linked with reduced mobility, loss of attractiveness, and lack of money.
- Excessive requests for attention, like indiscriminate approaches with persistent questioning, may function to force social interaction from others, who would pass by without comment if the attention seeker was quiet, preferring to 'let sleeping dogs lie'.
- The stress of relocation and adaptation to institutional living (where about 5 per cent of older people are located), represents a major social upheaval, especially when the move is rapid, and the mover ambivalent and still in the throes of life crisis.

Primarily psychological

Forgetfulness and memory impairment become an increasing concern for many. Clients can link everyday forgetfulness with 'Alzheimer's' or 'senility', and may develop unduly drastic or complex attempts to cover up or to cope in other ways, which impose more burden than the actual memory deficit. Confusion, disorientation, and progressive inability to think straight may succeed failing memory, but do not do so invariably. This type of problem may well be patchy, particularly in its early stages, so that episodic use of relatively convincing coping strategies can alternate with lapses during which the client can be aware that something is badly 'wrong' without being able to correct what is happening.

Anxiety, whether diffuse or relatively specific, accompanies many of the problems listed here, and appears in many forms. Depression, one of the most frequent and serious psychological challenges of ageing, similarly may appear in a variety of forms and degrees of severity. Often linked with depression, but worth considering in its own right, is demoralization. Low self-esteem and morale and a pervasive feeling of loss of control over one's own life may, to some extent, reflect the low social value of ageing and the aged in our society.

A preoccupation with bodily discomfort and the maintenance of physical functions, particularly bladder and bowel function, is characteristic of some elderly clients, particularly those who are depressed. Often chronic pain is experienced; but the client's signals complaining of pain can become augmented, and may function not only as a response to bodily state, but also as a means of operating on others to gain reassurance. Reaction to actual or anticipated loss—of social status, of economic or physical independence, of family or friends through relocation or bereavement, of one's own life—is of increasing concern in later life, and is often linked with depression or demoralization.

CERTAINLY A CHALLENGE

This is the phrase usually breathed by the awed clinical psychologist new to this client group, becoming aware that the above list could be twice as long and still not be truly comprehensive. However, the summary of practice which follows indicates that our resources are growing in response to the challenge. It remains the case that relatively few clinical psychologists devote all or even most of their time to this specialty; but this imbalance is being corrected as the positive contribution which can be made is recognized.

The tasks of a clinical psychologist concerned with older adults include the construction and administration of tests, particularly of competence in daily living, and carrying out counselling and therapy. Behaviour management programmes and therapeutic environments have to be developed and a positive part has to be taken within the multidisciplinary team in administering and managing these. The psychologist has to work with community services in encouraging co-operation and new approaches, and in monitoring the cost effectiveness of services; and act in relation to administrators as interpreter of research findings, as advocate of the needs of individual clients, and as a change agent working for the improved delivery of community care.

Assessment

It is of particular importance to use, and encourage others to use, a scientific approach. For this client group 'assessment' is too often invoked as a catch-all term, justifying emergency admission at the behest of hard-pressed community services or the client's despairing supporters. In these circumstances 'assessment' is rarely planned or related to design of treatment; it represents at best a breathing space while the multidisciplinary team seeks inspiration or moves on to the next task in hand.

There has been a shortage of psychological assessment instruments that are relevant for older people, and that have ecological validity in sampling the experience and activities of daily living. Some encouraging advances have been made in the area of brief cognitive assessment, but the user of a psychological assessment service, asking 'What will the results contribute to the management of this case?', still needs guidance. Appropriately, the specialist psychologist is increasingly likely to offer a user's manual for such a service, since data on techniques or tests for use with older people can be complex and conflicting.

Neuropsychological assessment, in memory clinics and other settings, can make a valuable contribution to diagnosis, to prognosis, to design of therapy for individual deficits, and certainly to the morale of some clients and their supporters. It can be a relief to hear that an observed specific impairment in cognitive functioning is not an indication of 'going mad' or becoming senile, that its causes can be understood and explained clearly, and that many other aspects of intellectual performance can be shown to be relatively normal. Tests such as the Revised Kendrick Battery have shown a way forward for attempts to establish the sometimes difficult differential diagnosis between dementia and depression in older people.

Many clinicians use criterion-referenced testing, evaluating the client's ability to meet a criterion specified in the test. For example in the assessment of testamentary capacity, or the ability to make a valid will, an old person's estimated ability to manage her or his own affairs, and make an informed decision on disposal of assets, may be evaluated most usefully by constructing a personalized multiple choice assessment of information and orientation with content selected for relevance to the direct demonstration of competence. There has also been progress in the objective assessment of family burden and strain felt by supporters of mentally frail older people living in the community.

Direct observation of behaviour, and of levels of engagement or constructive activity in institutional settings, can quickly point to priorities for management. For example a man was admitted to hospital from an old people's home as 'physically aggressive' and 'incontinent'. Nurses did immediate event recording when taking him to the toilet, recording any physical aggression or incontinence. In 25 consecutive observations he was wet once, and there was no aggression. Comparative observation of toileting approaches in the home and in hospital revealed that in the home, approaches by care staff fluctuated between the tentative and the over insistent, with frequent refusals by the resident and related incontinence, and an 'aggressive' response when this was pointed out. In the hospital, there was a more consistent and confident approach by the staff, winning the resident's compliance. Developing more assured behaviour of staff in the home through nurses' guidance, rather than concentrating on the resident's attributes of 'aggression' or 'wilful' incontinence, became the focus of a successful intervention.

Frequency, duration, timing, or intensity of a problem behaviour can be established by observation, as a baseline against which change can be evaluated. For example a woman who 'wandered' around a ward was reported by staff as doing this 'all the time'. Structured observation for 3 days, using time-sampling, taking in this case a 5-second observation hourly, revealed that this was not the case. She was walking about on 47 per cent of the observations; but settled behaviour coincided with activity initiated by staff, such as feeding, washing, and conversation. Again, how others were able to influence her behaviour became a focus for action.

Observer ratings, self-rating scales, and the varied techniques of naturalistic observation are favoured by psychologists; but it can be difficult to involve care staff, many of whom have difficulty in fitting structured observation into their notion of 'the real work' of care, and feel uncomfortable with what looks like a passive role while their colleagues are being visibly active.

PRINCIPLES OF INTERVENTION

There are 10 guiding principles for psychological intervention that are important for any client group, but particularly valuable for this relatively neglected and disadvantaged population:

(1) emphasize early action, producing minimal disruption for the individual;
(2) maintain the client's independence as far as possible;
(3) consult fully with the client and principal carers and supporters;
(4) establish the client's needs, and what incentives will help to meet those needs;
(5) reflect on the advisability or nature of an action before starting;
(6) work through carers and supporters in general;
(7) encourage objective assessment throughout intervention;
(8) set out action in small, specific steps, which are clearly understood;
(9) review progress with participants periodically;
(10) evaluate outcome and follow-up where necessary.

These guidelines are flexible. Despite point 6, for example, the psychologist needs to retain direct involvement with some clients to keep therapeutic skills sharp and to maintain effectiveness as a consultant. For some 'difficult customers' that no one else wants, there will be no alternative.

Reality orientation

Reality orientation (RO), the best-known training approach for 'confused' older people, has two main forms. 'Classroom' RO is conducted with a small group, or less frequently one-to-one; it cues, prompts, and selectively reinforces successive approximations to improved orientation. Information is shared with clients, recognition and repetition of general or personal information is encouraged, sensory stimulation is given, the environment is clearly and attractively labelled, and trainers are active in drawing out responses and offering correction or praise. Twenty-four-hour reality orientation, or 24RO, extends this approach as a model for consistent practice around the clock. RO is a philosophy of care rather than a specific treatment, and effectiveness has been difficult to evaluate. However, a specific aspect of RO, the use of directional signs to which residents' attention is persistently drawn by staff, has been shown to reduce wandering. Clinical psychologists have been active in developing individual applications of RO.

Validation therapy

RO is not always the approach of first choice with a 'confused' client. Validation therapy focuses on sharing and understanding the experience of the client as a prerequisite for reorientation. For example, Marjorie, a 68-year-old in a wheel-chair after successive strokes, distressed fellow patients and staff on a geriatric ward by repeatedly calling out, 'I'm going to have a baby!' Lecturettes on gynaecology and many other well-meant attempts at RO had proved of no avail, as her calling out continued. From her history it appeared that she had miscarried several times and had no children; it was felt that she might be reliving these experiences of distress and pain. Dialogue between Marjorie and a psychologist supported this view, and gradually they were able to progress through to her present predicament, and to explore how the ward team would have to take the place of her lost children, looking after her the best way they could. It was natural, it was agreed, for her to revert to her former experience of hospitalization, threat, and loss, and this did not make her the 'daft ha'p'orth' that she had felt herself to be. Thanks to nurses who gave her the necessary support in maintaining this insight, Marjorie's subsequent help seeking became more appropriate in expression, and less frequent; the cry 'I'm going to have a baby!' did not recur.

Psychotherapy or counselling

Many clinical psychologists face demoralized clients with an integrative model based on the capacities and strengths which normally develop in the course of growing old to overcome the demoralization which can be produced by the losses of ageing (Knight 1996). Successive levels of input are: meeting the material needs of the immediate situation; offering support and promoting efforts to stabilize self-esteem and morale; assisting the client to feel more in control of her or his life situation; and building positive, long-term changes in self-concept and self-esteem. For the client who is facing bereavement, or who is in terminal care, specialist counselling approaches may be added.

Reminiscence and life review

In reminiscence, small groups are encouraged to share memories, stimulated by newspaper files, sound archives, photographs, films, and other sources. Private as well as public recollections gradually emerge, and group members are prompted regularly to return to the present to compare 'things then' and 'things now', and to appreciate the many challenges they have faced.

Life review is a more personal, one-to-one therapeutic exercise in collaboration with a therapist, evoking pattern and meaning in a unique experience of life, and relating past events to present state within a sense of integrity. Integration of cognitive–behaviour therapy approaches, for example the analysis and working through of life traps identified in schema-focused therapy, is becoming more widely used by life review therapists.

Improving intellectual functioning

We tend to exaggerate the effects of ageing, which are less severe, more specific, and more amenable to efforts to cope than we might suspect. For example memory training programmes have drawn on a variety of techniques with success. These include: progressively lengthening by gradual increments the period of time over which memory is required; the use of external aids such as sign posts, colour coding of doors, and the use of diaries, notebooks, alarms, or other cues to prompt recall; and the use of internal aids such as visual imagery to build face–name links or identify places needing association with items to be remembered. Clients with relatively early or mild impairment can be expected to benefit most from such approaches in outpatient memory clinics, but their lasting effectiveness is uncertain.

Coping with anxiety and depression

Anxiety is common with older people, and is amenable to anxiety management training, although response tends to be slower and more difficult to sustain than with younger people, not only because in reality everyday life can hold more anxiety-provoking stimuli for vulnerable older adults but also because it is not uncommon for them to resist the psychologist's requests for self-monitoring. For example a not atypical initial reaction offered by a current client was: 'Oh dear. Another job!' Depression in late life is a major problem, yet antidepressants have a risk of serious side-effects with this age group, and the relapse rate after ECT is high. Prospects for cognitive therapy, in which the client is helped to identify and alter depressive patterns of thinking, having recognized their influence on mood state, are therefore of particular interest.

Starting therapy in a context of life review

Bill, a 74-year-old academic who had moved into a sheltered housing complex after heavy drinking had contributed to self-neglect, had identified himself as suffering from seasonal affective disorder (SAD), but this self-diagnosis had been set aside after exhaustive investigation co-ordinated by his GP, who then instigated referral for cognitive–behaviour therapy.

The client responded with glee to my invitation to state 'Why I can't possibly change.' He began, 'I am an academic—an academic is someone who knows what is wrong with an argument, not what is right . . .' He continued with a thorough and by no means unmerited critique of the pretensions of therapists, and explained that as a comparative youngster I could not presume to understand how he felt in having been flung on the scrap heap by the university's blinkered bureaucracy.

I acknowledged that it would indeed be difficult for me to understand without his help, and asked for his assistance in identifying an idea that ran through his life and related to his current condition. 'Of course!' Bill replied. 'It's not being good enough. I think even a person like you would understand that. I got a second class degree. I should have got a First. It hurt in 1948. It still hurts today. And that was just the start. Do you know what it feels not to be good enough?'

I suggested that even if I didn't, it was becoming clear that, with his assistance, I soon would.

Older people (and Bill proved to be no exception), have shown they can develop positive patterns of thinking and ability to cope in stressful situations, such as their admission to residential care. Self-monitoring as a prerequisite for introducing self-statements, such as 'This place is home now and I'm going to make the most of it', is a key component of therapy. In community health care studies, clients aged 60 to 80 have been shown to benefit from instruction on 'coping with depression'.

Reducing somatic preoccupation

For older people it is vital for them to recognize when they are not healthy so that they can take appropriate action. While many report increased bodily discomfort or pain, only a minority become excessively preoccupied. This minority can be an extremely vocal one, suffering and causing others to suffer, and becoming the target of intensive investigations and treatments which rarely yield long-term relief. A psychological intervention involves systematically withdrawing attention for complaining, giving attention and other rewards for 'well' behaviour, and above all encouraging distracting activities. These may include relaxation and the use of mental imagery to view discomfort and pain as controllable.

Rehabilitation

Psychologists are often asked to design and implement programmes for chronic psychiatric patients who return to the community after several decades of institutionalization. These programmes include modules of training in the activities of daily living and in social skills. It is increasingly common for psychologists to advise on incentive programmes for those older, post-stroke patients commonly described as 'lacking motivation'. The staffing of movers' groups is necessarily multidisciplinary, but often offers particular opportunities for a psychologist. These groups integrate rehabilitation effort by giving clients feedback on progress, using successful 'graduates' as models, and by sharing information on requirements of the community settings to which moves will be made.

Behavioural deficits and excesses

Many interventions with older adults in residential care are directed at overcoming a lack of normal activity (Fleming and Barrowclough 1996). Significant increases in constructive activity have been achieved by behavioural management procedures in, for example, self-feeding and personal hygiene. The basic approaches are those used for all client groups in these settings, such as helping the client to link specific desirable behaviour with particular features of the environment (stimulus control) and selectively reinforcing such behaviour.

Behaviour management can also reduce excess or high-rate behaviour. Excessive complaining has already been mentioned: significant reductions have also been achieved in, for example, inappropriate urinating, and with unwanted sexual approaches. Some of the main issues emerging in behavioural intervention with older adults appear below, since the clinical psychologist's participation is essentially as researcher, teacher, and consultant. In some respects—for example, in family therapy with the client and immediate supporters—the psychologist will be found to be directly intervening to meet social and psychological needs. Often, though, his role as a scarce resource may be found more productive in research, teaching, and consultancy.

CONSULTATION AND TEAMWORK

As clinical psychologists are generally in short supply for all client groups, the necessity of transferring psychological knowledge and skills to non-psychologists must be recognized. This is particularly true for work with older people, where even in a relatively well-staffed locality the number of psychologists will be very few.

Traditionally, though, the therapeutic process of developing knowledge and skills in the client (and, with family therapy, in immediate supporters), has been through direct intervention. This has been seen as the 'real work' of clinical practice, fundamental to job satisfaction. Less gratification has been perceived in consulting and teaching, viewed as a process of transfer of knowledge and skills to professionals, paraprofessionals, volunteers, and supporters. The traditional stance has been rooted in a tendency to perceive consultation and teaching as being primarily enforced by a lack of psychologists, and to consider the process one-sidedly as a depleting putting-in of expertise. Increasingly, though, the profession has come to appreciate the intrinsic value of consultancy as a mode of working, and to understand that in a joint effort to achieve change the consultant is recharged by the human potential drawn out by a successful intervention at this level.

Team or network?

With older people, as with other client groups, the multidisciplinary team is a generally recognized unit of clinical practice. In theory, such an entity should foster consultation and teaching, since shared problem solving and collaborative effort is implied. In practice, the working of the 'team' may create difficulties for consultation: members may protect expertise rather than share it in a transdisciplinary style; paraprofessionals from within the same agency may be seen as only marginal members; and, more importantly, the interests of clients and supporters are not represented directly within the team.

In clinical practice, the crucial venue for consultation and teaching is a specific support network, consisting of the client and other individuals with responsibilities in the assessment, management, and continued care of the older person. The most important criterion for effectiveness of consultation then becomes the condition of the network. If it is fine tuned and responsive to change in the client's situation, consulting within that network should be efficient. Knowledge and skills 'given away' in conventional training, rather than earned by shared effort within a care network, may be less likely to be integrated effectively in the form of increased psychological-mindedness in the non-psychologist.

GERONTOLOGY

Clients need to be understood in the context of gerontology, the scientific study of the normal and pathological changes occurring with ageing. In the social and behavioural aspects of this science the psychologist should be equipped as an information resource. A client may ask: 'What can I do about my failing memory?' A supporter: 'If we build a granny flat would it help?' A therapist: 'Why do so many patients get 'stuck' in our rehabilitation programme?' In some cases it may be desirable only to offer access to information, encouraging the enquirer to draw her or his own conclusions.

Within gerontology, the following themes are of particular clinical interest.

Support for supporters

It has been wisely said that families of impaired older people need to be supported by professionals, but not supplanted. Such support is provided by many agencies in face-to-face contact with families, ranging from small, *ad hoc* groups of supporters to organizations such as the Alzheimer's Disease Society. While there are a number of excellent community care projects, there is also overlap and muddle because many sources of support are involved, and beliefs differ about 'what carers really need'.

It is not uncommon for carers of persons with dementia to have very real doubts about the value of engaging with community support. Not all carers are willing, confident, well-informed or trusting. Their concern can often be expressed to a specialist support worker such as an Admiral Nurse in terms of 'I'm wasting your time' (or words to that effect.) Rather than making a reflex response of reassurance, it is important for the worker immediately to elicit the individual pattern of feelings and ideas behind such a comment, and to plan with the carer management of their time together so that both will appreciate that the shared time is being well spent.

Carers identify three main types of need: firstly emotional support, ranging from the reassurance of contacts with 'someone who listens' to intensive regular counselling where a care network is under intense pressure from guilt, anger, and physical exhaustion; secondly information about, and access to, resources such as attendance allowance, transport, aids, day care, or holiday relief; and thirdly advice on achieving insight into what is going on and developing ways of coping with disturbed feelings or behaviour. In responding to the third category of need, a key priority is for the psychologist to facilitate communication, as the following examples illustrate.

Des and his wife live half a mile from Des's father who suffers from dementia. The old man remains at home with intensive support from the couple who take turns to visit. Des is furious because his father keeps calling him 'Dad', and he is convinced that this is being done 'to wind me up'.

Asked whether this naming could simply reflect his father's understanding that they have changed places in the family in that the son is now taking care of his father, Des scornfully rejects the suggestion. Replying to the question 'What was the latest thing you've done for him?' Des reports that the previous night he had been with his father and wanted to make sure that the old man would be in bed and asleep before he left.

He had managed to persuade him to go to bed, but his father was 'obstinate' and refused to go to sleep, saying he was not tired. So what did Des do? He found a newspaper and read his father to sleep.

'Well . . .', reflects the psychologist.

'Well what?' Des retorts.

His wife leans forwards and says gently 'I'll explain when we get home, dear.'

The explanation must have been delivered successfully because in the following session Des is much more relaxed in talking to his father and begins openly to confront the fears that he has found in the reversal of their roles and his crisis of filial maturity.

Initial inability to understand also is shown by George, who is shamefaced as he reports that on Sunday evening he 'finally cracked' in losing his temper with his frail and confused mother-in-law, who lives with George and his wife. In his home 'office' he was struggling with his tax returns but kept losing concentration as mother-in-law roamed the house, repeating distractedly: 'I'm cold and I'm hungry!'

George tried explaining that his wife would soon be back from church and that she would then light the coal fire laid in the living room and prepare supper. Mother-in-law nodded in apparent understanding, only to return and repeat her complaining. Eventually in exasperation he took an executive decision to resolve the problem, lighting the fire and preparing her favourite supper with his own hands. He set supper by the fire, seated her with encouragement to enjoy the meal, and returned to his tax returns.

After 10 minutes he came to a tricky point and decided that he would take a break to peek round the living room door and enjoy the success of his solution. But he was surprised and disappointed to see that mother-in-law had gone, leaving supper untouched. He began to search, and eventually found her sitting in her room, rocking to and fro and murmuring: 'I'm cold and I'm hungry . . .' At this point he snapped, berating her for her stupidity and for having wasted his time, and dredging up many previous instances of her failing to appreciate what he and his wife were doing for her.

In subsequent discussion with a psychologist, George, with the assistance of his wife, was able to explore how emotional intelligence might have been used to understand mother-in-law's message in a less literal way, and to prepare and experiment with alternative responses that could meet her needs for contact and human warmth more effectively.

It has been suggested that the supporters who complain loudest get more than their fair share of assistance; that abuse of older people by their supporters is more frequent than is generally supposed; and that precipitate support may undermine families' commitment. The psychologist will be involved both in direct consultancy to enhance supporters' skills, and in indirect advice to them on how service and supporters' needs can be matched more closely, and in recommending how such issues as suspected abuse should be dealt with.

Assessment

The psychologist offers consultation to others who may wish to use, or adapt, psychological assessment. Advice may be required by community psychiatric nurses wishing to evaluate the level of burden on supporters, or by doctors dissatisfied with traditional brief 'mental state' examinations. Some specialized instruments—for example, neuropsychological evaluations—may be retained by the psychologist; but the case for retaining assessment as an exclusive function should be examined carefully, rather than be taken as for granted.

Behaviour management

Consultation is a recurring issue, particularly with care staff who may unwittingly be contributing to a client's undesirable behaviour. Consultation can draw on a 'menu' of procedures from which selection can be made according to carers' resources. An example is provided here, for the understanding and management of persistent excessive telephone calling by May, a widow living alone.

She had a lengthy psychiatric history marked by major mood swings and conflict with her husband and children. When she was bereaved, a son took her into his home, but within a few weeks this arrangement broke down and May was returned to her house, leaving her with an abiding sense of betrayal.

She complained to her children in turn and began to engage in lengthy and frequent 'phone calls citing her grievances, listing her physical and psychological complaints, reciting the events of her day, and relaying family gossip. In a single week-end one of her daughters clocked 128 calls from her. A family conference with her care manager and a clinical psychologist produced a menu of options for her children and their families which were reviewed for possible action.

1. Dealing with your feelings. Anger, or guilt (anger turned on yourself), is a common reaction to abuse. 'Phone calling that is over the top is a form of abuse and you have the right to do something about it. May has the right to know how what she does affects you. Rather than keeping your feelings bottled up it is helpful to you and May if you share them with her. Don't keep telling her 'we love you'—through gritted teeth!
2. Normal contacts. If May calls you or you call her and the contact remains normal—relatively brief, not too frequent, two-way and not just a monologue from her—go along with this. Better still, make it clear to her that 'it's good to talk' like this.
3. Bringing the contact back to normal. If she speaks too fast, ask her to speak slowly. If she begins to become unduly agitated, ask her to stay calm. Give her two reminders, and if she does not respond proceed to–
4. Cutting her short. If the conversation is not normal, and cannot be brought back to normal, make it clear to May that you are not enjoying the contact. You do not have unlimited time to listen while she holds forth. Already some of you have found ways of doing this. Use the way you find to work best and stick to it.
   (a) turning the tables, take the initiative by talking exclusively about yourself and your feelings;
   (b) have I got news for you, step in quickly to tell her in detail about the recent doings of your own family;
   (c) if I were you, lay down the law for her—move in to give firm advice about how she should live her life and get herself sorted out;

(d) other people have got problems too, when she talks about having a particular difficulty, point out that other people in the world have this too and ask her about their ways of coping;
(e) put the call on 'hold', leave the 'phone at arm's length, pick it up to put in a word occasionally, but otherwise rest your ears and think of other things.

Adapting care

While older adults whose behaviour presents a major challenge may need to be helped in adapting to their environment, the environment itself needs to be shaped, like a prosthesis, so that the person can be as independent as possible (Kitwood 1997). Psychological approaches to reshaping care take at least five interrelated forms: engagement sampling (which has been reinvented as 'dementia care mapping'); stimulation and activity programmes; planned changes to the physical environment which sometimes include adoption of Snoezelen apparatus from learning disability studies; reality orientation groups and 24RO; and behavioural management that consistently shapes and rewards constructive behaviour, while limiting attention given to behaviour of a destructive or needlessly dependent nature.

The significance of 'environmental docility' in impaired older people has been well documented by psychological research, indicating that as competence decreases external environment factors become progressively more important in determining behaviour. Occasionally a psychologist can be directly involved in planning the design of a new residential setting. In general, however, change is hard won, fought for in settings with many physical constraints. For example the demands of 24RO should not be underestimated. Working consistently to remind an impaired resident of reality and to maintain a positive attitude demands dedication.

Hazel, a care assistant, tried with a psychologist to build a more personal relationship with a resident by ensuring that the resident knew Hazel by name. Over several days the resident made 26 unsuccessful attempts, but number 26 held promise: 'Something to do with nuts, dear? Brazil? . . . No, Hazel!' Hazel sat slumped. Somehow, for her, it no longer seemed to matter that much. With enthusiasm born of relief the psychologist congratulated the resident and Hazel, rekindling some of Hazel's interest.

Psychologists have noted that certain routines in care of older people, such as bed-making or drug rounds, need no prompting.

Others, such as activity programmes or reality orientation, appear remarkably subject to extinction through neglect. It has been suggested that the former are more stable because they are more visible, so that neglect would be noticed, and that they are in any case secure as they are seen as the 'real work' of care. Perhaps they also involve less close personal contact with residents who are likely to be severely impaired, and whose response to contact is at best hesitant and limited.

Staff support

To work with this client group demands adaptive skills of a high order. There is a heavy demand for services, while resources tend to be scarce or ill-co-ordinated. Health-care networks can be fragile and their structure complex, rarely admitting of straightforward solution. The 'burn-out' syndrome linked with high absenteeism and low morale is not unknown in teams serving older people; and it is not uncommon for a psychologist to consult with others to give or receive support.

RESEARCH

The clinical psychologist is likely to be involved in fundamental research in clinical gerontology and in action research evaluating service, as well as participating in the work of other members with advice, general support, and collaboration if required. There is now a substantial body of research with older people. Effects of impaired memory and problem solving are beginning to be well understood, and compensatory programmes have been developed. A national memory clinics task group has been set up by PSIGE to collate views and evidence with the overall aims of placing such clinics within the wider context of services to people with memory disorders, and encouraging good practice. Research effort is growing, with a major need to evaluate a mass of findings.

To illustrate this point, it has been shown repeatedly that increased occupational therapy resources in continuing care bring a corresponding increase in the habitually very low level of constructive activity shown by most residents. When resources are withdrawn, activity reverts to its original level. Important questions then arise. In cosmetic terms increased activity looks good, but can it be shown to benefit residents? If it does, how can we devise intermediate types of occupational activity, attractive enough to engage both residents and direct-care staff who would be required to supervise in the therapists' absence?

Psychological research into intervention with older people has been remarkably inconclusive in some respects. For example RO is a well-known procedure which has been widely researched. According to some studies, it yields modest gains in intellectual functioning and considerable benefits for the morale of carers, who are able to interact with more confidence and report greater satisfaction with what they do. However, the rationale for RO is debatable, and it has been suggested that it is such a complex procedure that it is impossible as yet to conduct adequate research, as no evaluation could implement RO comprehensively or consistently enough.

Another area of uncertainty relates to research on psychological management of apparent incontinence, that is incontinence where no primary physical cause can be found. Outcome studies have produced mixed results, and one factor accounting for this is lack of care in screening subjects, so that some clients were included who could not have been expected to respond to psychological retraining. However, standards of research into the effectiveness of behavioural treatments for older people are improving, and a substantial body of literature is evolving which is beginning to come up with answers to the question 'what works for whom?'.

In terms of fundamental research in clinical gerontology, investigation of early psychological correlates of chronic brain failure, 'this epidemic of our time', is being pursued in Oxford and a number of United Kingdom centres; and a number of complementary investigations of provision and co-ordination of support for those who care for such clients are under way. The influence of dementia service development centres, the Alzheimer's Disease Society, and *The Journal of Dementia Care* has been notable.

It is important for the clinical psychologist working with older people to maintain a research interest in the relatively healthy. For example I have found that studying individuals over 65 active in the Oxford area in campaigning for improved economic, health, or social conditions for their peers has not only been a resource for community practice, but also has given a balanced perspective on this age group.

ADMINISTRATION AND POLICY MAKING

Apart from internal administration of a specialist professional service, the psychologist is expected to contribute to broader planning. There are four major goals.

1. Move toward a unified health and social care provision which recognizes the identity of interest between the sectors already mentioned.
2. Establish a service data base with objective assessment of clients' functioning, as a basis for classifying the categories of challenge.
3. Develop services' responsiveness to needs of clients and supporters. The Niskanen Effect—systematic bias in providing what suits the service rather than what clients necessarily require—is too frequent.
4. Support regular systematic audit of operationally defined care procedures. All too often, what is actually done in work with older people is left unresolved and unclear, and terms such as 'assessment' or 'support' conceal more than they reveal. Recent development of the United Kingdom HONOS-65 Scale is a hopeful sign that the introduction of a nationally recognized brief measure of outcome of clinical intervention may not be far away.

CONCLUSIONS

Work with older people is considered a distinctive specialty for a number of reasons: the universality of ageing, so that we face in clients our own potential future; the aversiveness of ageing for many of us; the relative frequency of premature termination of work through the client's death; the nature of the required knowledge base in social and behavioural gerontology; the need to master specialized assessment and treatment approaches; operation in age-segregated settings; the relatively high incidence of physical symptoms interacting with social and psychological problems; and a high frequency of iatrogenic complaints related to multiple treatments and idiosyncratic responses.

Also, we must consider: the prevalence of work through carers rather than directly with clients; family dynamics complicated by parent–child role-reversal, and expectations of paternalistic care; clients with a prolonged investment in current coping strategies, with strong resistance to change; older people's healthy scepticism of the psychological—'there's nothing wrong with my mind'; and comparatively greater evidence of barriers to communication—cognitive impairment, fatigue, and sensory impairment.

Within this specialty clinical psychologists have drawn attention to individual psychological needs, developed assessment procedures, devised therapeutic interventions to produce demonstrable change, and contributed to a substantial literature in clinical gerontology. Our need now is to ground our contribution more securely within the psychology of adult development and ageing, making a lasting contribution to the understanding of the process of late life, and the complex and often conflicting systems which enmesh older people.

Gerontophobia, a relatively common complaint among health-care professionals, is a suitable case for treatment. A treatment package may need to embrace not only *in vivo* exposure to a wide range of older people, but also the practical application of well-grounded theory to probe and shape assumptions of service providers and users.

Clinical gerontology, the scientific study of normal and abnormal changes in health-care needs with ageing, is the core knowledge unifying many health-related disciplines. The relevance of clinical psychology for late life is measured by practitioners' effectiveness in developing and applying this body of knowledge in partnership with other disciplines in response to the needs of older adults and their carers.

References

Fleming, I. and Barrowclough, C. (1996). *Positive approaches to assisting older people*. Psychological Corporation, London.

Kitwood, T. (1997). *Dementia reconsidered. The person comes first*. Open University Press, Buckingham.

Knight, B.G. (1996). *Psychotherapy with the older adult*. Sage, London.

Stuart-Hamilton, I. (1994). *The psychology of ageing. An introduction*. Jessica Kingsley, London.

Victor, C.R. (1991). *Health and health care in later life*. Open University Press, Milton Keynes.

Further reading

Biggs, S. (1993). *Understanding ageing. Images, attitudes and professional practice*. Open University Press, Buckingham.

Bond, J., Coleman, P. and Peace, S. (eds) (1993). *Ageing in society. An introduction to social gerontology*. Sage, London.

Holden, U. P. and Woods, R. T. (1995). *Positive approaches to dementia care*. Churchill Livingstone, Edinburgh.

Jacoby, R. and Oppenheimer, C. (eds) (1997). *Psychiatry in the elderly*. Oxford University Press, Oxford.

Woods, R.T. (ed) (1996). *Handbook of the clinical psychology of ageing*. Wiley, Chichester.

9

Working with offenders and antisocial behaviour problems

Ronald Blackburn and James McGuire

INTRODUCTION

The focus of this chapter is on work with people whose behaviour causes problems for others. Such work has traditionally centred on offenders whose antisocial behaviour is a function of psychological disorder or disability and who are consequently dealt with by the health-care system. However, it also includes efforts to rehabilitate offenders within the penal system and work with patients whose disruptive or violent behaviour poses threats within the health-care system or the wider community. Psychologists concerned with these problems work in a variety of settings, and an understanding of this area requires first some discussion of service provision at the interface between health care, the criminal justice system, and the social services.

TREATMENT OF OFFENDERS AND THE PENAL SYSTEM

The penal system functions to protect society from those who violate the criminal law, and does so through penalties which exact retribution, deter would-be offenders, or incapacitate the most harmful. The extent to which it also takes the offender's welfare into account reflects changes in attitudes to crime in the late nineteenth century, which have provided the basis for current services. The most important concern mentally disordered offenders and rehabilitation as a goal of the penal system.

Mentally disordered offenders

Legislation for detaining offenders excused legal punishment on the grounds of mental disorder originates from 1800. This led to the creation of the 'criminal lunatic asylum', and as the courts turned to physicians for advice on the mental state of offenders, forensic psychiatry developed as a medical specialty charged with overseeing the detention, care, and release of mentally ill or mentally handicapped offenders. Procedures for diverting mentally disordered offenders from legal punishment to health care were thus already in place at the time of the inception of the National Health Service (NHS), and these were effectively consolidated by the 1959 Mental Health Act for England and Wales, and its 1983 revision (Scotland and Northern Ireland have slightly different, though comparable, legislation).

The Act defines mental disorder as 'mental illness, arrested or incomplete development of mind, psychopathic disorder and any other disorder or disability of mind', and on medical evidence that an offender found guilty suffers from such disorder, disposal options available to the court include imprisonment or a fine, a probation order with conditions of inpatient or outpatient treatment, or a hospital order requiring compulsory detention in hospital. The Crown Court may additionally impose a 'restriction order', which prevents a detained patient from being discharged from hospital without the consent of the Home Secretary. However, the 1983 revision of the Act gave power to Mental Health Review Tribunals, which are independent judicial bodies, to discharge a restricted patient under certain conditions.

The majority of mentally disordered offenders dealt with under the Act are diverted to the NHS. Over 10 per cent of involuntary admissions to health-care facilities are admitted under a hospital order, although these make up less than 1 per cent of the total of offenders convicted of crimes other than motoring offences. Other offenders may also be dealt with as outpatients under a psychiatric probation order. Some offenders are therefore likely to be referred to clinical psychology departments in the course of ordinary NHS practice.

Of the most serious offenders, about 150 a year are admitted to the Special Hospitals. These are maximum security hospitals for patients who 'require treatment under conditions of special security on account of their dangerous, violent or criminal propensities'. There are four such hospitals in Britain, these being Broadmoor, Rampton, Ashworth (created in 1990 as an amalgamation of the former Moss Side and Park Lane Hospitals), and the State Hospital in Scotland. Together, they house some 2000 patients, four-fifths of them male. About 70 per cent have committed serious crimes such as murder, arson, or sexual assault, but the hospitals also admit prisoners who become mentally disordered while in prison, and psychiatric patients who exhibit serious violence in other hospitals. Clinical psychology departments were established in the hospitals in the 1950s, and these have developed in parallel with their NHS counterparts. Until 1989, the hospitals were administered directly by the Department of Health. However, in 1996, the English Special Hospitals became Special Health Authorities and are now more closely integrated with the NHS.

The treatment of mentally disordered offenders came under critical scrutiny during the 1970s, partly because of declining psychiatric facilities for patients requiring moderately secure containment, but also because research questioned the ability of clinicians to identify dangerous people. One consequence was the setting up during the 1980s of Regional Secure Units (RSUs) in the English and Welsh regions to provide 'medium' secure facilities for disruptive NHS patients and mentally disordered offenders not requiring the maximum security of the Special Hospitals.

RSUs provide a base from which a specialist service to the community can develop through liaison with the courts, the penal system, and community agencies, as well as the NHS and Special Hospitals. All secure units have established posts for clinical psychologists, resulting in a significant increase of psychological services for offenders. While the units are headed by forensic psychiatrists, and accept inpatients under the Mental Health Act, close working with agencies such as the probation service has allowed psychologists to establish outpatient services to offenders, such as sex offenders, who may not be disordered within the meaning of the Act, but whom the courts accept are suitable candidates for psychological treatment. Outpatient services may also be provided for individuals who have not broken the law but whose behaviour problems suggest a risk of antisocial behaviour.

The development of RSUs recognized the need for gradations of security and secure hospitals now form part of a wider network of custodial and community services. However, most mentally disordered people coming to the attention of the criminal justice system are relatively minor offenders whose needs overlap with those of disruptive or 'socially inadequate' non-offender patients. These needs were to some extent met by the locked wards of the traditional psychiatric hospitals, but hospital closures have left a gap in service provision for those who may be a social nuisance but are not a danger to the community. Recent Department of Health policies have affirmed a need to close this gap through the diversion of mentally disordered offenders to community programmes. Court-based diversion schemes have now been established in several areas through which disordered offenders are referred to community mental health teams. Clinical psychologists are frequently members of these teams, and in some instances have played a leading part in co-ordinating these services.

Rehabilitation of offenders

Although the number of offenders diverted from the penal system to mental health facilities has always been small, the treatment ethos has been extended to those who remain subject to legal penalties. Beginning with reforming efforts of eighteenth-century Quakers, legal punishment came to be seen as an opportunity to correct offenders, and the impetus to rehabilitate offenders was sustained by the development of psychology and sociology. Early psychoanalytic theories encouraged the view that many offenders not considered mentally disordered may, none the less, have personal adjustment problems. While more recent psychological theories view antisocial behaviour more in terms of failures of appropriate social learning than of intrapsychic conflict, the emphasis has remained on rehabilitation as a process of correcting individual deficits or problems.

During the 1970s, rehabilitation as a penal goal came under attack. In addition to questions about the ability of clinicians to forecast dangerous behaviour, research findings suggested that despite the range of therapeutic programmes provided for offenders, 'nothing works' in terms of reducing reoffending. However, more recent evidence has justified continued faith in rehabilitation (McGuire 1995; see below).

Nevertheless, rehabilitation has always been an uneasy bedfellow of the punitive goals of the penal system, and specialist therapeutic services have typically been available to only a limited extent. A few penal establishments in Britain have had visiting psychotherapists for some years, and a treatment prison run on therapeutic community lines was set up at Grendon Underwood in 1962. Since 1946, the English prison system has also had its own psychological service. The number of prison psychologists (currently some 150) is small relative to the prison population, and few of these are clinical psychologists. Much of the work of the service is therefore directed to the needs of prisons as social organizations, and includes training and support for prison officers, consultancy services for management and planning, and research into the functioning of prisons as well as the problems of offenders (McGurk *et al.* 1987). A particular emphasis during the last few years, however, has been the development of group-based programmes of psychological intervention dealing with problems such as anger, sex offending, and violence. The training of prison officers to carry out much of this work has permitted the implementation of programmes on a national scale.

PSYCHOLOGICAL PROBLEMS AND ANTISOCIAL BEHAVIOUR

There are no firm figures on the extent of psychological difficulties among offenders, but a substantial number have problems ranging from serious mental disorder to more focal and less serious disabilities, which may none the less warrant attention to improve their chances of rehabilitation. Research shows that anxiety, low self-esteem, poor impulse control, and problem-solving skill deficits are common among prisoners, and British estimates suggest that about a third have problems associated with alcohol and drug abuse or personality disorder. This last shades into interpersonal problems of varying severity.

The problems of offenders dealt with under the Mental Health Act are identified in terms of medicolegal categories of disorder. *Mental illness* is not defined, but generally covers the most serious mental disorders, such as schizophrenia, affective psychosis, or organic brain disorders. The majority of patients in Special Hospitals and RSUs fall in this category. *Psychopathic disorder* is 'a persistent disorder or disability of mind, whether or not including significant impairment of intelligence, which results in abnormally aggressive or seriously irresponsible conduct on the part of the person concerned.' *Mental impairment* and *severe mental impairment* refer to 'a state of arrested or incomplete development of mind which includes significant impairment of intelligence and social functioning and is associated with abnormally aggressive or seriously irresponsible conduct on the part of the person concerned' and hence essentially covers people with learning disabilities who are also 'psychopathic'.

The psychological problems presented by mentally disordered offenders overlap with those found in the mental health system generally. Mentally ill offenders, for example, exhibit problems of motivational and social deficits typical of long-stay patients, although they often also display socially unacceptable behaviour, such as aggression, which impedes their return to less restricted environments. Therapeutic goals are therefore to provide the necessary coping and interpersonal skills which will enable them to survive in their optimal environment, whether an open hospital, a hostel, or their own home.

It has been increasingly recognized that mentally impaired patients rarely need to be dealt with in maximum security because their problems are most commonly the *challenging behaviour* exhibited by some people with learning disabilities who are not necessarily offenders. Challenging behaviour includes a range of behaviours which may place the safety of an individual or of others in jeopardy, which may limit access to the full use of community facilities, or which may hinder access to a good quality of life. Such behaviours in turn may be a consequence of communication difficulties or other factors associated with learning disabilities. Within health-care services, the fundamental issue then becomes one of management of such behaviours by means which will be acceptable given the individual's disabilities, the needs of family and other community members, and also of staff groups and allied care providers.

About a quarter of patients in Special Hospitals, and a smaller proportion of those in RSUs, fall into the 'psychopathic disorder' category. This has always been a contentious category, not least because of its vague criteria, but also because of the doubts of many that 'psychopaths' are treatable in the health-care system. However, the term 'psychopath' has been much abused in Britain as a 'catch all' for a variety of socially problematic behaviours. Psychological research has emphasized a more strictly defined clinical category of *psychopathic personality* characterized by personality traits such as egocentricity, callousness or emotional coldness, impulsivity, and an antisocial lifestyle (Hare 1996). A significant minority of criminals show this pattern, particularly the more violent offenders. Psychopathic personality is not equivalent to the Mental Health Act category of psychopathic disorder. In practice, this category includes the more serious, violent and sexual offenders, some of whom may also show psychopathic personality. Other forms of personality disorder, however, are equally common among this group who are heterogeneous in the problems they present.

Personality disorders are identified by patterns of longstanding and persistent deviant traits that cause social problems for the individual and others. For example a tendency to be interpersonally exploitative, one of the traits defining narcissistic personality disorder, is likely to generate resentment and conflicts with others. Personality disorders are not confined to offenders, and are found among people with mental health problems more generally. However, some forms are commonly associated with antisocial behaviour, in particular antisocial and borderline personality disorder. Antisocial personality disorder, which overlaps with psychopathic personality, refers to a persistent disregard for and violation of the rights of others, as shown by a history of deviant behaviours such as deceitfulness, repeated physical fights or assaults, recklessness, financial irresponsibility, or lack of remorse over hurting or mistreating others. Borderline personality disorder describes a persistent pattern of instability of interpersonal relationships, self-image, and affects, as manifest, for example, in intense relationships that alternate between extremes of idealization and devaluation, an unstable sense of self, over-reactive moods, frequent displays of temper, recurrent suicidal gestures or self-mutilation, and self-damaging impulsivity in areas such as spending, substance abuse, or reckless driving.

Borderline patients pose particular problems of treatment and management because of their frequent rejections of help and the negative reactions their behaviour elicits in staff. Their self-harming tendencies, which may take the form of cutting parts of the body or swallowing foreign objects, often increase in institutional settings, and are particularly common among women detained in prisons or secure hospitals. However, these problems are also encountered in other health-care settings. Although these problems are not well understood, current views link them to the experience of abuse in childhood and the re-enactment in later life of ambivalent relationships with caregivers.

Treatment of these disorders entails changing long-established, self-defeating lifestyles. They are not generally amenable to medical forms of treatment, and psychological interventions are seen as the treatment of choice. However, psychologists typically redefine such disorders in terms of interpersonal skill deficits, dysfunctional cognitive styles, and belief systems relating to self or others.

The following case history illustrates some of the problems of offender patients in the psychopathic disorder category.

Gary was a young man with several convictions for indecent exposure (exhibitionism or 'flashing') and minor thefts. His most recent incidents of exposure, however, were accompanied by physical assaults on his female victims, and threats with a knife. Interviews revealed violent fantasies of rape and killing females, depressed mood, and a history of social avoidance. He also had considerable sexual problems, including anxieties about social and sexual interactions with females, erectile failure when he attempted intercourse, excessive masturbation, and frequent urges to expose himself. His violent fantasies were traced to the termination by a girlfriend of a brief adolescent affair, which he attributed to her becoming a 'prostitute', an interpretation resulting from her developing an interest in wearing heavy make-up and provocative clothes. He felt intense hatred towards women he perceived as 'prostitutes', and this occasioned his recent assaults. In addition to feeling depressed, he was also frequently tense and anxious, and felt a failure in most areas of his life. He also had a long record of unemployment, partly due to his lack of skills, but also to impulsively leaving his jobs, and was inclined to get into financial difficulties because of heavy gambling and drinking.

Gary's antisocial behaviour is therefore associated with more general problems of distorted interpersonal beliefs, mood disorder, and inappropriate social behaviour, and he displays some of the characteristics associated with borderline personality disorder. He is also of limited ability and deficient in social skills, and his problems centre particularly on sexual difficulties and social anxiety, associated with an idiosyncratic view of women. Psychological treatment needs to address these multiple problems.

However, antisocial behaviour is often associated with more focal psychological difficulties which do not amount to serious mental disorder. This is illustrated by the case of Alan, a man in his late thirties referred to a clinical psychologist by his general practitioner.

Alan had become increasingly worried by what he described as an inability to control his temper, a problem of which he had become aware over a period of several months. In the worst incident, he had seen some youths outside his house apparently tampering with his car. He experienced feelings of rage, and shouted furiously at them. When they ran off he pursued them in his car, attempting to run one of them over in a sustained episode of anger which lasted more than 20 minutes. Afterwards he became extremely concerned over the harm he could have done. Clinical assessment showed that Alan had a number of problems in his life and was experiencing bouts of anxiety. He also had financial difficulties. Now in his second marriage, he was still locked in a number of disputes with his first wife. He worked as a security officer but had had warnings that he might lose his job due to repeated lateness. He had a history of heavy drinking, and was having more and more arguments both at home and at work. Though he did not have a formal criminal record, Alan admitted to having occasionally been involved in fights. The overall pattern of his difficulties was explored and he was offered a 'clinical formulation' of the possible connections between them and their relationship to his temper control problems.

ROLES OF PSYCHOLOGISTS

The kinds of service provided by clinical psychologists for offenders vary according to their work setting and the legal procedures through which they receive their clients. For example psychologists attached to

RSUs spend much of their time working with clients in the community, while those in security establishments work within the constraints of a closed setting, which may itself create problems for both inmates and staff.

Models of service delivery parallel those found in health care generally. Most commonly, the psychologist is a member of a unit multidisciplinary team of staff responsible for the care of a group of patients. In the Special Hospitals, for example, the team usually consists of a consultant psychiatrist, a social worker, a psychologist, and a nurse ward manager, while teachers and occupational therapy staff may attend team meetings as appropriate. Psychologists working in secure settings also provide consultancy services for professionals outside the team. However, this calls for a range of assessment and treatment tasks, which are considered in more detail below.

In a team context, the psychologist does not receive referrals as such, but rather negotiates the kind of involvement most likely to be productive. This has the advantage that the more pressing psychological problems are defined by the psychologist, rather than a referring agent. Collaboration between disciplines is also more likely in a team system. For example the psychologist may work with nursing members in devising and implementing a rehabilitation programme for a particular patient, or with the social worker or psychiatrist in running a therapy group. Similarly, team psychologists are more likely to participate in group decision making about patients with whom they are only indirectly involved, and can contribute an alternative perspective on such issues as the granting of parole. In community oriented services, however, psychologists are likely to receive referrals from a variety of agencies.

Forensic psychology

Work with offenders is now commonly identified under the umbrella term of 'forensic psychological services'. However, 'forensic psychology' specifically describes a particular legal role in which psychological findings are used to assist legal decision making, and it is not synonymous with clinical work with offenders. Nevertheless, it is a role which some clinical psychologists exercise regularly. A pioneer in this area is Professor Lionel Haward who has achieved recognition as an expert witness by providing evidence to the courts for many years. He believes that clinical psychologists are particularly well placed to develop the role of forensic psychologist more generally because of their research training, and that they may assist the courts in more than purely clinical matters. His own contribution has included evidence in obscenity trials as well as commercial disputes (Haward 1981).

In criminal cases, the forensic role of the clinical psychologist may include the presentation of psychometric findings on the characteristics of an offender, an assessment of likely response to treatment, or the setting up and reporting of a psychological experiment to clarify a critical point of evidence. An important development regarding the acceptance of psychological evidence in courts of law occurred through the widely publicized case of the 'Tottenham Three'. The trio in question were defendants accused of the murder of a police officer during the Broadwater Farm Estate riots in North London in 1985. All had confessed to this crime but later retracted their confessions. One of the defendants was initially assessed by a clinical psychologist but the evidence so obtained was not heard in court.

When the case was later taken to the Court of Appeal, the applicant was seen by Dr Gisli Gudjonsson, a clinical psychologist who has conducted extensive research on the phenomenon of 'false confession' and has investigated factors such as interrogative suggestibility which had been shown to influence these occurrences. The report he prepared raised serious doubts concerning the veracity of the confession obtained prior to the original trial. In 1991, this evidence was examined and ruled admissible by the appeal judges who additionally commented that expert psychological evidence would have assisted the jury in the original hearing of the case. This case has been regarded as creating legal precedence, and has had a number of implications for the status and usage of psychological evidence in courts of law (Gudjonsson 1992).

Dangerousness and risk assessment

The prediction of dangerousness is one aspect of forensic psychology in which those working with offenders engage regularly and is a critical requirement in legal decisions to detain a person under a hospital order or to release a restricted patient from secure facilities. However, as was noted earlier, the capacity of psychiatrists and psychologists to forecast future dangerousness has been shown to be limited. The difficulty lies not only in our limited knowledge of the causes of dangerous behaviour, but also in common biases in human judgement established by psychological research to limit the accuracy of decision making. For example, clinicians may selectively focus on psychological disorder while ignoring established *risk factors,* that is events or experiences known to be precursors of harmful behaviour. In addition, appropriate information about risk is often inadequately documented or communicated between professionals. This has been observed by several inquiries into serious incidents within clinical services and violent acts committed in the community by discharged psychiatric patients.

Although the difficulties of making accurate predictions of future behaviour have to be accepted, it is now recognized that *risk assessment* is a systematic process that occurs in a variety of settings and that clinical decision making about future harmful behaviour can be improved by structuring the assessment task. In particular, it is not informative to assert that a person is or is not dangerous. Rather is there a need to gather information that permits the clinician to specify not only whether certain risk factors are present that make the person more likely to engage in harmful acts, but also the type of harm, the probability of the behaviour occurring, the type of victim, and the time frame in which the behaviour may occur. The goal of risk assessment is *risk management*, that is the prevention of harm. This has to be an ongoing process and not simply a one time prediction.

Several approaches to assessing the risk of violence have recently been developed. For example one procedure developed by Canadian psychologists is based on research on violence and entails a detailed assessment in which the clinician examines evidence in three areas (Webster *et al.* 1997). First, the individual's history is examined to identify risk factors such as previous violence, alcohol or drug abuse, or psychopathic personality traits. Second, a clinical assessment of current state is made to determine characteristics such as response to treatment or the presence of violent fantasies. Third, evidence is obtained on variables which may affect risk in the immediate future, such as the availability of social support or the likelihood of compliance with treatment plans or medication. The results of the assessment permit both a qualitative and quantitative judgement about the likelihood or probability of future violence.

Advocacy

Clinical interventions normally terminate when client and therapist agree that therapeutic goals have been achieved. In secure psychiatric settings, however, legal powers of discharge rest with the consultant psychiatrist for patients detained under a hospital order, and with the Home Secretary or a Mental Health Review Tribunal for those detained under a restriction order. Psychologists who assume responsibility for a major part of a patient's treatment are therefore often obliged to take on the role of patient's advocate after treatment has ceased. The prime task then becomes to convince other team members, government officials, or a Tribunal that sufficient change has occurred for discharge or transfer to less secure conditions to be appropriate.

Offenders whose crimes are morally repugnant or difficult to comprehend invite little public sympathy, and are viewed with caution not only by officials responsible for public safety, but also often by care staff. There may therefore be strong resistance to arguments that an offender is ready for discharge, even when these are buttressed by objective measures of change. In functioning as an advocate, then, the psychologist must defend a psychological interpretation of the patient's behaviour, marshal evidence of change from clinical observations and psychological assessments, and present this in written reports or verbal arguments at team meetings or Tribunal hearings. While these arguments are not always accepted, the following kind of success may be sufficient to prevent demoralization.

Peter was admitted to a Special Hospital following an attack on three youths with a knife. For some months prior to the attack, he had been unemployed, isolated, withdrawn, and unkempt in appearance. The attack appeared unmotivated, and schizophrenia was diagnosed. While several psychiatrists subsequently commented on the absence of psychotic symptoms, the label persisted, and his rather odd, withdrawn, and unco-operative behaviour in hospital was attributed to persisting psychosis. The team psychologist, who was asked to evaluate Peter's social interactional skills, found him initially anxious and unforthcoming, but gradually learned that prior to the offence he had become depressed and left his job because of the death of a workmate for which he blamed himself. On his occasional walks, he had been taunted by the three youths for his unkempt appearance, and after they attacked him on one occasion, he bought a knife for protection. The offence followed further taunting and fears that he was about to be assaulted again. His unco-operative behaviour in hospital reflected resentment at what he saw as punishment for justified self-defence.

Psychological testing showed no evidence of psychotic symptoms or cognitive impairment, but clearly indicated that Peter was an anxious, introverted, rather hostile, but unaggressive and socially unskilled person. While some of the team remained convinced that Peter was psychotic and dangerous, the psychologist presented an alternative formulation, relating his offence behaviour to depression and limited coping skills, and his hospital behaviour to anxiety and resentment. After a few sessions of anxiety management, Peter became more relaxed and co-operative. The team subsequently accepted the psychological formulation, and recommended his transfer to less secure facilities.

Staff support

Psychological treatment methods may be of limited value for many mentally disordered offenders, and, for much of the time, the primary therapeutic needs of such patients are likely to be medication, nursing management, or regular counselling. However, while many offenders present few problems of management within an institution, their offences may invite negative reactions from staff, and some may be disruptive and unco-operative. High-security establishments also often dictate an emphasis on security and containment, and a mistrust of inmates, which conflicts with therapeutic goals. Staff who work directly with offenders may therefore find their work stressful because of conflicting aims and uncertainties in their dealings with patients, particularly in units containing a high proportion of individuals with borderline personality disorder. Similar problems arise in high-security prisons.

One role for psychologists in such settings is to provide staff support based on psychological understanding of the problems that arise in therapeutic relationships. This most commonly takes the form of group sessions, in which staff are encouraged to examine the basis for their negative reactions to particular individuals and alternative explanations for inmate behaviour. Sessions may also focus on coping skills required for inmate management, including training in basic behavioural techniques.

Consultancy

Psychologists sometimes provide consultancy services to support management. Some psychologists, for example, have developed particular skills in dealing with hostage-taking situations, and provide advice when such incidents arise. While these are rare in mental health settings, they have become more frequent in prisons during the past decade. They call for skills of negotiation and of monitoring the state of hostage-takers and their relationship with the hostage if the incident is to be terminated without harm to the latter.

Consultancy may also be provided for other agencies. In recent years, the probation service has been required to work with an increasing proportion of 'higher-risk' offenders and consultation with psychologists is now common in many areas. Some consultative work consists of discussion and advice concerning the delivery of treatment services for individuals at risk of sexual offences. Alternatively, it may be much more extensive. It may, for example, include design of specialized manuals for working with offenders who are placed on probation with additional requirements to attend group programmes in probation centres. In this case, the psychologist's involvement may range from preparing and piloting materials, to staff training, evaluation, preparation of project reports, and advice to management. Several well-established, probation-based activities have been developed in this way, including programmes or courses focused on life skills, offending behaviour, aggression and anger management, and problem-solving training.

CLINICAL ASSESSMENT OF OFFENDERS

As in other areas of clinical psychological practice, emphasis has shifted from providing diagnostic and prognostic information from psychometric tests to more direct involvement in treatment. Nevertheless, broad-based assessment combining interviews, tests, and individualized measures, and providing reports for others continues to be important in work with offenders. Apart from identifying and monitoring specific problems which are the focus of psychological treatment, objective psychological measurement may contribute to the way in which other staff deal with a patient—for example by providing explanation and understanding of an offender's behaviour, as in the case of Peter described above. Moreover, those responsible for decisions to release mentally disordered offenders frequently rely on objective evidence of how far problems contributing to dangerous behaviour have been resolved, even though direct psychological intervention may have been negligible.

Psychological assessment of offenders draws on a variety of procedures commonly used in other health settings. These include standardized tests of intelligence, personality traits, social attitudes, and neuropsychological functioning, and also more specific, often unstandardized procedures to assess emotional reactions to particular situations, beliefs about the self and others, or problem-solving skills. Methods used more particularly in work with offenders are illustrated by approaches to the evaluation of aggressive and sexual problems.

Assessing violent offenders

Assaultive behaviour tends to be an attempt to control a situation which the aggressor finds threatening, and is now generally understood in terms of cognitive processes and interpersonal skills. For example research with violent delinquents has shown that they readily jump to conclusions about the intentions of others, and fail to consider future consequences. They also frequently lack skills for resolving minor conflict, and they minimize the harmful effects of their behaviour. Assaults occur most commonly when people believe, whether mistakenly or not, that their physical or psychological well being is intentionally threatened or thwarted by another person. Aggression is a likely outcome when they are in the habit of resorting to coercion to obtain their ends, lack skills for resolving conflict by non-aggressive means, or fail to consider long-term consequences as a result of temporary situational factors, such as domestic stress or alcohol intoxication. The commission of an assault therefore invites questions about the immediate situation and how the offender perceived it, the relationship to the victim, and the offender's habitual interpersonal behaviour patterns. Answers suggested by the initial interview are explored and tested out by means of general and specific assessment procedures.

A general assessment of personality characteristics can provide initial evidence of the personal factors which may contribute to assaultive acts. For example not all criminal assaults are committed by habitually aggressive people. For *overcontrolled* people, who are typically unaggressive and have difficulty expressing feelings of anger, the assault may be a last resort when threat seems overwhelming. Peter, whose case was referred to earlier, is an example of such a person. Others may be *undercontrolled*, and resort to violence frequently as a result of easily aroused anger, and a lack of controls in the form of concern for others or future consequences. One of the authors has developed a standardized questionnaire, the SHAPS (Special Hospitals Assessment of Personality and Socialization) to assist in making this kind of distinction. It consists of 213 questions requiring 'yes' or 'no' answers (for example 'Are the people who run things usually against you?', 'Do you easily get impatient with people?', 'Do you often get so annoyed when someone pushes ahead of you in a queue, that you speak to them about it?'). Answers are summed to yield scores on 10 scales (Lie, Anxiety, Extraversion, Hostility, Shyness, Depression, Tension, Psychopathic deviate, Impulsivity, Aggression). These are converted to standard scores to permit comparison with, for example, adult males in general. The more a score diverges from average, the more likely is the trait to be a dominant feature of the person's behaviour. For example, Peter was found to have rather hostile, suspicious attitudes, and was prone to depressed mood and tension. He was also inclined to be shy and introverted, controlled (low impulsivity), and unaggressive.

This kind of general picture indicates typical behavioural styles which may identify potential problem areas for treatment, but it is simply a first step in assessment, which will usually include more specific tests, such as measures of anger arousal. Observations from sources other than the offender's self-report are also obtained. In particular, structured or semistructured interviews are increasingly used in the assessment of personality disorders. These specify questions and 'probes' to elicit information relevant to the variables or traits to be assessed. One such procedure now widely used in work with offenders is the Psychopathy Checklist (PCL) developed by a Canadian psychologist, Robert Hare (Hare 1996). This consists of 20 items relating to the characteristics that distinguish psychopathic personality, for example 'conning/manipulative', 'lack of remorse or guilt', 'impulsivity', 'failure to accept responsibility for own actions'. The interviewer carries out a semistructured interview to explore aspects of the offender's behaviour and lifestyle which may demonstrate these traits and related information is also gathered from the individual's records. Each PCL item is then given a rating of 0 (clearly absent), 1 (possibly present), or 2 (definitely present), and a total score across the 20 items derived. A total of 30 or more is considered to reflect marked characteristics of psychopathy. Research has established that high scores on the PCL are associated with a greater likelihood of further offending, particularly violent offending, and this measure is now commonly included in risk assessments.

More individualized measures include structured methods such as the Repertory Grid. This examines the dominant themes in people's interpretations of their interactions by means of comparisons of perceived similarities and differences in evaluations of significant people and events. Less structured are diary records or logs, in which the person notes incidents arousing anger and aggression, and the associated thoughts and coping attempts. Finally, assessment methods not relying on self-report include observer rating scales in which staff estimate the frequency of particular behaviours, such as 'gets involved in heated arguments' or 'demands attention to his own needs', from which everyday styles of interaction can be assessed. Role-plays may also be set up in individual or group settings to examine how the person deals with provocation, and the kinds of interpretation and expectation elicited by such events.

Assessing sex offenders

The assessment of sex offenders is equally multifaceted, and requires attention to general interpersonal styles and expectations, beliefs about the victims of sexual assaults, knowledge of sexual matters (which is frequently deficient), fantasies used during masturbation, and specific skills in heterosexual interactions. Sex offenders often develop deviant preferences for children or vulnerable victims because they lack adequate skills of interacting and forming intimate relationships with adult females. These can again be assessed to some extent by diary records, role-plays, and specific self-reports.

One of the more central concerns in assessing sex offenders is the strength of interest in particular kinds of sexual partner or practice. The most valid measure of this in males is penile tumescence to sexual depictions. In *penile plethysmography*, small erectile changes in the penis are measured by means of a thin, mercury-filled rubber tube or a lightweight calliper-like device which encircles the penis, and which transmits a continuous electrical signal to a graphical recorder. Stimuli are presented under laboratory conditions, and may be slides portraying targets of possible interest, such as pictures of nude children, videotapes of varying types of sexual activity, or audiotaped descriptions. The procedure usually involves comparing tumescence to different stimuli, from which sexual preference can be determined. For example rapists often show greater arousal to portrayals of non-consenting coercive sex (usually simulations by professional actors in short videotaped segments) than to mutually consenting sexual interaction.

Penile plethysmography is clearly a sensitive procedure, which raises ethical issues about the often pornographic materials used. Psychologists in the Special Hospitals have therefore agreed a code of practice to cover the protection of the materials, informed consent of patients who participate, and the conduct of staff who administer the assessment. The method also raises practical and technical issues which have been the subject of considerable research. For example some patients can suppress their response by using distracting thoughts. While there are sometimes pressures on psychologists to use it as a 'lie detector' in cases where an offender claims to have lost his deviant interests but verification is difficult to obtain, such use is contraindicated, as well as being ethically dubious. The procedure is most useful as one component of assessment in monitoring the treatment progress of well-motivated patients.

TREATMENT INTERVENTIONS

Offending behaviour is usually only indirectly the target of psychological treatment, although there are several reports in the literature, mainly from North America, of psychological clinics specializing in specific categories of offender, such as drunk drivers, minor sex offenders, or shoplifters. It has been found, for example, that shoplifting is commonly associated with distorted beliefs about the crime (for example, 'It won't harm anyone', 'Shopkeepers deserve it'). Cognitive therapy groups have therefore been set up in which these beliefs are challenged. However, clinical psychologists in Britain are more likely to deal with such problems when they are referred to a mental health setting. Within this context, intervention needs to address the psychological variables that are functionally related to the offending behaviour. Some of these may be the emotional and social problems dealt with by clinical psychologists in other settings, but others are likely to be deviant cognitions and skill deficits common among offenders.

Psychological interventions with offenders vary with the orientation of the psychologist, which may be behavioural, psychodynamic, or cognitive. However, cognitive–behavioural approaches have dominated recent developments, and will be emphasized here. It is now recognized that to improve the likelihood of an impact on future recidivism, programmes of intervention for offenders must contain a number of inter-related elements. There is no single cause of crime and in the vast majority of cases multiple factors are involved. It follows that changing the behaviour of someone involved in persistent law-breaking will mean that a number of areas of need must be addressed. Offenders may require social skills training, but they may also display low self-control, or antisocial attitudes and values. They may additionally have concomitant problems of substance abuse, social disadvantage, and disorganized lifestyles. For each individual, the pattern of these difficulties will vary and it is essential that a careful assessment be conducted to establish the nature of risk factors and 'criminogenic needs' (personal and social factors that contribute to criminal activities). Some of the approaches developed by psychologists for carrying out such assessments and for designing appropriate forms of intervention have already been described. Outcome evidence (see below) provides empirical support for this general approach and has delineated some of the associated features of 'likely-to-succeed' programmes and services. While to date, the bulk of this work has been carried out in North America, both prison and community services in the United Kingdom have recently initiated programmatic work in which the findings of this research are being implemented.

Similar approaches have also been increasingly applied in mental health settings dealing with antisocial behaviour problems. In facilities for the learning disabled, for example, a behavioural or cognitive–behavioural approach is commonly adopted to deal with challenging behaviour. Functional analysis of the problem behaviour is a basis for positive programmes of intervention which, in order to be effective, must be tailored to the specific skill assets and deficits, and environmental opportunities both of the person involved, and of others such as relatives or carers working with him or her. Over recent years, there has been a shift of focus towards 'constructional' or non-aversive behavioural methods, and to attempts to marshal community resources in the client's interests. It has been shown that cognitive–behavioural approaches can be adapted and successfully implemented with members of this client group.

The treatment of personality disordered offenders has traditionally been viewed pessimistically. The traits of psychopathic or antisocial personalities, for example, often make them resistant to therapeutic interventions because they are unwilling to acknowledge personal deficits. However, treatment research in this area is recognized to be inadequate and there is little basis for the claim that 'nothing works' with this group. Some guidelines drawn from research on offender treatment more generally are beginning to emerge (Lösel 1998). Treatment methods based on cognitive–behavioural and psychoanalytic principles have also been applied with some success with borderline patients. However, this is an area currently in need of further research and development.

Treatment of violent offenders

Violent offenders are not homogeneous, and hence do not respond to any single treatment approach. Among those who are aggressive with some frequency, aggression may serve different purposes. A distinction is commonly made between *instrumental* aggression, in which aggression secures some desirable goal (for example in robbery), and *angry* aggression, which relieves a state of anger. For those who use aggression instrumentally, the problem is to change a style of behaviour which is maintained by rewarding consequences. In institutional settings, contingency management has been used to deal with repetitive aggression. Aggressive acts may be followed by loss of rewards or privileges, or by 'time out from reinforcement', that is brief removal from the opportunity to engage in rewarding activities. Alternative ways of attaining desired goals can also be taught. At least some aggressive offenders lack non-aggressive, assertive skills, and may generate conflict by their confrontational style. Social skills training focusing on conflict resolution has therefore been used in some programmes.

Recent approaches give greater weight to cognitive processes and the content of social beliefs. The ability to recognize interpersonal problems, generate alternative solutions, test these out, and act on the most appropriate has been found to be deficient in socially deviant populations, including aggressive delinquents. In problem solving training, everyday problems posing a barrier to the attainment of a goal (for example when someone wishes to watch a different TV channel) are examined in terms of the sequence of steps from problem recognition to resolution. Training consists of instructions and modelling, role-plays, and feedback, and may include the use of self-instructions. The aim is to generate a generalizable skill in which encounters with interpersonal problems will produce constructive resolutions rather than confrontation and aggression. Aggressive offenders also commonly hold distorted beliefs, such as that violence is legitimate, that it enhances one's image, or that victims suffer little. In group contexts, change has been achieved by having offenders develop and present arguments refuting these beliefs.

Most acts of serious violence probably involve angry aggression, although a proneness to experience excessive anger characterizes some overcontrolled offenders as well as the more habitually violent. *Anger management* is a treatment package originating in the work of an American psychologist, Raymond Novaco, which has become increasingly popular in work with offenders (Howells *et al.* 1997). The programme may be conducted with individuals, though more commonly in groups, and aims at regulation and control of the experience of anger so that it can lead to constructive interpersonal outcomes. Attention is paid to four interrelated components thought to be significant in anger arousal (Fig. 9.1): external triggering events; cognitive appraisals of these events, including the person's self-statements (private speech); anger arousal, which is experienced as tension; and behaviour when angry, which may include avoidance as well as aggression.

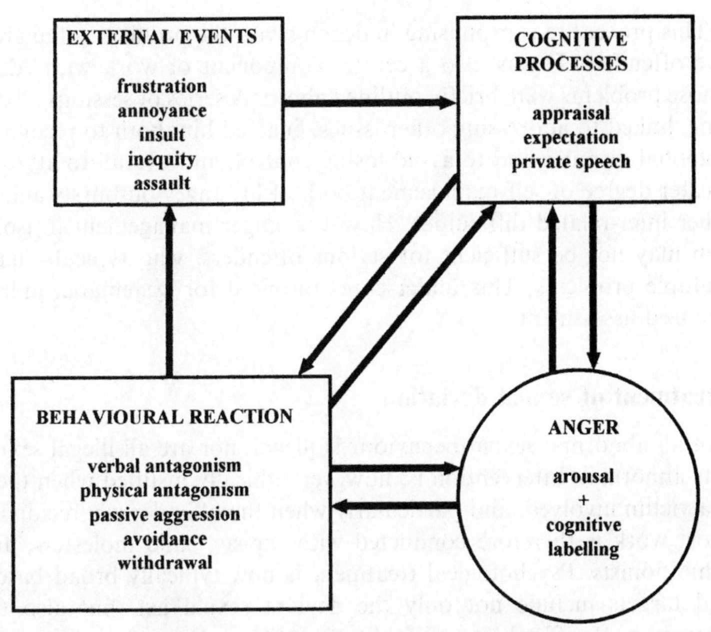

Fig. 9.1 Novaco's model of anger.

The programme proceeds through three stages. The first is *cognitive preparation*. The patient is introduced to the rationale of the programme, is given an instruction manual, and begins a diary record of anger experiences, both to facilitate awareness of the relation between anger and self-statements, and to monitor progress. Diary incidents form a basis for examining cognitions in subsequent sessions, when the conditions eliciting anger are reviewed, and distinctions made between justified and unjustified anger. At the *skill acquisition* stage, the patient is taught how to reappraise anger-eliciting events in terms of possible alternative intentions on the part of the source of anger, to shift from a personal to a task orientation in confronting difficulties, and to employ self instructions during an angry exchange. The self-instructions are statements which guide coping attempts ('can handle this'; 'Resolve the problem, not the feeling'), and provide self-reinforcement ('I'm handling this situation well'). Relaxation training is given as a further self-control skill, and skills of assertion and negotiation are taught using modelling and role-play. The third stage is *application practice*, in which developing skills are applied and tested in graded simulated anger situations.

This procedure is promising in dealing with the problems of aggressive offenders. It was also a central component of work with Alan, whose problems were briefly outlined above. A series of sessions of this type, linked to addressing other issues, enabled him both to recognize potential disputes and to avoid losing control, and overall to attain a greater degree of self-management both of his angry outbursts and of other inter-related difficulties. However, anger management in isolation may not be sufficient for serious offenders, who typically have multiple problems. This underscores the need for systematic, individualized assessment.

Treatment of sexual deviation

Not all abnormal sexual behaviour is illegal, nor are all illegal sexual acts abnormal. Intervention is, however, ethically justified when there is a victim involved, and particularly when the offender is a recidivist. Most work is therefore conducted with rapists, child molesters, and exhibitionists. Psychological treatment is now typically broad based, and targets include not only the deviant sexual act, but also the interpersonal difficulties and faulty cognitions which often support it.

Several procedures have been developed for use with individuals. The central aims of behavioural treatments are to modify sexual preferences by enhancing non-deviant arousal and reducing deviant arousal. Procedures for enhancing arousal include masturbatory reconditioning, which involves associating orgasm with non-deviant sexual stimuli. The patient is required to switch his sexual fantasies during masturbation from his arousing deviant fantasies to socially acceptable fantasies as orgasm approaches. He carries this out as 'homework' over an extended period. Fading is a laboratory method with similar aims, in which pictures of adult females are superimposed on pictures of the preferred sexual stimulus when arousal level is high, as monitored by the plethysmograph.

Reduction of deviant arousal can be achieved by chemical suppression of male hormones, although this itself does not facilitate learning of non-deviant behaviour. More common has been the use of aversion therapy, in which portrayed or fantasized deviant acts are associated with brief electric shocks or foul odours. However, this procedure raises ethical concerns, particularly when applied to compulsorily detained offenders. Covert sensitization is an alternative approach to 'compulsive' problems, based on operant principles of punishment and negative reinforcement. This relies on the patient's imagining aversive effects of the behaviour to be eliminated, rather than on the physically unpleasant stimulation of aversion therapy.

Part of the treatment programme for Gary, one of the detained offenders described earlier, aimed to deal with his indecent exposure, since his urges to expose himself persisted in hospital, and on a few occasions he exposed himself to female staff. In this case, covert sensitization began with a behavioural analysis of the sequence of antecedent events and thoughts leading to exposure and its usual consequences. Tape recordings were made portraying these events in incidents described by Gary. Certain consequences he identified as aversive (shame, physical pain, fear of arrest) were described on the tapes as occurring at critical points in the behaviour sequence. A final scenario described him exercising control over his urges early in the sequence, and the rewarding consequences of this. The tapes were played for an hour in 12 weekly sessions, and Gary also listened to them on his own between sessions. His self-monitoring of urges to expose himself revealed a decline from an average of two to three daily prior to treatment to less than one a month 6 months after treatment, and no further incidents occurred. While his urges were not completely eliminated, he described them as controllable and less powerful.

It should be noted that in Gary's case, this procedure was only one component of treatment, which also included cognitive therapy for depression, heterosocial skills training, and counselling to deal with his stubborn, self-defeating behaviour. In general, modifying sexual preferences is unlikely to have a durable effect unless accompanied by modification of wider patterns of beliefs and social behaviour. Rape, for example, is frequently associated with anger and humiliation of the victim, and may serve more of an aggressive than a sexual function, expressing hostility towards women. Additionally, a high proportion of rapists have difficulties in sexual performance, such as erectile failure or premature ejaculation, which occur in their normal sexual relations as well as during the rape. These problems are addressed by confronting attitudes towards females and sexual behaviour, by anxiety-reduction methods, and by treatment of sexual dysfunction where appropriate.

As well as the individualized treatment procedures described above, group programmes for sex offenders have also been developed by psychologists in prison settings and in the community. The largest-scale illustration of this in Britain has been the prison-based Sex Offender Treatment Programme which commenced in 1994, and which by 1997 had an intake of approaching 600 prisoners per year. This entails a series of structured sessions focusing on such issues as the causes of offending, attitudes towards victims, sexual assault cycles, cognitive distortions, and self-control of deviant sexual arousal. Given that many of the prisoners participating in this work are serving lengthy sentences, a full-scale evaluation is not yet available. In the community, several shorter, though essentially similar, programmes located mainly in probation services were evaluated in what became known as the STEP project (Beckett *et al.* 1994). Preliminary results of this project provided encouraging suggestions that those placed in the programmes were less likely to offend than comparison groups not placed in the programme.

Systematic programmes for sex offenders which have been followed up have generally been found to reduce the rate of reoffending among those treated, compared with those not receiving treatment. This is not always dramatic, particularly in the case of rapists and exhibitionists. However, psychological treatment of sex offenders, and indeed of offenders generally, is more analogous to remedial education than to medical treatment, and the notion of 'cure' as the goal is inappropriate. The most realistic goal is often to enable the offender to manage his problems without reoffending, and drawing on work from the addictions field, many programmes for sex offenders focus particularly on *relapse prevention*. This entails training the individual in self-management skills of self-monitoring and coping in high risk situations to avoid the re-emergence of previous deviant behaviour. This may require periodic support over several years. In these terms, an occasional lapse or temptation as a result of unforeseeable stress does not necessarily represent treatment failure.

The effectiveness of treatment of offenders

Not all offenders have treatable emotional or social problems, but evidence suggests that psychological disabilities among apprehended offenders are more prevalent than in the population at large. Clinical services are therefore justified whether or not these problems are the cause of offending, and this applies as equally to those receiving legal punishment as to those diverted to the mental-health system. In these terms, the effectiveness of treatment must be judged by clinical criteria of alleviating distress and disability, and not simply by effects on criminal behaviour.

Nevertheless, humane concerns for the well-being of offenders also include their future conflict with society, and the prevention and reduction of offending is both a legitimate and an expected goal of psychological services to offenders. This has been clouded by widespread pessimism about the utility of these and other professional services aimed at the rehabilitation of offenders, because of the earlier evidence that 'nothing works'.

However, evidence concerning the realistic possibility of reducing rates of offender recidivism through psychologically-based forms of intervention has accumulated steadily in recent years (McGuire 1995). In a series of meta-analytic research reviews since 1985, the 'nothing works' position has been contradicted and gradually undermined. By the mid-1990s, it was estimated that the number of controlled research studies focused on evaluation of outcomes in offender work had exceeded 700. A relatively consistent trend is observable amongst the findings of these studies. Overall, the net effect of a wide range of interventions on recidivism rates was a comparatively modest reduction of approximately 10 per cent. But some forms of intervention, particularly those based on the principle of 'deterrence' or involving increased levels of punitive sanctions, were associated with *increased* rates of reoffending. In contrast, other programmes of work which targeted individuals at high risk of reoffending, focused on their 'criminogenic needs', and employed multimodal, skill-oriented and cognitive–behavioural methods, yielded reductions in recidivism of, on average, 25 percentage points.

CONCLUSIONS

This chapter has emphasized some of the more distinctive problems dealt with by clinicians working with offenders. However, crimes occur in social contexts which provide not only stress or temptation, but also encouragement for antisocial behaviour. Psychological treatments therefore need to look beyond the individual, and support the development of new cognitive and behavioural skills in the offender's natural environment. Increased opportunities for working with antisocial behaviour problems in the community are thus likely to enhance the effectiveness of interventions.

Psychological services nevertheless represent only a part of the network of facilities provided for offenders and, given the small numbers of psychologists working in this area, it would be unrealistic to expect that the currently available services will have a major impact on 'the crime problem'. However, for every serious offence prevented, there is one less victim. This is, perhaps, an ample justification for psychological intervention.

References

Beckett, R., Beech, A., Fisher, D. and Fordham, A. S. (1994). *Community-based treatment of sex offenders: an evaluation of seven treatment programmes*. Home Office, London.

Gudjonsson, G. (1992). *The psychology of interrogations, confessions and testimony*. Wiley, Chichester.

Hare, R. D. (1996). Psychopathy: A clinical construct whose time has come. *Criminal Justice and Behavior,* **23**, 25–54.

Haward, L. R. C. (1981). *Forensic psychology*. Batsford, London.

Howells, K., Watt, B., Hall, G., and Baldwin, S. (1997). Developing programmes for violent offenders. *Legal and Criminological Psychology,* **2**, 117–128.

Lösel, F. (1998). Treatment and management of psychopaths. In *Psychopathy: theory and research and implications for society* (D. J. Cooke, A. E. Forth, and R.D. Hare eds). Kluwer, Amsterdam.

McGuire, J. (ed) (1995). *What works: reducing re-offending: guidelines from research and practice*. Wiley, Chichester.

McGurk, B. J., Thornton, D. M., and Williams, M. (eds) (1987). *Applying psychology to imprisonment*. HMSO, London.

Webster, C.D., Douglas, K.S., Eaves, D., and Hart, S.D. (1997). *HCR-20: Assessing risk for violence, version 2*. Mental Health, Law, and Policy Institute, Simon Fraser University, Vancouver.

Further reading

Blackburn, R. (1995). *The psychology of criminal conduct: theory, research and practice*. Wiley, Chichester.

Hollin, C. R. (ed.) (1996). *Working with offenders: a psychological sourcebook for rehabilitation*. Wiley, Chichester.

Howells, K. and Hollin, C. R. (eds) (1993). *Clinical approaches to the mentally disordered offender*. Wiley, Chichester.

10

Working with alcohol and drug misusers

Ray Hodgson

In 1979, the Royal College of Psychiatrists produced a special report on Alcohol and Alcoholism in which they emphasized that: 'The scenes of our concern must embrace houses, streets, offices and factories, courts and prisons as well as consulting rooms, casualty departments and hospital wards. It must include the families and children, neighbours, workmates and the other road-users who are inevitably and repeatedly going to be involved.' This statement could be directed at all clinicians working in the alcohol and drug service, including clinical psychologists. In fact, clinical psychologists tend to perceive themselves as clinical and community psychologists, since a great deal of their work is directed towards community services and community interventions. Clinical psychologists are usually involved in community alcohol teams and community drug teams, if such teams exist in their district. They also co-operate with other sectors and organizations, including education, social services, the police, probation, and employers.

Some of this work will be described in the following pages; but the first priority must be to outline the psychological model of addiction that most clinical psychologists adopt.

CHANGES IN DEFINITIONS AND THEORIES

The simple disease model of alcoholism and drug addiction suggested a dichotomous categorization into normal drinkers or drug users on the one hand and alcoholics or addicts on the other. This 'all or none' model has now been overtaken by a rather more psychological approach, which emphasizes a continuum of dependence and views drug use as an acquired, motivational state rather than a disease. This emerging psychological model embraces the following basic assumptions:

1. *Drinking and drug use is learned.* We learn about alcohol and drugs from parents, peers, books, films, and the broadcast media. Some of

the effects will be learned in this way. Others are learned through direct experience; and the likelihood that a person will have direct experience of heavy drinking or drug use will depend upon a wide range of psychosocial factors, including occupation, personality, subculture, price, and availability. Numerous direct experiences are involved, some of them powerful and others more subtle. Reducing and avoiding anxiety is one of the most frequently reported effects; and, among those who are becoming more dependent on drugs, quickly passing from an agitated state of withdrawal back to normality is a powerful reinforcing experience.

2. *Psychosocial processes are crucial.* In both social drinkers and those who are more severely dependent, it has been shown that expectations about the effects of drinking and not drinking are important predictors of behaviour (see Hodgson 1988). The excessive drinkers' expectations of positive effects from drinking predict drop-out from treatment. Furthermore, the expectation that alcohol reduces tension predicts relapse better than factors such as marital status, employment status, living environment, participation in aftercare programmes, and social support. One crucial psychological construct is perceived self-efficacy or the perceived ability to cope with reduced drug consumption. In a recent study, it was found that outcome expectancies (defined as the costs and benefits expected to result from a reduction in alcohol or drug consumption) did not predict consumption at follow-up, whereas self-efficacy expectations did. This finding suggests that an important treatment goal is to change self-efficacy expectations.

During the last 20 years, psychologists have initiated a rich vein of experimentation on the effects of expectations as opposed to the direct pharmacological effects of alcohol. The balanced placebo design has been widely used in these studies. Subjects are given either alcohol or a soft drink. In the 'given soft drink' condition, subjects are either led to believe that they are consuming alcohol (placebo) or that they are consuming soft drink. Similarly, in the 'given alcohol' condition, subjects are led to believe that they are consuming soft drink (balanced placebo) or alcohol. This design permits the separation of the effects of alcohol consumption from the effects of a cognitive set or expectation. There is a large and growing body of research which demonstrates the effect of a cognitive set on a range of social behaviour including aggression, sexual arousal, and self-disclosure.

Relapse and recovery are also strongly influenced by social factors. The available evidence indicates that social networks, marital cohesion, and job satisfaction are particularly influential. Finally, within a psychological model great emphasis is placed upon the development of cognitive self-control skills and the way in which such skills can be impaired.

3. *Learning is influenced by physiological adaptive processes.* Tolerance occurs, following drug use, when the same dose begins to have a reduced effect and, therefore, a larger dose is needed to achieve the same effect. The development of tolerance and withdrawal symptoms is usually explained by invoking the concept of an adaptive response which counteracts the effect of the drug. For example insulin produces low blood sugar, whereas the compensatory–adaptive process results in high blood sugar levels. There is now a great deal of support for the hypothesis that such an adaptive process can be conditioned to external cues and expectancies. For example some studies have looked at the effects of a placebo challenge. If an excessive drinker is led to expect alcohol but is actually given a placebo then a compensatory reduction in heart rate can be observed, rather than the drug effect which is an increase in heart rate. There can now be no doubt that adaptive processes are involved, and future debate will be about their exact contribution to dependence. At what point in a drink or drug user's career are these processes involved? Can they be reversed? To what extent are learning and conditioning involved?

AN INTEGRATED MODEL OF CHANGE

Clinical psychologists dealing with alcohol and drug misuse have been strongly influenced in recent years by the integrated model of change proposed by Prochaska and DiClemente (1986). Their model brings together three psychological domains. The first involves *stages of change*. The second covers the *processes of change*, and the third emphasizes the different *levels of change*. These three dimensions will be considered in some detail, before moving on to discuss ways of helping people to change.

Stages of change

It is often assumed that there are just two types of addict. There are those who are desperate to change, and those who have absolutely no intention of changing. According to this view the one group is given help, whereas the other group is confronted with the facts about drug misuse until they are sufficiently motivated to accept help. In fact, this view is not supported by the evidence. Motivation to change is complicated and fluctuating. Furthermore, confrontation is not usually the best method of encouraging change.

Prochaska and DiClimente (1986) have carefully researched the way in which changes occur and concluded that there are at least four stages. In the *precontemplation stage* the drug user does not intend to change in the near future. This could be because the perceived benefits of drug use still outweigh the perceived costs, often because the costs are played down through ignorance or denial. Drug users who try to change but fail sometimes slip back into this stage. The *contemplation stage* covers that period when the costs and benefits are being reappraised, and ability to cope with behavioural changes is being assessed. This stage can last a few minutes or a few years. In the *action stage* a pledge has been made, and positive steps are being taken. Finally, the *maintenance stage* begins a few months after successful change. In this stage vigilance is still relatively high, in an attempt to prevent relapse.

The following brief case description illustrates these stages, as well as the fact that there is not usually an orderly progression from one stage to the next. Stable changes are only achieved after many unsuccessful attempts.

Mr T is a successful doctor who has had to struggle with a drink and drug problem at various stages throughout his career. He went to medical school during the sixties, and started to drink excessively whilst living in a hall of residence in the centre of London. Almost every night a group of friends had three or four pints in the pub, sometimes at 10 p.m., after studying during the first half of the evening. Heavy drinking in this situation was socially accepted, even though it caused regular arguments with his girlfriend and a noticeable lack of vim and vigour in the morning. Mr T was not even contemplating change. The immediate pleasures of a carefree evening in the pub by far outweighed the delayed negative consequences. During this period he was in the *precontemplation stage*. During the next 6 to 10 years Mr T used a range of drugs as well as alcohol, and there were many times when unpleasant negative consequences forced Mr T to consider change. This *contemplation stage* would often last for days or weeks. Occasionally Mr T would be ready for action and would move into the action stage, when he set limits and planned alternative activities. More often than not he would, however, slip back from the *contemplation* or *action stage* into the precontemplation stage.

Whilst working as a junior doctor he continued to use drugs and drink heavily. He would often take a swig of whisky to get to sleep or to calm himself down. He recognized that he was risking his whole career; but his attempts to change always eventually failed, and he would then resist even contemplating change. He would slip back into the precontemplation stage, and remain there until he again reappraised the risks or discovered a new way of attempting to change. For most of the 10 years after qualifying, Mr T was in the *precontemplation stage*. Quite often he was contemplating change, sometimes he was ready for action and, occasionally, he moved into the action stage. When last seen he had been in the *maintenance stage* for several months. He now sticks to a few simple rules, and is aware that certain mood states (for example tiredness), and certain situations (for example travelling alone) are high-risk cues, and have to be given special attention.

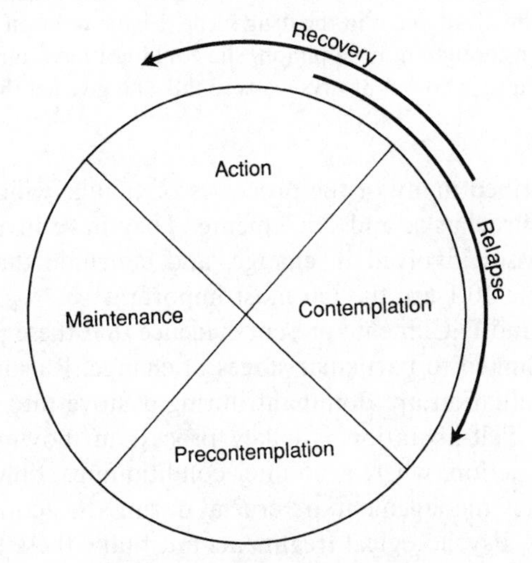

Fig. 10.1 Stages of change.

One of the mistakes that is often made when attempting to help a problem drinker or drug misuser is to assume a readiness for action and discuss coping strategies prematurely. The ambivalence of wanting to change but not wanting to change is frequently experienced, and motivation can vary from day to day. Furthermore, a person in the contemplation stage needs a different approach from a person who is ready for action. In this chapter the approaches that clinical psychologists usually adopt will, therefore, be considered as they relate to stages of change (see, for example, Miller and Rollnick 1991).

The processes of change

As a drug user moves through the stages of change, whether slowly or rapidly, different *change processes* come into play. Consider, for example, the following brief case history of a young drug user who successfully changed.

At the age of 23, after 5 years of drug misuse, Elaine was deserted by her long-standing boyfriend. He could not cope with her mood swings and could not stand her drug-using friends. This event forced her to think a great deal about her future and, during the next 6 months, she made two important decisions. First, she moved out of central London, away from her friends and haunts. Second, she signed on for a full-time course in photography. At first she resolved not to go anywhere near her friends in central London; but, after a few months, she discovered that she could occasionally visit them without being tempted to get involved again in the drug scene. Elaine went on from strength to strength, even though, in her opinion, she could not have survived without the help of an Aunty who was always ready to talk and give her the support that she needed.

Elaine described many of the processes of change which have been identified by Prochaska and DiClimente. They have investigated the various processes involved in change, and conclude that those displayed in Table 10.1 are the ten most important.

Prochaska and DiClimente present evidence that these processes are differentially linked to particular stages of change. Raising awareness and self-re-evaluation are dominant during a move into the contemplation stage. Self-liberation is a key process in moving from contemplation to action; whereas counter-conditioning, stimulus control, and contingency management are crucial during the action and maintenance stages. Psychological treatments must take these findings into account.

Levels of change

The third factor is the level or extent of change, whether produced by a psychological therapy or by natural psychological and social changes. One level is that of a circumscribed problem. For example stopping smoking with the help of nicotine chewing gum might leave untouched a whole range of psychological and social systems. The next level involves maladaptive thought patterns. The cognitive–behavioural treatment of depression would be working at this level. Interpersonal and family approaches consider even more extensive psychological systems; and it is suggested that the last level involves deep intrapersonal conflicts. One of the important decisions that a clinical psychologist has to make is the level and extent of change that is achievable.

Table 10.1 Processes of change

1. *Raising awareness*: This can be the result of a therapeutic intervention or, alternatively, a life event. Elaine was forced to face the fact that her drug misuse would almost certainly have a detrimental effect on her future social relationships.
2. *Self-re-evaluation*: Taking stock of one's current situation often precedes cognitive and behavioural changes. What are my talents and skills? What do I want to achieve?
3. *Social–environmental re-evaluation*: Elaine realized that she was locked into a social network of drug users and decided that, for her, a change of environment was called for.
4. *Self-liberation*: At some stage during change a feeling of freedom and confidence is experienced. Perceived self-efficacy, or ability to cope, is an important milestone and a predictor of future success.
5. *Social liberation*: When Elaine visited her friends in London she realized that she was now socially more skilled and was not compelled to use drugs when in the presence of her old friends.
6. *Counter-conditioning*: This process involves replacing drug use with other leisure or work activities—for example an obsession with photography in Elaine's case. At another level it is the process of counteracting craving and temptation by replacing drug thoughts with other thoughts.
7. *Stimulus control*: Avoiding powerful drug cues or desensitizing them through cue exposure is one component of the more behavioural approaches to treatment.
8. *Contingency management*: If abstaining from drugs (or sensible drinking) leads to immediate benefits then the new lifestyle will be reinforced. One year after moving out of London, Elaine was sure that a life without drugs was more rewarding than her life as a drug user.
9. *Dramatic relief*: Catharsis and conversion sometimes occur during psychological treatment, during a religious experience, or after a drug-related catastrophe. Sometimes a dramatic change in attitudes occurs after a less obvious trauma (for example an experience of impotence).
10. *Helping relationships*: Self-help groups, befriending schemes, and professional counselling are based upon the belief that it is easier to change with the help of a sympathetic friend or professional. Elaine considered this to be crucial in her case.

The integrated model described above helps to put an addiction problem in perspective and enables the therapist to ask a number of relevant questions, the main ones being:

- What stage of change has this person reached?
- What change processes should be the focus of attention?
- What is the level and extent of change that is being considered?

HELPING ALCOHOL AND DRUG MISUSERS WHO ARE NOT READY FOR ACTION

Although clinical psychologists are able to apply a range of action-oriented treatments, these have to be introduced at the right time. A common mistake, which is made by therapists of all persuasions, is to tell substance misusers how to change when they are not yet ready to change. We would not try to force tennis lessons on to a child or an adult who had no intention of playing tennis—although, of course, we might exert an influence in more subtle ways. Many people with alcohol or drug problems will want help and will co-operate; but there will also be a number of clients who are resistant to any intervention. This applies especially to advice which is given at an early stage in the development of dependence. Here are two examples from a recent World Health Organization investigation which demonstrate how difficult it can be to engage a client's motivation and co-operation in working towards behaviour change.

Example from Mexico

Mr P was a 38-year-old man who worked as a security agent. He usually had some guns with him. Mr P lived with one woman, who had three girls, but they weren't married. He did not have a regular schedule at work; sometimes he worked at night, sometimes at noon. He was very reluctant to receive any advice, since 'all that stuff is useless and the information is only for young kids who do not know what they want'. He was very aggressive during the interview. Mr P did not change at all.

Example from Bulgaria

A 48-year-old baker, married with two children had been drinking excessively for more than 20 years—mostly beer but sometimes brandy. During his first meeting with a health worker he was co-operative and didn't deny his drinking problem, but added 'I want to stop but I can't. Nobody can help me because I have no willpower. I am weak and I like drinking more than I like my wife and children. Friends forced me to stop, but I couldn't and I can't. That is all.' He still drinks too much, but now works on a farm. Otherwise, nothing has changed.

Of course, it has to be accepted that some people with drug and alcohol problems are going to resist all offers of help. Nevertheless, most people who are excessive users of alcohol or drugs are in the precontemplation or contemplation stages, and most of them do eventually try to change. This section is about ways of helping and influencing people who are not yet ready to change radically their patterns of substance misuse but are stuck in the precontemplation or contemplation stages.

Overview

The first point to make is that excessive drinkers and drug users might not be ready for action if the action means giving up alcohol or drugs, but might be ready for a range of other types of action. For example they might be ready to learn about the known effects of drugs, and the psychology of addiction. *Motivational counselling* (Miller and Rollnick 1991) draws a client into this type of discussion in an attempt to restructure attitudes and beliefs. The therapist encourages the client to see connections between substance misuse and personal problems, and attempts to gently nudge the client from precontemplation to contemplation, and possibly to the action stage. Clients might also be ready to discuss *harm limitation*. There are many methods of reducing the harmful consequences of drug misuse which might be acceptable since they do not involve giving up drugs altogether (for example switching alcoholic beverages, needle exchange). Furthermore, a client might be ready to take action and accept help in dealing with a range of drug-related *psychosocial factors* such as social skills and anxiety. Finally, one important influence, which is under the control of the therapist, is the *therapeutic style*. It has been shown that therapists who adopt an empathic, non-confrontational approach are more successful than those who rely upon warnings, threats, and confrontations. This whole approach emphasizes motivation and stages of change rather than 'cures'. A service which is only interested in cures will drive away clients who are not ready to be cured, and will demoralize therapists who have nothing to offer the contemplators and precontemplators. On the other hand, a service which focuses upon motivational counselling, harm limitation, changing underlying psychosocial factors, and developing an empathic therapist style is good for the client and good for the therapist. Clients are less likely to drop out, and therapists are less likely to burn out.

Motivational counselling and therapeutic style

The core objective of motivational counselling is to restructure beliefs and expectancies about the costs and benefits of substance misuse. This is achieved by avoiding confrontation and instead adopting the following approach:

1. Creating a supportive empathic relationship which facilitates an accurate description of drug use, drug-related problems, and the expected consequences of behaviour change.
2. Giving the client clear feedback about the relationship between drug use and personal problems, as well as the psychosocial factors which appear to be influencing drug use. Helping the client to correct any cognitive distortions that make change difficult to contemplate (for example, 'I've tried to stop six times; there is no point in trying again').
3. Helping the client to consider possible alternatives to excessive drug use and then to make decisions.

Van Bilsen and Van Emst (1989) were involved in a drug treatment service which changed from a traditional outpatient methadone clinic to an approach which revolves around motivational interviewing. They describe in Table 10.2 a number of major differences between the two approaches.

This psychological approach to drug users in the contemplation and precontemplation stages is spreading throughout the specialist alcohol and drug agencies, especially in the United Kingdom. Now is the time to direct resources towards well-designed evaluations of motivational interviewing, and especially of the effectiveness of this approach within primary health care and social work settings.

Psychosocial changes and harm reduction

Drug and alcohol abusers who are not ready to pledge themselves to total abstinence will often be willing to consider some psychosocial changes (for example developing social skills) or some harm limitation strategies. Psychological and social interventions will cover the whole range of problem areas, including the following (see, for example, Watts 1990):

Sleep difficulties	Social confidence/skills
Anxiety disorders	Obsessions and compulsions
Depression and boredom	Family and work relationships
Sexual/marital problems	Job-finding skills
Violence	Coping with frustration/craving

Table 10.2 Motivational interviewing versus a traditional approach

Motivational interviewing	Traditional approach
Denial/telling lies	
• Denial and telling lies are seen as interpersonal behaviour pattern (communication) influenced by the interviewer's behaviour.	• Denial and telling lies are seen as a personal trait of the heroin addict/junkie, requiring heavy confrontation by the interviewer.
• Lies and denial are met with reflections.	• Lies and denial are met with argument/correction.
Labelling	
• There is a general de-emphasis on labels. Confessions of being a junkie or being an irresponsible heroin addict are seen as irrelevant.	• There is a heavy emphasis on acceptance by patients that they are junkies or addicts. Self labelling or confession is often an important part of group therapy.
• Objective evidence of impairment is presented in a low-key fashion, not imposing any conclusion on the client.	• Objective evidence of impairment is presented as a dire warning, as proof of a progressive disease, and of the necessity of complete abstinence.
Individual responsibility	
• Emphasis on personal choice regarding future use of heroin.	• Emphasis on the disease of addiction, which reduces personal choice.
• Goal of treatment is negotiated, based on data and preferences.	• The treatment goal is always total and lifelong abstinence.
• Controlled heroin use is a possible goal, though not optimal for all.	• Controlled heroin use is dismissed as impossible.
Internal attribution	
• Within limits the individual is seen as able to control and choose.	• The individual is seen as helpless and totally unable to control his/her own heroin use.
• The interviewer focuses on eliciting the client's own statement of concern regarding the heroin use.	• The interviewer presents his/her own tough assessment of the evidence to convince the client that he/she has a problem.

Harm reduction approaches might involve some moderation or drug substitution. Methadone maintenance, for example, helps the drug user to keep withdrawal symptoms at bay and avoid some of the harmful consequences which are associated with purchasing and injecting heroin (for example infection, theft, and arrest). A brief period of supervised abstinence within a hospital or community setting can help to reduce harm by allowing the body to recover from many of the toxic effects of alcohol and drugs. A period of abstinence also facilitates self-re-evaluation and contemplation, as well as a general appraisal of physical health. Problem drinkers are sometimes happy to consider moderating their consumption or substituting a low alcohol beer on some occasions, even though total abstinence cannot be contemplated.

When moderation is not accepted, there are still a range of possible harm-reduction strategies. Needle-exchange schemes provide a good example. By providing drug users with a good supply of clean needles and discouraging needle-sharing there is less chance of infection, and thus the spread of AIDS will be curtailed in this high risk group.

In some families the spouse and children are repeatedly exposed to harmful and sometimes dangerous situations. One harm limitation strategy is to help them to solve some of the problems which occur during a period of excessive alcohol or drug use.

Psychosocial interventions and harm-reduction strategies can lead to health gain in the drug users and their families. They also keep the family in touch with services, so that problems can be monitored and any motivational changes can be acted upon. Attitudes towards drugs often change following a life event such as marriage, the birth of a child, or simply reaching the age of 40.

Before moving on to psychological approaches which are appropriate to the action stage, the following case described by Baldwin (1991) illustrates the way in which a precontemplator was nudged into the action stage.

Ken is a 22-year-old man who was referred by the district (magistrates') court for assessment for an Alcohol Education Course. At the time of referral, he was drinking 3 or 4 days each week, with an average intake of between 100 and 120 units during these sessions. Ken started the assessment interview by saying: 'I don't mind answering your questions, but I won't be going on the course, because I don't have a problem.' This was countered with 'It's not for me to tell you if you have a problem or not; it's up to you to decide that for yourself. Let's take a look at your drinking and see how you're doing just now.'

A detailed behavioural analysis was used to examine the functional relationship between Ken's drinking and offending. For each offence, Ken was asked about the preceding events. In particular, he was asked to focus on whether or not drinking had occurred prior to the offence. Further questions about whom he was with, doing what, where, and in what way produced this summary statement from the interview:

'Ken, what you seem to be saying is that you've been lifted five times before, and again last month. Each time you've been caught by the police, it's been after a long drinking session. Every time, you've been drinking for at least 5 hours; you've never been lifted before half-past ten, and always on a Friday or Saturday night. Gary has always been with you, and usually John as well. You've always been caught in the High Street, or in the Royal Terrace. Every time it's been because you've been making a noise in the street, or because you've damaged someone's property on the way home. What do YOU think? IS there a connection between your drinking habits and getting into trouble with the police?'

Despite a clear functional relationship between heavy drinking sessions and subsequent offending behaviours, Ken had not been aware of this. When asked, he had attributed his arrests and detention to a bias amongst police officers. This belief was also challenged, and Ken was asked to 'plot' his offences on a city map. His six offences formed a straight line between a city centre pub and his flat.

Ken's lack of insight and distorted belief system were systematically challenged during the interview. His drink-related physical health and social problems were reattributed to alcohol consumption. Ken was assisted to view his problems as an *understandable pattern* rather than a *random set of unconnected events.* He subsequently decided to attend an Alcohol Education Course to help him with his drinking and offending behaviours.

ACTION STAGE: PSYCHOLOGICAL APPROACHES TO THERAPY AND BEHAVIOUR CHANGE

A psychological model of drug misuse places a great deal of emphasis upon the high-risk personal and social events which lead to temptation, as well as the more enduring psychological states and environmental situations which can influence the way in which a high-risk event is perceived. Consider the following example:

Lorna, a female heroin addict aged 27, left hospital on a Monday morning and survived for 2 weeks without even wanting to inject. The first weekend was a very lonely and depressing experience. Her feelings of helplessness were exactly those feelings that were usually associated with a desire to use drugs. Lorna knew who to telephone to get a dose, nevertheless she did not experience a strong craving. During the second weekend her ex-boyfriend moved in with her, and although he was a drug user she had a good weekend and was not tempted.

The following week was a bad one, and resulted in a recurrence of her drug habit. She explained that on this occasion she felt very depressed and, furthermore, drugs were easily available. She could not resist the urge when she watched her boyfriend injecting.

These interactions between psychological processes, social environment, and drug availability are usually a major focus of a psychological analysis. The following are some of the examples of well-researched psychological treatments, although it should be noted that most of the research described in this section concerns alcohol dependence (see Hodgson 1994).

1. Coping skills training or relapse prevention

In principle this approach is very simple. Just as a golfer carries around a bag of clubs designed to cope with different situations, so the addict has to devise and practise coping skills to deal with high risk situations. The strategies can be attempts to avoid cues arising in the first place, or they can be methods of coping with unavoidable cues. In one study this approach was tested with hospitalized problem drinkers, although it should be emphasized that the method can also be used with problem drinkers or drug users in community settings. High-risk situations were considered under four headings, namely: frustration and anger, social pressure, negative emotional states, and intrapersonal temptation.

The intervention consisted of eight group sessions spread over a period of 4 weeks, during which specific situations were identified and ways of coping with them were discussed and rehearsed. This kind of practice led not only to an increased ability to think of coping strategies, but also to a decrease in the duration and severity of relapse episodes up to 1 year later.

Here are some examples of the cognitive and behavioural coping strategies that are commonly used:

Accepting craving: Sometimes it is difficult to do anything about craving or the urge to use drugs or alcohol, especially in social situations. One solution is to stop fighting, but recognize the fact that the craving will eventually subside. Sometimes seeing the craving as a bodily symptom, like 'flu, can help to put it in perspective. Sometimes seeing it as a storm that will pass over also helps. Whatever the image used, it has to counteract the thought that craving is an unstoppable biological process.

Social skills: In a social situation it is very easy to give in to social pressures, especially if coping strategies have not been rehearsed. It only takes a few seconds to say yes and start to inject. Saying no and providing a good reason must be rehearsed until it becomes second nature (for example, 'I'm trying to experiment to see what I'm like after 6 months without drugs'). Social skills training usually involves role-playing and real-life practice of difficult activities (for example conversation, assertion).

Social contact: Sometimes just talking to a supportive friend can help to reduce craving. Alcoholics Anonymous recognize the power of social contact, and every member has a sponsor or buddy who can be contacted if urgently needed. Psychologists sometimes make use of a similar approach.

The aim of coping skills training is to develop a range of simple coping skills and to rehearse their use in specific tempting situations until they are readily available when needed. One analogy is that of an airline pilot practising ways of dealing with emergencies.

There is good evidence that this approach is useful and effective, even though there are also numerous occasions when addicts will say: 'I knew exactly what I ought to do but 1 didn't feel like doing it.'

2. Social and marital interventions

It has been argued that if the problem drinker or drug user is interacting well with his family and community, then sobriety will be reinforced and excessive drinking will be curtailed. Trials of such a community reinforcement approach have now been completed by Nathan Azrin and his colleagues, and these suggest that increasing social and job-finding skills and improving marital relationships can have a strong beneficial effect (Meyers and Smith 1995). Although these trials involved fairly intensive work with severely dependent drinkers, many of the strategies can be used among the broad range of clients commonly encountered in community work. This community reinforcement approach is mainly behavioural or action-oriented. For example their approach to marital counselling attempted to change day-to-day interactions in such a way that both partners benefited. Twelve specific problem areas were discussed, including money management, family relations, sex problems, children, social life, attention, neurotic tendencies, immaturity, grooming, ideological difficulties, general incompatibility, and dominance. The husband and wife together constructed a list of specific activities that each would agree to perform in order to please or help the other spouse. This list typically included preparing meals, listening to the partner with undivided attention, picking up the children from school, redistributing the finances, visiting relatives together, and spending a night out together. Absolute sobriety was requested of the husbands by all of the wives as part of this agreement. For unmarried patients living with their families, similar procedures were used. For those patients living alone, attempts were made to arrange a foster family who would regularly invite the patient to their house.

The social and job counselling procedures also focused upon interactions and skills. Furthermore, a former tavern was converted into a self-supporting social club for the clients and provided a band, jukebox, card games, dances, picnics, snacks, bingo games, films, and other types of social activity. Alcoholic beverages were banned from this club, and any member who arrived at the club with any indication of having been drinking was turned away.

Changing family and community interactions is a major focus in the psychological treatment of many disorders (for example schizophrenia), since there is a wealth of evidence that psychological disorders are influenced by the social context.

3. Cue exposure

It has been argued that experiencing a strong desire to use drugs or alcohol is not unlike the compulsive urge to wash or check described by people suffering from an obsessive–compulsive disorder. Indeed, there are so many similarities that it could be argued that methods which have been successfully used to treat obsessive–compulsive disorders might be successful in treating people suffering from drug dependence. One very powerful method, usually called cue exposure, involves repeated exposure to the cues that trigger or influence the compulsive behaviour.

The evidence relating to the effectiveness of cue exposure in the treatment of drug and alcohol dependence is very promising but still not conclusive. This is an important area crying out for further research. In one series of studies directed by the author, severely dependent drinkers were given a priming dose of alcohol, in a safe environment, and then encouraged to resist consuming more of their favourite beverage. To briefly summarize this research programme, we were able to demonstrate that consuming alcohol did have a priming effect, but mainly in those who were severely dependent. We also produced evidence to support the view that this priming phenomenon is not simply related to expectancies, but is probably also a function of psychophysiological cues produced by the consumption of alcohol. After completing a number of individual case studies on cue-exposure treatment we decided to carry out a controlled study to test the hypothesis that repeated cue exposure would result in a gradual reduction of the priming effect both within and across sessions.

In this study we encouraged a number of volunteers from an Alcoholism Treatment Unit to consume a priming does of alcohol in a safe environment and then resist consuming further available alcohol. All ten volunteers were severely dependent on alcohol. Fig. 10.2 displays the combined ratings of desire to drink across six cue-exposure sessions, results which clearly indicate that a priming effect was produced, that desire for more alcohol decreased during each session, and that, after six sessions, the priming effect had almost completely disappeared. Furthermore, a similar decrease did not occur in a control condition involving only imaginable exposure.

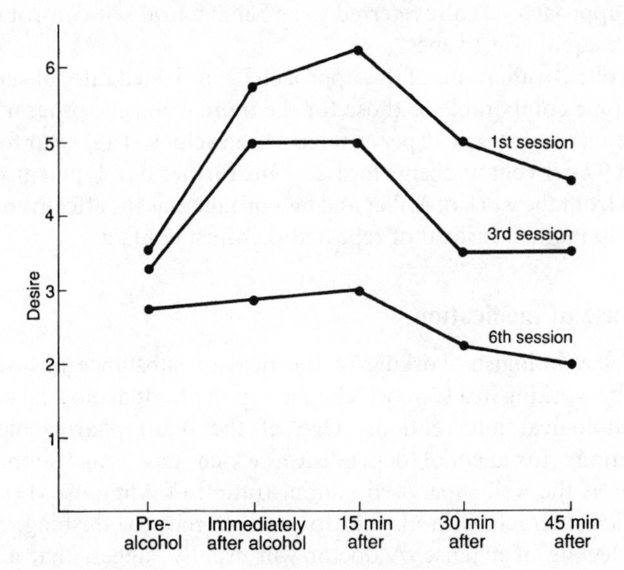

Fig. 10.2 Reduction in desire after six sessions of cue exposure.

We viewed this as a process study rather than a treatment study; nevertheless, we did demonstrate that alcoholics exposed to cues do respond in a very similar way to those who suffer from obsessive compulsive problems. These preliminary studies did not follow patients up after discharge from hospital and did not attempt cue exposure outside the safe environment of the hospital. Such a comprehensive investigation has still not been completed.

A person who is dependent on drugs or alcohol has had thousands of training trials over many years so that modifying the habit will be very difficult. Nevertheless the notion that relapse prevention approaches should ideally involve exposure to cues is still gaining support (Drummond *et al.* 1995).

4. Controlled drinking

During the 1970s there was a rapid increase in the number of research reports evaluating the effectiveness of controlled drinking as a treatment goal for problem drinkers. In general the early studies were very positive, with success rates at 1-year follow-up averaging between 60 and 70 per cent. However approaches typically used in these studies were very time consuming. Later studies have used a less time-consuming approach, usually referred to as behavioural self-control training, with equal effectiveness.

Controlled evaluations of this approach have yielded rates of successful outcome comparable to those for the more extensive programmes. Average success rates of 70 per cent have been achieved at 1-year follow-up, with 97 per cent of clients located. One further development which emerges from the work of Miller and his colleagues is the effectiveness of a self-help manual instead of repeated therapist contact.

5. The use of medication

Clinical psychologists working in the field of substance misuse will usually be working in a team which relies upon pharmacological as well as psychological interventions. One of the main pharmacological interventions for alcohol dependence, which has some supportive evidence, is the well supervised administration of Antabuse (Disulfiram) which interacts with alcohol to produce nausea, flushing, and a general feeling of malaise. A doctor will usually suggest that a third person supervises the administration. This additional support from a nurse or helper, a relative or friend, is considered to be a crucial component of this approach to treatment.

The most common approach to the treatment of opiate dependence involves the long-term use of methadone. This drug blocks, to a large extent, the euphoric effect of heroin (opiate blockade) and also reduces withdrawal symptoms. Doses above 60 to 70 mg/day have been shown to reduce the likelihood of relapse. Methadone maintenance is also linked to a reduction in crime as well as a reduction in needle sharing.

It should be emphasized that medication is only one component of treatment and one of the roles of a clinical psychologist is to advise on the need for psychological interventions.

BRIEF INTERVENTIONS

There is growing evidence that a very brief intervention, when given at the right time, can provide a cue to action. A person in the contemplation stage might need just a little more information about harmful effects or perhaps a simple way of coping with temptation. For example in one study the brief counselling was carried out by a nurse within a District General Hospital setting. In the months following discharge, patients receiving this intervention (1 hour maximum) had fewer alcohol-related problems than a randomized control group. Other studies have confirmed these results.

Clinical psychologists have been at the forefront of these developments, since stages of change and motivational interviewing are key concepts relating to the development of brief interventions. Miller and Sanchez have reviewed a number of studies which have demonstrated the effectiveness of brief interventions in reducing alcohol consumption and problems. They summarized the common components of these studies using the acronym FRAMES, which stands for: Feedback, Responsibility, Advice, Menu, Empathy, and Self-Efficacy.

The assessment of health and social status followed by FEEDBACK of results is included as a key component in most brief interventions. The feedback might be of liver functioning or of the possible link between excessive drinking and sexual, marital, social, or work problems. Personal RESPONSIBILITY for change is emphasized. The aim is to promote internal attributions of responsibility for change rather than encouraging a reliance on doctors or psychologists. ADVICE to change is a third common element. Advice given sensitively by a high-status or respected person can be 'a cue to action' and move a person from one stage of change to the next. Sometimes, advice to change is accompanied by a MENU of specific recommendations from which to choose. The counsellor or change agent's ability to EMPATHIZE with a problem drinker has been shown to influence outcome; and the development of confidence in ability to cope (i.e. SELF-EFFICACY expectations) is also important.

The proven effectiveness of brief interventions is an important finding which changes the way in which we view a comprehensive drug and alcohol treatment service. Instead of using scarce resources to proliferate hospital treatment units, the first priority must be to ensure that each community has a widespread network of low-cost interventions. These could be based within a primary care setting, a community, or a District General Hospital outpatient department. Training and advising health and social workers about low-cost psychological interventions is a key role for clinical psychologists. Pamphlets and manuals should be easily available from health centres, social services, pharmacists, and other centres involved in providing help. One main objective should be to ensure that it is relatively easy to get some advice and support directed towards changing outcome and efficacy expectancies. Higher-cost alternatives would then be developed only for clients who require more intensive help, and only when there is good evidence that such approaches are likely to be effective.

PREVENTING ALCOHOL AND DRUG MISUSE

Clinical psychologists working on drug or alcohol problems will, more often than not, be involved in advisory committees or community teams which have a wider remit than treatment and rehabilitation. District Health Authorities should be looking at the best way of using resources in order to produce maximum health gain for their resident population. Obtaining the correct balance between prevention, early interventions, treatment, and rehabilitation is a difficult task, but one that is attracting the interest of clinical psychologists. Undoubtedly more could be done to prevent drug and alcohol problems. In the previous section it has already been noted that early identification and the provision of brief interventions should be one component of a community response. But early interventions are not applicable or acceptable to every excessive drinker or drug user. Health promotion or prevention strategies must also be directed towards the wider community in an attempt to prevent problems occurring in the first place. Just one investigation will be described, which demonstrates how clinical psychologists sometimes link up with other services in order to develop and evaluate new approaches.

This investigation was carried out by a clinical psychologist and a police officer, and is based upon the hypothesis that the police can have a powerful preventive influence on drink-related problems simply by reminding both the publican and the drinker that excessive drinking can be illegal. They were able to evaluate the effectiveness of a community policing strategy which was implemented in an English seaside resort during the summer of 1978 and then withdrawn the following year. Public houses in the harbourside area of the town were visited by two policemen, and the first step was to remind licensees of their responsibilities under the licensing legislation. The licensees and the police agreed to co-operate fully in an attempt to ensure that the law was observed, particularly as it relates to under-age drinking and serving alcohol to those who are already intoxicated. During the summer months the selected premises were then visited regularly. Two or three uniformed officers amicably, but very conspicuously, checked for under-age drinking or the presence of persons who were the worse for drink. The checking was very thorough, and was designed to bring home to both staff and patrons the seriousness of their intention to enforce the licensing laws.

In order to test the effectiveness of this preventive exercise the rates of recorded crime and public order offences for the summer of 1978 were compared with those for the year before as well as the year after. Such an analysis did indeed suggest that crime in 1978 was 20 per cent less than would be expected from an extrapolation of the figures for 1977 and 1979. The implication that this change resulted from the alteration in police practice is supported by two additional pieces of evidence. First, this result was not apparent in a control town within the same tourist region. Second, the reduction in 1978 was greater for alcohol-related crimes than for those, such as burglary and theft, which are not strongly related to alcohol consumption.

This study suggests that a comparatively minor change in police practice, albeit a major change in policy, produced results which would be quite dramatic if they could be replicated throughout the world.

Of course, clinical psychologists are not employed by the NHS in order to spend all of their time influencing organizations outside the NHS. Nevertheless, enlightened NHS managers are beginning to realize that it is the responsibility of the health services to work together with other organizations in order to prevent accidents, illness, and disease. Clinical psychologists and other health professionals working on drug and alcohol problems have formed alliances with the police, probation officers, magistrates, licensees, education departments, trade unions, social services, and the voluntary sector in order to prevent alcohol and drug misuse.

NEUROPSYCHOLOGICAL IMPAIRMENT

Clinical psychologists have specific skills in psychometric testing and have, therefore, been closely involved in studying the relationships between substance misuse and cognitive impairment. More specifically, research on the effects of excessive alcohol consumption has developed very rapidly during the last 10 years.

In alcoholics, the characteristic pattern of cognitive impairment relates to tests of abstraction, memory, visuospatial ability, verbal fluency, planning and organization, and shift of set. Several groups of workers have also found impairments in social drinkers; but there is still some debate about the exact type of impairment and the cause. The continuity hypothesis is that the alcoholic Korsakoff patient, the severe alcoholic, and the heavy social drinker all suffer from similar deficits along a single continuum of alcohol-related cognitive impairment. In a recent study, investigators administered a range of neuropsychological tests that are sensitive to impairments in alcoholics to three groups of healthy male social drinkers. The subjects were divided into three groups according to their daily alcohol consumption (40 g or less, 41–80 g, 82–130 g). Subjects consuming more than 80 g per day (about 5 pints of beer) were found to be performing at a significantly lower level than the other two groups on these tests. The pattern of deficits found in these heavy social drinkers is less severe, but otherwise similar to that found in severely dependent drinkers. These impairments are also similar to those which occur during alcohol intoxication. Clinical psychologists are now paying much more attention to these cognitive deficits. In both prevention and treatment it is important to consider the psychological consequences of such impairments.

CONCLUSIONS

The role of a clinical psychologist in the alcohol and drug services is both varied and interesting. Most psychologists will be involved in assessment, psychological treatments, community interventions, prevention, teaching, and management as well as research and development. It should be added that other types of psychologist also provide a service within this field (for example, research psychologists, health psychologists, counselling psychologists). Furthermore, a great deal of psychological work is carried out by other professions. What is certain is that a clinical psychologist can bring useful skills to bear upon addictive behaviour. If we consider only the treatment of alcohol problems, the effectiveness of a psychological approach is supported by the available evidence. For example a recent review of the treatment–outcome literature for alcohol problems concluded that the following interventions have good scientific support for their effectiveness: self-behavioural marital therapy, self-control training, community reinforcement, social skills training, and stress-management training. These treatments are psychological, and were originally developed by clinical psychologists.

Although this chapter describes a psychological model which implies that treatments should be matched to clients, recently published research suggests that even the most convincing matching hypothesis should always be questioned. Project Match (Project MATCH Research Group 1997) is the largest and statistically most powerful psychotherapy trial ever conducted. A total of 1726 clients were randomly assigned to one of three psychological treatments, namely, Cognitive–Behavioural Coping Skills Therapy, Motivational Enhancement Therapy, or Twelve Step Facilitation Therapy. Ten client characteristics were assessed in order to test 16 a priori matching hypotheses (e.g. Motivational Enhancement Therapy will be most beneficial for those who are less motivated). All three treatments were associated with substantial reductions in drinking but there was only limited support for the matching hypotheses and the supportive evidence was not as simple as predicted. For example outpatient clients who were less motivated to change, ultimately did significantly better if they had received Motivational Enhancement Therapy but initially they appeared to benefit more from the Cognitive–Behavioural approach. This important study is just a first step in attempting to ascertain how treatments can be matched to client's needs. It suggests that we should be cautious but does not negate the need to tailor interventions to client characteristics.

Finally, it should be added that work in this field is sometimes difficult and frustrating. Relapse is the norm, and, to quote Mark Twain, 'You can't throw a habit out of the upstairs window. You have to lead it gently down the staircase step by step.'

References

Baldwin, S. (1991). Helping the unsure. In *Counselling problem drinkers* (eds R. Davidson *et al.*), pp. 39–57. Tavistock/Routledge, London.

Drummond, C., Tiffany, S.T., Glautier, S., and Remington, R. (1995). *Addictive behaviour: cue exposure theory and practice*. Wiley, London.

Hodgson, R. J. (1988). Alcohol and drug dependence. In *Adult abnormal psychology* (eds E. Miller and P. J. Cooper), pp. 299–317. Churchill Livingstone, Edinburgh.

Hodgson, R.J. (1994). The treatment of alcohol problems. *Addiction*, **89** 1529–1534.

Meyer, R.J. and Smith, J.E. (1995). *Clinical guide to alcohol treatment*: the community reinforcement approach. Guilford, New York.

Miller, W. R. and Rollnick, S. (1991). *Motivational interviewing: preparing people for changing addictive behaviours*. Guilford, New York.

Prochaska, J. O. and DiClimente, C. C. (1986). Towards a comprehensive model of change. In *Treating addictive behaviours processes of change* (eds W. R. Miller and N. Heather), pp. 3–27. Plenum, New York.

Project MATCH Research Group (1997). Matching alcoholism treatments to client heterogenity; Project MATCH post treatment drinking outcomes. *Journal of Studies on Alcohol*, **58**, 7–29.

Van Bilsen, H. and Van Emst, A. (1989). Motivating heroin users for change. In *Treating drug abusers* (ed. G. Bennett), pp. 29–47. Tavistock/Routledge, London.

Watts, F. N. (1990). *The efficacy of clinical applications of psychology*. Shadowfax, Cardiff, Wales.

Further reading

Beall, A.T., Wright, F.D., Neuman, C.F., and Leise, B.S. (1993). *Cognitive therapy of substance abuse*. New York, Guilford Press.

Bennett, G. (ed.) (1989). *Treating drug abusers*. Tavistock/Routledge, London.

Bonner, A. and Waterhouse, J.M. (1997). *Addictive behavoiur: Molecules to mankind: Perspectives on the nature of addiction*. St Martin's Press, London.

Orford, J. (1985). *Excessive appetites*. Wiley, Chichester.

11

Clinical health psychology in general medical settings

Dorothy Fielding and Gary Latchford

INTRODUCTION

The last 15 years have seen an unprecedented upsurge of interest in the application of psychological theory and practice to health care and physical health problems. Within psychology, this growth in interest has been demonstrated by the increasing numbers of national and international groupings of psychologists showing an interest in health and a proliferation of journals catering for the large numbers of researchers and clinicians working in this area.

There are a number of reasons for these developments. Illness and health are clearly important and interesting fields for psychologists to research, offering the possibility of producing real and significant practical benefits to patients. However, two other points are also worthy of mention. First, it is now clear that lifestyle factors, such as poor diet, smoking, and lack of physical exercise, play an important role in the causation of major illnesses, such as heart disease, cancer, and stroke. Health programmes aimed at encouraging individuals to change these behaviours are becoming standard components in primary and secondary prevention of these diseases.

Second, improvements in medical care have led to increasing numbers of patients surviving with chronic and debilitating conditions. A new set of problems has emerged for health services—that is helping these patients cope with distressing physical symptoms, a reduction in their quality of life, and sometimes a complex number of drug and other treatments. The focus for any intervention which aims to tackle these problems is invariably psychological.

Progress in health psychology research is leading to increased understanding of these issues, offering possibilities for developing therapeutic strategies aimed at changing behaviour, reducing distress, and facilitating adaptation to the demands of an illness. For example two important areas of study have been opened up by attempts to describe the experience of illness (Leventhal *et al.* 1984) and the range of coping strategies used when individuals try to adapt to lifelong illness (Moos 1995).

There have also been corresponding developments within clinical psychology. Although an interest in psychological interventions for patients with physical illnesses began more than 30 years ago, a growing awareness amongst medical practitioners of the importance of psychological factors, both in assessment for medical interventions and in the process of physical recovery following medical interventions, has led to increasing demands upon clinical psychology services.

In recent years, the number of health-related referrals to clinical psychologists has risen dramatically and the range of medical specialties seeking psychological services has widened. Moreover, in the United Kingdom, a radical reorganization of the National Health Service and the formation of Trust Hospitals in the early 1990s led, in some areas of the country, to the development of clinical psychology departments whose sole focus is to provide psychology services within acute hospital settings.

THE WORK AND WORK SETTINGS OF CLINICAL HEALTH PSYCHOLOGISTS

The work of clinical psychologists in medical settings has recently been named clinical health psychology (Belar and Deardorff 1996). In general, clinical health psychology can be thought of as the application of the theory and practice of psychology (including clinical psychology) to health and illness. In this it is distinct from the emerging profession of health psychology, which does not involve face to face work with patients, and the more established areas of behavioural medicine and health promotion, which have applied psychological concepts to the practice of medicine and prevention of ill health, respectively. Clinical health psychologists offer therapeutic and consultation services for patients and staff within a variety of health-care settings (Table 11.1).

Many clinical psychology departments, even those based in community settings, will occasionally be referred a patient who has a physical illness. For community-based departments, most of these referrals will come from general practitioners although there may be some psychologists who work in teams that specialize in the community care of patients with physical problems, such as physical disability or head injury. Community departments with links to general hospitals will also receive referrals from medical consultants.

Table 11.1 Work settings of clinical health psychologists

Setting	Examples
Community	GP Clinic Unit for physically disabled adults Head injury team
Hospital	
Anaesthetics	Pain management team Palliative care team (terminal illness)
Women's services	Assisted conception team (IVF treatment) Abortion clinic
Children's services	Paediatric intensive care Paediatric renal unit
General medicine	Diabetes outpatient clinic Cardiac rehabilitation team
Surgery	Trauma ward Cancer unit
Personnel	Staff counselling service Health promotion unit Staff development unit
Commissioning/health authority	Health education unit Public health department

However, in some areas of the United Kingdom there are also psychology services whose main focus of work is with physically ill patients These services are mostly located within large acute hospital trusts. Such departments will see patients across the age range from the very young to the elderly and psychologists will work with both inpatients and outpatients.

Inpatient referrals offer psychologists the opportunity to work with patients much closer to crisis (e.g. following road traffic accidents or sudden, life-threatening illness). Such work can be particularly challenging. For example carrying out a counselling session at a person's bedside, in ward day room, or on a dialysis unit does not afford the privacy of more usual therapeutic settings.

Many clinical health psychologists work individually with patients. For example a psychologist may be referred a patient who has chronic pain, someone who is recovering from a heart attack and is depressed, or a patient with a chronic condition such as rheumatoid arthritis who has problems adjusting to the implications and losses associated with the illness.

Some psychologists work in staff consultancy in a hospital unit or ward . For example a psychologist may be asked to facilitate a staff group on an intensive care unit to allows discussion of staff issues which, if unresolved, might impair patient care. At an organizational level, a psychologist may work with personnel managers on a project examining organizational contributions to staff stress. Yet others may work alongside health promotion staff in devising community projects to promote health and fitness. In addition to work at an individual or organizational level, clinical health psychologists will also be involved in research in collaboration with medical practitioners, surgeons, health and academic psychologists, or other members of the clinical team.

Figure 11.1 summarizes some of the influences (knowledge and skills) on the practice of clinical health psychology, the areas or setting in which practice is carried out, the levels at which interventions may be made, and the focus or function of those interventions. The following sections in this chapter provide more detailed examination of these *influences* and *applications*.

INFLUENCES — THEORETICAL FRAMEWORKS

Clinical health psychology draws upon a broad range of theories and concepts which have been applied to health and illness as well as the cognitive, behavioural, and psychodynamic models of mainstream clinical psychology mentioned earlier in this volume. For example within health psychology, the Health Belief Model (Becker *et al.* 1977) and Moos' conceptual framework (Moos 1995), which considers the role of personal (e.g. coping strategies, self-esteem) and social resources (e.g. social support, social networks) in health and illness, have all proved influential.

The Illness Representation Model (Leventhal *et al.* 1984) is a relatively new model which has attracted much academic and clinical interest. This is an attempt to examine an individual's understanding of their illness (based upon their objective experience and subjective emotional responses) and how they cope with the threat the illness poses. In this self-regulatory model people are seen as active problem solvers who are building up a picture of their illness and what they need to do to cope with it, and then evaluating their efforts at coping. The

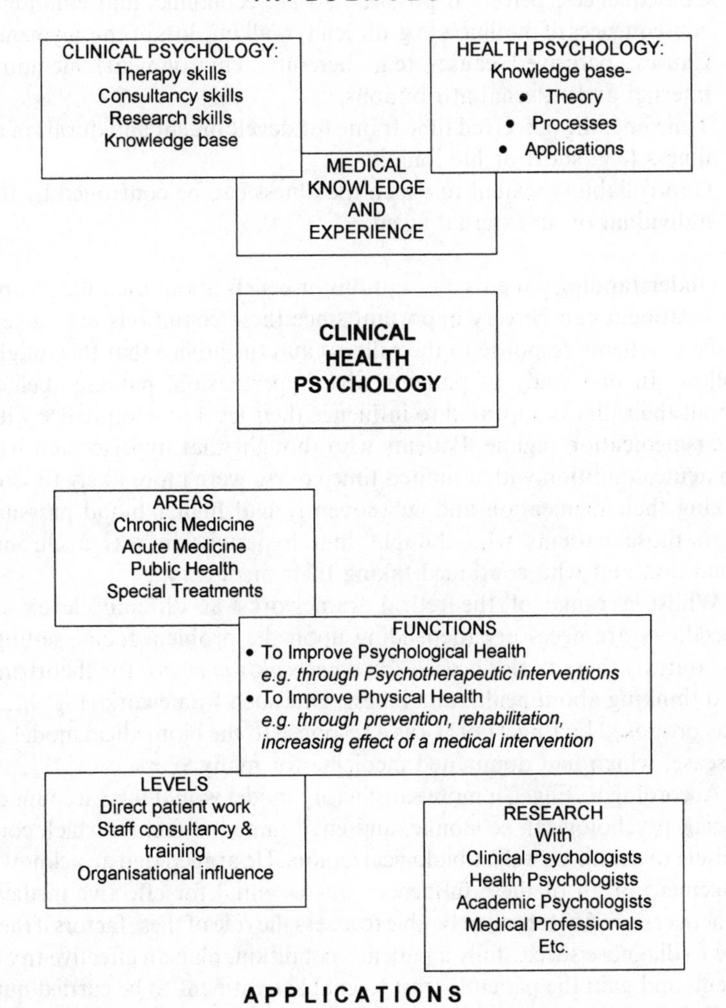

Fig. 11.1 Influences and applications in clinical health psychology.

structure of cognitive representations, proposed by Leventhal, is perhaps the best known part of the model and provides a framework for understanding individual differences in adjustment to illness. Cognitive representations commonly involve five attributes:

1. Identity: beliefs about the identity of the illness, based upon symptoms (e.g. pain), concrete signs (e.g. bleeding), and labels (e.g. heart attack).

2. Consequences: perceived physical, social, economic, and emotional consequences of the illness (e.g. difficulty walking, loss of employment).
3. Causes: perceived causes (e.g. heredity, environment) including internal and external attributions.
4. Time line: the perceived time frame for development and duration of illness (e.g. short or life long).
5. Controllability: extent to which the illness can be controlled by the individual or an external agent.

Understanding patients' perceptions or beliefs about their illness and its treatment can be very important since these cognitions may determine a patients response to their illness and the advice that they might follow. In one study of patients with hypertension, patients' beliefs about their illness appeared to influence their level of compliance with their medication regime. Patients who thought that hypertension was an acute condition with a limited time course were more likely to stop taking their medication and subsequently had higher blood pressure than those patients who thought that hypertension was a chronic condition and who continued taking their medication.

Whilst a range of theoretical frameworks at different levels of specificity are necessary (depending upon the problem focus, setting, or context) there is also a need for a *general framework* for theorizing and thinking about health and illness. One such framework (Fig. 11.2) was proposed by Engel (1977) as a response to the biomedical model of disease, which had dominated medicine for many years.

According to Engel, a more satisfactory model would take account of social, psychological, economic, and environmental factors which contribute to health, as well as biological factors. He argued that an acknowledgement of all of these influences was essential for effective medical practice, since doctors must be able to assess the role of these factors if they are to diagnose successfully a patient's condition, plan an effective treatment, and gain the patient's trust to enable treatment to be carried out.

Engel's biopsychosocial model of disease has gained increasing support in recent years since, despite the intense focus upon disease mechanisms in medical research, biological factors have failed to account for the wide variations in morbidity and mortality in different segments of the population. A critical body of evidence has begun to emerge, which clearly shows that health and socioeconomic status are intimately linked. Individuals in favourable economic circumstances are more healthy on a range of health outcome measures when compared with those in less favourable circumstances. Furthermore, this association cannot be totally attributed to variations in unhealthy behaviour, such as smoking, or a greater exposure to environmental hazards within the poorer sections of society.

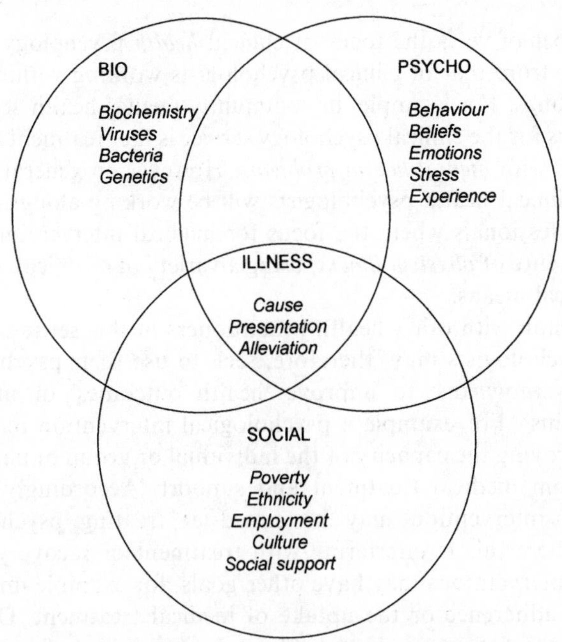

Fig. 11.2 A graphical representation of the biopsychosocial model of health and illness.

Interestingly, income distribution within society appears to be particularly important. In one study, when nine western countries (Australia, Canada, Netherlands, Norway, Sweden, Switzerland, United Kingdom, United States, West Germany) were compared on a number of health variables, overall life expectancy was found to correlate with *inequality* of income distribution within those countries. Put another way, life expectancy is greater in those countries where the poorer members of society share more of the countries wealth.

These seemingly academic issues are of great importance in the practice of clinical health psychology since the discipline must draw upon models which emphasize both social and psychological influences on health. In addition, if interventions in clinical health psychology are to be widely effective they should be capable of operating at individual, family, organizational, and community levels which take account of the multiplicity of variables contributing to ill health.

THE FOCUS OF CLINICAL HEALTH PSYCHOLOGY INTERVENTIONS

In a number of ways the focus of clinical *health* psychology services may differ from that of clinical psychologists working within mental health settings. For example, in community mental health settings, a prime focus for the clinical psychology service is the treatment and care of patients with *mental health problems*. However, in general medical settings, clinical health psychologists will be working alongside other health professionals where the focus for medical interventions is the control or cure of *physical illness*, using a variety of chemical, surgical, and physical means.

In common with other health practitioners in this setting, clinical health psychologists may, therefore, seek to use their psychological skills and knowledge to improve 'health outcomes' or maximize 'health gains'. For example a psychological intervention may focus upon improving the capacity of the individual or group of patients to benefit from medical treatment and support. Accordingly, a psychological intervention may be aimed at treating psychological distress where this is interfering with treatment or recovery. Alternatively, interventions may have other goals, for example improving treatment adherence or the uptake of medical treatment. On other occasions the focus may be to reduce the frequency of behaviours (smoking, excessive alcohol consumption) which contribute to ill health. The following section and Table 11.2 summarize the key areas for the focus of psychological interventions in clinical health psychology.

Psychological distress interfering with treatment, recovery, or affecting quality of life

Receiving a diagnosis of a serious and debilitating physical illness can be frightening and very unpleasant event. For many, the early stages of illness can be experienced as a loss of control over daily life, a feeling that may be reinforced by a period of hospitalization in which even basic freedoms such as choosing what time to sleep or eat is, to large extent, decided by others. In other senses, too, patients who are ill find themselves dependent upon others, looking towards medical staff to provide a cure, alleviate suffering, or provide some answers about what is wrong with them and what they can expect in the future.

Table 11.2 Focus and level of interventions with selected examples

Focus	Levels	Intervention examples
Psychological distress *Example: depression following a heart attack*	Individual/group	Psychological assessment Psychological therapy
	Consultancy	Input to other staff (e.g. cardiac rehabilitation team) focused on increasing psychological knowledge, giving advice on managing care, and indirect therapy work
	Organizational	Advising on provision of psychological care (e.g. psychological component in services for patients after a heart attack or angina)
Poor treatment outcomes *Example: pain and distress following surgery*	Individual/group	Preparation for surgery/counselling Pain management procedures
	Consultancy	Education of nursing staff focused on psychological methods of preparation for surgery
	Organizational	Advising on provision of psychological care (e.g. routine screening of patients undergoing day surgery and change in procedures of theatre staff)
Poor adherence to medical treatment *Example: paediatric patients on dialysis*	Individual/group	Psychological therapy using self-monitoring techniques, removal of barriers to adherence, target setting and self-generated rewards
	Consultancy	Input to other staff focused on increasing psychological knowledge, giving advice on managing care, and indirect therapy work
	Organizational	Investigate staff methods of dealing with non-adherence Advising on new methods based on psychological principles (e.g. development of child-friendly software package to provide information on weight gain and give positive feedback)
Inappropriate uptake of medical treatment *Example: patient with somatic symptoms of anxiety referred to medical services*	Individual/group	Psychological therapy as an alternative medical treatment to e.g. anxiety management strategies
	Consultancy	Input to other staff (e.g. advice on managing patients and indirect therapy work)
	Organizational	Advising on organization of services, increasing knowledge, and establishing referral routes to psychology

Table 11.2 *contd*

Focus	Levels	Intervention examples
Behavioural risk factors for illness *Example: smoking*	Individual/group	Psychotherapy/counselling for lifestyle change
	Consultancy	Input to other staff on psychological approaches to lifestyle change (e.g. teaching motivational interviewing techniques)
	Organizational	Health promotion interventions within community settings
Problems in delivery of health care *Example: staff stress leading to poor relationships with patients*	Individual/group	Counselling individual staff members
	Consultancy	Workshop for junior doctors (e.g. advice on stress and teaching self-care skills)
	Organizational	Conducting a study on factors affecting stress levels across the organization and producing recommendations (e.g. provision of staff counselling services and training packages)

It is no wonder, then, that such a threatening experience can have serious psychological consequences. Anxiety and depression are common reactions among patients who are physically ill. Prevalence rates of 25 to 30 per cent have been noted in some patient groups. Particularly at risk are patients with life-threatening or chronic, painful, disabling, and disfiguring diseases (e.g. cancer or rheumatoid arthritis). However, although such reactions are common, they may also have a significant impact upon the recovery of the patient and the effectiveness of treatment.

One example of a major, life-threatening disorder is coronary heart disease. In this condition the arteries supplying the heart with blood are narrowed by plaques of fatty substances such as cholesterol (a process known as atherosclerosis or 'hardening of the arteries'). This results in reduced blood flow and can lead to a sudden, complete blockage of an artery. If a blockage causes the death of the heart muscle being supplied by that artery, this is known as a heart attack.

Coronary heart disease is one of the major causes of premature death in the western world. Understandably, following a heart attack many patients are very anxious. However, for individual patients, anxiety will vary over time. Studies tracing the progress of patients through treatment suggest that anxiety is highest at admission to the coronary care unit and immediately after transfer from coronary care to the hospital ward. Anxiety falls rapidly over the next week, rising prior to discharge, and falling to the lowest level 4 months post discharge. Anxiety levels may rise again when uncertainty about the ability to cope with the aftermath of the illness is greatest, as for example on return to work or when symptoms such as chest pains (angina) return.

There are several powerful reasons for psychologists to be involved in work with cardiac patients. First, behavioural factors such as smoking and diet are very important in the development of heart disease. Second, psychological factors have been shown to be crucial in successfully coping with symptoms of the illness such as angina (pain caused by episodes of insufficient blood flow to heart muscle due to narrowing of arteries). The role of psychological factors can be seen clearly in relation to recovery in the brief case descriptions shown below.

Psychological factors and recovery from myocardial infarction (MI): case vignettes

Mr S. is a 49-year-old man who had his first MI 5 weeks ago. He seemed to have coped very well but his wife confides to his GP that he has been running up and down stairs each night to 'test himself out'. He is also planning a long distance walk. His wife tells the GP that her husband was very proud of his efforts to keep fit prior to his heart attack. She is worried that he will bring on another attack if he does not take things more carefully.

Mr E. is extremely anxious following his first MI a month ago and has visited casualty twice believing he was having another MI. He tends to interpret any changes in bodily symptoms (heart beating more quickly) as signs that he is having another heart attack

Mr B. is a 56-year-old long distance lorry driver who has become extremely angry and verbally aggressive to medical staff following his admission to hospital after a heart attack. He was clearly worried about losing his driving license but it was difficult for staff to tolerate or understand his behaviour which was threatening to disrupt the cardiac rehabilitation programme and impede the recovery of other patients. Much later it emerged that Mr B's last visit to hospital was when he was 6 years old and his mother had died. He was fearful of hospitals and angry with doctors for their failure to save his mother.

Following a heart attack it is quite possible for patients to improve their physical fitness even beyond pre-illness levels, yet many continue to lead restricted lives. Moreover, there is no simple relationship between the severity of the heart attack and the extent of the patient's recovery afterwards. Interestingly, some of the best predictors of how well a patient will recover—for example whether they will return to work or how often they will need further medical help—appear to be psychological. For example a patient's subjective beliefs about the cause of their heart attack, that is their 'causal attributions', have been found to predict recovery rate independent of other variables such as age, education, or disease severity.

Psychological distress is also predictive of patient recovery. Although for the majority of patients levels of anxiety and depression fall during the recovery process, for a significant minority (around 30 per cent) high levels persist. Patients with raised anxiety or depression levels are less likely to return to work, are more likely to be hospitalized, and once hospitalized are more likely to have increased lengths of stay.

Prolonged psychological stress of this nature in patients with physical illness is an important focus of intervention for clinical health psychologists. Psychological states such as depression and anxiety have many implications for successful delivery of treatment. Patients may not feel motivated to participate in an intervention such as physiotherapy, for example, and may neglect important self-care tasks such as taking medication. In addition, the relationship between patient and health professional is inevitably placed under greater pressure, and there is a risk that communication will be adversely affected.

Also important in this area is predicting those who are most likely to show such sustained reactions. For some patients, psychological problems existed before they became physically ill but for others facing stressful events with few social supports or resources is the crucial issue. The presence of good social and family support systems has been found to be predictive of good psychological adjustment in patients with cancer, rheumatoid arthritis, and diabetes, as well as those recovering from coronary heart disease. For this reason a number of clinical health psychologists have attempted to focus interventions on improving social support via community or family networks.

Psychological and physical complications in stressful medical procedures

A great many medical procedures are stressful to patients. The reasons for the stress of the procedure may vary. Some patients are concerned about the pain or discomfort that they may experience, others are concerned about a loss of control, as for example when they are anaesthetized and lose consciousness. Other procedures, such as rectal examination or urinary catheterization, may be embarrassing for some patients and therefore stressful. Some procedures may be risky or even life threatening. Yet other procedures may be simply unfamiliar to the patient and they may not know what to expect.

In addition, a patient's reaction may also be influenced by the outcome of the procedure. An otherwise quite minor surgical intervention may be experienced as stressful and painful where the outcome is uncertain and important to the patient. This may be the case where surgical procedures are undertaken to diagnose an unexplained illness or where the outcome of the surgical procedure is greatly prized, such as surgical procedures used in assisted conception treatments where couples, infertile for many years, hope that surgical interventions will eventually lead to them having a baby.

Procedures may also be stressful because they disrupt an individual's life or daily routine. In a study of children and young people with renal disease who were attending hospital three or four times a week for hospital haemodialysis, 85 per cent of patients and 70 per cent of principal carers mentioned practical problems as one of the most difficult aspects of treatment (Brownbridge and Fielding 1994). A great many practical problems were reported by parents and children. For example a great deal of time was taken up in dialysis treatment with patients and parents travelling quite long distances between hospital and dialysis centre. Parents were required to take much time away from work, with consequent financial problems, and children reported that treatment interfered greatly with school, normal play activities, family, and social life.

Whilst patient discomfort and distress are obviously important in their own right, they are potentially of even greater significance since they can influence the technical success of the medical procedure. In extreme instances, of course, a patient may be so fearful that he or she refuses to undergo the procedure at the last minute. In the case of surgical interventions, this can be time wasting and costly with loss of staff and theatre time. However, even when patients do attend, their anxiety may effect treatment making processes longer and more difficult to carry out. Inserting a dialysis needle into a vein or removing a plastic surgery dressing when a patient is tense are likely to be problematic and give rise to more pain for the patient. In addition, during surgical procedures, psychological distress will be accompanied by physiological changes which may make the patient more physically vulnerable during the procedure and therefore more likely to experience complications.

Numerous studies have now shown that patients who are anxious prior to surgery are most likely to report postoperative pain, require more analgesic medication, stay in hospital longer, and report more anxiety and depression during their recovery period. For these reasons psychological interventions aimed at reducing psychological distress before and during medical interventions are particularly important.

Poor uptake or adherence in medical treatment

Surveys of medical practitioners indicate that one of the most distressing features of their practice is the failure of patients to follow medical advice or carry through treatment regimes that have been prescribed. This may be shown in many ways including: failure to keep appointments, premature dropping out of treatment regimes, discharge from hospital against medical advice, or a failure to take medication as prescribed. Some case examples are given below.

Problems in treatment adherence: case vignettes

Ms Y. is 28 years old and was diagnosed with Type I diabetes 8 years ago. Her control has always been poor. She tries to keep her diabetes from others as much as possible and believes that a cure for it will be found very soon. She feels that she is doing her best at controlling it and that there is nothing more that she can do.

Mr T. is 18 years old and has end-stage renal failure. His illness was diagnosed when he was 11 years old. The illness developed very suddenly and he was put on hospital haemodialysis 3 weeks after the first symptoms were noticed. Two years after starting dialysis, he received a kidney transplant and although this went well at first, after only 1 year the kidney failed, damaged by the disease that had caused kidney failure in the first instance. Mr T. was put on continuous ambulatory peritoneal dialysis (CAPD) a treatment that can be carried out by the patient at home but which requires meticulous care over the sterilizing of equipment and the carrying out of 'bag changes'. Although he preferred this form of dialysis, whilst on CAPD he had several episodes of peritonitis and he had to return to haemodialysis because his peritoneum had been too badly damaged to continue with this treatment. He was referred for help because of difficulties adhering to the fluid restrictions involved in the haemodialysis regime.

Mrs C. has failed to turn up for a number of appointments at the renal outpatient clinic. Whilst her renal disease has not progressed to the extent that she requires dialysis, it is important that she attends the clinic so that staff can take blood samples and monitor her plasma creatinine levels to determine her progress and, if possible, halt the development of her disease. Staff cannot understand why she does not attend and feel annoyed by her behaviour. Following referral to the psychology department, it is discovered that she has a severe needle phobia which started when she was a child resulting from an occasion where she witnessed her father being given a wrong injection and having an epileptic fit.

Although the precise level of treatment non-adherence is difficult to determine and estimates vary, it has been suggested that on average one-third of patients fail to co-operate with medical recommendations given to them in short-term treatments. In the case of medication, some estimates are even more striking; for example it has been said that around half of all medicines prescribed to patients are not actually taken.

Studies have shown that the extent of treatment non-adherence varies considerably, depending upon: health professional variables such as the type of advice and the way that advice is given; patient variables such as the perceived severity of the illness, the perceived advantages and disadvantages associated with the behaviour change required by the medical practitioner; and social and environmental variables such as socioeconomic status or family cohesiveness.

The nature of the patients illness and the treatment regime will also be important. For acute illnesses with unpleasant symptoms which are alleviated by medication, adherence may be comparatively high. In a chronic illness, such as end-stage renal failure which requires complex, lifelong schemes of treatment including a highly restricted diet and fluid intake, adherence may be more difficult to achieve.

The effects of not adhering to treatment are well documented. Around one in five hospital readmissions are related to patients not following treatments. In many conditions, not following medical advice can have serious physical consequences. In Type I diabetes, for example, in which the body lacks insulin to break down sugars in food, the person has to monitor food intake and self inject with insulin in the right amounts and at the right time. Insulin usually has to be injected several times a day for the rest of the person's life or diabetes quickly becomes life threatening. In addition, if the amount of sugars in the blood is not kept down to a recommended level, the person faces an increased risk of a number of secondary complications (including blindness) at a later age. Even though the threat of secondary complications is distressing, very many people with diabetes struggle to follow the suggested treatment, and this pattern is repeated in many chronic illnesses.

With rates of non-adherence as high as those quoted above and the implications in terms of poor treatment outcomes and excessive costs to health-care providers, it is not surprising that clinical health psychologists are involved in interventions programmes for patients who have difficulty adhering to treatment regimes.

Inappropriate uptake of medical treatment

Patients presenting with multiple, unexplained complaints represent a huge problem for the health services. It is estimated that up to half of all medical outpatients in the United Kingdom experience bodily symptoms that cannot be explained in terms of organic pathology, and in half of these cases there is underlying anxiety and depression.

In a smaller number of patients, these problems become chronic. Around 5 to 7 per cent of the primary care population in the United States meet the criteria for a diagnosis of somatization disorder—a condition in which psychological problems are presented as physical symptoms such as fatigue, dizziness, and pain. For some patients this takes the form of hypochondriasis, a disorder in which the patient becomes preoccupied with the possibility that they have a serious disease. The usual response from medical practitioners is to offer reassurance. Unfortunately, this seldom has any lasting effect, and in many such cases patients will press for further consultations and investigations, all producing at best a temporary relief from worry.

The financial consequences of treating this group of patients may be huge. United States estimates suggest that their health-care costs are nine times the national average and one United Kingdom case report estimated that over £250,000 of surgical and medical treatment was given to one patient with a chronic somatization disorder. However, apart from these financial considerations, research has also shown that patients with somatization problems report greater disruption to quality of life than most other chronic conditions.

Research in the United States and the United Kingdom reveals that the psychological nature of these problems tends not to be detected by staff in general medical settings. Patients are often put through timely and expensive diagnostic tests which produce no useful findings and cause further disruption to the patient's life.

Somatization disorder is not the only reason for inappropriate medical treatment. Another, rarer group of patients present with dissociative (or conversion) disorders. These patients unconsciously present with quite dramatic symptoms that mimic an organic disease. Sometimes this is easy to diagnose. More often, the presentation of such patients is very ambiguous.

Other reasons for inappropriate medical treatment includes factitious disorders such as Munchausen syndrome. In this rare, but challenging, condition patients present to medical practitioners with a variety of faked and self-induced symptoms. When challenged (often after lengthy investigations and treatments) they may present at a different hospital with a new identity. A single patient may cost the health service many hundreds of thousands of pounds.

Finally, a small group of patients with body dysmorphobia (delusions about a body part, such as the size of the nose) often seek medical treatment such as plastic surgery for their perceived deformity. The needs of such patients are never met by medical intervention, the focus of the delusions simply shifting to another body part.

A major role for clinical health psychologists working in medical settings is the assessment and treatment of patients with somatization problems. Also important is assisting other staff to recognize such conditions and the development of co-ordinated systems of medical care to avoid multiple and inappropriate medical interventions.

Behavioural risk factors for illness

In recent years, increasing attention has been given to the role of lifestyle factors which may place individuals at risk for developing particular diseases. In the United Kingdom, the Health of the Nation document produced by the Government in July 1992, outlined the main targets for reduction of illness in the years up to the millennium. The five targets chosen (heart disease/stroke, cancer, HIV/sexual health, mental illness, and accidents) were radically different from those that would have been drawn up in the last century. Then, most common causes of death were infectious diseases, such as tuberculosis, which were tackled by medical interventions such as vaccination and public health interventions such as sanitation. The causes of death outlined in the Health of the Nation document are different. Heart attacks, strokes, and cancers, for example, are all multiply determined. They do not depend on the actions of an infectious agent—rather they are largely dependent upon the actions of the individual, for example whether they smoke, whether they drink alcohol, what they eat, and how much exercise they get.

Smoking is the single biggest risk factor for a number of diseases, and accounts for 30 per cent of all deaths from cancer. The Government set stringent targets. By the year 2000, the Government hoped to achieve a 33 per cent reduction in cigarette smoking and 40 per cent reduction in the overall consumption of cigarettes. By the year 2005, the following were to be achieved: 35 per cent reduction in the consumption of fatty acids; 25 to 30 per cent reduction in obesity; and 30 per cent reduction in the prevalence of drinking beyond safe limits (e.g. 21 units for men and 14 units for women).

The Health of the Nation paper, whilst not fully addressing the multiple influences on these behaviours (including powerful socio-economic factors) (Bennett and Murphy 1994) and hence the difficulty of achieving the targets, clearly emphasized the importance of fundamental lifestyle changes which are necessary to impact on the Nation's health and the primary and secondary prevention of disease .

Clinical health psychologists working in a range of settings, from primary care to acute hospitals, cannot fail to address these important domains. In this they need to work closely with a number of other health professionals including public health doctors, physiotherapists, dieticians, and experts in health promotion.

Problems in the delivery of health care

People who are ill are emotionally vulnerable. In this state, their experience of treatment is very important. Many different factors will influence this experience, from the written information they receive before an appointment to the physical environment of an outpatient clinic. Although there are a large number of factors within the health-care environment which may effect patient progress, it is useful to group them under three headings:

- communication with health-care professionals;
- the social climate of health-care settings;
- the work environment of health-care staff.

In studies seeking patients' views about the health care that they have received, the most consistent complaints are those concerned with *communication* between health-care professional and patient. There is now a substantial body of knowledge linking improved doctor–patient communication to reduction in patient distress, improved patient satisfaction with treatment, improved compliance with treatment, reduced pain, and improved rates of recovery. Nevertheless, many health-care staff are understandably cautious about giving information, particularly when it might lead to patient distress. The giving of emotionally laden information or 'bad news' is another area where there may be communication difficulties. Based upon the research findings in this area, communication skills training has become important in medical training. Clinical health psychologists involved in medical education and research in doctor–patient communication have played key roles in this area.

Although interpersonal relationships with health-care professionals are important, other factors such as the *health-care setting* (hospital wards, outpatient clinic, accident and emergency department) can be a significant source of stress for patients. Physical and architectural features, hospital or unit policies and procedures, the working practices of outpatient and inpatient units, can all have direct effects on patient care.

In one survey of four hospital inpatient wards, patients showed high rates of dissatisfaction with aspects of their ward environment (Fig 11.3). Undertaking such assessments of heath-care settings can be important as a starting point to improve patients' environment and general well being. Clinical health psychologists may work alongside nursing and other staff to find ways of improving ward procedures and facilities. Using patient views to introduce individual choice and a sense of control during hospital inpatient stays or treatment can be important in improving health outcomes.

Finally, health-care settings provide a *work environment for staff* as well as a treatment environment for patients. These two components can be closely related. Staff who feel unsupported from work colleagues or managers can find it difficult to provide supportive care for patients. In addition, high work loads can lead staff to use less-time-consuming methods of care which can reduce patient choice and control and reinforce dependency. If harnessed, staff attention and positive expectations can be a powerful factor helping to motivate patients who are in pain or distress or coping with the disabling and restrictive consequences of disease.

In recent years, there has been increasing awareness of the effects of staff stress, poor morale, and dissatisfaction with the work environment in health-care settings. In one recent study of junior hospital doctors, nearly 20 per cent were said to be suffering from 'occupational burnout' (emotional exhaustion, depersonalization, non-achievement) resulting from long working hours and being on call. Additional pressures were organizational difficulties, insecurity associated with future posts, and risks of litigation by patients (Humpris *et al.* 1994). The more junior doctors (house officers) showed greater levels of stress than more senior doctors (registrars and senior registrars).

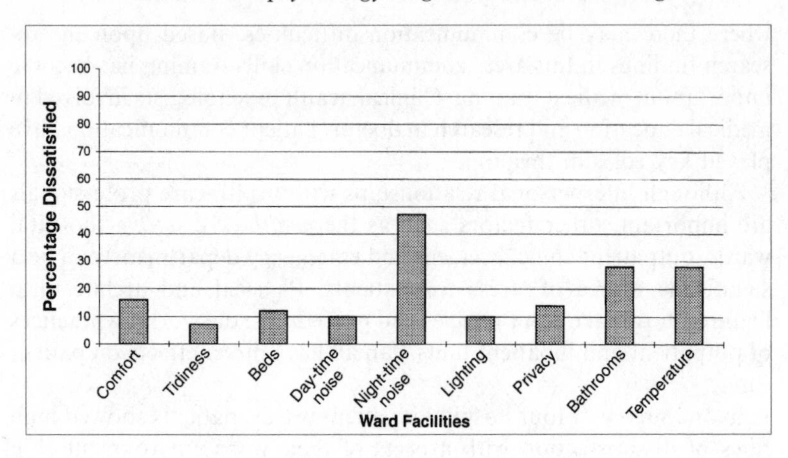

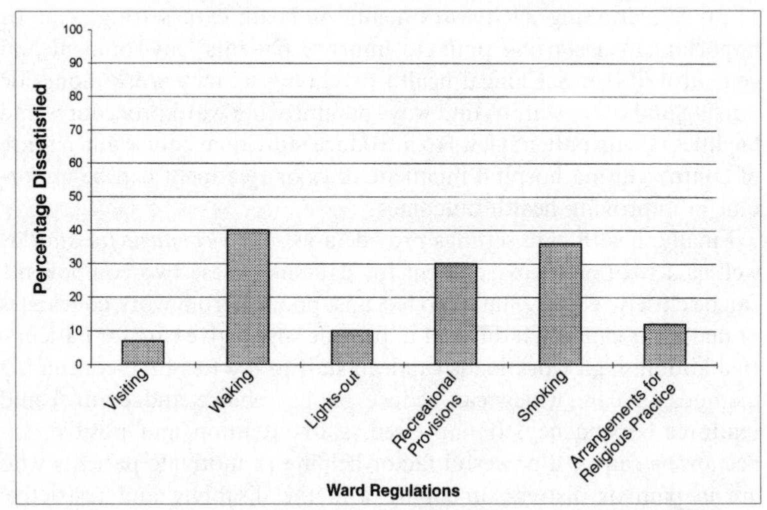

Fig. 11.3 Percentage of patients dissatisfied with each aspect of ward regulations or facilities.

Similar high levels of stress have been found for nursing staff, although the sources of stress are somewhat different. Staff with high stress levels are more likely to be dissatisfied with their jobs and are likely to show more absence through sickness than staff with lower stress levels. All of this has serious implications for a health-care system where there is growing evidence that job satisfaction in health professionals is an important predictor of job performance, patient satisfaction with treatment, and patient adherence to treatment.

The three areas described above show the importance of psychological factors in health-care settings, whilst also illustrating that the role for psychological skills and knowledge is much broader than psychological treatment of the individual patient. Clinical health psychologists are always likely to be a scarce resource within acute settings yet the need for psychological skills among health professionals is great. Psychologists, therefore, need to concern themselves with effective ways of spreading psychological knowledge and skills within the setting in which they work for the benefit of all patients who are being treated. For this reason the following sections and Table 11.2 illustrate the work of clinical health psychologists at different levels (individual, group, organization, and community).

APPLICATIONS—INTERVENTIONS

Assessment for psychological interventions

A thorough description of assessment methods in clinical health psychology is beyond the scope of this chapter. In work with individual patients, many of the assessment tools and methods described elsewhere in this volume are also appropriate. Accordingly, in an attempt to provide a formulation in an individual case, psychologists will rely upon careful interviewing and the use of a range of questionnaires to measure mood, quality of life, social support networks, coping strategies, and so on. Behavioural diaries may also be helpful in examining the frequency of illness-related problems or variations in mood (pain levels, palpitations, epileptic fits, anxiety during medical procedures). Observation can also be particularly important. A psychologist may accompany a patient when undergoing a diagnostic procedure (e.g. having a blood sample taken or undergoing a scan) or during treatment (e.g. 'needling' during haemodialysis), recording various aspects of the patient's behaviour whilst they are undergoing the procedures.

Psychologists will also draw upon a range of other, and sometimes newer, measures which are being developed in health care (Bowling 1995). One important and developing area is the *measurement of illness cognitions* alluded to earlier in this chapter. Generic assessments such as the Medical Outcomes Study Short Form or SF-36 (Ware and Sherbourne 1992) can be useful as measure of change across all clinical conditions, whilst other condition-specific measures, such as the ATT-39 assessment of emotional adjustment for diabetes (Dunn *et al.* 1986), may be used where the psychologist has a specific treatment focus.

However, there are numerous other measures in this rapidly expanding field (measurement of functional ability, health status, social networks and support, measures of life satisfaction and quality of life) which may prove useful.

Regardless of the mode of assessment, an important part of the assessment process is to decide at which level to intervene. Table 11.2 gives some examples of different levels of interventions for the same problem focus. Clinical health psychologists are a scarce resource so where problems are common (e.g. anxiety in patients following a heart attack, stress before medical procedures) it may be most appropriate to intervene at a ward or unit level. However, in some cases where the psychological problems of individual patients are particularly severe (e.g. severe phobias) it may be impossible to undertake medical procedures at all without a individual-based psychological intervention taking place first.

In other instances, a patient referral to a psychologist may be more indicative of staff difficulties within a ward or unit than the individual patient's problems. Staff who are overworked or under pressure temporarily may find it more difficult to deal with patients who are demoralized by setbacks in treatment than would usually be the case. In such instances, interventions with the staff may be more important than direct treatment of the patient.

Interventions with individual patients

Individual or group interventions for physically ill patients who are psychologically distressed, inevitably utilize similar psychotherapeutic models to those used by clinical psychologist colleagues in other specialties. Cognitive–behaviour therapy, for example, is widely used with patients with a variety of physical health conditions. Therapy for such patients does not involve denying the reality of the patient's illness. Instead, it is concerned with helping the patient to make a realistic appraisal of their situation whilst recognizing the emotional impact of the illness. With such patients, therapy may also involve an appreciation of other issues that are relevant. For example a patient experiencing the loss of freedom after becoming paralysed may also be re-experiencing earlier losses, such as loss of a parent during childhood, and it may be important to acknowledge this in the context of therapy.

In working with individual patients, Moos (1995) has stressed the importance of a conceptual framework which assesses both personal resources (self-esteem, illness cognitions coping styles) and environmental resources (life stresses, social networks, family relationships). He describes one patient with severe back pain and high blood pressure (Mrs M) where an assessment and intervention in the patient's social life was crucial to later recovery. Mrs M had become depressed following her husband's death. Assessment revealed a high number of life stresses (bereavement, sudden loss of income, failure to gain promotion at work) and an overall lack of support from children and other relatives. Although she had so far coped by detachment and avoiding confronting her difficult situation, following therapy she was able to use her coping strengths (logical analysis and seeking support) and with the help of a friend joined a women's bereavement support group. This provided opportunities to share her loss with others but also to build up a less stressful and more supportive life situation.

For patients who are making inappropriate demands on medical services the treatment approach will be different. In patients with *somatization disorder* described earlier in this chapter, emphasis may need to be placed upon the role of 'catastrophic' misinterpretation of bodily symptoms which seem to be important in maintaining the disorder. In such cases cognitive–behavioural treatment involving the identification of automatic thoughts ('I may have a stroke'; 'I'm suffocating, I'm having a heart attack'), challenging these thoughts, the use of distraction and relaxation techniques, and activity scheduling have all been found to be useful.

Over the last 10 years a number of successful individual and group psychological treatment strategies have been developed for various specific syndromes such as somatization disorder and chronic fatigue syndrome. Controlled studies show that such interventions tend to work, producing better long-term outcome than routine medical treatment. For many patients, however, a major problem remains engaging them in appropriate treatment. When somatization disorder is accurately diagnosed by medical staff, for example, patients may often be unwilling to be referred to a psychologist or psychiatrist. For such patients, a consultancy approach is the most effective use of resources. In general, management guidelines for such patients emphasize improved communication between the staff involved.

There always remains, of course, the unlikely possibility of a misdiagnosed organic illness, which means that it is essential to retain some medical contact. There is widespread acknowledgement that because such patients are so difficult to treat effectively, early prevention should be a priority

Finally, clinical health psychologists are often referred individual patients because of *poor adherence*. Much of this work involves psychological therapy aimed at helping adaptation to illness. It may be, for example, that the emotional shock of a diagnosis of a chronic disease such as diabetes produces an element of denial in which the patient will do only what is necessary to stay alive—have daily injections—but takes no care about diet or timing of injections. A diagnosis may produce strong psychological reactions such as depression, grief, or feelings of helplessness, which sap motivation to control the illness.

Notwithstanding this, adherence to complex regimes may also be difficult. In the patient with end-stage renal failure described earlier (Mr T.) treatment by haemodialysis regime involved a complex set of changes in lifestyle including:

- attendance at dialysis sessions three times per week (4 h per session);
- fluid restrictions—700 ml per day (approximately three cups);
- dietary restrictions of potassium intake (e.g. fresh fruit, vegetables nuts, and whole grains);
- dietary restrictions of sodium (e.g. salt);
- dietary restrictions of phosphate (e.g. diary produce).

It is clear that in many conditions such as this, the aims of the medical staff and the aims of the patient may be quite different. Patients may choose not to follow a treatment, balancing instead immediate gratification against long-term costs. In such cases the traditional approach of instructing the patient in what to do will simply not work. Instead, the reasons for the choices made by the patient need to be addressed, together with any practical and emotional blocks to appropriate self care being carried out.

In an approach which utilized both behavioural and psychotherapeutic methods (Brownbridge 1991) a psychologist worked with a number of patients who had difficulties adhering to their renal medical regime. The behavioural approach was collaborative in style and involved:

- education;
- review of existing strategies to decrease fluid intake;
- diary records of daily drinking patterns (including situational, cognitive, physiological cues);
- assessment of the consequences of overdrinking (physiological, cognitive, interpersonal, etc.);
- 'brainstorming' of strategies to reduce drinking (distraction, sucking ice cubes, etc.).

Evidence of the effectiveness of the psychological intervention in helping Mr T. improve his adherence to fluid restrictions is provided in Table 11.3. The table shows the number of days the patient stayed in hospital as an inpatient as a result of fluid overload and the number of days he was dialysed during the behavioural and psychotherapeutic intervention. Days in hospital decreased through treatment. Psychological distress as measured by a personal questionnaire also decreased through the duration of the project (Fig. 11.4).

Table 11.3 Numbers of days spent as a hospital inpatient as a result of fluid overload and number of days dialysed during the three phases of the study

		Phases of study (duration 6 weeks each)		
	Baseline	Behavioural	Developmental intervention (1st 6 weeks)	Follow-up intervention
Days in hospital	11	2	0	0
Days dialysed	23	20	18	21

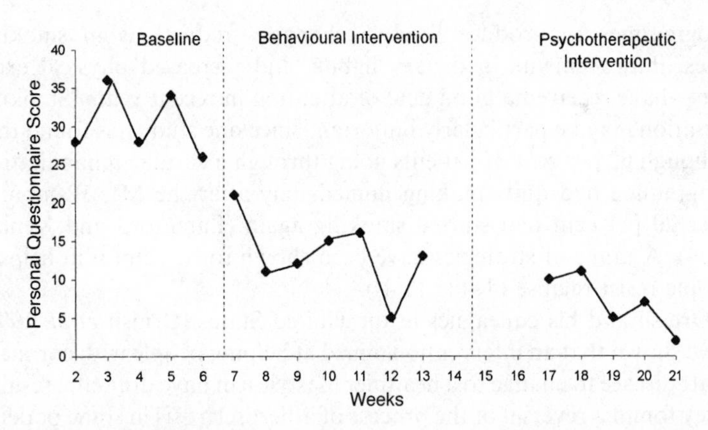

Fig. 11.4 Mr T's score on a personal questionnaire measure of overall psychosocial distress for each week of the study.

Working in teams

Clinical health psychologists may also work as part of a team of other health professionals. This may involve the psychologists offering advice on the psychological care of particular patients, offering supervision for psychological work, and training in relevant areas of psychological knowledge and practice. It may also involve joint clinical work with other professions.

A good example of joint working can be seen in a number of *cardiac rehabilitation programmes* within the United Kingdom. These are short exercise-based programmes offered to patients after a heart attack which have been shown to produce a wide range of benefits, including increased survival. Psychological changes during the programme, such as increased confidence, are well documented. Clinical health psychologists are often involved in the provision of this service.

Although recently the subject of some debate, when considered overall the evidence for effective psychological interventions for people with coronary heart disease seems overwhelming. Interventions are focused on three main areas:

- lifestyle change;
- psychoeducational interventions;
- psychological therapy for anxiety and depression.

Lifestyle change

Programmes to produce lifestyle changes—reductions in smoking rates, improvements in dietary habits, and increased physical exercise—have received a good deal of attention in recent years. Smoking cessation may be particularly important since one study has found that although 62 per cent of patients going through a cardiac rehabilitation programme had quit smoking immediately after the MI, 12 months later 20 per cent had started smoking again (Latchford and Kendal 1994). A range of strategies have been shown to be helpful in helping people resist relapse (Table 11.4).

Ornish and his colleagues in the United States (Ornish *et al.* 1990) have shown that an intervention aimed at helping people with coronary heart disease to change to a healthier lifestyle can have dramatic results. They found a reversal of the process of atherosclerosis in some patients attending an intensive programme aimed at producing substantial change in exercise and dietary habits. Patients attended for 8 h every week. Whilst such programmes are labour intensive and therefore costly, these workers have pointed out that this treatment option is much cheaper than surgery. Furthermore recent, less intensive interventions appear to achieve comparable results.

Table 11.4 Guidelines for smoking cessation

1. Use the cycle of change model	match intervention to stage of change plan for the possibility of relapse allow for the possibility of several attempts incorporate a follow-up to review progress
2. Use education	present using interactive studies acknowledge positive aspect of smoking present immediate benefits and long-term risks
3. Acknowledge social influences	invite partner to session use social support where available
4. Increase self-efficacy	emphasize understanding of why change is difficult give responsibility for change to patient let patient choose strategies
5. Use psychophysiological model of addiction/dependence	use nicotine patches etc. as adjunct if necessary use monitoring to identify difficult places, times, and situations plan for difficult situations: avoid at first, then return (gradual exposure in order to extinguish conditioned response) rehearse coping skills/strategies in advance use relaxation and cognitive skills for stress management

Psychoeducational interventions

As noted earlier, many patients hold erroneous beliefs about their heart attack. Particularly important are false beliefs about the causes of coronary heart disease and heart attacks in particular—if a patient believes that stress causes heart attacks, for example, they may have great problems in resuming their previous lifestyle. Similarly, many patients become unnecessarily phobic of activities that they believe may contribute to a heart attack, such as sexual activity. Knowledge of what the heart does and what constitutes a heart attack varies widely but can be very inaccurate. Beliefs such as a 'I will never be healthy again' are clearly unhelpful to recovery. More positive beliefs, which acknowledge the possibility of physical recovery and the role of the individual in this are much more helpful, and may avoid an unnecessary life of disability and worry. Challenging erroneous beliefs requires a sensitive intervention, and cognitive therapy seems a useful model. When adopted as part of an exercise programme (such as in the work of Bob Lewin *et al.* 1992) this approach has been shown to be extremely effective.

Psychological therapy for depression and anxiety

As noted earlier, many patients (around 30 per cent) continue to have serious psychological problems long after having a heart attack. These are not necessarily the patients whose prognosis is particularly poor or those who have had a more severe heart attack. Such patients can benefit from some of the individual psychotherapeutic approaches mentioned elsewhere in this volume, although such approaches must clearly incorporate some of the features of the psychoeducational approach mentioned above, since erroneous beliefs about the heart attack may well be contributing to the persistent psychological disturbance.

In practice, most cardiac rehabilitation takes place in groups. Although these can be very effective, the evidence also suggests that the patient's spouse and family should be involved in all aspects of rehabilitation so that social support is maximized. It also seems wise to screen all patients for psychological symptoms following a heart attack and offer individual sessions to those in need.

Another area where team working has proved fruitful is the management of *chronic pain*. There has been a growing recognition over the last 30 years that there is a limit to the effectiveness of medical treatments for chronic pain and the possibility of psychological interventions have been explored. This has come about largely because of changes in the way pain has been conceptualized. The model of pain proposed in 1965 by Melzack and Wall has been very influential since it gave recognition to the importance of central brain processes in pain perception. For example psychological factors, such as expectation, and mood states, such as depression, have been shown to play a major part in the experience of pain. This has stimulated a number of attempts to translate the model into effective psychological interventions.

The behavioural and psychological methods of pain management which followed have been subject to many well-controlled studies, which have demonstrated very clearly the effectiveness of behavioural and cognitive–behavioural techniques at reducing pain and pain-related distress. Group interventions are often used, and a common component is a graded activity programme for patients who have become less active over time in response to pain, in which they are encouraged to gradually increase levels of activity.

Clinical health psychologists who work within a hospital pain service may work alone or within a multidisciplinary pain management team, which may include anaesthetists, physiotherapists, occupational therapists, nurses, and pharmacists.

Organizational and community interventions

Earlier sections in this chapter have commented upon the importance of spreading psychological skills and knowledge to other health-care staff in order to maximize effects on patient care. Psychologists working at an organizational level may work with other health-care staff to introduce new *systems of care* or *information provision* based on psychological principles. One example of this arises in surgical settings.

Technological advances now allow many surgical techniques to be carried out through natural openings in the body (endosurgery) or through small incisions with fibre optic directed instruments (laparoscopy). Such procedures have radically transformed the nature of much surgery, which can now be undertaken with local rather than general anaesthesia and with much less medication and much shorter hospital stays. Some surgeons, concerned about high levels of anxiety among patients, have invited psychologists to work together with other staff in an attempt to improve the information and preparation given to patients attending hospital for day surgery.

Because there is often little or no chance to provide care following day surgery, presurgical interventions can be very important as a means of preparing patients for the problems they may face in the post-operative period. Such interventions should reduce anxiety and improve recovery rate. Psychologists have long been involved in evaluating the effectiveness of a variety of psychological techniques for reducing stress and producing a better outcome. Many different approaches have been described, either singly or in combination, including the provision of information about the operation or the bodily sensations that the patient is likely to feel, relaxation training, and psychotherapeutic interventions.

Does psychological preparation for surgery work? The evidence now seems very clear that it does. A variety of benefits seem to be obtained—the most significant being that patients who have preparation for surgery feel better, leave hospital sooner, and require less medication for pain than those who have not received preparation.

Organizational intervention may also be helpful in the case of staff stress. One study (Fielding and Snowden 1996) adopted a problem solving approach. These workers (a psychologist and personnel manager) enlisted senior managers support in analysing the causes of stress in the organization and in generating ideas to address the problems of stress in their own departments and in the organization as a whole. Key features of the approach were:

- to promote ownership of the results;
- to devise an interactive process where results could be fed back and solutions generated;
- to translate findings in ways that could be clearly communicated;
- to generate actions that could be practically implemented;
- to involve key managers who could take the action forward.

A group of 32 senior managers and a sample of 272 staff in an large teaching hospital took part in the project. Staff and managers were surveyed using an occupational stress indicator. The survey identified a number of sources of stress. Results were fed back to managers and staff in a number of workshops. Within the workshops, staff and managers discussed interventions to reduce stress and finally a framework for organizational stress interventions was devised (Fig. 11.5). In the final stages of the project a number of changes were introduced and the results were evaluated.

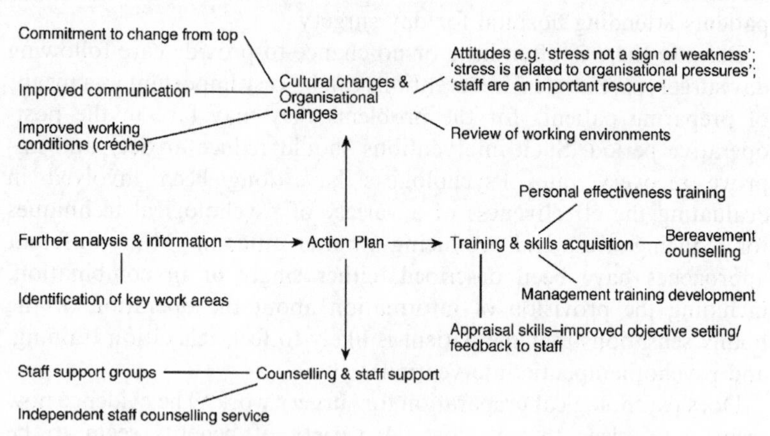

Fig. 11.5 Strategies to reduce stress levels for staff.

A continual evaluation of the organizational changes introduced to reduce stress levels appears to be particularly important. In a separate study, which addressed the issue of junior doctors hours, rota changes introduced to reduce doctors hours actually increased staff stress and reduced job satisfaction. The study showed that junior doctors levels of stress were greater when they were working in a new full shift system (8–12 h shifts) than when they were working on the traditional on-call rota (one night in six).This was surprising in view of the fact that the total hours worked in the full shift system (59.8 h per week) was less than in the on-call system (72.7 h per week). The study concluded that some 'new deal' rotas may increase psychological morbidity and reduce job satisfaction.

So far, we have not commented on community interventions in clinical health psychology. Traditionally, many clinical health psychologist have tended to focus on individual and team interventions rather than work at a community level. However, the climate of opinion is changing with growing recognition of the role of powerful social and environmental forces on health related behaviour. The present Government's emphasis on removal of social inequalities may be an important factor in helping to facilitate the development of community interventions. The recent creation of 'health action zones' may be a further impetus in this direction.

We have seen that some of the illnesses that are the main causes of death in western societies are to a large extent determined by lifestyle. If the incidence of these diseases are to be significantly reduced, then it is clear that people will need to change their behaviour. Medical professionals have been aware of this for some time. Unfortunately, whilst there is evidence to suggest that advice from a GP on smoking cessation is considered credible by patients, advice giving and confrontation is extremely ineffective at achieving behaviour change. Instead, direct confrontation tends to provoke defences in the patient, and the behaviour becomes more entrenched. Medical professionals have therefore looked to psychology for models of more successful intervention strategies.

The transtheoretical model (Prochaska and DiClemente 1984) with its associated stages of change (from precontemplation through to action and maintenance), is the most frequently cited framework for interventions in addictions, and its usefulness in other health-care settings is becoming increasingly recognized.

Nonetheless, achieving behaviour change on the scale necessary to affect the incidence of these diseases is a huge task. Two recent, large-scale attempts to induce changes to a healthy lifestyle in primary care in the United Kingdom (OXCHECK and Family Heart Study) have produced small changes which were commonly seen as disappointing by the medical profession . The future, perhaps, lies in bringing together the aims of large scale community interventions and a sophisticated model of behaviour change such as that of Prochaska and DiClemente, with associated recommendations for successful interventions targeted at the motivation to change of individual patients. However, such community interventions will also need to take into account the social context of behaviour. For instance, one study of working class women suggested that for these women smoking was a rational choice, and a way of controlling stress resulting from their adverse social and material circumstances. In socially deprived settings, community interventions will need to acknowledge and find ways of addressing the multiple variables that contribute to the maintenance of smoking behaviour.

Clinical health psychologists rarely seem to become involved in the area of primary prevention (health promotion aimed at preventing illness), though it seems to be an area in which clinical psychologists have much to offer. They are more often involved in secondary prevention (preventing a reoccurrence of an illness, such as in cardiac rehabilitation), and this may reflect current referral routes. Nevertheless within hospitals, as we have seen, there remains a great deal of scope for developments at a consultancy and organizational level; so that clinical health psychologists may become more involved in secondary prevention in the future. The hospital environment in which many clinical health psychologists work provides a 'window of opportunity', in which patients are more likely to change unhealthy behaviours than at any other time of their lives.

CONCLUSIONS AND THE FUTURE OF CLINICAL HEALTH PSYCHOLOGY

Health services are amongst the biggest employers in the western nations. They are huge organizations working within changing political, economic, and scientific contexts. Change is constant and inevitable, though often challenging. In the last 20 years, our knowledge of the psychological context of health and illness has changed; we have tried to describe some of the implications of this and the ways in which clinical health psychologists are active in reacting to, and adding to, these changes.

In many ways, medical treatment can be seen as a collaboration between doctor and patient. In such a situation, the traditional view, which sees a patient as a passive recipient of health care, is not just inaccurate, it risks missing issues which have huge implications for the physical and psychological well being of the patient and staff, and the economics of the entire health system.

To be effective, clinical health psychologists need a good understanding of: the knowledge base of health psychology, the area of medicine in which they specialize, the clinical skills which are an essential part of clinical psychology, and the wider organizational context in which they work. Many clinical psychologist are also active in contributing to this knowledge base and research is a high priority, with many opportunities for collaboration with academic health psychologists and colleagues in the health professions.

As in other specialties within clinical psychology, the field is changing and expanding constantly. Recent years have seen a number of striking developments in medical technology, for example genetic testing is now possible for a number of inherited diseases and assisted conception programmes are increasingly successful. However, these new technologies have generated new moral and ethical dilemmas with psychological consequences for those involved. Psychologists are increasingly being asked to contribute to these new areas of work and the need for psychological interventions is being recognized. For example recognizing the stressful nature of infertility treatment and the difficult treatment choices that couples are required to make, the Human Fertilization and Embryology Authority places a legal requirement upon assisted conception units to provide counselling services to all couples entering treatment programmes.

What of the future of clinical health psychology? There is undoubtedly a growing enthusiasm for the specialty within the profession, which seems to be shared by those purchasing health services. One reason for the latter is the growing evidence of the cost effectiveness of many psychological interventions within medical settings. The reason for the former, we suggest, is that the field is so interesting! Once the, sometimes, formidable requirement to become familiar with medical literature (which surpasses even the discipline of psychology for jargon) is mastered, a psychologist working in this area finds that he or she may deal with a huge variety of problems and clients, which span the whole spectrum of human experience.

References

Becker, M.H., Haefner, D.P. and Maiman, L.A. (1977). The health belief model in the prediction of dietary compliance: a field experiment. *Journal of Health and Social Behaviour,* **18**, 348–66.

Belar, C. and Deardorff, W. (1996). *Clinical health psychology in medical settings: A practitioner's guidebook* American Psychological Association, Washington.

Bennett, P. and Murphy, S. (1994). Psychology and health promotion. *Psychologist*, **7**, 126–128.

Bowling, A. (1995). *Measuring health. A review of quality of life measurement scales.* Open University Press, Milton Keynes.

Brownbridge, G. (1991). *Psychological intervention to improve treatment adherence in adolescents undergoing haemodialysis: a preliminary study.* Unpublished MSc dissertation, University of Leeds.

Brownbridge, G. and Fielding, D. (1994). Psychosocial adjustment and adherence to dialysis treatment regimes. *Paediatric Nephrology*, **8**, 744–749.

Dunn, S.M., Smartt, H.H., Beeney, L.J. and Turtle, J. R. (1986). Measurement of emotional adjustment in diabetic patients: Validity and reliability of the ATT39. *Diabetes Care,* **9**, 480–489.

Engel, G. (1977). The need for a new medical model: A challenge for Biomedicine. *Science,* **196**, (4286), 129–136.

Fielding, D. and Snowden, D. (1996). Stress in hospital staff: Research to aid management action. *Proceedings of the British Psychological Society*, **4**, 4.

Humphris, G., Kaney, S., Broomfield, D., Bayley, T. and Lilley, J. (1994). Stress in junior hospital medical staff. *NHS Management Executive (Medical Manpower and Education) Report.*

Latchford, G. and Kendal, S. (1994). Smoking cessation in cardiac rehabilitation. *Health Psychology Update,* **18**, 10–13.

Leventhal, H., Nerenz, D. and Steele, D.J. (1984). Illness representations and coping with health threats. In *Handbook of psychology and health, Vol. IV: social and psychological aspects of health* (A. Baum, S.E. Taylor, and J.E. Singer eds). LEA, Hillsdale NJ.

Lewin, B., Robertson, I., Cay, E., Irving, J. and Campbell, M. (1992). Effects of self-help post-MI rehabilitation on psychological adjustment and use of health services. *Lancet,* 339 (8800), 1036–1040.

Moos, R. (1995). Development and applications of new measures of life stressors, social resources and coping responses. *European Journal of Psychological Assessment,* **11**, 1–13.

Ornish, D., Brown, S.E., Schwerwitz, L. W., *et al.* (1990). Can lifestyle changes reverse coronary heart disease? *Lancet,* **336**, 129–133.

Prochaska, J.O. and DiClemente, C.C. (1984). *The transtheoretical approach: crossing traditional boundaries of therapy.* Dow Jones Irwin, Homewood, Il.

Ware, J.E. and Sherbourne, C.D. (1992). The MOS 36-item Short-Form Health Survey (SF-36). *Medical Care,* **30**, 473–483.

Further reading

Broome, A. and Llewelyn, S. (1995). *Health psychology: processes and applications*, (2nd edn). Chapman and Hall, London.

Nichols, K. (1993). *Psychological care in physical illness*, (2nd edn). Chapman and Hall, London.

Ogden, J. (1996). *Health psychology: a textbook*. Open University Press, Buckingham.

Sarafino, E. (1994). *Health psychology: biopsychosocial interactions* (2nd edn). John Wiley, New York.

And if you want to get a taste of clinical work, we would recommend the series of books published by the BPS on counselling for physical illness. We especially like:

Shillitoe, R. (1994). *Counselling for diabetes*. BPS Books, Leicester.

12

Clinical psychology and primary health care

John Marzillier

Clinical psychologists have traditionally worked as specialists in health care. They have been attached to hospitals, special units, or other institutions, and have applied their psychological knowledge and principles to the problems of the particular client group. In the field of mental illness, for example, clinical psychologists have often been attached to psychiatric teams, carrying out specialized assessment, and treatments (see Chapters 2 and 3). Centres for those with learning difficulties, neurology departments, adolescent units, Regional Secure Units, Special Hospitals, physical rehabilitation centres, paediatric departments, are all specialist services to which clinical psychologists have contributed a specialized service. Their work is illustrated in various chapters of this book.

However, the people seen by the various specialist services constitute only a small percentage of those who experience similar problems in the community at large. In the United Kingdom, around 90 per cent of people who consult with health problems are not referred on to specialists but are managed by GPs and other primary care workers. The significance of this is illustrated in the notion of different *levels* of care (see Fig. 12.1).

Goldberg and Huxley (1980), from whom the idea of levels of care is derived, suggest that of 250 people with psychiatric disorders found in the community (level 1) only 17 will in fact reach the specialist psychiatric services (level 4). Of these 17, only a certain indeterminate percentage will come to the attention of clinical psychologists. Goldberg and Huxley describe how between each level of care certain filters come into operation. For example between the presentation of a psychiatric disorder in primary care (level 2) and its recognition (level 3) is a 'detection filter', indicating that a substantial number of psychiatric disorders remain undetected. Equally, of those detected (level 3) only a very small number are in fact referred on to psychiatrists (level 4), indicating the operation of a 'referral filter'. Clinical psychologists also receive direct referrals of patients from GPs, and so are

	the community	primary medical care		specialist psychiatric services	
	level 1	level 2	level 3	level 4	level 5
	morbidity in random community samples	total psychiatric morbidity, primary care	conspicuous psychiatric morbidity	total psychiatric patients	psychiatric in-patients only
one-year period prevalence, median estimates	250 →	230 →	140 →	17 →	6 (per 1000 at risk per year)

	1st filter	2nd filter	3rd filter	4th filter
characteristics of the four filters	illness behaviour	detection of disorder	referral of psychiatrist	admission to psychiatric beds
key individual	the patient	primary care physician	primary care physician	psychiatrist
factors operating on key individual	severity and type of symptoms psycho-social stress learned patterns of illness behaviour	interview techniques personality factors training and attitudes	confidence in own ability to manage availability and quality of psychiatric services attitudes towards psychiatrists	availability of beds availability of adequate community psychiatric services
other factors	attitudes of relatives availability of medical services ability to pay for treatment	presenting symptom pattern socio-demographic character-istics of patient	symptom pattern of patient attitudes of patient and family	symptom pattern of patient, attitudes of patient and family delay in social worker arriving

Fig. 12.1 The pathway to psychiatric care. (Reprinted with permission, from Goldberg and Huxley 1980.)

subject to a similar filtering system to that which affects psychiatrists, or they may receive many of their referrals from specialist physicians (for example neurologists, psychiatrists), and in the latter instance be subject to yet another filter. Operating as specialists in the health-care system means that clinical psychologists will only see a fraction of the psychological problems presented by people at large. To a certain extent this protects the psychologist from being subjected to a larger volume of clients that she or he can cope with. But in other respects it results in a selective, and at times idiosyncratic, service to clients which is dependent more on the nature of the 'filters' than on the applicability of the service to particular problems or clients.

Over the past 25 years, clinical psychology has established closer and more direct links with primary health care. Some psychologists have carried out specialist treatment sessions on general practice premises. Others have forged close links with health visitors and community nurses. There have also been examples of individual psychologists working full time in primary care, serving the needs of one or more teams. In some parts of the country, the whole adult mental health psychology service is physically based in a general practice or community centre. This 'move into the community' has also been seen in the work of other mental health professionals, psychiatrists and nurses in particular. It reflects a general climate of change in mental health in which the traditional reliance on specialized care, particularly in terms of large mental hospitals, is giving way to the idea of 'care in the community'.

In the last decade, there have been very significant changes in the organization of mental health services in the United Kingdom. Political changes in the structure and funding of the NHS, begun under the last Government, have resulted in greater emphasis on, and more power to, primary care services (Department of Health 1996). GP fundholding was initiated in which general practices over a certain size were given the opportunity to hold their own budgets and to commission the specialist services they wished. This led to practices influencing the type of mental health care they felt most appropriate and, in many instances, fundholding practices employing counsellors, psychologists, or other mental health workers directly to work in their practices. Although GP fundholding was abolished by the incoming Government, on the ground that it resulted in a two-tiered system of access to specialist care, the principle of a primary-care-led service was retained.

The other significant change has been the mushrooming of community mental health teams, often organized on a locality basis serving the mental health needs of a small community. These teams consist of several health professionals working together to provide what should be a speedy and efficient service to GPs and other referrers. Clinical psychologists have become part of such teams, either directly as a member of the team, or attached to the team as a consultant, or occasionally as the manager of the team. The way this has worked is discussed later on in the chapter.

Clinical psychologists have therefore found themselves working increasingly in primary care settings and within a health service that is increasingly primary care led. This was generally welcomed at first since it freed psychologists from too close a relationship with psychiatry and allowed for greater flexibility and development in the sort of work that could be done. However there is a snag. Clinical psychology is a very scarce resource. Already hard pressed adult mental health services are at risk of being swamped by an increasing volume of work resulting in even longer waiting lists and the inability to meet the wishes of the primary care purchasers who are then likely to turn elsewhere. How clinical psychology has sought to respond to this dilemma is a theme of this chapter.

PRIMARY HEALTH CARE

Primary health care describes the nearest contact that individuals have with their local health service. It is one of a number of tiers of health care, as Table 12.1 indicates.

Table 12.1 Population size, level of care, and professional service

Population	Level of care	Professional/premises providing care
Family unit (1–10)	Self-care	Friends; non-professional helpers; (only one in four of all symptoms are taken to professional medical worker)
50–50 000	Primary	Single-handed general practitioner; group practice; health centre practice; polyclinic
50 000–500 000	Specialist	Genral hospital and specialist clinic
500 000–5 000 000	Super-specialist	Regional or super-specialist hospital or clinic

Primary health care is concerned with the delivery of services to a small, local community of up to 50 000 people. In developed countries, this is achieved through doctors, who act as 'gatekeepers' to the specialist hospital services, diagnosing and treating the vast majority of patients themselves and referring on those who need a specialist assessment or treatment.

The organization of primary health care differs from country to country. For example in some countries such as France the vast majority of doctors work single-handedly, whereas in the United Kingdom the majority of general practitioners collaborate in partnerships (i.e. groups of doctors co-operating together) or interdisciplinary teams. The funding of primary health care differs too. In a few countries, such as Denmark, New Zealand, and Britain, the service is centrally funded by government taxation. However, the majority of countries operate under a pluralist system of compulsory health insurance, private insurance schemes, and direct payment to doctors. In the United Kingdom, the primary care doctor is a generalist (hence the term general practitioner) who provides personal and medical care to individuals and families within his practice irrespective of their age, sex, and illness. But in other countries patients may call directly on specialists such as paediatricians or gynaecologists, who will have a specific responsibility for the category of patients within their area of expertise.

Primary health-care team

There has been a trend in some countries for primary-care physicians to work in collaboration with other professionals in the form of a primary health-care team. The core of the team is a group of GPs who directly employ the practice manager, secretaries, receptionists, and practice nurses. In the United Kingdom, up to 70 per cent of the salaries of these professionals can be claimed back by the general practitioner from central government. In addition, a number of other professionals work in general practice either as employees of the GPs or under their own managers. Health visitors, attached social workers, counsellors, psychiatrists, and clinical psychologists all can be found working in primary care and to a greater or lesser degree can be part of the primary care team.

PSYCHOLOGICAL PROBLEMS IN PRIMARY HEALTH CARE

What psychological problems present in primary care? This is a difficult question to answer, because the term 'psychological problems' is vague and open to many different interpretations. The Goldberg and Huxley study focused on diagnosed psychiatric disorders such as depression, schizophrenia, and anxiety. But the range of psychological problems that people have is considerable, from everyday problems of life such as marital discord, stresses at work, worries about bringing up a family, or being bullied at school, as well as major psychiatric disorders. In addition, many purely physical illnesses can have psychological consequences, for example the need to adjust to a permanent disability, the impact of a chronic illness on family and friends, or the effect of surgical disfigurement on feelings of self-esteem and acceptance by others. Fortunately, people do not perceive most psychological concerns as problems for which they seek professional help. Most people cope with their psychological problems themselves and, as far as we can tell, they cope reasonably well. This is an important point for health-care professionals to remember, since many of the minor worries and concerns that people experience will 'resolve themselves' without the need for intervention. There is some risk that professional help can have a negative effect, crystallizing ordinary worries as 'illness' or 'disorders', with the implication that remedies need to be sought in order for these apparent 'illnesses' to be treated. For example it is now well recognized that the prescription of minor tranquillizers, benzodiazepines, for anxiety has in many instances been unnecessary and potentially harmful, creating a state of psychological and physical dependency and reinforcing the view that emotional states are chronic disorders requiring treatment.

Prevalence of psychological problems

Because of the vagueness of the term 'psychological problems', it is difficult to get a clear picture of their prevalence in primary care. When GPs are asked to assess the percentage of their consultations that include psychological problems, they estimate about a quarter; but the range of estimates is large, varying from 0 to 100 per cent! In one study, a clinical psychologist sat in on 366 consultations, and he and the doctors separately rated consultations for 'psychological relevance' (McPherson and Feldman 1977). The psychologist rated 12 per cent of all consultations as 'quite' or 'highly relevant', whereas the GPs rated 18 per cent. The correlation between the psychologist's and the doctor's ratings was very low, indicating substantial disagreement about which consultations were the psychologically relevant ones.

These subjective estimates may say more about the 'psychological mindedness' of the GP rather than being a reliable or accurate assessment of psychological disturbance in primary care. Not only will GPs differ in their readiness to perceive psychological problems, but patients will vary in their readiness to present such problems to particular GPs. In this way some doctors may genuinely never be presented openly with a psychological problem, while others will be inundated with them. An alternative approach to the assessment of prevalence of psychological problems is to concentrate upon specific and discriminable categories of disorder, such as psychiatric illnesses.

Prevalence of psychiatric illness

A distinction can be made between 'formal psychiatric illnesses' such as neurosis, schizophrenia, manic-depressive psychosis, and those physical disorders or social problems with a psychological or psychiatric component. Even with regard to formal psychiatric diagnoses, estimates of their prevalence in primary care are quite variable. It has been estimated that between a quarter and a third of all illnesses treated by GPs are psychiatric illnesses, and that in one year about 14 per cent of a GP's patients will consult for psychiatric disorders. By far the most common disorders are the minor affective illnesses, that is anxiety, depression, and mixed anxiety–depressive states. Many psychiatric disorders that present in primary care will not be detected by the GP; this has been termed 'hidden psychiatric morbidity'. For example Goldberg and Bridges (1987) found that, while almost one-third of all consecutive new illnesses presenting in general practice were classifiable as psychiatric according to established diagnostic criteria, GPs rated just over half of these as 'entirely physical'. Moreover, pure psychiatric illness (i.e. without physical concomitants) was uncommon. Most psychiatric symptomatology is masked by somatic and physical complaints. Thus, although exact estimates of the prevalence of psychiatric illnesses are difficult to achieve, research has shown that these illnesses—particularly the minor affective disorders—are very common and that, further, a substantial number of them are not detected by the GP.

Mrs Barnes is an example of 'hidden psychiatric morbidity'. She consulted her GP because of persistent insomnia, and after a brief chat was prescribed sleeping tablets. However, Mrs Barnes's presenting complaint masked a more deep-rooted anxiety. She had been experiencing intrusive fantasies of harming her children, and was terrified that she might be driven, against her will, to kill them. These fantasies kept her awake at night. Her anxiety was beginning to develop an obsessional quality; she hid away knives and sharp objects, and would recite ritualistic phrases to forestall the possibility of harm occurring.

Mrs Barnes was eventually referred to a clinical psychologist, and successfully helped to deal with her anxieties. Many patients are like Mrs Barnes in that they present with a physical complaint (for example headaches, physical tension, skin problems, tiredness) which, on further analysis, reflects underlying psychological problems. These physical symptoms have been described as the patient's 'ticket of entry' to the consultation.

An alternative approach to attempts at assessing prevalence of psychological problems is to ask what sorts of problems would be most effectively dealt with by clinical psychologists. It is these problems that will then tend to be more usefully referred. Several clinical psychologists have sought to categorize psychological problems from this perspective. One of the most influential attempts has been that of Kincey (1974) (Table 12.2).

Kincey's five categories describe the broad problem areas that clinical psychologists tend to come across in their specialist work. In this way of working, the role of the psychologist is essentially that of therapist, and in a sense they are simply transferring their normal therapeutic skills to a different context (for example from psychiatric clinic to GP clinic). Surveys of GPs' attitudes to clinical psychologists suggest that these are, by and large, the problems that they would tend to refer. They also tend to want psychologists to provide a treatment service, particularly one that is brief and responsive to demand. However, important as the therapeutic service is, it represents only one of a number of ways that clinical psychologists may work in primary care.

THE WORK OF CLINICAL PSYCHOLOGISTS IN GENERAL PRACTICE

General practice has been the most fruitful ground for the work of clinical psychologists. Over the years GPs have begun referring many more patients directly to specialist psychological services, rather than through the medium of psychiatric clinics, and this has resulted in a better knowledge of what the service can provide. Closer collaboration has been achieved when clinical psychologists have worked directly in general practices providing a therapeutic service to the primary care team. The major problem however with a therapeutic service of this sort is that it will be inevitably selective and limited to some practices and not others. There are only 2,500 clinical psychologists in the United Kingdom, working in all specialties and settings. Even if all clinical psychologists stopped working for their specialist services-hardly desirable or feasible-there would still be too few psychologists to go round. This has led to psychologists examining different ways of working in general practice.

Table 12.2 Five categories of psychological problem amenable to clinical psychological intervention (adapted from Kincey 1974)

Category	Description
(a) Problems of anxiety and stress	Generalized anxiety, panic attacks, phobias, obsessional ideas or rituals, psychosomatic or stress-induced illnesses, e.g. migraine, asthma
(b) Habit disorders	Various habitual behaviours that lead to personal distress, ill-health or social problems, e.g. smoking, obesity, bulimia, problem drinking, enuresis, encopresis, drug addiction
(c) Educational, occupational difficulties or decisions	Choice or transition points throughout life-span, e.g. leaving school, change of job, retirement. Problems that arise in the educational–occupational context, e.g. study problems, lack of confidence and social skills
(d) Interpersonal–social–marital problems	Problems arising out of relationships with others, e.g. shyness, unassertiveness, marital discord, psychosexual problems, antisocial and aggressive behaviour
(e) Psychological adjustment to physical illness and other significant life events	Adjustment to psychological trauma of illness and hospitalisation. Adjustment to chronic disability. Childbirth Accident. Terminal illness. Death.

Brief specialist treatments in primary care

Most clinical psychologists working in primary health care have worked in an essentially similar way to their traditional role in a clinic setting, that is, they have carried out specialist psychological assessment and treatment on the patients referred to them by GPs. Specialist assessment consists, in the main, of the assessment of cognitive abilities by means of psychometric tests, for example the assessment of intelligence and memory. This is much less common than a therapeutic service, but it can be useful in physically handicapped or impaired patients, where a formal assessment will reveal the pattern of their intellectual abilities and disabilities. Assessment of intelligence and attainments (reading, spelling, arithmetic) can also be of value in gaining a picture of the all-round abilities of school children. (Educational psychologists, who are attached to schools, are usually the more appropriate professional group for this type of service.)

Specialist treatment has been predominantly in the form of cognitive–behavioural methods for people with emotional problems such as anxiety, depression, obsessions, and phobias, and for those with habit disorders, relationship problems, or problems in living (see Table 12.2 earlier). This approach consists of short-term treatments using psychological principles to achieve clearly defined and agreed goals. For example for an agoraphobic patient with anxieties about going out on her own, the goal might be to go to the local shopping centre on her own with the minimum of anxiety. For a patient with an eating disorder such as anorexia or bulimia, the goal might be to establish a more normal eating pattern and to modify abnormal attitudes to eating (for a fuller description of this approach see Chapter 2). Clinical psychologists working directly on general practice premises tend to spend rather less time in treatment sessions than when working in specialist clinics. In a careful study of clinical psychologists' work in general practices, it was found that, on average, a patient received 3.7 treatment sessions or about 2.5 hours treatment time (Robson *et al.* 1984). This was about half the time spent per patient in a local specialist clinic. An additional benefit of a treatment service on general practice premises is therefore that less time is spent with each patient.

The effectiveness of cognitive–behavioural therapy in primary care

How effective is a brief cognitive–behavioural therapy in a general practice setting? There have been only two controlled studies of the therapeutic work of clinical psychologists in general practice. In the first study (Earll and Kincey 1982), 50 consecutive referrals by the GPs to the clinical psychologist were randomly assigned to either treatment or control groups. Apart from patients needing to be 15 years of age or older, with no evidence of psychosis or organic brain disease, and not to be involved in any treatment elsewhere, no specific criteria for patient suitability were used. Kincey's guidelines were given to the GPs, and the majority of patients had anxiety-based problems. Patients in the treatment group were seen by one clinical psychologist, who followed a behavioural self-control approach. On average patients received 7.7 sessions of treatment over 16.3 weeks. Patients in the control group were treated in whatever ways the GP felt appropriate.

The results of this study showed that during their treatment with the psychologist, the patients took significantly less psychotropic medication than the control patients, but that there were no other statistically significant differences between the two groups (for example in terms of prescription for other medications, consultation rates, or number of outpatient attendances). At 7-month follow-up, 85 per cent of the treated patients reported that they had been helped to some extent or a great deal by the clinical psychologist. However, there were no statistically significant differences between the treated and control patients on psychological measures of emotional distress, life satisfaction, and personal control. Moreover, the differences between the groups in terms of prescription of psychotropic medication had disappeared, with the patients in the treated group tending to increase their medication during the follow-up period .

This study therefore failed to show that referral to a clinical psychologist was of clear benefit to patients. Although 85 per cent of the patients treated were satisfied with the service, and there was a reduction in the prescription of psychotropic medication during treatment, there were no significant differences between treated and control groups at follow-up. A major problem in interpreting the study is the fact that one psychologist carried out all the treatment, confounding the evaluation of a clinical psychology service with that of a particular clinical psychologist. The small numbers of patients in each group also made statistical significance between the groups difficult to achieve.

The second controlled study (Robson *et al.* 1984) avoided the methodological shortcomings of the Earll and Kincey study while following an essentially similar design. Four hundred and twenty-nine patients were randomly assigned to either a treatment group consisting of psychological treatment from one of four clinical psychologists working in the general practice, or a control group, which consisted of management by the GP. Treatment was up to a maximum of 10 weeks and, as reported earlier, averaged 3.7 sessions or 2½ hours of psychologist time. Patients were assessed on psychological measures, prescription costs, consultations, and hospital appointments at various stages after the end of treatment up to 1-year follow-up. Kincey's categorization was used, with the majority of patients having anxiety problems (47.9 per cent), interpersonal problems (17.4 per cent), and habit disorders (16.2 per cent). In addition, 13.7 per cent of patients were referred because of depression.

The results of this study were more favourable to psychological treatment. Patients treated by the clinical psychologists showed significantly greater improvement in their presenting problems than control patients immediately after treatment and up to 34-weeks follow-up. They made significantly fewer visits to the GPs during treatment and up to 24-weeks follow-up, and received significantly less psychotropic medication during treatment and up to 1-year follow-up. Control patients improved steadily over time, but at a lesser rate than those treated by the psychologists; at 1-year follow-up the control did not differ significantly from the treated group on most measures except for the cost of psychotropic medication (higher for controls). Robson *et al.* (1984) concluded that the patients treated by clinical psychologists in this study showed an accelerated improvement compared to controls, with less frequent consultations and less expenditure on medication. Results, therefore, supported the value of a clinical psychologist service in a general practice setting.

The research described above suggests that, for the most part, some psychological problems presenting in general practice resolve themselves over time, albeit more slowly than with psychological help. This may well be true for the milder types of problems, but is not necessarily true for others. In evaluating their clinical psychology service Milne and Souter (1988) found that while on a waiting-list patients showed little or no improvement, but made significant gains during and after cognitive–behavioural treatment. They suggested that for more chronic and difficult problems psychological treatment is necessary.

This point is important in view of recent developments in the United Kingdom with regard to the seriously mentally ill. The Government has made the treatment of the seriously mentally ill a priority, with the result that mental health workers, including clinical psychologists and those working in community mental health teams, have had to direct their time and efforts to this much more difficult group. Whether brief interventions such as cognitive–behavioural therapy are helpful for this group of patients is uncertain. In fact where cognitive–behavioural therapy has been applied to more severe psychological problems such as personality disorders, treatment has tended to be longer, for example one to two years of once weekly therapy. If clinical psychologists working in primary care find themselves seeing more severely disturbed patients for longer periods of time, what happens to the anxious and depressed patients that up to now they have helped? What seems to have happened is that GPs, particularly those who have had control of their own budgets, have employed counsellors instead.

Counselling and counselling psychology

In the last five years, there has been a huge increase in counsellors working in general practices to the extent that about half of all practices in the United Kingdom have a counsellor attached to them in one form or another. Many have been employed directly by the GPs while others have been employed by clinical psychology agencies to work alongside psychologists. One value of counsellors to financially pressed purchasers is that they cost less than clinical psychologists. Unlike psychologists who have other managerial, teaching, and administrative responsibilities, counsellors spend almost 100 per cent of their time in direct client contact. Therefore, they seem better value for money. However, this assumes that counsellors can provide a similar service to clinical psychologists and that there work is of proven effectiveness. A survey of outcome studies of counselling in primary care showed that most studies failed to demonstrate positive benefits for counselling (Roth and Fonagy 1996). Only when counselling was directed at a specific target (e.g. postnatal depression) or based upon a specific model of therapy (e.g. interpersonal psychotherapy) were clear benefits shown.

While a few clinical psychologists have reacted against the employment of counsellors in primary care, most have embraced this development, recognizing it as an inevitable product of market forces in a changing health service. Those with a longer memory recall the hostility of many psychiatrists to the rise of clinical psychology and do not wish to engage in the same professional defensiveness. There are also significant advantages to be gained for both parties when counsellors work within a clinical psychology service, as shown by Shillitoe and Hall (1997). Counsellors can benefit from being part of an organized service with regular meetings, supervision, training opportunities, etc. Clinical psychologists can gain from contact with professionals with a high level of therapeutic expertise and experience of one-to-one work. The recent creation of a Division of Counselling Psychology within the British Psychological Society has resulted in a new profession of Counselling Psychologists combining a theoretical background in academic psychology with a highly structured and personalized training in therapeutic work. It remains to be seen whether this new profession provides a significant challenge to clinical psychology (see Chapter 14).

Consultancy and collaborative work

A clinical psychologist may work collaboratively with GPs and other members of the primary health-care team, either by working together with them on individual cases or by carrying out specific projects. There are some obvious advantages to a collaborative approach, not least of which is the fact that it makes more efficient use of clinical psychologists' time and skills. Consultation between clinical psychologists and primary care workers can be at various levels. At its simplest, there may be informal meetings over coffee and lunch in which cases are discussed, possible referrals mooted, and information about treatment (medical and psychological) shared. A step up from this is joint work on individual cases (for example marital disorders, sex therapy), in running a group, or in family therapy. Deys *et al.* (1989) described a collaborative project between clinical psychologists and a GP, taking a family systems perspective and team approach to treatment. As part of ongoing therapeutic work with families, the therapist (sometimes the GP, at other times the psychologist) was observed by other team members through a one-way screen. Immediate consultation was available when the therapist desired it. Team consultation of this sort is standard practice in a family systems approach, and has the advantage of immediate and specific clinical relevance. At another level, clinical psychologists have run training courses or workshops for GPs and other primary care workers with the aim of teaching specific skills. One example is the teaching of anxiety-management skills (relaxation, target-setting, planned practice) to primary care workers with the aim of their using these skills as an alternative to medication or simple advice. Care must be taken to evaluate how effective primary care workers are in the use of such skills.

Working with health visitors

A good example of collaborative work is that between child clinical psychologists and health visitors. This can take the form of joint work, as for example running a group for parents of preschool children with sleeping difficulties. Sleep problems in preschool children are quite common, and consist of difficulties in settling, frequent waking, and disturbances to sleep routines, for example being taken into the parents' bed. While many parents will cope without help, others find the disturbance to their own sleep and the child's sleep distressing and emotionally draining. Health visitors, because they routinely visit parents with young children, are often the recipients of the parents' worries, and are frequently asked if they can help in any way.

Behavioural management of sleeping problems involves careful record keeping, analysis of the individual's problem in terms of contingencies maintaining the behaviour, and establishing agreed goals and working gradually towards their attainment. An example of the behavioural management is that of a 4½-year-old girl, Linda, who refused to go to bed in the evenings and fell asleep on the settee in front of the television each evening, after which she would be taken up to bed. She then woke between 12.00 and 1.00 a.m. and wandered, as if sleepwalking, into her parents' room. Linda would then get into her parent's bed and sleep the rest of the night without waking. If her parents attempted to put her to bed in the evening or at night she screamed and if left alone would come and find them. The main goal established was that Linda should go to sleep in her own bed. The advice on management involved:

(1) bath time to precede bedtime immediately;
(2) Linda to have a story read to her in bed for about 20 minutes; and
(3) the parent reading the story was then to stay in the room until Linda was asleep, but was to have minimal interaction with her, for example they could read a book, knit, etc.

Later advice involved the parent gradually withdrawing from the room before Linda was asleep, for instance sitting outside the room, then on the landing, and finally downstairs. These procedures successfully led to the resolution of the settling problem. The straightforward nature of procedures should not disguise the real difficulties there can be in implementing them successfully. The value of collaborative work lies in the clinical psychologist's expertise in behavioural management combined with the health visitor's extensive knowledge of parents' difficulties with young children.

TAKING A SOCIOCONSTRUCTIVE PERSPECTIVE

Much of the health-care system is dominated by a medical or pathological model of problems. Thus people are seen as 'patients' who have 'illnesses' which are expressed in terms of 'symptoms' that require 'treatment' or 'cure'. This model has fuelled a huge pharmaceutical industry resulting in a large part of the GP's role being seen as prescribing medication. Many psychologists have gone along with this model and sought to develop treatments for 'illnesses' such as anxiety or depression, implicitly endorsing the view that the problem resides within the individual. However an alternative view—known as the socioconstructivist position—emphasizes the importance of seeing problems in their social context and, as a consequence, seeking social as well as individual change. For example many people come to doctors and psychologists complaining of stress for which they may be offered anxiolytic medication and/or stress management. Yet if the stress is a result of huge pressures at work, serious financial difficulties, intolerable housing conditions, or seemingly insuperable family demands, then merely focusing on the individual's symptoms ignores the major maintaining factors and leaves the individual vulnerable to further stress in the future. Moreover, requiring experts—whether psychologists, doctors, or counsellors—to pronounce what is 'wrong' and prescribe 'therapy' risks undermining the individual's capacity to help themselves.

Jones, Moss, and Holton (1997) describe a consultation approach to adults with mental health problems that reflects a socioconstructivist position. The consultation is provided by two psychologists, one of whom conducts the interview while the other observes. After a break, the two psychologists discuss the consultation in the presence of the client with the observing psychologist focusing attention on the social context. The aim is to make the client aware of alternative narratives, putting their concerns within their life context, including social and economic factors. The psychologists offer information about sources of support in the local community and focus the discussion on what the client can do the effect changes themselves. Arriving at an alternative construction in this way, they claim, can often effectively dissolve the problem.

A similar approach is described by Partridge *et al.* (1995) based upon the systemic model used in family therapy. In their work the consultation is carried out by an interviewer in the presence of a team of mental health workers. The team's role is to reflect on the processes going on in the consultation:

> The most unusual component of the session is the reflecting team discussion, when client and interviewer are invited to listen to the reflections of the observers. The team reflections include a description of the problem and the client's explanation of it, the generation of alternative explanations and an exploration of the alternative epistemologies underlying these. This might include identifying strengths and beliefs, reframing problems and exploring dilemmas . . . All reflections are presented tentatively, in keeping with the idea that no one perspective is automatically privileged above others. The session is concluded by inviting the client to reflect on the team discussion and, as a result of this, joint decisions are made about 'next steps'.

This use of a team of workers may seem luxurious in a health-care system where resources are severely limited. However, Partridge *et al.* (1995) report both a reduction in their waiting list from 18 months to 3 to 4 months and a dramatic reduction in the numbers of clients opting to go on for individual therapy, thereby saving much needed resources. What remains to be seen is whether such a service is beneficial in the long run. There is also the danger of endorsing a simplified dichotomy; either the patient is treated (whether drugs or psychotherapy) or they are helped to find solutions themselves. In practice patients may need some help first before they can find solutions themselves. Most psychological therapies are constructed in such a way as to encourage patients to sort out problems for themselves (see Chapter 2).

RESEARCH IN PRIMARY CARE

An important part of the training of clinical psychologists is in research skills and methodology. In their undergraduate degree, psychologists are taught experimental methods of inquiry and are required to carry out and report a research project using appropriate statistical analysis. In their postgraduate training, they are taught to apply these research skills to clinical problems and are required to carry out several research studies (see Chapter 1). Carrying out clinical research may be part of a clinical psychologist's job description (though not in all cases), and up to one day per week may be made available for research. For various reasons—the pressure of clinical commitments, competing interests, awareness of the snags and pitfalls of research work—the majority of trained clinical psychologists are not actively involved in research. Yet their contribution as researchers may well be of particular value in primary care. Some ways in which clinical psychologists could carry out collaborative clinical research are now considered.

Detection and identification of psychological problems

Knowledge about what psychological problems present in primary care is still only rudimentary. By focusing on discrete and widely identifiable categories of disorder, such as anxiety, depression, and obsessions, where standardized assessments have been developed, there is scope for psychologists to uncover the extent to which such problems present in the community and to primary care workers such as health visitors, district nurses, and GPs. It is also of interest to find out more about the natural histories of psychological problems since, as was mentioned earlier, many problems will be resolved without any professional intervention. Clinical psychologists, with their knowledge of psychological problems and ways of assessing them, could fruitfully collaborate with other specialists, particularly those with experience in epidemiology such as public health doctors. The knowledge gained from this type of inquiry will be of practical use in, for example, helping to determine what problems need intervention.

Psychological aspects of the work of primary care professionals

It has been increasingly recognized that a large part of the work of doctors, nurses, receptionists, health visitors, and others who work in primary care is 'psychological'. At its crudest, this refers to the importance of interpersonal skills and behaviour in professional work—which, of course, would also apply to medicine in general. But a singularly important feature of primary care is the frequency of contact with people, over 95 per cent of whom will visit their GP at least once in five years. A large part of primary care work entails dealing effectively with people, whether it is in making appointments, in changing dressings, in one-to-one consultations, or in clinics. Psychologists and other social scientists have become interested in the process of communication in primary care, and in particular in what factors aid and what impede effective communication (Pendleton and Hasler 1983).

The failure of many patients to adhere to the treatment regimens suggested by doctors and others is in part due to deficiencies in communication. While most patients report being satisfied with the communication they receive from their doctors, a substantial minority (between 35 and 40 per cent) report dissatisfaction. Psychological studies of doctor–patient communication have highlighted some of the factors that affect satisfaction. For example many communications from doctors are too complex for patients to understand, too long to be adequately recalled, and are delivered in a way that fails to take into account the patient's existing knowledge and beliefs. Psychological studies of the processes of remembering and forgetting can be useful in designing more effective communications. People tend to remember information presented at the beginning of a message (the primacy effect) and at the end of a message (the recency effect); whereas the bit in the middle—which often contains important information about the treatment and its effects—is less well remembered. Equally, information that is concrete, emphasized as important, and repeated will be more easily remembered. It is obvious that well-established psychological knowledge such as this can be practically applied, as indeed it has begun to be.

PREVENTION AND HEALTH PROMOTION

There has been an increasing awareness that primary health care is one of the most fruitful fields for the prevention of illness and the promotion of health. The GP in particular has been seen as potentially a major agent of change, although other primary care workers such as practice nurses and health visitors are also important. About two-thirds of patients consult their doctors in one year, and the availability and accessibility of the GP creates many opportunities for health education and promotion. The doctor too is generally a respected and trusted figure whose advice is taken seriously. For example studies of GPs giving advice to smokers to quit smoking have clearly demonstrated that a small but significant number of smokers successfully give up directly as a result of that advice. In recent years, doctors and other primary care workers have become more and more involved in promoting health, from straightforward activities such as immunization and screening to education and advice on aspects of lifestyle.

Clinical psychologists have also begun to direct their attention to prevention and health promotion. This makes sense, since it is primarily psychological change that is necessary to achieve a healthier lifestyle. For example there is an accumulating body of evidence linking diet, particularly one high in saturated fat and low in fibre, with coronary heart disease and certain cancers. If people can shift their eating habits, then they will reduce the risk of these very common diseases. What is required is a change in attitude (i.e. being prepared to recognize that a change in diet is important for health) and in behaviour (viz. to adopting a healthier pattern of eating). The GP, practice nurse, or health visitor may well be the best means of seeking to instigate change, but how should his or her advice be given? Clinical psychologists, whose daily business is seeking to change attitudes and behaviour, could work closely with primary care workers to maximize the effectiveness of their interventions.

While there has been most emphasis on prevention and health promotion in physical health, some attention is beginning to be paid to mental health promotion. Newton (1988) has analysed the research into major psychological disorders such as depression and schizophrenia and suggested a number of psychological preventive measures. These range from practical help to ensure greater security for infants and young children, thereby hopefully reducing the risk of depression and anxiety in later life, to better means of identifying and helping those at most risk of serious breakdown. As Newton points out, there is a growing body of knowledge about psychological conditions which could form the basis of much needed research into prevention and mental health promotion.

COMMUNITY SERVICES

The work of clinical psychologists in primary care has predominantly been with the general practice team. This is not surprising, since clinical psychologists are health-care professionals with already-established links to GPs, nurses, and other health-care staff. In the transition to primary care, clinical psychologists have extended their customary ways of working, and general practice has been a most fertile ground. However, as was illustrated earlier in Fig. 12.1, many more psychological problems exist in the community than actually present or are recognized in general practice. Awareness of this has led some clinical psychologists to work directly 'in the community'.

Community mental health teams

The transition from the institutionalized care of the mentally ill to 'care in the community' has been accompanied by the widespread development of community mental health teams (CMHTs). A CMHT consists of a group of different mental health professionals who work closely together in order to provide a service to the local community, particularly to GPs. A team might consist of one or more community psychiatric nurses, an occupational therapist, a social worker, clinical psychologist, and a psychiatrist, although the latter more commonly acts as in conjunction with the team rather than as a full member. Referrals come from GPs and other local sources. The team offers a range of therapeutic interventions—usually short-term pragmatic treatments. Groups are often run, such as stress management, assertiveness training, or a group for the bereaved.

The aim of the community team is to be more responsive to local needs and to avoid the lengthy waiting lists that have bedevilled referrals to specialized mental health services. In addition, it is hoped that there would be a reduction in the stigma associated with psychiatric services, the benefits of a multidisciplinary approach, and their ability to offer psychological interventions that are pragmatic, brief, and effective. However, CMHTs also have their problems. Some clinical psychologists report that working in 'democratic' teams can lead to a loss of professional identity and a diminution of specialist skills—the philosophy can be that 'everyone can do everything' (Anciano and Kirkpatrick 1990). Others report being overwhelmed by the number of referrals, and that allocation to team members can be arbitrary rather than based upon matching client needs to professional skill. Clinical psychologists can find themselves torn between being a core team member working directly with clients and a consultant advising other professionals.

Community psychologists

Community psychology is a term that first appeared in the United States to describe a radical shift in applied psychology away from individual psychotherapy in a professional health-care context to an approach that views psychological problems from an ecological viewpoint. Community psychology emphasizes the critical importance of social and environmental forces in the determination of human behaviour problems, and favours what is loosely described as a 'systems oriented' approach to intervention. There is also the recognition that many mental health problems are the product of social and political conditions such as poverty, unemployment, racism, and urban deprivation, and that changes in these social conditions are required in order to make much impact on these psychological problems. Community psychology, therefore, seeks to embrace a broader perspective on mental health and illness than is currently adopted by most clinical psychologists. Homelessness is a prime example. Lack of employment and family difficulties can force young people to move to large cities in search of work. However, without resources, friends, or other support, they find themselves living rough, unable to find either work or accommodation. The problems that ensue—hopelessness, depression, alcohol and drug abuse—are as much a product of the social system as the individual.

There are in fact few community psychologists *per se* outside the United States, probably because there does not exist a career structure in the health and social services. Some clinical psychologists have sought to take more of a community psychology perspective in their work. This entails a deliberate move away from individual treatments to attempts to produce or provoke changes in social systems, for example by working closely with voluntary groups seeking social and political change, by taking an advocacy role in the pursuit of the rights of the mentally ill and the learning disabled, by working in or with Social Services Departments, and by helping to establish and support self-help groups. To date, this community role has been relatively little developed; but as political and financial constraints directly affect the health-care system, this is a role that may become increasingly important.

SUMMARY

Clinical psychologists have worked in primary care for many years. There are various ways in which they have contributed to the service. Firstly, a treatment service is offered similar to that provided in outpatient clinics. Up to now this has been the commonest and most preferred service. While research has provided some support for the effectiveness of such a service, the small number of clinical psychologists means that a purely therapeutic role is bound to be limited and selective. In the last five years, there has been a growth of counsellors either employed directly in general practices or working in clinical psychology services. A new profession of counselling psychology has also emerged. These developments provide a challenge to the therapeutic work of clinical psychologists in primary care. However, there is an increasing number of services which combine clinical psychologists and counsellors to the benefit of both professions. Secondly, a consultative service can be provided in which the skills and knowledge of psychologists are used to help other primary care workers. One example is the close collaboration between child clinical psychologists and health visitors. Thirdly, some clinical psychologists have sought to develop innovative methods of working based upon a systemic or socioconstructive model of problems. Consultations are designed in order to find alternative ways of seeing problems which reflect the influence of the social context. Clients are aided to find their own solutions as an alternative to individual therapy. Fourthly, research can be carried out into various aspects of primary care work; doctor–patient communication is one example. Finally, clinical psychologists can participate in health promotion and prevention programmes, many of which are carried out in primary care settings. Advice on diet and smoking are two examples. While clinical psychologists have, on the whole, worked in primary care through the medium of general practice, this is not the only way of working. Some clinical psychologists have begun to work directly in the community either as community psychologists or as part of community teams.

References

Anciano, D. and Kirkpatrick, A. (1990). CMHTs and clinical psychology: the death of the profession? *Clin. Psych. Forum,* **26,** 9–12.

Department of Health (1996). *Primary care: delivering the future.* Department of Health, London.

Deys, C., Dowling, E., and Golding, V. (1989). Clinical psychology: a consultative approach in general practice. *J. R. Coll. Gen. Pract.*, **39,** 342–4.

Earll, L. and Kincey, J. (1982). Clinical psychology in general practice: a controlled trial evaluation. *J. R. Coll. Gen. Pract.,* **32**, 32–7.

Goldberg, D. and Bridges, K. (1987). Screening for psychiatric illness in general practice: the general practitioner versus the screening questionnaire. *J. R. Coll. Gen. Pract.,* **37**, 15–18.

Goldberg, D. P. and Huxley, P. (1980). *Mental illness in the community. The pathway to psychiatric care.* Tavistock, London.

Jones, S., Moss, D. and Holton, R. (1997). A consultation service to adults referred as having mental health problems. *Clin. Psychol. Forum*, **105,** 21–6.

Kincey, J. A. (1974). General practice and clinical psychology—some arguments for a closer liaison. *J. R. Coll. Gen. Pract.,* **24**, 882–8.

McPherson, I. and Feldman, M. P. (1977). A preliminary investigation of the role of the clinical psychologist in the primary care setting. *Bull. Brit. Psychol. Soc.*, **30**, 342–6.

Milne, D. and Souter, K. (1988). A re-evaluation of the clinical psychologist in general practice. *J. R. Coll. Gen. Pract.*, **38**, 457–60.

Newton, J. (1988). *Preventing mental illness.* Routledge and Kegan Paul, London.

Partridge, K., Bennett, E., Webster, A. and Ekdawi, I. (1995). Consultation with clients: an alternative way of working in adult mental health. *Clin. Psychol. Forum*, **83,** 26–8.

Pendleton, D. and Hasler, J. (eds) (1983). *Doctor-patient communication.* Academic Press, London.

Robson, M. H., France, R., and Bland, M. (1984). Clinical psychologists in primary care; controlled clinical and economic evaluation. *Brit. Med. J.*, **288**, 1805–8.

Roth, A. and Fonagy, P. (1996). *What works for whom? A critical review of psychotherapy research.* Guilford Press, New York.

Shillitoe, R. and Hall, J. (1997). Clinical psychologists and counsellors: working together. *Clin. Psychol. Forum*, **101,** 5–8.

Further reading

Feldman, M. D. and Christensen, J. F. (1997). *Behavioral medicine in primary care: a practical guide.* Appleton and Lange, Stamford.

France, R. and Robson, M. (1997). *Cognitive behaviour therapy in primary care.* Jessica Kingsley, London.

Onyett, S. (1995). *Making community mental health teams work: CMHTs and the people who work in them.* Sainsbury Centre for Mental Health, London.

13

Working with others

John Hall

A small number of clinical psychologists practice on their own, seeing patients who refer themselves directly, with minimal contact with other psychologists or other therapists or health care staff. The majority of psychologists are involved with members of other professional groups from the very moment that a referral is made. Equally importantly, many psychologists will be involved at some time with the immediate family of the patient they are seeing, as well as with informal carers.

As well as working with members of health care professions, clinical psychologists are likely to be working with staff of voluntary and charitable organizations, to be in contact with staff of local authorities, and to be responding to groups representing the consumers of health care. This last group of people will normally have no professional training, may know little of the shared assumptions of health care workers, and may indeed be actively challenging some of those assumptions. Clinical psychologists in all these circumstances have to be able to build therapeutic alliances with all who can contribute to better health care.

Apart from a psychologist's concern with identified patients and their families, many psychologists will be concerned with other aspects of the local health-care system, such as helping to run a day centre, planning a new service for people with AIDS, or conducting an audit of community services for children with disabilities.

COMMUNICATING WITH OTHERS

All psychological work with people requires good communication. Some forms of physical health care, such as emergency resuscitation, can be given without any spoken or written communication. However, most care or treatment involves some spoken communication, even if it is only to require some simple response such as opening your mouth or rolling over. For most patients, good quality care and treatment requires a two-way transfer of information, which takes account not only of the understanding of basic facts, but also the ability to put that information into practice. For psychological treatments in particular, psychologists must understand complex emotional states, about which the patient may feel at least reticent and possibly highly embarrassed. A core skill for all psychological work with patients is the ability to listen to them, to understand how they feel and think, and to communicate back to them in a way which helps them to feel valued, understood, and in control of what happens to them.

Psychologists are interested in several aspects of this information-exchange system, not least because some health-care staff may not appreciate how difficult many patients find it both to provide and to retain the relevant information. Some patients may have defective senses, so that an electronic communication aid, giving a visual display of what is required, may be needed. Improved communication is related to compliance—given that often only a third of oral medication is taken as prescribed by outpatients, how can that rate be improved? Guidance may be needed to make sure that the huge range of information sheets and forms used in any hospital are comprehensible to the wide range of both staff and patients who must use them. A substantial proportion of patients, certainly 10 to 15 per cent, will not be highly literate, and will not understand high-level vocabulary words. This suggests the use of various indices of 'readability' to make sure that instructions are generally comprehensible, although the simplistic application of such formulae is open to criticism.

Another approach is to look at the emotional implications of information conveyed to the patient, examining, for example, whether fear-arousing messages to patients work. Do they lead to more compliance with prescribed treatment by patients? Some studies suggest that fear arousal cannot be strongly advocated on present evidence. However, an approach which examines just the way in which the doctor or patient evaluates information is criticized by Tuckett and Williams (1984). Their social–psychological or sociological analysis also draws attention to the social setting within which information is exchanged, particularly examining the degree of control exerted by health-care staff in their communication with patients.

There is now a wealth of useful psychological guidance on many aspects of communication between health-care staff and patients, relevant not only to highly qualified staff, but to portering or domestic staff who may have to deal with a disturbed or violent patient or visitor.

WHO ARE THE OTHERS?

There are three main groups of people who clinical psychologists encounter in their work. First and most important are their patients or clients—the generic term 'users' is increasingly employed to indicate the recipients of health care services. Often of equal significance with them are the relatives and informal carers of service users, since, as in the case of people with a chronic physical disability such as multiple sclerosis, they may be a major resource in the continuing care of the person identified as the patient.

Second are health-care and related professional staff, such as doctors, or speech and language therapists, but also social care staff, such as residential care workers, and educational staff, such as teachers.

Third, and of growing significance in many countries, are workers in voluntary and charitable agencies who, for example, offer residential care for people with severe chronic conditions, and also information and support for often highly specific groups of sufferers. These workers can be an invaluable first point of call. Many of them may themselves be relatives of sufferers, or former sufferers, and may be both advocates for alternative forms of service, and critics of existing services. They may not share the assumptions of professional staff, but by their questioning and prodding can undoubtedly improve the quality of local services.

Working with users and their families

Traditionally, health-care staff decided what was best for patients, and scant attention was paid to engaging patients as actively as possible in all decisions relating to their care and treatment. Taking users seriously has a number of different aspects. Only recently have the concerns of patients themselves begun to be important in the planning of health services and in assigning priorities. What may then emerge is that the users of a day centre may value it more for offering a safe and non-exploitative place to go during the day, rather than the carefully constructed and planned activities which take place in the centre. Unless the user's *first* priorities are met, they may well not continue to use the services provided.

Beresford and Croft (1993) have suggested a number of guidelines to follow when consulting users, such as building as few assumptions as possible into the questions set, offering both individual and collective discussions, and making the experience positive, by making the setting attractive and offering a warm welcome. There is a risk that users may be seen as token members of planning groups, expected to give their time free while professional staff have all expenses paid. Participation in planning—or research—should involve some feedback of results, if the exercise is not to prove demanding and sterile. A striking first-hand account of the experience of patienthood by Chadwick (1997), himself a possessor of a PhD in abnormal psychology, stresses the importance of knowledge about the condition he had, the pathogenic implications of the term 'discharge' as conveying a sense of being chucked out or rejected, and the importance of at least some loose structure or texture to daily life.

A particular issue of psychological significance is the best way of supporting patient choice, by providing information about the effectiveness of the services offered to them. Both evidence based medicine and patient choice have developed as a reaction to what has been seen as the excessive authority given to doctors, and the combination of these two has been described as offering a paradigm shift within medicine. It offers an active partnership model of the relationship, acknowledging four main elements: patients are not uniform in what they want, and hence the roles of patients and doctors must be flexible; arguments and discussion are positive elements in helping patients to decide what they want; patients want emotional support and help when making decisions as well as information and technical skill; and the health professional needs to ascertain the patient's values so that any support, advice, and arguments are informed by those values (Hope 1997).

All of these arguments apply just as well to the relatives of patients. There are however additional points which need to be considered. Relatives may have a very different interest in the outcome of a consultation than the identified patient, so that evaluating their contribution to a discussion about the patient should take into account what their agenda may be. This may well be the case when the relative is also the main carer of the patient, when the burden, or better the impact, of caring needs to be considered. In some circumstances it may be more important to meet the needs of the caring relative before the patient. The concept of 'relapse' normally places the focus of change within the patient, whereas an apparent relapse may sometimes be more of an indication that the *carer* has reached the limits of their endurance.

The concept of 'profession'

The idea of a profession relates mainly to the possession of particular skills and knowledge. It may also relate to pay and status, or to patterns of authority. As striving for 'professional' status by occupational groups has been a constant theme in this century, sociologists have tried to identify the characteristics of a profession, suggesting that a profession is defined by: possession of a body of specialized knowledge; a monopoly of practice in a field of work; an acceptance that fellow members of a profession are adjudged competent to assess the work of a member; and an ideology of service to clients.

Different health-care professions, and the boundaries between them, have arisen because the amount of technical information is so great, and the range of skills so varied, that no one person could possibly be expected to be conversant with them all. These boundaries are not fixed, nor are they impermeable. New demands upon the health-care system, for example the requirement for better knowledge of physics in the growing field of brain imaging techniques, has led to the demand for new skills which did not reside in existing health-care professions, and which then had to be imported from those without a conventional professional membership. But given boundaries do exist. An important part of a clinical psychologist's job is to recognize the boundaries, and to work with people at the boundaries and on the other side, and maybe changing the boundary in the process. Some people live on two sides of a professional boundary, being trained in more than one health-care profession. Indeed, a proportion of clinical psychologists have previously been nurses or therapists of some sort (such as occupational therapists) before retraining as psychologists, and an increasing number of members of other professions will have studied psychology to degree level while remaining in that profession.

The establishment of distinct professional groups in health care developed gradually from the middle of the last century, in England dating from the establishment of the General Medical Council for doctors in 1858. However, the continuing development of a profession is affected by external pressures, including the financial rewards of a job and availability of people able to do the job, as well as by internal pressures such as the level of competence demanded by patients and employers. This process is alive today, as shown by the changing length and type of training of clinical psychologists in different European countries, and by the impact of the move to graduate-level degree training for most therapist groups.

The introduction of the term 'semi-professions' by Etzioni indicates that some professions may be more professional than others! Certainly within health-care professions, medicine has achieved an ascendancy over a number of clinical care groups, to the extent that they may control, or 'prescribe' the therapeutic actions taken by members of those groups. In a number of European countries, medical colleagues may still have a considerable degree of control over the work of psychologists in public health settings. Where the medical profession does not have prescriptive or legal control over another group, and where it cannot be seen to possess knowledge which encompasses that of the other group, then negotiation has to take place on how members of each profession relate to doctors, with the possibility of an interprofessional boundary change as discussed above.

The rapid development of counselling as a profession or 'semiprofession' has been a challenge to medical, and indeed to psychological, ascendancy in primary care settings. The issues now being negotiated between clinical psychologists and counsellors parallel in some ways the negotiations which have taken place in the past between doctors and clinical psychologists.

Professional views and standards thus have a range of functions. They clarify the nature of the task each group can perform and they provide a set of guidelines of interprofessional conduct. They can protect both professional and client. Conversely, professional differences can be over-rigid, and can fail to cope with changing patterns of health need and professional skill. They can hamper collaboration in helping individual patients and they can lead to confused communication. Understanding the ethos of other professions is a prerequisite for working with them.

Working with doctors

Doctors are, in virtually every country, the most influential professional group in health care. Because of the central position of doctors in any health-care system, it is essential that as a group they are aware of the clinical implications of developments in psychological theory and practice, and are aware of how psychologists can both provide a service and assist them to modify their own practice accordingly.

In most countries, there is a clear separation between the 'general practice', 'family medicine', or 'primary care' type of practice, and the specialist practice of a particular branch of medicine, such as neurology, in a 'secondary care' setting. While in Britain these two areas of practice have been highly separated, it is now likely that these two areas will be related in ways more similar to that in many European countries, where a family doctor will also have an associated specialist practice. The relationship between these two branches of practice is changing, but the family doctor usually occupies a key position in the continuing care of the individual patient, and has a pivotal role in referring, or 'steering' patients to specialized treatments.

Patterns of training for doctors are also changing. Although different countries have a differing emphasis on preclinical experience, traditionally the neophyte doctor first studies 'preclinical' subjects, such as physiology and biochemistry, before being exposed to 'clinical' subjects by direct contact with patients who are attending clinics and wards associated with the medical school. This separation means that trainee doctors cannot be expected to integrate easily their medical 'clinical' knowledge with their preclinical knowledge. There have thus been attempts to introduce some clinical contact and training in clinical skills much earlier in the basic 'scientific' training, and correspondingly to introduce some scientific topics at a time when they can be related to clinical phenomena. All of these developments have prompted a growth of interest in the process of professional acculturation by medical students and in the process of acquisition of the relevant human practice skills, and have thus promoted a development of behavioural sciences teaching from the very beginning of the medical course. From a psychological viewpoint, the more that relevant teaching of topics such as doctor–patient communication can be integrated with early clinical experience, the more trainee doctors are likely to absorb a psychological perspective to their work.

After basic training, doctors usually follow some course of specialized training. Some medical specialties have a high proportion of psychological content in their future training, the best examples being paediatricians and psychiatrists. In these specialties some knowledge of developmental psychology (for example parent–child bonding and normal language development) and social psychology (for example the social psychology of small groups) respectively is essential, so that clinical psychologists come to have a specialized teaching role for these specialties. This implies that psychologists with the relevant professional knowledge are themselves available not only to become familiar with the clinical practice of the specialty, but to help the trainee doctors become aware of some of the conceptual issues in their fields. When clinical psychologists work closely with specialist doctors, there is scope for co-operation, but also for competition and tension, over, for example, responsibility for particular areas of work or what priorities to establish in responding to very high levels of demand. The publication of joint guidelines on psychological therapies by the British Psychological Society and the Royal College of Psychiatrists (1995) is an example of co-operation on the corporate level. Mutual understanding of mind-sets, and acknowledging potential areas of role-confusion, is needed as a basis for interprofessional collaboration at the individual level (Hall 1996).

Public health, or community, medicine is also of special interest to psychologists, with the growing interest in health promotion and illness prevention and the accompanying emphasis on understanding the impact of the total environment on health status. The growth of health psychology as a separate area of practice reflects this interest, as discussed later in this chapter.

Working with nurses

Nurses constitute the largest staff group in a health-care system. They are the people who will have the closest day-to-day contact with patients in hospital, and who both in hospital and in the community have to carry out the most personal tasks for people who cannot look after themselves. A group of nurses on a ward often have to provide a 24-hour service every day, so that at any time of the night they may have to deal with medical—or psychological—emergencies or sudden outbursts of disturbed behaviour. While a particular doctor will have medical responsibility for a patient, many of the minor—and indeed major—worries of the patient will be shared with and solved by the first available nurse, who may be relatively junior and inexperienced.

Nurses are the people in a hospital who potentially have the greatest knowledge of a patient's day-to-day behaviour. They also often have the closest, if not the only, personal knowledge of patients' relatives. Equally important is the fact that careful observation of ward interaction between nurses and patients shows that it is the more junior or less well-trained staff who usually interact more with patients. From a psychologist's viewpoint, perhaps the less well-trained staff actually have more potential to change patients' attitudes and behaviour than the better trained senior staff who are necessarily involved in other tasks. If that view is correct, it carries major implications for the design of staff training programmes, both for who should be trained and for the level of knowledge and literacy that can be assumed of all trainees.

In community teams for people with mental health problems and learning disabilities, community nurses are likely to be the largest group. They are most likely to be the 'key worker' for a patient or client, thus co-ordinating the input of all the staff involved with them. It is in these settings that psychologists are most likely to have close day-to-day working relationships with nurses, and part of the way in which such teams develop is the respect that arises from close working with sometimes demanding and needy patients.

Because nursing is numerically the key caring health profession, continued recruitment of nurses is essential to a health-care system. A lot of psychological attention has accordingly focused on the way in which interest develops in potential nurses, and why voluntary withdrawal from training is much more common for nurses than for other health-care groups. Young nursing students are confronted with illness, suffering, and dying in a way that young people starting other jobs are not, exposing student nurses to considerable personal stress, and suggesting that nurses should be helped to develop mechanisms for coping with this stress and should be well supported in this learning process.

The demands made on nurses vary widely from one setting to another, so that some nursing, such as that in operating theatres, is highly technical and physically intrusive, while other fields of nursing, such as work with people with learning difficulties, are primarily interpersonal and social. Some nurses work entirely within a specialist unit, such as a coronary care unit, and others, such as community psychiatric nurses, work entirely in the community. If there is pressure for patients to be discharged early from inpatient care, then community nurses will take on some tasks that would otherwise be the responsibility of hospital-based nurses. In some European countries, such as Belgium, community psychiatric nurses do not exist, so those tasks may simply not be carried out. Some countries train nurses as polyvalent; some specialize from the start of basic training; some specialize after a common basic training. Basic standards of training vary greatly, ranging in Europe from completion of primary studies to university admission level, although those countries who are members of the EC have signed an agreement which will lead to more consistency in standards of training.

For all these reasons, the assumptions that can be made about the level of psychological knowledge and skill in nurses vary greatly. Yet there are an increasing number of reputable nursing journals and texts that demonstrate an increasing psychological sophistication among at least a proportion of nurses. As more nurses become psychologically informed—partly as a product of people being doubly qualified as nurses and psychologists—this sophistication, and demand for more psychological orientated training and support, is growing.

An important aspect of the developing professional autonomy achievable by nurses is the level of specific therapeutic skills they may now possess. The concept of 'clinical nurse specialist' or 'nurse therapist' indicates the idea of a nurse practising independently, perhaps as a cognitive therapist or as a family therapist. In many areas these nurse therapists will be working alongside, possibly supervised by, and even in the same professional department as, clinical psychologists.

BURN-OUT IN HEALTH-CARE STAFF

One of the appeals of working as a doctor or a nurse is the idea of 'working with people'. Many texts on psychology and nursing, for example, focus on the interpersonal elements of nursing, often described as nurse–patient interaction. From the patient's point of view, the quality of human relationship with those looking after him or her is extremely important, as is evidenced by such phrases as 'a good bedside manner'. Qualities such as warmth, sensitivity, and respect for the patient are encouraged in all sorts of care situations, quite apart from their value in more intense one-to-one therapeutic relationships.

However, while patients may want such qualities in the staff about them, it is not easy for those staff always to display them. Some settings are associated with higher levels of stress, so that nurses on medical wards show higher levels of stress than nurses on surgical wards. Wards with high rates of death on them, such as intensive care units and terminal care units, are also associated with high stress levels. The end result of this type of stress has been called 'burn-out'. Burn-out describes a range of responses to increased emotional demands, such as emotional detachment, cynicism, and an unwillingness to admit to having emotional needs. Burn-out can be seen, of course, in a number of other professional groups where there are high personal and emotional demands, and where there may be a lack of support from others, such as ministers of religion and policemen.

What can be done about this? From a psychological point of view, it may be possible to offer a psychological analysis of burn-out, and then do something to relieve the problem. Personal Construct Theory, a theory put forward by Georg Kelly, proposes that people are essentially trying to make sense of the world around them, and relate events according to their own constellation of 'constructs', which are based on each individual's own life history and beliefs. The relevance of this to coping with the burn-out is that it helps to explain what is happening to both patient and nurse in what may be a very confusing situation. For the patient, all sorts of strange things will be happening, with threatening medical procedures and an endless stream of strange new people, each anxious to ask about this or take a drop of blood for that. A general approach to the patient which accepts that they will all interpret these events differently, and positively need help to make sense of their experiences, will offer more support to the patient. For the nurse, it emphasizes the value of exposing hidden anxieties; a hidden anxiety cannot be tested or rejected.

A nurse in the front line may then want support from others alive to these anxieties and stresses, and with some skills in resolving them. Parry (1990) points out the major role of social support in times of stress; that social support consists of information and practical components, as well as emotional ones; and that social support does not just happen, but has to be obtained or elicited from those about us. People who feel unsupported in a stressful professional situation may therefore have help potentially available to them, but be unsure how to elicit that help. The literature concerning patterns of social interaction in lonely and depressed people suggests how to help people elicit help. If some people in a situation feel support and others do not, what can we observe about the supported people that differentiates them from the others? This type of analysis, applicable to patient and staff alike, could give an added dimension to more straightforward advice usually given to staff feeling under pressure.

Nurses are of course the same as everyone else, and it is sometimes simplistic to assume burn-out is the cause of problems that individual nurses may be encountering. There is an increasing range of excellent self-help literature for many problems of everyday life, a good example being the book covering a wide range of issues, including study skills and improving your memory, by Butler and Hope (1995).

Working with remedial therapists

After doctors and nurses, the members of the various therapeutic professions are the most numerous, dignified by such catch-all phrases as 'professions allied to medicine' (PAMs) or 'ancillary professions'! The diversity and differentiation already noted in nurse training is even greater with this group. While in Britain the two major professions in this group are physiotherapy and occupational therapy, kinesitherapy and ergotherapy are parallel titles used in other countries.

The importance of these professions is that, for many patients, they provide the main rehabilitative daytime activity for patients in hospital, and are the main therapists in day centres. Many of the activities are highly intensive, and may involve much physical contact between therapist and patient. The importance of touch as a therapeutic tool in itself is increasingly recognized in general nursing, often linked to a use of simple aromatherapy techniques. Apart from the technical nature of the therapy offered, physical therapists also potentially offer a strongly supportive relationship to their patients, this being particularly apparent when patients are recovering from traumatic accidents. People who have, for example, had a severe spinal injury—often active young men—will spend several months having regular physiotherapy with usually young women therapists. In this setting, as in others, physical therapists need to know how to use the relationships they become involved in, and how to cope with the issues that may arise.

There are many specific issues in different therapies that can be analysed in psychological terms. Just as many people do not comply with a prescribed medical regime, so some people do not use a prosthesis or physical aid as prescribed, and need instruction and guidance to use it properly. Should activity regimes provide a relatively modest level of stimulation for, say, two or three hours, or provide a more demanding level of stimulation for half an hour?

The significance of other therapists to psychologists lies either in the length of time they are in contact with the patient, or in the significance of the particular skills they offer to the patient. Speech and language therapists are a particular group of therapists concerned to alleviate defective speech patterns, and to correct acquired speech defects after, for example, a stroke. They have a special training in speech development and linguistics, and thus necessarily need to be familiar with a number of psychological concepts. Dieticians give advice to a wide range of patients on the diet that may reduce or prevent the risk of certain conditions, and contribute significantly to their long-term management. Dieticians have become more closely associated with psychologists in recent years because of their joint interest in bulimia and anorexia, the two psychogenic eating disorders, and the increased incidence of obesity in developed countries can only lead to more co-operation.

Working with social workers and care managers

The boundary between health care and social care has always been loose and movable, yet people's needs often require that the two systems of care work closely together, when national social institutional policies have created two separate systems. In a number of European countries one ministry or agency provides both services. Within the United Kingdom, there are major differences between England, where the health and social services agencies are separated, and Northern Ireland, where one agency organizes both services. However, there are moves to consider the creation of unified health and social agencies in some areas such as mental heath services. Issues such as differing degrees of responsiveness to local political opinion, the load of statutory duties (such as the procedures for taking children who are 'at risk' into residential or alternative foster care), differing methods and time scales of financial budgeting, and differing styles of professional accountability, may loom large as organizational matters requiring resolution. This suggests that a considerable degree of political sophistication is required from a clinical psychologist working with both health and social care agencies.

To the extent that the organization of services dictates the training and roles, there is thus a huge diversity in the range of work undertaken by 'social workers'. There may be generic field workers providing a comprehensive service to a population, including everything from arranging adoptions to supporting the families of people currently in prison. There may be specialist field workers funded by religious or voluntary bodies providing services to a particular client group such as those dependent on alcohol; there may be specialist workers attached to day or residential units, such as a day care centre for elderly people. Social services agencies may also be commissioning agencies, providing 'care managers' who assess the need for services of an individual and then provide a budget for those services to be bought from possibly a number of providers.

In some of these functions, a social services department may not directly employ staff with skills to provide the best sort of help for some groups of clients. In Britain, one of the greatest uses made by social services departments of clinical psychologists is in providing advice on day care, on fostering and adoption of children, or in special residential settings for children. It is likely that a social services department will be presented with other highly specific demands; such as developing a community programme for substance abusers, or providing parenting programmes for families at high risk of breakdown. In Britain, some social services departments directly employ psychologists to offer these services, and of course in those European countries where health and social agencies are combined such services would be routinely expected of clinical psychologists. In a number of countries, social welfare provision is provided through charitable agencies, and there has been a trend in Britain towards a greater range of 'provider' agencies. Thus both social services departments and a wide range of voluntary agencies may also seek advice from clinical psychologists, when the psychologist's role with respect to these agencies may become that of a 'consultant' as well as a clinician.

Working with other professions

In addition to the main professional groups already mentioned, clinical psychologists work with a number of other professions, or people working in health care who do not readily fit into conventional existing professions.

Chapter 4 describes the work done by psychologists with children. Depending on the way in which countries organize their health and education services, there may be one integrated profession of child psychology, seeing children with problems irrespective of how the problems present, or two separate professions of educational and child clinical psychology. In a similar way, clinical psychologists may often have very close links with teachers, particularly if the psychologists are working in a special day or residential unit (for example for disturbed adolescents, for children who have committed serious offences and are in special units, or for multiply-handicapped children). The careful attention now paid to child abuse has lead to new groupings of workers in this field, so psychologists may be more closely involved with foster parents and health visitors (known in other countries as public health nurses).

The emergency (police, fire, and ambulance) services have not traditionally been seen as allied to clinical psychology. However, the clinical research work done on post-traumatic stress disorder (PTSD) has highlighted both the role these services have as being 'first there' for major incidents involving loss of life, serious injury, and violence, and the risk these groups face of 'flash-back' memories, and of PTSD following the harrowing scenes they may face. Although not seen as an emergency service, prison staff similarly have to deal with violence both to others and themselves, and some staff face similar risks to emergency service staff. There is increasing demand from all of these services for psychological help in staff training, early detection of PTSD, and postincident debriefing.

There is currently a substantial growth in the numbers of those training as counsellors, partly perhaps because of a greater willingness to admit to psychological difficulties, itself a product of better public awareness in this field. The most common basis for generic counsellor training is essentially a Rogerian or person-centred approach, or counsellors may be trained within a specific conceptual framework, such as humanistic counselling. People without a full counselling training may work within a particular problem area, such as substance abuse, and still be called counsellors. Training courses exist at many levels, from brief introductory courses of a few hours, sometimes relying on heavily on correspondence course methods, to demanding 3-year courses with high standards of professional supervision. The British Association for Counselling (BAC) is the main accrediting body for counsellors in Britain, with similar bodies in Europe. A number of psychology graduates now train in this way, having a training specific to the work they do, and sometimes as part of a team which may be led by a clinical psychologist. A special issue of *Clinical Psychology Forum* (Shillitoe and Hall 1997) was devoted to examining the issues raised by clinical psychologists and counsellors working together.

Working with other psychologists

There are a number of fields of applied psychology other than clinical psychology. Forensic psychologists work with offenders and the courts, and may be expert witnesses as well as having contact with individuals. Organizational or work psychology—formerly called industrial psychology—is concerned both to fit work to people, by designing equipment displays for example, and to fit people to work, by use of selection procedures and industrial training programmes. In a number of European countries counselling psychology is a major field of applied psychology; but in Britain counselling has historically developed largely outside the professional practice of psychology. The British Psychological Society has now recognized counselling psychology as an area of professional practice in its own right, and approved training courses leading to Chartering (see Chapter 1). Given the continuing shortage of qualified clinical psychologists, a clinical psychology service may decide to employ a counselling psychologist, if the skills of a counselling psychologist are appropriate to a post. This is most likely to be working in a primary care setting, and least likely to be in fields such as neuropsychology and learning disability. The interface between clinical and counselling psychology is likely to develop rapidly over the next few years, given that in many areas, particularly those with smaller populations, the clinical psychology service effectively manages or co-ordinates most psychological treatments.

Similarly the field of health psychology has also achieved recognition by the British Psychological Society as an area of independent professional practice. While historically many of the academic leaders in health psychology have been clinical psychologists, increasingly psychologists are working in health-care settings in health promotion, clinical audit, and conducting research into population-based health practices, such as the effectiveness of health screening programmes. A major new text (Baum *et al.* 1997) explores many of the topics in this field, such as the fascinating area of risk perception, covering the way in which individuals judge the risk to themselves of some event occurring, such as a serious injury from a road traffic accident compared to the risk of cancer. The issues raised for clinical psychology by these emergent related professions is discussed in Chapter 14. A number of clinical psychologists also obtain further professional training in occupational or organizational psychology and continue to work in the NHS, where the skills they acquire in, for example, task design, occupational selection, and the management of change can be invaluable.

A significant issue now facing all applied psychologists in health-care settings is how best to co-ordinate the activities of psychologists who are fully qualified in one or other branch of applied psychology, and at the same time to offer support and continuing education to those psychology graduates working in health-care settings who may no longer identify themselves as psychologists, but who want to update their knowledge in this field.

TEAMWORK

Good teamwork has been mentioned in several other chapters in this book, such as Chapter 6, dealing with work with physically disabled people. Teamwork obviously assumes the existence of a team—a group of people who work co-operatively with each other. Teams may be formed primarily for clinical work, and many psychologists will spend part of their time as a member of a clinical team. Teams may also exist mainly for management purposes, and more senior clinical psychologists may be members of a number of management teams or groups.

Teams in health care vary in their composition and fall into three categories. They may be made up of groups of people of the same profession, who usually are of varying levels of expertise and experience within that profession. Thus nursing teams will consist of one or more ward charge nurses or head nurses who clearly organize the work of registered or qualified nurses, and a number of assistant or learner nurses. Secondly, teams may be made up of members of different professions, where a member of one specified profession—usually medical—specifies the work of the whole team: an excellent example is the group of staff in an operating theatre, where the operating surgeon is very clearly in charge of the operation.

A third option exists: where members of different professions are in the team, but where no one profession inevitably carries prime responsibility for all the work done by a team. Such multidisciplinary teams may have either a management function or a clinical function—sometimes both. Clinical psychologists most commonly work in teams of this third type. Multidisciplinary teamwork is seen by some as impeding clear executive action, and by others as the only acceptable way for members of different professions to work together. In either case the issues raised are central to the way in which psychologists relate to members of other professions, and work with them.

Typically a clinical psychologist will be contributing to a multidisciplinary clinical team, where staff are appointed to or seconded to the team for all or part of their work. The activities of this type of team include: the acceptance, diagnosis, and assessment of new cases; the discussion of cases as a group; the determination of appropriate treatment; and the organization of follow-up after treatment. The key questions which immediately arise in such groups are: Who does what? Who is the leader? and Who is responsible for what? The allocation of tasks among members of a team is determined by a number of factors. Usually members of a team will contribute specific skills and knowledge derived from their particular professional training, and will have other more personal knowledge, such as knowledge of a particular locality or of a particular local voluntary group, which may be highly relevant to who does what with a particular patient. A psychologist working in a community learning disability team, for example, might be expected to contribute particularly to decisions on individual care programmes, and to the design of treatment programmes for specific behavioural problems. The British Psychological

Society (1988) has produced some very helpful guidelines on methods of team working.

The concept of a 'key worker' is becoming increasingly widely accepted, so that one person is designated as the main link or liaison with an identified patient, so that specific professional skills are seen as secondary to the development of a positive one-to-one relationship between key worker and patient. This principle is enshrined in the 'Care Programme Approach', which is a semistatutory procedure in Britain in mental health services to ensure that adults with severe mental illness living in the community remain in contact with treatment services. The 'practice assumptions' of a profession also dictate how work is allocated. Some professions, of which medicine and clinical psychology are examples, organize their work on the assumption that a patient expects to see one individual member of that profession exercising their professional skills during their episode of illness. While this is also true for community nurses, hospital nurses, on the other hand, are organized on an 'agency' assumption, so that nurses will change shifts and even wards during the course of a patient's illness.

As far as management teams are concerned, any health authority will lay down clear lines of authority, and should establish clearly where, in the last resort, responsibility for action lies. Management needs to be constantly reviewing service priorities, not least by interpreting data on the efficacy of different types of treatment, for example. Clinical psychologists obviously have a role in contributing to management in this way, and if they possess the confidence of their employers or colleagues they can appropriately be the chairpersons of such teams in, for example, planning a new type of service for people with learning disabilities, or can become managers or clinical directors of a range of services for mentally ill people, or become project managers.

Leadership of teams may be vested in a member of any professional group who possesses the relevant experience and knowledge. Sometimes leadership in such groups rotates among members according to a set pattern. Sometimes the appropriate leadership of a team may apparently be settled by appeal to the purpose of the team. The example of child community teams—teams of child psychiatrists, psychologists, psychotherapists, and social workers—illustrates how different professional orientations may then impose their own pressure on leadership questions. A health-centred orientation, stressing the child's health, suggests medical leadership; an educational orientation, suggesting classroom adjustment and attainment, might favour psychological leadership; a social orientation, emphasizing the effects of family and social conditions, might indicate social work leadership.

Yet the nature of work with disturbed children is such that for any group of children seen, some children will have presenting problems mainly in one sphere, others problems in another sphere. There is no uniform solution to leadership in such teams. What is certain is that as professions other than medicine—not only psychology—offer an increasing proportion of experienced and competent staff, so their involvement in the leadership of teams is bound to increase.

The title of teamwork is often applied to what is in reality a different style of joint working, which is better described as a network. In a number of settings, a professional will be in regular contact with members of other professions, but contact will be primarily by telephone or by letter. It is vitally important that communication is good between members of a network, as in a team; but in networks, the team as a whole often do not meet face to face. With the move to dispersed community services, health-care staff inevitably move away from the patterns of joint working produced by working on a common site, to patterns of working more resembling a network than a team. This carries with it the need for members of the network to meet together from time to time for supervision and support. If this shift is not recognized, staff may be left working with little personal support, with the associated risk of work dissatisfaction and loss of morale.

Since teams are groups of people, a number of findings of social psychology, particularly of the psychology of small groups, help to explain why teams do what they do. In any group there needs to be a balance between activities aimed at achieving the group's common objectives, and activities aimed at meeting the social and interpersonal needs of group members. Different group tasks require different levels of thinking and working, so that some group members will then be satisfied with one type of activity, while other group members will be satisfied by others. Team loyalties can become so strong that they supersede other loyalties or responsibilities that individual members should at least be bearing in mind, so that group tasks become subtley modified, and a team heads off in a direction different to that which was intended.

TEACHING AND TRAINING HEALTH-CARE PROFESSIONS

A major issue in meeting rising expectations of health care is how to teach effectively the skills, competencies, and knowledge required. This assumes in turn competent teachers, not only for basic training of the major health-care professions, but also for the ongoing in-house training of unqualified staff. It is a highly demanding task to design an educational programme that will produce a range of specific skills from groups of learners who are highly heterogeneous in ability and prior experience. Teachers in the health-care field need, for example, to be able to plan objectives relevant to local needs and to design curricula and plan instructional strategies to provide varied routes for achieving these objectives. They must also be able to evaluate their own teaching and consider such issues as teacher effectiveness. All of these activities presuppose some knowledge of the extensive educational and psychological literature on these topics. To take but one example, knowledge of educational evaluation techniques is important to any health-care professional who has to do any teaching. Evaluation of a teaching course is usually limited to some assessment of how much knowledge the student has acquired, largely because this type of assessment, involving some sort of set essay or factual questions, is easy to set up and use. In many situations competence at a skill is the desired outcome, whether it be a specific practical skill, such as learning how to take blood-pressure with a mercury sphygmomanometer, or a more complex interpersonal skill, such as knowing how to assess the risk of self-harm of someone who you are seeing for the first time.

Psychological knowledge is thus relevant to a wide range of teaching and training situations in a health-care system. More specifically, we can consider teaching and training members of other professions in psychological knowledge and skills-not forgetting the training of psychologists by members of other professions in *their* skills.

Teaching psychology to other professions

The demand for teaching of psychological topics from other professions is growing. The statutory training syllabuses for many health-care professions now require what may be dozens of hours of psychological teaching. Some syllabuses still imply that the best way to introduce psychology is by teaching a watered-down academic course on general psychology. This approach is nearly always inappropriate. Most trainees come to psychology expecting it to provide the answer to questions their discipline prompts, so a more appropriate introduction is to explore immediately, from a psychological viewpoint, practical problems the trainee encounters. These might include: how to prepare someone for surgery; how to assess the risk of a person being violent; or how to control pain. Most of these topics can be presented in a way that integrates theory with practice, and presents psychology as relevant to the trainee.

The boundary between 'the clinical psychologies' and related disciplines, such as ethology or anthropology, is sometimes unclear, and increasingly psychology is taught as one component in a 'behavioural sciences' course embracing these related disciplines, such as medical sociology. It is usually helpful for a clinically experienced psychologist to be involved in both planning and teaching such a course, working with other colleagues to offer a balanced programme.

Psychology does pose some problems, when deciding how to teach it. Many trainees in health professions come to the subject ignorant of the experimental aspect of the subject. Ask almost any group of health-care students to name a well known psychologist, and Freud will come top of the list every time. Some students come with what almost amount to fantasies about the subject, and attribute to the subject an explanatory power that is quite unrealistic. The attention paid to animal experimentation in some fields of psychology can be off-putting to some students, who may either see reference to animal studies as a reductionist account of human behaviour, or who may object to *all* animal experimentation on principle. For all these reasons, careful thought has to be given in planning the teaching of psychology to other professions, especially at the beginning of the course.

Training in psychological treatment skills

One important consequence of the development of treatment procedures by clinical psychologists is the acknowledgement that members of other professions may be fully capable of learning to use those procedures. Where demand for psychological treatments is high, there will be heavy demands upon the limited numbers of the most skilled staff, both to see the most complex cases and to train others. Skilled staff are thus a scarce resource, to be used strategically. A comprehensive review of clinical psychology practice in Britain (MAS 1988) suggested a three-tier model of psychological skills, which translates into a training strategy. Level 1 psychological skills are those which need to be possessed by all health-care workers; level 2 skills are specific but limited skills, as for example those used in a particular mode of psychological treatment; level 3 skills imply a comprehensive psychological knowledge, and will normally only be possessed by a qualified psychologist. Thus any staff capable of working at level 3 should concentrate their clinical work at that level, and should be enabling others to carry out level 2 or level 1 work.

Psychologists are also involved in training other groups of staff or would-be therapists in other types of skills. The range of skills is considerable, including: basic counselling skills; treatment of sexual dysfunction; psychological care of children in hospital; and educational techniques for severely handicapped children at home. The range of people so trained may also be wide, extending beyond family doctors and community nurses to parents, church workers, and voluntary workers in telephone help-lines and day centres. An example is the well-validated series of parenting skills programmes developed by Webster-Stratton (1997), aimed at families with conduct disorders, offering a structured series of teaching/learning sessions to parents in groups.

When a psychologist becomes involved in direct skill training a number of practical issues become important. Very often the learners have never read a psychological book in their lives, and need to acquire some sort of general psychological perspective along with the particular skills they are acquiring. Scheduling teaching or training sessions into the lives of often very busy learners means that considerable flexibility in fitting in the sessions may be needed, including, for example, sessions at 10 or 11 p.m. for night staff in a ward or hostel. Despite these demands and problems, many psychologists find this form of training to be one of the most stimulating areas of their work.

Most psychologists in Britain take the view that psychological skills can be usefully acquired by others. In view of the relatively small number of psychologists compared to doctors, nurses, and other therapists (let alone parents and spouses!) perhaps most clinical psychologists should be actively engaged in 'giving away' or sharing their skills alongside their continuing clinical practice, within the three-tier model of skills given above.

EVALUATING THE SERVICES PROVIDED

Other chapters have described some of the ways in which psychologists have evaluated the services they themselves provide. For most psychologists, such an evaluation of their own effectiveness, or the effectiveness of the particular unit or team with which they work, will be relatively limited in scope, and often concerned with outcome for the patient. There is now an increasing pressure for health-care services to demonstrate their effectiveness on a much broader scale, often under circumstances where close experimental control or manipulation of the service is impossible. A range of terms is used to describe this concern about effectiveness, including evidence-based health care, quality assurance, audit, and clinical standards. While some of these terms may differentially emphasize the views of users of the service, or the views of professional providers, they are all concerned with demonstrating the effective and efficient application of resources to identified problems.

This pressure to evaluate effectiveness derives from a number of sources. There is public concern about the extent to which the widespread discharge of patients with severe mental illness has not been accompanied by proper community provision. Government may be concerned that public money is used in the most cost-effective manner. Professions may themselves be aware that new patterns of service cannot be convincingly demonstrated to be superior to the old. A spreading interest in some so-called 'alternative' or non-conventional therapies is generating new techniques and services that also need appraisal.

Clinical psychologists have a number of contributions to make to evaluating services in concert with the other professions who provide them. One contribution is in identifying stated objectives for a service as a set of desired outcomes which are attainable, measurable, and sufficient to justify a programme. The objectives or desired outcomes should be stated in advance in such a way that relevant baseline or preintervention measures can be obtained. An evaluation should also turn away from what one profession alone might see as a desirable outcome, to those outcomes which might be desired by patients and by others, such as direct-care staff. This requires that all those groups contribute to the evaluation procedure, and that the results of the evaluation are comprehensible to all those who contribute. Evaluation reports then have to be readable by direct-care staff, not just published in scientific journals, and they have to be readable by the planners and managers who may have to make difficult decisions of resource allocation on the basis of those results.

Researchers often hope to find some single global outcome measure that encompasses everything of potential interest. 'Quality of life' is such a concept, used to supplement the usually simple but essentially rather arid measures of survival or cure rate relevant to some conditions or operations, such as stroke or coronary bypass surgery, where the patient may still encounter significant limitations of everyday activity. Any clinical intervention will, of course, only affect the function or behaviour to which it is directed, and while the quality of *care* may be improved, it may be rather grandiose to suggest that 'quality of life' will be affected by possibly a rather limited intervention. The concept of quality of life may thus need to be carefully defined, if in any particular study it is to be a valid and useful measure. In some fields of physical rehabilitation indices of Activities of Daily Living (ADL) have been used as global outcome measures. These are less relevant for people with a primarily non-medical disability, where more comprehensive indices, including information on social activity, are required. All of these more comprehensive measures raise issues of reliability, validity, sensitivity to bias, and utility under service conditions with which psychologists are likely to be familiar.

SUMMARY

Clinical psychologists work closely with a wide range of other professions and people. The significance of these other people to the life of the individual patient varies considerably—they may be making a highly sophisticated diagnostic decision, or they may be engaged in practical 'hands-on' care. There is a psychological component to most of the work they carry out. How does the first person to meet a new patient entering a particular service obtain the most significant information from the patient reliably and quickly? How can direct-care staff be helped to maintain an individualized and relevant care plans month in, month out? How can users of services remember the key facts about their high-risk condition so that they can self-treat themselves as effectively as possible in an emergency?

Current practice suggests that clinical psychologists have a number of key functions with respect to other staff in a number of different areas of health care, not just in the better known areas such as mental health and work with children. They can help to promote clear and uncluttered communication between everyone concerned with the individual patient. They can facilitate team working. They can be a resource of relevant psychological knowledge. They can work to help others acquire psychological knowledge and skills. They can support staff facing difficulties and stress in their work. They can help to ensure that the most effective treatments are chosen. Lastly, they can help to show that those treatments are effective.

References

Baum, A., Newman, S., Weinman, J., West, R. and McManus, C. (1997). *Cambridge handbook of psychology, health and medicine*. Cambridge University Press, Cambridge.

Beresford, P. and Croft, S. (1993). *Citizen involvement*. Macmillan, London.

British Psychological Society (1988). *Responsibility issues in clinical psychiatry and multi-disciplinary teamwork*. British Psychological Society, Leicester.

British Psychological Society and Royal College of Psychiatrists (1995). *Psychological therapies for adults in the NHS—a joint statement*. British Psychological Society, Leicester.

Butler, G. and Hope, T. (1995). *Manage your mind*. Oxford University Press, Oxford.

Chadwick, P.K. (1997). Learning from patients. *Clinical Psychology Forum*, **100**, 5–10.

Clinical Psychologists and Counsellors Working Together (1997). *Clinical Psychology Forum* (special issue) (eds R. Shillitoe and J. Hall), **101**, pp. 4–43.

Hall, J. N. (1996). Working effectively with clinical psychologists. *Advances in Psychiatric Treatment,* **2**, 219–225.

Hope, T. (1997). Evidence-based patient choice and the doctor-patient relationship In *But will it work, doctor?* (eds M. Dunning, G. Needham, and S. Weston), pp. 20–23. But will it work, Doctor? Group.

MAS (Management Advisory Service) (1988). *Review of clinical psychology services*. Management Advisory Service, Cheltenham.

Parry, G. (1990). *Coping with crises*. British Psychological Society, Leicester.

Tuckett, D. and Williams, A. (1984). Approaches to the measurement of explanation and information-giving in medical consultations: a review of empirical studies. *Social Science Medicine,* **18**, 571–580.

Webster-Stratton, C. (1997). Early intervention for families of pre-school children with conduct problems. In *The effectiveness of early intervention: second generation research* (ed. M.J. Guralnick), pp. 429–454. Paul H Brookes, New York.

Further reading

Davis, H. and Butcher, P. (1985). Sharing psychological skills: training non psychologists in the use of psychological techniques. *Br. J. Med. Psychol* (special issue), **58** (3).

Ham, C. (1994). *Management and competition in the new NHS*. Radcliffe Medical Press, Oxford.

Jaques, E. (1978). *Health services: their nature and organisation, and* the role of patients, doctors, nurses, and the complementary professions. Heinemann, London.

14

Overview and implications

John Marzillier and John Hall

In Britain fifty years ago, there were only a handful of clinical psychologists, working as technician scientists in psychiatric hospitals. Like physicists and biochemists they were 'backroom boys', whose contribution to health care consisted of highly specialized scientific investigations, mainly in the form of psychometric tests and investigations. In many other countries in Western Europe, clinical psychologists did not exist. Only in the United States, had clinical psychology any appreciable history and a developing professional identity. In the late 1990s, the picture is very different. Clinical psychology has become an established profession in most European countries, in the English-speaking areas of Australia, New Zealand, and South Africa, and in South America. Some countries such as Britain have seen a rapid increase in the number of clinical psychologists, particularly over the last decade.

Most importantly, as is illustrated in the chapters of this book, clinical psychologists are front-line workers in many spheres of health care. Clinical psychologists have had a practical impact in such diverse clinical fields as child health and working with older people, in pain management and neurological disability, and by their contribution to staff training. For many other health-care workers, psychological insights and skills have become important and sometimes central to health care.

The preceding chapters of this book have provided illustrative accounts of the practical working of clinical psychologists in various settings. In this chapter we describe some of the common themes that emerge from those working practices and tentatively discuss their implications for both clinical psychology and health care in general.

THEORY AND PRACTICE

Clinical psychologists have traditionally seen themselves as 'scientist–practitioners' or 'evaluator practitioners' whether their work is in teaching basic skills to people with learning difficulties, in carrying out intensive psychotherapy with disturbed adolescents, or in evaluating the success of a new day-care regime for older adults. What does the term 'scientist–practitioner' mean? In Chapter 1 we describe how the profession of clinical psychology is based upon a growing knowledge base (the science of psychology), and how the training of clinical psychologists entails using that knowledge for beneficial ends. The application of scientific and systematic knowledge is therefore a fundamental feature of clinical psychology, which distinguishes it from the practical 'common-sense psychology' that all of us use in everyday life. For example, in Chapter 4 we can see how knowledge of normal child development is essential to understanding when a particular behaviour becomes a significant problem. Understanding of the stages and processes of developmental change in young children enables the psychologist to assess a problem in its appropriate context and to tailor interventions to suit the developing child. The same point may be made for adults too, though the process of development takes place over a longer period of time and reflects social and cultural influences, as in the transition from young adult to parent or from worker to retired person. The importance of these longer-term developmental trends has been recognized in training by the requirement to study lifespan development as one of the core courses. Models of 'science' too are changing, so that psychology has itself grown by, for example, the development of more qualitative methods of research, alongside quantitative methods, and the increasing knowledge of brain and behaviour relationships through the new information provided by brain imaging techniques, as described in Chapter 7.

Scientific knowledge consists of facts embedded within theory, and psychology is driven by various, often competing, theories about human behaviour. Theories are vital. They are the lifeblood of our attempts to make sense of our behaviour. Clinical psychology has been influenced by several theories, notably theories about learning processes, and many have directly guided clinical practice. Cullen and his colleagues in Chapter 5, for example, describe how functional analysis, a method of assessment derived from learning theory, provides a productive way of helping people with learning disabilities. The behavioural treatment of anxiety illustrated in Chapter 2 arose directly from experimental studies of conditioning in the laboratory. Theories about the way memory operates in terms of different processes directly influence the memory retaining programmes that Carpenter and Tyerman use for the head-injured patients (see Chapter 7). The interplay between theory and practice is not simply a one-way relationship, but a reciprocal one. Studies of the way memory is disturbed in head-injury patients help psychologists understand more about the way memory normally works.

Theories and ideas derived from cognitive psychology have become increasingly influential in clinical psychology. Cognitive models and methods have come to dominate the psychological treatment of mental health problems such as anxiety, depression, panic, post-traumatic stress, eating disorders, chronic fatigue, and many others (Clark and Fairburn 1997). The basic tenet of the cognitive approach is that emotions, and concomitant emotional disorders, are mediated through the meanings and interpretations people give to their experiences. Currently, interest lies in uncovering the specific features of cognition and how they relate to various emotional states. For example Clark's cognitive model of panic, described in Chapter 2, is based upon specific misapprehensions of bodily changes (increased heart rate, feeling of faintness) which become locked into a cycle of increasing panic. Certain developments within cognitive psychology, such as modular processing and the variety of interacting processing systems, open the possibility of integrating different models of therapy. One example is Teasdale and Barnard's (1993) Interacting Cognitive Subsystems model, which postulates that mental activity reflects the collective action of nine specific subsystems, each with its particular function. Although each of these subsystems can contribute, directly or indirectly, to the experience of emotion, one subsystem, the *implication subsystem*, plays a key role. It integrates information from a variety of sources (sensory, proprioceptive, propositional), all of which are important in changing beliefs and emotions. The experiences of bodily changes, as occurs in some emotional focusing therapies, can be as important or more important than verbal methods such as cognitive and psychodynamic psychotherapy. In an exciting development Power and Brewin (1997) have brought together ideas from cognitive therapy, psychoanalysis, cognitive psychology, ethology, humanistic, and existential therapies to develop an integrationist approach to theory and practice in psychotherapy. Cognitive psychology provides a modern framework for the study of the dynamic unconscious, for example, linking psychoanalysis and cognitive constructs and methods.

The scientist–practitioner model also entails the application of *scientific principles* in clinical practice. The design of formal assessment measures (such as the neuropsychological tests described in Chapter 7, questionnaires used to assess specific problems such as delusions, and rating scales used to assess treatment outcome) involves the scientific procedures of item analysis, scaling, and factor analysis in order to produce assessment tools that are scientifically reliable and valid, and sensitive to change. Many other psychometric instruments or tests have been developed using similar scientific principles, such as the British Ability Scales for assessing the intellectual abilities of children. Attention to these scientific principles enables the psychologist to develop assessment measures that are free from gross errors such as bias, poor reliability, or invalid inferences, so that greater confidence can be placed in the results of the assessment.

The use of scientific principles is also evident in the systematic evaluation of treatment methods. This can take the form of clinical research trials, such as the evaluation of a cognitive intervention for panic disorders, or the careful assessment of individual cases. Data on the problem in question may be collected by means of a self-monitoring record (by observation, or by other means), before, during, and after treatment, thereby providing evidence on the extent to which change occurred. Research strategies suitable for the single case have been developed which give the clinician–researcher greater confidence in the validity of the treatment outcome, when large numbers of patients cannot be included in a treatment trial.

The 'practitioner' component of the scientist–practitioner model should not be overlooked. Working with clinical cases demands many practical skills. These range from the subtle, interpersonal skills involved in psychotherapy to the diplomatic skills required for working with other staff. These skills are acquired not so much from scientific principles and procedures, but as a result of practical experience. Clinical psychologists, like other professionals, can only be scientists to a degree. They must also learn to be creative and sensitive practitioners, and while some skills training occurs in professional courses, many skills are learnt from personal experience.

Psychology is about people

Underpinning the work of clinical psychologists in various settings is a fundamental concern with the rights and values of patients as people. As Garland states in his account of work with older people in Chapter 8: 'While old people do have some unique concerns, they are basically just people who have been around longer than us.' Cullen and his colleagues in Chapter 5 describe the 'normalization' philosophy which has been a major influence on work with people with learning difficulties, which implies that they should not be segregated from the community, but treated as equal members with equal rights and privileges. This may be all too rarely achieved. A similar argument can be made with respect to the care of adults with severe mental illness, where the philosophical ideas of providing care which is minimally restrictive have similar impact (see Chapter 3).

Concern about the rights and values of people can be found in different aspects of the work of clinical psychologists. It can be seen in the respect for the dignity and worth of the client in psychotherapy, where an open and non-judgmental attitude is adopted by the therapist and the client is able to discuss painful, personal concerns in an atmosphere of acceptance and trust. It is very much a part of the advocacy role which may be required with regard to the rights of disabled people and, as described by Blackburn in Chapter 9, with regard to offenders. It can be found in the need to protect children and young people from abuse and exploitation by parents and other adults.

This essentially ethical statement is also reflected in the view that most psychological problems are not different in kind from the problems all of us experience. For example problems of anxiety, depression, sexual difficulties, addictive behaviours, are part of a continuum, and are experienced by most of us. Recent research suggesting that experiences very similar to auditory hallucinations are reported by a proportion of adults with no other psychiatric symptomatology reinforces the view that we should first of all seek an explanation based on normal psychological mechanisms, before assuming that a pathological process is operative. Professional help may be sought when the problems become too intense or severe to be managed on their own, or cause too great a disruption to normal life. Even in cases where there is clear evidence of a biological deficiency (for example in some conditions leading to learning disability), a psychological approach will emphasize the commonalties with normal experience. People with learning difficulties have to learn skills like other people, following the same principles of learning. People with physical illnesses experience the normal psychological reactions to pain, trauma, and isolation that all of us experience from time to time. This is not to say that there are not unique or peculiar features to having learning difficulties, or being severely depressed, or in undergoing major surgery. But it is with the experiences and behaviour of *people* that psychology is ultimately concerned, and there is much to be gained from recognizing the continuity of such experiences across all conditions and problems.

ASSESSMENT AND INTERVENTION

The common clinical strategies of assessment and intervention are exemplified again and again in the various chapters of this book. Whatever the setting or whatever the population worked with, clinical psychologists are concerned to provide a thorough assessment of the problem, a psychologically-based method of intervention, and a systematic evaluation of the outcome.

(a) Assessment

Three important characteristics of assessment stand out. Firstly, assessment should be in response to a significant clinical question. In the past, clinical psychologists were sometimes asked to assess the patient's 'IQ', often without any real consideration of the value of such information. General practice in clinical psychology in Britain has changed to replace these essentially descriptive assessments by more practical and specific questions, the results of which will have a direct bearing upon the patient's clinical state. In the case of learning difficulties, for example, Cullen and his colleagues contrast an IQ assessment, which is of little practical use, with an assessment that seeks to understand why a child with learning difficulties might giggle and run away whenever she is asked a question. This type of information is of practical use, since the information can be used to help the child improve her communication skills. In the field of physical health a simple diary record sheet can be used to assess what factors provoke a woman's anxiety about chest pains and headache. Understanding the factors that lead to such anxiety (antecedents) can not only help us to understand it better but to plan methods of change.

This leads to the second major characteristic of assessment, which is that it contributes to an analysis of the factors that cause and maintain problems. This is known generally as a *functional analysis,* or as a *case formulation*, since it is concerned not merely with the description of the problem, but with the function it has for the patient in question and for the patient's family, and the way in which different predisposing factors may interact with specific 'trigger' precipitants. This type of analysis can be applied to very precise patterns of behaviour, such as the triggering of an aggressive outburst in a psychiatric resident, or to more complex psychological relationships. The successful treatment of problems such as depression, anxiety, and eating disorders depends upon a sensitive and careful assessment of how these problems relate to other important aspects of people's lives. If a person's self-worth is strongly determined by believing herself to be slim and attractive, then understanding that relationship is necessary for successful therapy.

It is precisely because a functional analysis provides information about the causes and consequences of a problem that it leads on to the third major characteristic of assessment, which is that it provides the basis for intervention. The information provided is useful precisely because it suggests ways of achieving change. Identification of different maintaining factors then implies that some modification of those factors will change the main problem of concern, which might be, for example, parental reactions to a child's sleeping problems (see Chapter 12).

Assessment is not simply confined to an individual and his problems. There are various levels of assessment; for example intrapsychic, interpersonal, social, institutional, familial, etc. In Chapter 3 Hall illustrates how assessment can be concerned with the characteristics of a residential care setting (in this case a psychiatric hospital), taking into account the behaviour of ward staff, administrators, and doctors, as well as the residents. Such an approach has sometimes been called a *systems* approach, since the assessment is concerned with the interaction between various systems. Thus a child's antisocial behaviour can be seen in terms of the relationships between him and his various family members or between him and his peers at school, each of which describes a particular system of interactions. Whether assessment is concerned with problems at an individual level or at a systems level, similar strategies will be found—namely the concern with a specific practical question, a systematic analysis of the various maintaining and causative factors, and the generation of specific treatment objectives.

(b) Intervention

Psychological interventions are concerned with promoting beneficial change using psychological procedures and principles. Much of this book is about change, which ranges from reducing confusion in elderly residents by means of reality orientation, to helping a sufferer from rheumatoid arthritis cope with the consequences of chronic pain. Although the specifics of treatment vary according to the type of problem and the population concerned, it is possible to identify several common features.

Firstly, clinical psychologists are very much concerned with teaching specific skills. It requires skills for a person with learning difficulties to learn to tie his or her shoelaces, and equally it requires skill for a diabetic child to learn a programme of managing their insulin intake, or a brain-damaged person to recognize the sounds and names of letters. Skills training draws upon some well-established procedures such as modelling or demonstration of the skill in question, repeated practice, informational feedback, reinforcement or incentives, and homework tasks.

A second common feature of interventions is the reduction of fear or anxiety. Cognitive–behavioural treatments of phobias and anxieties are described in detail in Chapter 2. Anxiety is a characteristic not only of psychological problems but also of many physical problems, where it can exacerbate the problem and delay treatment, and where the reduction of fear and anxiety has both physical and psychological benefit.

The third aspect of treatment that is worth noting is the emphasis on the role played by cognitive processes such as thoughts, attitudes, and beliefs. This is particularly evident in the treatment of depression by cognitive therapy, when people may have beliefs about themselves—that they never do anything of which other people approve, for example—or attributions about the impact of external events upon their lives, which are triggers for their patterns of mood change (see Chapter 2), but is applicable in other problem areas too. For example the motivation to overcome physical disability will be directly influenced by the extent to which the patient's attitude is positive and his or her expectations are realistic. Modifying beliefs similarly draws on well established methods, using external facts to challenge beliefs which are inconsistent with evidence of everyday living

Most patients are strongly motivated to seek change. They desperately want to overcome their problems or disabilities. In other cases, motivation is itself a problem, as is seen in the apathetic behaviour of the most severely mentally ill patients. Some psychological treatments are directly concerned with increasing the patient's motivation for change, as in token economy programmes described in Chapter 3. In psychological terms, motivation is not some predetermined state or personality trait, but a product of the various factors that maintain and cause behaviour. The successful treatment of addictions will, in part, depend upon the person's ability to create and sustain strong incentives for change to counteract those of the addiction in question, as discussed in Chapter 10.

In psychological terms, interventions are concerned with four major processes: the change in *behaviour,* such as the acquisition of certain skills; the change in *emotions,* such as the reduction of fear or anxiety and the elevation of depressive mood; changes in *cognition,* such as the modification of attitudes and beliefs; and *environmental* change. In the latter category, more attention is paid to the controlling factors in the person's environment. These factors may include the physical environment in which the person lives—such as the facilitating and enabling effect of having lifting equipment in the home for someone with severe limitations of muscular strength—and the social environment, such as the attitudes of the immediate family towards someone with a history of domestic violence.

RESEARCH, EFFECTIVENESS, AND EVALUATION

(a) Research and effectiveness

The single word 'research' covers a number of different functions or tasks. They usually refer to the process of conducting a research project—of *producing* research. The tasks include the formulation of the initial research question, which may be of the form:

- Which of these two treatments will be best for this individual patient?
- Has this patient benefited as much as they will ever do from this treatment?
- Will it be more efficient in terms of staff time to treat these six patients with similar problems individually, or as a group?

When at least the initial question is reasonably clear, the potential researcher will begin to read the relevant literature:
What else has been done in this field?
They will consider:

- What outcome measures would be most appropriate?
- How many patients should I include in the study?
- What statistics should I use in interpreting the data collected?

While all of these questions are sensible, from a clinical point of view perhaps the most important question is the potential impact of the proposed study upon clinical practice. This means that the results of the study must be useable by others, in the sort of real-life clinical setting where such patients are normally seen. The value of a study is then seen in the way in which others—not the researcher—critically appraise the research from their point of view, and decide to put the research findings into practice. But if the original study, let us say a study of the effectiveness of a brief cognitive treatment for severe anxiety in a primary care setting, was carried out in suburban Leiden in the Netherlands—a prosperous University town—would the results be applicable in a deprived, industrial, urban area in the British Midlands? The only way to check that would be to carry out an outcome study in the British setting, using the same outcome measures as used in the initial study.

Rather than rely on the results of one study only, it would obviously be sensible to see what other similar studies have been carried out in other countries. Meta-analysis is a method of combining the results from several different but similar studies together, so that since the size of the patient sample is then greater, there is a greater probability of any differences being significant, and also the methods shows how stable the treatment effect is across different settings. Meta-analysis can only be helpful if there are clear criteria for which studies have been included. Rosenthal (1995) puts forward a powerful argument that meta-analysis is the most appropriate method to cumulate the findings of psychological research, and that the approach renders obsolete a number of traditional statistical procedures commonly used in psychological research. The studies included may only be those which have been published, but scientific journals tend not to publish negative or non-significant findings, so published articles may inflate the apparent treatment effect. Given that any researcher can only be fluent in a limited number of languages, the studies reviewed may not include those published in minority languages, even though the studies may be of high quality.

What all of these points lead to is the realization that the implementation of research into clinical practice—the *consumption* of research—requires just as much skill as the conduct of the study in the first place. This realization has led to the approach called evidence-based medicine, or evidence-based health care. This approach requires that the best available evidence for the treatment of any given condition should be systematically reviewed, and that clinical practice should be based on those treatments with the best proven effectiveness. A number of 'Cochrane Centres' now exist within an international World Health Organization-sponsored network, each of which prepares systematic reviews on particular common conditions—for example the international centre for systematic reviews on the effectiveness of treatments for schizophrenia is based in Oxford, and employs psychologists in doing this work.

This does not mean that the double-blind, randomized, controlled trial reigns supreme as the only research method of value. That would deny the need for initial exploratory research into new methods—the creative aspect of research. It would also ignore the fact that for some psychological treatments especially, true blind trials are impossible, since both the patient and the therapist are fully aware of what treatment is being used. What it *does* mean is that where reasonable evidence does exist that one intervention is more effective than another, that should be preferred.

This apparently simple principle is contributing to a revolution in the way in which health care is being delivered in some countries, most obviously in the United States, where what is known as 'managed care' is transforming health-care practice. In the United States, the main organizations funding health care, known as Health Maintenance Organisations (HMOs), impose strict limits both on the number of sessions a psychologist can offer a patient and on the duration of any hospital admission which is needed. This is having a major impact on psychological practice, leading to the search for briefer and more effective treatments which will be funded under these regulations. Both the HMOs and the professional bodies concerned are issuing clinical practice guidelines (Nathan 1998), which may either be true guidelines, in the sense of offering non-prescriptive guidance, or they may dictate precisely what a given therapist may do. In Britain, with a publicly-funded health-care system, a similar pressure is apparent, illustrated by the Government's announcement in 1998 of a national body for clinical excellence in the NHS, which will be given powers to ensure that health authorities commission services based on the best available evidence.

All of these changes are driven by a number of factors. Cost is one of them—as the costs of health care rise greater than the cost of living, so any funding agency will be concerned to contain costs. Increased public concern about the quality of health care is another factor, which itself is fuelled by the increasing availability of good information on effectiveness, which in turn arises from developments in information technology and data collection created by professional health-care researchers. Together these factors have transformed the need for all health-care staff to be able to appraise research themselves, and to implement research findings in their local setting. This constitutes a major opportunity and challenge for all psychologists in the health-care system.

(b) Evaluation and quality

This emphasis on research implementation goes alongside a continuing emphasis on the audit and evaluation intervention programmes. Evaluation approaches specify in advance the goals of treatment and, by then monitoring the attainment of those goals, see directly whether treatment has or has not been successful. It is also possible to include aspects of evaluation other than outcomes, such as the acceptability of planned interventions to users. While the concept of service evaluation is well established, a number of other terms—such as quality assurance, audit, standard setting, peer review, and consumer satisfaction—are used with varying degrees of precision to describe related ideas and procedures.

Evaluation can occur at different levels, and with respect to different criteria and measures. A model for evaluating psychotherapies, for example, could embrace the interests of the client, of the professional, and of society. Clients are primarily interested in personal changes, such as reduced distress and increased happiness. Professional staff will view change in terms of the theoretical model underlying their interventions—so that some therapists would regard changes in specific symptoms as of less value than changes in beliefs. From society's viewpoint, therapies are valued in terms of social norms and standards, to the extent that they reduce 'problems' that are socially visible, such as people who are both homeless and mentally ill.

Ideas of quality—quality assurance, quality of care, quality of life—are perhaps the most important after ideas of service evaluation. Definitions of components of quality look rather similar to the components of an evaluation study—referring to effectiveness and efficiency, for example—but in addition components such as accessibility and equity tend to be added. Accessibility describes the ease of access to a service—this is determined not just by the distance from home to clinic, but by the cost of travel (including parking charges) and by the average waiting time at the clinic. Equity describes the extent to which a service is available to a population in need of a service, irrespective of age, sex, income, or employment status. Quality assessment also takes account of the passage of the client through the total episode of care, in the course of which the client will be seen by members of different professions, may be seen on several different sites, and may require fundamentally different types of service—a diagnostic service, a rehabilitative service, and perhaps terminal care. The emphasis on quality essentially takes the view of the consumer of the service more seriously, and assumes a more multidimensional perspective towards effectiveness.

The different levels of evaluation are important, since not only do they contain different perspectives and values, but the type of evaluation determines what measures are used. Financial considerations can result in a concern with gross measures of change, such as how many people are admitted and discharged from a hospital, or assessing the efficiency of a treatment service in terms of numbers of people treated in relation to staffing. The problem with these measures is that they do not reflect either the client's perspective (being discharged from hospital need not result from psychological improvement) or the professional's perspective. Knowing the logistics of a therapeutic service tells us nothing about its quality and aims. Concern with evaluation therefore is not simply with cost, effectiveness, and efficiency, although these will be important, but with psychological change from the perspective of both client and therapist.

WORKING WITH OTHERS

Day-to-day practice of clinical psychology inevitably results in close contact with other people. This is illustrated in the many examples of collaborative work in the various chapters of this book. In Chapter 13, Hall discusses the different forms such collaboration can take and some of the issues arising out of it.

The most common form of collaboration is that of joint work on clinical cases, in which the specialist skills of psychologists combine with those of nurses, health visitors, physiotherapists, doctors, and other professionals. Psychological assessments and interventions combine with the work of physiotherapists and occupational therapists with brain-damaged patients. Health visitors and psychologists can effectively combine in group treatment for parents of sleep-disordered preschool children. In these and other examples successful collaboration depends upon mutual sharing of specialist skills and knowledge. This is of benefit not only to the patient but also to the different professionals, who in this way will learn about each other's particular contribution. Collaborative work is particularly valuable, since so many problems are multidimensional. The nature of work in intensive care units indicates the value of monitoring and treating patients' psychological states—in particular their anxieties—which may inhibit their response to prescribed medical treatment such as exercise. There are also ways in which various aspects of physical treatment may have adverse psychological effects, as when the technology of modern obstetric medicine can interfere with the mother's emotional response to her new baby.

In addition to collaborative work, there is a clear role for psychologists in training and supervising others in procedures informed by psychological principles. Recently a distinction has been made between training and 'consultancy'. Training implies an explicit objective of the transfer of knowledge and skills, and the systematic creation of a training programme or regime to attain those objectives. Many psychologists are already involved in training others in psychological skills, such as counselling and cognitive therapy. In doing this it is important that those being trained are not only given a thorough training in practical skills, but they should also become familiar with the psychological perspectives and theories that underlie those skills. The best training courses involve fairly lengthy and thorough training in both theory and practice.

Consultancy, on the other hand, implies a structured response to a particular presented problem, where the psychologist formulates the problem psychologically, and then guides and supports the people in direct contact with the person-with-the-problem, offering them the psychological knowledge and skills necessary for that particular presented problem. Consultancy is usually time limited, and does not lead to another trained person, but is a time-efficient way to make the best use of limited psychological time.

A consultancy model of working is advantageous in its own right—a substantial proportion of the problems encountered by, say, a community psychiatric nurse will not need the specialized skills of a clinical psychologist or psychiatrist; but nurses will be better able to help their clients by the availability of consultancy. However, it is undeniable that this model of working has been stimulated by the continuing shortage of clinical psychologists.

In the first edition of this book, a national vacancy rate for clinical psychologists of 14 per cent for England was given, and in the second edition a 22 per cent vacancy rate in 1990 was quoted. With the advent of NHS Trusts it is no longer easy to establish overall vacancy rates, but the shortage continues. Expansion of training depends crucially upon adequate supervised placements, so there are limits to the extent to which training can be quickly expanded. There is in fact a shortage in Britain of staff in several health-care professions, including nurses, occupational therapists, and psychiatrists, and similar constraints upon rapid expansion of training apply to them. Thus there is a concern shared with other professions in making the most effective use of limited human resources. Although other some other European countries may be overproducing some groups of health-care staff, there is little likelihood of mass migration in the numbers required to correct these shortages.

FUTURE PRACTICE AND CHALLENGES TO CLINICAL PSYCHOLOGY

It is possible to discern several trends in practice that give some hint as to how clinical psychology is developing. We have already referred to some of these—notably the increasing application of psychological methods in various health fields and the increasing emphasis on collaborative work with other professional groups. Four other features are also evident: changing models of health and medicine, the rise of other applied psychology professions, the move to community care, and the challenge of long-term disability.

(a) Changing models of health and medicine

A traditional view of the health service is one in which doctors assisted by nurses apply their skills and expert knowledge to treat illnesses. While this is a large part of modern medicine, it has become increasingly obvious that illness and disease will never be eradicated by technological medicine alone, that much of ill health is a product of the social and environmental conditions in which people live, and that many of the most notable improvements in health have come about as a result of societal change. Diseases such as typhoid fever, cholera, and rickets were virtually eliminated in Western countries by changes to sanitation and improvements in material conditions. Poverty is still a major determinant of ill-health, as a glance at the disparities in health between First and Third World countries will confirm. Even in the relatively affluent United Kingdom, those who live at or below the poverty line are much more vulnerable to illness and premature death. Illness therefore cannot be seen simply as an individual's misfortune; health is in a large part a social and economic concept.

The socioeconomic dimension of health and disease has mostly bypassed the attention of health professionals, including clinical psychologists. This may be because it is seen as a 'political' issue, and therefore touches uncomfortably upon the many inequities that govern our lives in general. However, this situation is rapidly changing. The spiralling costs of health care have resulted in a radical restructuring of the health-care system in Britain and America, introducing 'internal markets' whereby different sections compete for often scarce resources. One result has been to make the disparities in health much more visible, as well as forcing professionals to confront the socioeconomic issues that underlie clinical practice at all levels. How can comparisons be made between better care for long-term mentally ill patients, on the one hand, and the care of AIDS sufferers on the other? Should resources be directed to more sophisticated (and expensive) technology for cardiovascular surgery or to a programme of health promotion to prevent the onset of coronary heart disease? These decisions—which had always been implicitly made—are now openly debated, because their economic basis is manifest. Clinical psychologists, like other health-care professionals, cannot afford to ignore the debate: their very existence is threatened by the implications of the decisions taken by managers and others. Some NHS clinical psychology services, for example, have already been privatized in an effort to reduce health-care costs. The politicization of the professions is an inevitable result of increasing social and economic pressures on health care.

Another area of fast-growing awareness is that of environmental factors in health and illness. Over the last decade, media attention has been focused on world-wide disasters such as famine, earthquakes, political oppression, war, enforced migration, flooding, oil spills, and nuclear accidents. It is impossible to ignore the massive effects that are produced by such disasters, not only at the point of impact but across the globe. At a related level there is growing concern about the damage inflicted on our environment by the consequences of our industrially-fuelled, consumer-led way of life. There are direct and indirect effects on health of acid rain, nuclear waste, urban decay, and motorway expansion programmes amongst other things. The 'greening' of our society is only a small beginning in the process of social change that is necessary not only for improved health but for the continued existence of the planet. A model of health that ignores the environment is just not possible.

There is a growing public interest in health and medicine. Scepticism about the value of many medical treatments has been fuelled by well-publicized examples of apparently effective treatments proving to be ineffective and sometimes harmful. The consumer of health care is forced more and more to follow the old legal adage, *caveat emptor* ('let the buyer beware'). The use of tranquillizers for the treatment of anxiety is a good example. Recognition that barbiturates were highly addictive drugs led to their replacement by benzodiazepines, which were hailed as revolutionary, non-addictive, and harmless. However, in the 1980s, it was belatedly acknowledged that benzodiazepines were also capable of producing dependency, and moreover could, with chronic use, lead to permanent effects on the brain (Catalan and Gath 1985). Tens of thousands of people who have become dependent on these drugs felt betrayed by their doctors; some have initiated legal action against the drug companies that made the tranquillizers. In this climate of scepticism and uncertainty consumers have been turning more to alternative medicine (alternative to conventional medicine) and to 'complementary medicine', which coexists with conventional medicine. There is a belief that such medicine is safer, more environmentally friendly, and less likely to be subject to economic pressures. The emphasis on a *holistic* model (i.e. one that sees mind and body as inextricably linked) is also attractive: too often modern medicine has concentrated on physical change at the expense of psychological care.

Models of health and medicine are therefore in flux. Social, environmental, and economic factors on the one hand underline the importance of large, external, world-wide influences on health, which are difficult for the individual to control. On the other hand, the consumer is anxiously seeking greater knowledge and control over his or her own health, being aware of the need to take active steps to avoid illness and ensure good health; the continued emphasis on a healthy 'lifestyle' is an example of this concern. The conflict can produce its own problems. Anxieties about potential hazards to health are increasing, such as worries about HIV infection and their impact on Western societies.

Where does clinical psychology fit into this picture? In physical health the importance and value of taking psychological factors into account needs to be stressed, not only in terms of a holistic approach to the individual but in the planning and management of the health system as a whole. Some clinical psychologists have taken steps into management and thereby taken the opportunity to apply psychological concepts and principles to health care at a different level. It remains to be seen what impact they may make.

At a more specific level, the contribution of clinical psychology to health could take a number of forms. Firstly, more individual assessment and treatment programmes could be developed, for example for stress management for those at risk for coronary heart disease, for counselling services for actual and potential AIDS sufferers, and for psychological help for the terminally ill and their relatives. Secondly, there could be an expansion in the numbers of psychologists able to offer counselling and consultation services in general hospitals, and thereby to begin to influence the way health care is delivered in those settings. This would conform to the wider role for clinical psychologists envisaged in the MPAG report on clinical psychology in Britain. Thirdly, there is a powerful role for psychology in the promotion of health, advising on the strengths and limitations of strategies for changing lifestyle, for example. Fourthly, there is still a paucity of good research on psychology and health; too many ideas are put forward without attention to proper understanding or careful evaluation. Finally, clinical psychologists, like other health-care professionals, will need to be much more active in lobbying governments to take a broader view of health and to recognize that resources are essential at all levels of health care.

Clinical psychology is a small profession within a changing health-care system. How may it respond to the challenges that these broad issues throw up? One way is through the recognition that psychological help is not just about assessing and treating damaged or ill individuals. The systemic approach, illustrated at various points in this book, points to the importance of social systems in determining and maintaining psychological problems. Family therapists, for example, see a child or adult's problems not as something internally generated, but as a response to forces within the family (see Chapter 4). Change is sought systemically. Similarly, Western society is a system in which psychological problems are embedded. An unemployed single parent in high rise, poor quality housing in an area of drug abuse and high crime may well be depressed, anxious, and addicted to instant and unhelpful 'solutions', such as drinking, smoking, and the lottery. Should clinical psychologists seek to change this person's behaviour, mental state, and cognitions? Or would it be better if social, environmental, and political changes were more actively sought, as some critics of the profession have argued (e.g. Pilgrim 1997)? This is not a new dilemma, and it is one that is relevant to all forms of health care. A better lifestyle would reduce the chances of coronary heart disease, but should we stop cardiac surgery? It is a matter of balance. It may be that in the 30 years over which clinical psychology has come of age in the United Kingdom, there has been too much emphasis on individual care, and not enough on systemic and neighbourhood analyses and solutions.

(b) The rise of other applied psychology professions

In the past decade, two other professional psychology groups in particular have flexed their muscles in the market place, *health* psychologists and *counselling* psychologists. How do these two groups relate to clinical psychologists? How does their work differ?

In Chapter 11, Fielding and Latchford describe clinical health psychology, which they define in terms of the work of clinical psychologists in general medical settings. This is an extension of the way clinical psychologists work in other settings, such as staff training, consultancy, and organizational change. The skills and knowledge of clinical psychology are brought together to bear on psychological problems arising in a general hospital such as St James in Leeds. But their chapter also illustrates the value of a *non-clinical* approach to health care, for examples problems that arise in the delivery of health-care services. This is what is meant by *health psychology*. Many aspects of medicine, from the training of medical students to the way health-care staff communicate, are fundamentally influenced by psychological factors. Health psychologists show how attention to psychology, in terms of both theory and practice, can greatly influence health care. A recent comprehensive textbook demonstrates the huge amount of knowledge that there is already in this field (Baum *et al.* 1997). Health psychology has become a specialty in its own right. Although many health psychologists are clinical psychologists who have gone on to specialize in health care, as both Dorothy Fielding and Gary Latchford have done, a more direct route is available. Postgraduate courses in health psychology now exist which enable psychology graduates to train directly as health psychologists. A Division of Health Psychology was created within the British Psychological Society in 1997. What this will mean is that posts within the NHS which in the past might have been seen as suitable for clinical psychologists alone may now be taken by health psychologists. Given the shortage of clinical psychologists this is a healthy development as it brings more psychologists into the health system as well as providing a training that is specifically geared to the issues and problems of health care. A disadvantage is the potential loss of the clinical approach, although this will depend on the ways in which health psychology practice evolves and health psychology training is organized.

Counselling psychology shows a similar pattern of development. In the past, psychology graduates in the United Kingdom who wanted to work therapeutically with individuals and groups would have to train as clinical psychologists, apart from the very few who trained to work as child psychotherapists. This excluded a large number of psychologists, because each year nine out of ten applicants to clinical psychology courses are turned down: there are simply not enough training places. At the same time there was a strong movement to improve the more psychotherapeutic training of psychologists, which is limited in clinical psychology courses where so much else is covered. The British Psychological Society has developed a 3-year Diploma in Counselling Psychology, the completion of which would lead to Chartered status as a counselling psychologist, with eligibility to join the Division of Counselling Psychology within the Society. University courses to match this standard also exist—the demand for places on the City University, London, course now matches the demand for clinical psychology places. The training is intensive in both theory and practice and has a strong emphasis on acquiring specific therapeutic skills. In addition, a programme of personal development is a required part of training. Thus counselling psychologists completing the Diploma have become proficient in the enterprise of psychological therapy, an obvious asset when applying for many posts. A possible disadvantage is the loss of the broader base of clinical experience that underpins clinical psychology training, which has been seen as its strength over the years.

There seems little doubt that as long as clinical, health, and counselling psychology remain separate branches of applied psychology, there will be competition from the graduates of different courses in applying for jobs in the NHS. Given the shortage of trained psychologists, this is not a problem. However, some countries such as the Netherlands and America already train more psychologists for health work than can be employed there. As illustrated in Chapter 2, clinical and counselling psychologists can work very effectively together to provide a more comprehensive and flexible service in adult mental health. The same is true for clinical and health psychologists in general medical settings. It will be interesting to see how the applied psychology professions can work together, doubtless not without some territorial clashes, over the next decade.

(c) Community care

There has been a strong trend towards the provision of community care for mentally ill people, older adults, and people with learning difficulties. This has arisen partly from a positive concern to make services more accessible to the communities they serve, partly from concern about the standards of care and accommodation in older institutions, and partly out of financial reasons, since the rundown of such hospitals was seen as leading to savings in terms of both labour and capital costs. In many areas, clinical psychology services have moved in part or wholly 'into the community', both in terms of the place where they do their clinical work, and in terms of the organizational framework within which they work. One immediate question arises—what constitutes appropriate community care?

One important objective for community care is that treatment facilities should be as accessible as possible for the person in need. In this way existing community support such as family and friends can remain in contact, especially during crisis periods. A second objective is that there should be organizational collaboration between different professional and voluntary agencies. This permits greater continuity of care and the possibility of preventing minor problems turning into major ones. Thus a vital feature of community care is the establishment of close links between secondary care specialists, such as psychologists, and primary care staff. There is a need too for the various specialist groups to work together to avoid duplication of skills and contradictory advice and practices. The practice in Community Learning Disability Teams, in which specialists take a consultancy role in relation to the activities of front-line workers such as care workers, is one example of how a community service can be developed. In addition to providing psychological advice and supervision, a clinical psychologist can contribute to a community care programme by working closely with the different groups or teams. This might entail, for example, the setting up of staff support groups or training groups whose function would be to improve communication and provide a forum for the sorting out of interprofessional problems.

While there may be benefits for users of a community service, it does not follow that staff also benefit. A move to community work not only involves the acquisition of new skills, but also changes working practices that may have significant psychological effects. While there is limited information about the psychological problems and stresses of a transition to community care, community-based nurses and others are relatively isolated from their own professional group, and may miss out on the informal support and management communication which goes on in larger settings.

The ideal of care in the community, however, needs to be tempered with the realities and limitations of both local receptivity and health service practice. The closure of large mental hospitals in Britain, Italy, and other parts of Europe has led to some seriously ill and vulnerable patients being left without any form of proper care. Whatever the benefit to the many who have moved to a settled life in a normal house and street, others have ended up wandering the streets or languishing in prison cells. The community does not always care, as is shown in the opposition of local people to the establishment in their neighbourhood of psychiatric hostels and homes for disabled people. The NIMBY phenomenon ('not in my back yard') does not only apply to the dumping of nuclear waste.

In Britain, social services are funded from a different budget from that of the health service. It has therefore been seen as financially beneficial to hard-pressed health service managers to close down expensive hospitals, releasing much-needed cash from the sale of often valuable land, and to transfer care of the long-term mentally ill to the local authority. Local authorities, however, have also been severely cash limited. In this situation, successive British governments have explored ways to bridge the gap between the two systems of funding, by special funding mechanisms such as 'Mental Illness Specific Grants', and by considering the establishment of joint agencies for all mental health services. The result of this confusion has been an inevitable failure to provide the hostels and staff to care for those who are mentally ill or in need of long-term support.

Another issue has been the changes to the management of the health service in the United Kingdom, whereby there is a split between *purchasers,* now called *commissioners,* on the one hand, whose role is to buy health care from hospitals and other resources, and *providers* on the other, who contract to provide the services. This 'internal market' has highlighted the costs of the various services, and has brought in an element of competitiveness between different service providers. Because resources are finite, and opportunities for generating further income are in practice limited, the internal market has led to a squeeze on both community provision and hospital provision, both of which are at risk of being curtailed as managers desperately strive to maintain basic health care out of inadequate budgets. There are now proposals to include family doctors more closely in the commissioning process, and to reduce the competitive element in the service contracts which are agreed.

For clinical psychologists, community care is a more satisfactory way of delivering psychological services to many groups of people: the service is brought closer to the individual; the model of care is less medical; there is opportunity for local communities to take on more responsibility for the care of their members; professionals can work closely with local groups and thereby disseminate their skills and expertise more widely; and preventive and educational measures can be implemented more easily. But if resources are not adequate, and the appropriate structures not put in place, community care will not be successful, and those most in need will suffer enormous deprivation.

Movement to a community care model is by implication a move away from an institutional care model, so that it can be simplistically seen as a pendulum slowly swinging on a unidimensional axis. In that sense, the pendulum in many parts of Europe has swung as near to the community care end as is practicable. A need remains for some centralized resources, especially for the most disabled, and to offer respite for families for whom care is a heavy burden. Indeed, there are now calls in Britain for an increase in institutional provision, if only for more semisecure provision for those severely mentally ill who are considered to be at risk to themselves or to others. Community care is multifaceted, and is defined not only by care in the community, but by closer links between primary and secondary care services, and by an emphasis on early intervention.

(d) The challenge of long-term disability

The application of psychology to health care should reflect the health problems and needs of a population. If that population and those needs change, then the priorities of the health-care system should also change. Kaprio (1979) pointed out a decade ago that

> Europe is becoming healthier, death rates are falling, and patterns of need are changing . . . Pathological conditions determined by a combination of genetic, environmental, and behavioural factors are beginning to dominate the health scene and intrude into family and community life.

This places great emphasis on the notion of need for care, a topic that has only recently attracted the attention of psychologists. A key article by Bradshaw (1972) differentiates between: normative need—as expressed by a professional; felt need—where need equals want; expressed need—felt need turned into action; and comparative need—where need is perceived to exist in members of a population because others with equal need receive a service. Need is often expressed as someone X needs Y for purpose Z, when the nature of Z is itself often obscure. The related concept of dependency draws attention to the person's lifespan experience of receiving support and help as a determinant of care elicitation. Developing formal means of need analysis may be a major psychological contribution to long-term care.

Clearly increasing attention needs to be paid to the health-care needs of the increasing numbers of people of all ages who have a disability. There is a growing population of young adults with non-degenerative but irreversible handicaps with considerable expectation of life, who require specialized help to adapt to their disabilities. The development by the WHO of a classification of Impairment, Disability, and Handicap, to match the classification of disease, is indicative of the growing significance of chronic disability in health care. Psychological adaptation to disability, both by the person with the disability as well as by families and carers, is thus of increasing importance.

Changed patterns of family life also have an effect on the care of those with chronic conditions. The increasing proportion of single-parent families, and of families where children have had successive different parents through divorce and remarriage, is likely to reduce the amount of support available to a child within such families. The greater availability of work outside the home for women, and the greater proportion of older people with fewer children to look after them means that care for older people within their own families is less likely to be available. This suggests an increased need for information and guidance to families with a handicapped member, to enable them to cope better and longer with the relative, and exploring ways to encourage men to become carers.

Clinical psychologists have not traditionally been concerned with care—as opposed to cure. Recently there have been a number of comments on the need for psychologists to adopt a more ameliorative or rehabilitative model of intervention, accepting in so doing that positive treatment does not always work—and may be viewed as a failure. Several aspects of care stand out as demanding attention from psychologists. What psychological processes are involved in the vigilance, risk taking, and decision making of care? How is care elicited and terminated, and what features of the cared-for elicit care? Why do people want to care when there is no pre-existing emotional or social attachment to the other? Since one in four of the readers of this book are likely to require care at some time in their lives, simple self-interest alone suggests we look at some of these questions (Hall 1990).

INTERNATIONAL TRENDS IN THE DEVELOPMENT OF CLINICAL PSYCHOLOGY

Clinical psychology as a discipline varies in some aspects of orientation and structure from country to country. It is instructive to compare developments within Europe to the present position within the United States, traditionally seen as the 'market leader' in clinical psychology. In those European countries where a number of psychologists are available for employment, the main areas of employment tend to be health, education, correction, and employment/vocational guidance. Psychologists may also be employed in applied research units, and by the public services and armed forces (such as the police and army) to assist with training, support at times of stress, and equipment design.

There are a number of organizational changes affecting British and European health and professional psychological services, including changing United Kingdom policies on the funding and structure of health-care agencies, and EC changes in the acceptability of professional qualifications. Jansen (1986), in reviewing common trends in five European countries regarding mental health and social welfare policy, points out the shared emphasis in the countries studied on adequate social support systems, on integrated health-care systems and on support of the co-ordinated care system by a social welfare system which allows for community-based care. Thus there are a number of political assumptions shared by European countries relevant to the delivery of publicly-funded psychological services.

In 1991, article 27 of the Treaty of Rome of 1957 was implemented (by EC Directive 89/48/EEC), which provides for the mutual recognition of professional qualifications in member states. The existence of the EC directive will give a powerful thrust towards increasingly common procedures in licensing and certification of psychologists in public services. The EC regulations will both force and encourage clinical psychologists in Europe together more, and there is likely to be more interchange of psychological knowledge within the EC. This is facilitated by the European Federation of Professional Psychologists Associations (EFPPA), which co-ordinates the work of the different national organizations, and is now preparing common statements about different areas of applied psychological work. All of these moves have the capacity to create a professional psychological community potentially large enough to challenge some of the implicit assumptions of the American psychological community, which ever since the

'Boulder' Conference of 1948 has guided clinical psychology internationally.

Meanwhile, the position of clinical psychology in the United States has not remained static. Moghaddam (1987) has suggested that there are three worlds of psychological research and practice: the first consists of the United States alone, the second comprises the 'other developed nations', and the third the developing nations. Moghaddam goes on to suggest that the traffic of psychological knowledge has mostly been one way—from the first world to the second, and from the first and second to the third, even though 'there are few important ideas of contemporary psychology that are North American in origin'. This analysis suggests that European countries may have imported psychological ideas from the first—the American—world of psychology, which are not necessarily those most relevant to their needs, or consistent with their political and social values and institutions.

What gives an added edge to this view is the impact that managed care is having on the practice of clinical psychology in the United States. Bobbitt, Marques, and Trout (1998) have reviewed the implications of managed care for the profession, and conclude that managed care is likely to be a long-term feature of American funding arrangements, and carries with it a probability of reduced funding for 'routine individual psychotherapy'. There has also been an expansion of private professional schools of clinical psychology in the United States—not affiliated to any University. Given that not all of schools are accredited by the American Psychological Association, and that there are not now enough accredited internship placements for the graduates of these programmes, there is now an oversupply of clinical psychologists, not all of whom are trained to agreed standards, who are in direct competition with other therapists. This only illustrates starkly the point that any profession has to both respond to and assertively engage with changes in the wider environment, and that we need to continually re-examine what psychology is best suited to the needs of public services.

SUMMARY

Clinical psychology has developed very rapidly as a profession, both numerically and in the range of client problems that are now presented for treatment. A continuing interplay between theory and clinical practice has meant that new areas of psychological research and theory have become of practical significance. The continuing concern of psychologists with assessment has been modified to emphasize those aspects of behaviour and experience more directly related to client problems and treatment. The growing range of effective psychological interventions has increased the interest of both clients and other professionals in them, leading to an important growth in collaboration with and training of other professionals.

Public views of health and illness are changing, and the health needs of the public are changing. Part of that change is a readiness to look at non-medical forms of help, and to take more personal responsibility for health care. The practice of clinical psychology supports both of these changes, and offers many useful concepts and procedures to assist them.

References

Baum, A., Newman, S., Weinman, J., West, R. and McManus, C. (1997). *Cambridge handbook of psychology, health and medicine*. Cambridge University Press, Cambridge.

Bobbitt, B. L., Marques, C. C. and Trout, D. L. (1998). Managed behavioral health care: current status, recent trends, and the role of psychology. *Clinical Psychology: Science and Practice*, **5**, 53–66.

Bradshaw, J. (1972). A taxonomy of social need. In *Problems and progress in medical care* (ed. G. McLachlan), pp. 71–82. Oxford University Press, Oxford.

Brewin, C. (1988). *Cognitive foundations of clinical psychology*. Erlbaum, London.

Catalan, J. and Gath, D. (1985). Benzodiazepines in general practice: a time for decision. *British Medical Journal*, **290**, 1374–6.

Clark, D. M. and Fairburn, C. (1997). *Science and practice of cognitive behaviour therapy*. Oxford University Press, Oxford.

Hall, J. N. (1990).Towards a psychology of caring. *British Journal of Clinical Psychology*, **29**, 129–4.

Jansen, M. A. (1986). Mental health policy: observations from Europe. *American Psychologist*, **41**, 1273–8.

Kaprio, L. A. (1979). *Primary health care in Europe*. WHO Regional Office for Europe, EURO Reports and Studies No. 14, Copenhagen.

Moghaddam, F. M. (1987). Psychology in the three worlds. *American Psychologist*, **42**, 912–20.

Nathan, P. E. (1998). Practice guidelines: not yet ideal. *American Psychologist*, **53**, 290–9.

Pilgrim, D. (1997). Clinical psychology observed (reprise and remix). *Clinical Psychology Forum*, **107**, 3–6.

Power, M. and Brewin, C. (1997). *The transformation of meaning: integrating theory and practice*. Wiley, Chichester.

Rosenthal, R. (1995). Progress in clinical psychology: is there any? *Clinical Psychology: Science and Practice*, **2**, 133–49.

Teasdale, J. D. and Barnard, P. J. (1993). *Affect, cognition and change: re-modelling depressive thought*. Erlbaum, Hove.

Further reading

Powell, G., Young, R. and Frosch, S. (eds) (1993). *Curriculum in clinical psychology*. British Psychological Society, Leicester.

Rutter, D. R. and Quine, L. (ed.) (1994). *Social psychology and health: European perspectives*. Avebury, London.

Glossary

Adherence. Term finding favour as an alternative to compliance, used to denote the extent to which a patient follows the course of treatment suggested by their doctor. It is often thought to imply that this is more of a collaborative process than the previous term.

Advocacy. Pleading, defending, or interceding on behalf of another. In psychological usage, refers to advocacy on behalf of handicapped or disable people (such as people with learning difficulties) to enable them to have access to a range of benefits within the complex welfare, social care, and health-care systems, and to improve the quality of those systems as used by them.

Agoraphobia. From the Greek 'fear of the market place'. Characterized by fear of being away from a place of safety, usually the home. Low self-esteem and excessive dependence on others are features.

Alternative and complementary medicine and psychologies. Non-traditional theories and techniques of disease and treatment, such as osteopathy and aromatherapy. The terms are often used interchangeably, although strictly alternative medicine refers to medical practices which are not acceptable to conventional medicine, while complementary medicine refers to practices which are compatible with (and not infrequently themselves practised by) conventional medicine. Alternative psychologies are based on a variety of doctrines and philosophies, often including elements from psychodynamic schemes of thought, neurophysiological studies, mystical or esoteric philosophies, and so-called 'unexplained' phenomena.

Amnesia. Disruption of memory processes, either partial or total, including memory loss and impairment of new learning.

Anger management. A programme of treatment designed to help people understand and control their feelings of anger. Developed by the psychologist Novaco it is a skills training approach in three stages (monitoring anger experiences, acquisition of adaptive behaviour, and role play in simulated anger situations).

Anorexia nervosa. Loss of weight usually due to persistent fasting or excessive dieting. Amenorrhoea is also common, as are fear of fatness and disturbed body image. Almost entirely found in girls and younger women.

Anxiety. Feelings of apprehension and unease in response to real or imagined threat. Anxiety consists of: *physiological reactions,* such as increased heart rate, sweating, and trembling; *behavioural responses,* such as avoidance; and *cognitive disturbance,* such as worrying thoughts or frightening fantasies. There are a variety of clinical anxiety states, for example generalized anxiety and phobic anxiety.

Anxiety-management training. The use of behavioural treatments of anxiety in the form of a skills training approach. Anxious patients are directly taught methods of managing their anxiety such as relaxation and planned practice, either individually or in a group.

Applied behaviour analysis. Applied behaviour analysis is the application to problems of social importance of the concepts and methods associated with the philosophy of science known as radical or operant behaviourism. Behaviour itself is its fundamental subject matter, and it is not an indirect means of studying something else, such as cognition or mind or brain.

Assessment.
Behavioural: psychological measurement procedures which focus on the behaviour which is to be treated, or which is likely to change, at the time it occurs and without making any assumptions about underlying causes or variables.
Psychometric: psychological measurement procedures which measure assumed traits or characteristics, typically involving comparison of the patient with appropriate norms, and often conducted in a face-to-face assessment setting.

Assisted conception. The term used to describe a number of different medical procedures which help couples who are otherwise unable to have children.

Autogenic relaxation/ autogenic training. Self-initiated, imagery-based method of relaxation.

Backward chaining. This is a process whereby a task is broken down into its components and the final link in the chain of components is taught first. This is then followed by reinforcement. When the person is able fully to complete the final component the penultimate component is taught, and so on back to the beginning of the chain.

Baseline. An assessment, or the results of an assessment, carried out before treatment has started and normally continued until the measure is stable or steady.

Behaviour therapy. Method of psychological treatment developed in the 1950s, derived from experimental studies of conditioning and learning. The focus of treatment is on overt behaviour, using psychological principles to achieve specific behavioural goals. Often contrasted with **psychodynamic** psychotherapy, where the focus is more on achieving insight or personality change.

Between-groups design. An experimental design where two or more different groups are studied, one receiving the experimental treatment and the other(s) receiving control or comparison treatments. In some such designs all groups receive all treatments, but in a different order.

Biofeedback. The process of learning to control the autonomic body functions using visual or auditory cues.

Biopsychosocial model. This is a model that recognizes the reciprocal relations among the biological, psychological, and social aspects of health and illness. In this model the onset, cause, and treatment of physical illness are best understood as involving each of these levels of analysis. It is a conceptual framework rather than a unifying theory.

Bulimia. Disturbance of eating characterized by excessive preoccupation with food—a pattern of binge eating and self-induced vomiting or laxative abuse. Occurs mainly in young women of slightly older age-range than anorexics. See **anorexia nervosa.**

Case-management. The provision of a single person or team to assume responsibility for long-term care and support to a client, regardless of where the client lives or which agencies are involved. The case manager must work in the community, sometimes intensively, and serves as a helper, service broker, and advocate (see **advocacy**).

Child abuse. Serious physical, mental, or sexual assault, neglect, or exploitation of a child, by implication referring particularly to that initiated by someone (well) known to the child. Includes intentional acts of omission as well as repeated excessive violence and incest; being subject to abuse may lead to profound disturbance in later adulthood.

Cholesterol. A fatty substance found in animal cells and body fluids, it is known to crystallize along the walls of arteries and is thought to be implicated in heart disease.

Chronic. Long term or lasting. For example chronic pain is used to refer to pain which persists after healing has taken place and serves no useful function.

Client-centred therapy. Developed by Carl Rogers in the 1940s, CCT aims to help clients explore their feelings in the context of a warm, empathic, and trusting relationship. Therapy is seen as personal growth rather than treatment, and the approach eschews specific techniques or procedures.

Clinical psychology. The application of psychological theory and practice to a broad range of problems—mental and physical—for which people seek help.

Cognition. A general term to cover all aspects of knowledge—perceiving, thinking, imagining, reasoning, etc. Contrasted with affect or feeling. It is maintained by some that all emotions are cognitively processed and by others that emotions are at times directly experienced.

Cognitive–behavioural therapy. Describes the combination of behaviour therapy and cognitive therapy in which, generally, behavioural procedures are used to change cognitive processes. It is a more liberal form of behaviour therapy in the recognition paid to thoughts and beliefs in understanding and changing psychological problems.

Cognitive therapy. The prime focus is on patients' thinking processes, with the goal of changing distorted or unrealistic thoughts and beliefs. Methods vary from Socratic argument to behavioural procedures.

Community psychology. The application of psychological theory and practice to people living in natural communities, and to the problems encountered by people in that setting.

Compliance. The process of following a treatment prescribed by a doctor.

Conditioning. The process by which a particular response comes to be elicited by a stimulus, event, or object other than that to which it is the natural or reflexive response.

Classical conditioning: the association in time of a neutral stimulus (for example a bell) with a reflexive stimulus (for example food) so that a conditioned response (for example salivation) occurs to the neutral stimulus.
Operant conditioning: the process by which behaviour is modified by systematically varying its consequences (rewards and punishments).

Constructional approach. A constructional approach is one which deals with a person's problems by establishing new behaviours or by re-establishing behaviours which have been lost. It avoids focusing on the removal of behaviour by whatever means. The 'constructional question' would be 'if you didn't have this problem, what would you be *doing,* what would you be like?' A constructional approach gives particular recognition to how a problem first occurred or developed or is maintained.

Control group. A group of patients or people in all respects similar to the main group, except that they are not subjected to the treatment or condition that is being experimentally investigated.

Coping. An adaptive way of dealing with stress or threats.

Coping skills training. A problem-solving approach which first identifies cues and high-risk situations leading to temptation or relapse. Then alternative ways of dealing with these high-risk situations are systematically explored.

Counselling. A helping relationship in which the counsellor seeks to enable the client to explore his or her concerns and to find ways of resolving them. Counselling is a form of psychological treatment, although generally its focus is on less disturbed clients and it often takes place in non-medical settings, for example student counselling.

Cue exposure. An approach to psychological treatment which involves deliberate exposure to those cues or high-risk situations which provoke desire or compulsion. Prolonged repeated exposure, whilst at the same time resisting temptation, leads to a gradual reduction in desire.

Depression. Feelings of sadness and hopelessness, and lowered bodily activity. Clinical depression is characterized by a reduction or increase in appetite, disturbances of thought and movement (these usually being slowed down or occasionally agitated), lethargy, poor concentration, feelings of guilt and self-blame, and general loss of interest in previously enjoyed activities.

Diabetes. A chronic disorder in which insulin, a hormone which is essential in breaking down carbohydrates in the body, is either not produced or not utilized properly. Diabetes can be controlled, but not cured.

Dysphasia. Disruption of speech or language processing.

Educational psychology. The application of psychological theory and practice to educational methods, and to problems encountered by people in the educational process.

Evaluation. The process of finding the value of a treatment, by formally determining whether it is effective, efficient, and acceptable, in achieving predetermined objectives.

Event-sampling. A behavioural assessment technique where only a proportion of the key events are observed thoroughly, although all events are recorded; this technique is particularly appropriate for complex key events demanding very detailed observation.

Forensic psychology. Psychology as applied to the legal process; sometimes also used generally to describe the application of psychological theory to the assessment and treatment of offenders.

Functional analysis. The analysis of the relationship between a key event, and the preceding, concurrent, and following events, to see if there is any association between them. If such an association is found this functional relationship can be used to develop a treatment strategy.

Goal planning. A systematic approach to setting goals, specifying who will do what, under what conditions, and to what degree of success.

Haemodialysis. In patients with kidney failure, the process of removing blood from an artery, purifying it, and returning it to a vein.

Health belief model. Developed by Becker, initially to predict whether people engaged in preventative health behaviour such as attending screening, but later applied to a wide variety of health settings.

Health psychology. The application of psychological theory and practice to the beliefs, behaviour, and experience of people relating to their health, both when they are well and when they are ill.

Hypertension. Abnormally high blood pressure.

Hypnosis. An altered state of consciousness in which the hypnotized person responds to external suggestions allowing events to be experienced as if they were actually occurring. It has been successfully used as an anaesthetic and analgesic in selected subjects, as a form of psychotherapy, and it has been closely studied by experimental psychologists.

Intelligence. General mental ability and specialized abilities such as numeracy, verbal reasoning, and perceptual skills. There is a long-standing controversy over the extent to which general intelligence (called G) exists over and above a variety of specialized abilities. The Intelligence Quotient (IQ) describes a way of measuring intelligence using psychological tests.

Learning. The process by which knowledge and behaviour are acquired and understood. *The laws of learning* refer to basic principles formulated by psychologists in the scientific study of learned. behaviour. *Learning theory* describes the body of theoretical knowledge on the processes involved in learning.

Learning disability/intellectual impairment. The following definition has been proposed by the American Association on Mental Retardation in December

1990. '[Learning disability] is manifested as significantly sub-average abilities in cognitive functioning, accompanied by deficits in adaptive skills. These deficits in adaptive skills may occur in one or more of the following areas: communication, self-care, social skills, functional academics, practical skills, leisure, use of community, self-direction, work, and independent living. Adaptive deficits often coexist with strengths in other adaptive skills or other areas of personal competence.'

Meta-analysis. A statistical method used to evaluate the results of large numbers of outcome studies and arrive at a figure that summarizes the overall effect (effect size). It has become the preferred method of assessing outcome in psychotherapy.

Milieu therapy. A method of psychotherapy that arose in the context of institutional care of psychiatric patients. The total environment or milieu, including staff and patients, is designed to be a 'therapeutic community', conducive to the patients' psychological welfare and recovery.

Morbidity. The nature and frequency of specific mental or physical conditions in the population, often expressed as the number of contacts or notified cases for every 1000, say, of the population.

Motivational counselling. An approach to counselling which emphasizes a supportive, empathic relationship, a non-confrontational approach, exploration of the benefits of behavioural change, and helping a client to make choices about coping strategies and alternative activities.

Needs, and need analysis. In experimental psychology a need refers to a deficiency or lack in terms of a postulated goal, which may be physiological. It has acquired a secondary meaning in clinical psychology practice, referring to a lack of appropriate clinical service for a person with a health-care problem. Need analysis consists of formally establishing the needs for psychological and health care of a population or an individual, examining normative, felt, expressed, comparative, and met and unmet need.

Neuropsychology. The study of the relationship between brain structure and pathology, and behaviour and experience.

Normalization. The use of culturally normative means to establish, enable, or support behaviours, appearances, and interpretations which are as culturally normative as possible (compare **social role valorization**).

Obsession. Irrational idea or thought that persists against one's will. Often accompanied by ritualistic, compulsive behaviour. Common obsessions are of checking, contamination, and harm to oneself or others.

Personality. The integrated organization of the physical and psychological characteristics of an individual, including intelligence, emotionality, and social behaviour, in the way that the individual presents himself to others. *Personality traits* describe general characteristics of the individual, for example impulsive, social, taciturn, etc. *Personality, types* describe major patterns of personality, for example introvert, neurotic.

Personality disorder. A pattern of deviant or extreme personality traits relating to beliefs and feelings about the self and others and control of behaviour that impairs the person's social functioning. *Antisocial personality disorder* is the form most commonly identified among offenders and violent people. Other forms, such as *borderline* or *avoident personality disorder*, are common among people seeking help for social and emotional difficulties.

Phobia. Intense fear and avoidance of harmless events or objects. There are a variety of specific phobias, for example of insects and animals, and also social phobias and **agoraphobia.**

Post-traumatic amnesia. The interval following a brain assault between the time of injury and the reinstatement of continuous day-to-day memory.

Post-traumatic stress disorder (PTSD). A syndrome or set of presenting problems arising as a consequence of the experience of an unusual, sudden, and major threat or distressing event, such as serious harm to oneself or one's close family, or sudden destruction of one's home. The consequences may include intrusive distressing recollections of the event, recurrent distressing dreams, persistent avoidance of places and stimuli associated with the event, and persistent symptoms of increased arousal, such as disturbed sleep.

Processes of change. Part of a model of change developed by psychologists Prochaska and DiClimente in analysing the way people seek to change well-established behaviours such as smoking. Processes include *raising awareness* and *self-liberation* which are linked to particular **stages of change**.

Progressive muscular relaxation. A widely used method of relaxation based upon repeated contraction and relaxation of muscle groups. Often used as part of **anxiety management**.

Prompts, physical and verbal. A prompt is help given to a person so that they may complete a task. A verbal prompt is essentially an instruction or some spoken help; a physical prompt is manual guidance.

Psychoanalysis. A method of psychological treatment, developed from the work of Freud, which focuses on the uncovering of unconscious conflicts by predominantly verbal means. Significant features of psychoanalysis include free association, interpretation, and the development of transference, whereby strong emotional feelings experienced in other relationships are 'transferred' to the therapist. Classically a lengthy and intensive therapy lasting several years, although briefer and less intensive forms have also been developed.

Psychodynamic. A term derived from psychoanalytic theory, describing the interplay of mental and emotional forces and the way these affect behaviour and mental state.

Psychopathic disorder. A medico-legal category in the 1983 Mental Health Act for England and Wales in which abnormally aggressive or seriously irresponsible behaviour is attributed to 'a persisting disorder or disability of mind', usually interpreted in practice as a personality disorder. The term should be distinguished from the clinical concept of *psychopathic personality*, which describes a more specific form of personality disorder characterized by callous, egocentric, and impulsive traits, and which is similar to *antisocial personality disorder*.

Psychotherapy. General term for any treatment by psychological means designed to reduce personal distress, raise morale, or help solve personal or social problems. Sometimes used to describe verbal methods of therapy in contrast to **behaviour therapy,** although this distinction is not consistently used.

Psychotropic. A term used of drugs with an effect on psychological function, behaviour, or experience. The term can cover a wide range of substances, but is usually taken to refer to those drugs most frequently used in psychiatry (for example major tranquillizers or antidepressants).

Punishment. Describes the way the probability of a response is reduced by the presentation of an aversive consequence.

Questionnaire. A list of questions seeking information about a person's attitudes, knowledge, or traits, often self-administered, and thus easy to use, and often used for surveys.

Rating scale. A list of questions or statements about a person which are judged or rated, typically by another person (the rater) about the extent to which they occur. The observation or rating procedure is usually well-defined.

Regional secure unit (RSU). A medium-secure health service facility for disruptive psychiatric patients and mentally disordered offenders. RSUs were set up in the English and Welsh regions following the recommendations of the Butler Committee in 1975 as a complementary facility to **Special Hospitals.**

Rehabilitation. Procedures for helping disabled patients to return to society after illness and to maximize their general functioning. It is applied both to institutionalized psychiatric patients being returned to community settings and to physically handicapped people being helped to recover from or adapt to their disability.

Reinforcement. Describes the process in operant conditioning by which a response is strengthened by its consequences. *Positive reinforcement* describes the strengthening of a response by presenting a stimulus (for example a reward). *Negative reinforcement* describes the process of strengthening a response by taking away an aversive or unpleasant stimulus (for example by the removal of loud noise or shock). Not to be confused with **punishment.**

Reliability. The extent to which a measurement procedure gives consistent or closely similar results when applied more than once, under similar conditions, to the same person or group. When the measure is applied by two or more different users (or raters or testers) the degree of consistency or similarity is a measure of interuser (or -tester) reliability.

Renal failure. Condition in which the kidneys, which remove toxic substances from the bloodstream, fail to work. It can be either reversible (acute renal failure) or progressive (chronic), leading to complete loss of functioning (end-stage renal failure).

Repertory grid. A psychometric assessment method developed from George Kelly's personality theory which seeks to describe the way people construe their world.

Rheumatoid arthritis. A chronic disease of unknown cause characterized by inflammation of the arteries, particularly in smaller peripheral joints, which causes varying degrees of pain, stiffness, swelling, and joint deformities in sufferers.

Room management. Room management is a system of a number of clients may be influenced by two or three staff members. The system whereby the behaviour involves designating specific roles for the room manager (such as ensuring that materials are available for all clients and that crises are dealt with) and an individual helper (whose job is to move around the room systematically prompting clients to work with materials).

Schizophrenia. A major psychiatric disorder characterized by disturbances of thought, flattened, or inappropriate emotions, delusions, and hallucinations, usually in the form of imagined voices. Tends to occur in young adults in acute form, and can become chronic.

Self-monitoring. Assessment procedures that involve people in recording their own behaviour by suitable charts or diaries, or by suitable physiological devices.

SF–36. This is a short version of a battery of questions used in the medical outcomes study in the United States. It covers a range of areas, including physical and social limitations, pain, mental health, and health perceptions, and is increasingly used as a measure of health status and treatment outcome in the United Kingdom.

Single-case designs. An experimental design where one person receives a series of treatments or conditions in a carefully planned sequence, with some conditions possibly repeated (but where the sequence minimizes the effect of early conditions on later conditions).

Social role valorization. Enhancing the social role of people or groups of people at risk of being socially devalued. There is an important distinction between the valorization of the role of the person, and the value of the person themselves.

Social skills training. The use of didactic procedures of modelling, role-playing, and feedback, to train people in 'social skills'. 'Social skills' refer to specific features of social behaviour that result in successful interaction. These range from specific non-verbal behaviours, such as eye contact or gesture, to complex patterns of interaction.

Special Hospital. A maximum-security hospital for patients whose violent or criminal behaviour is deemed to require treatment under conditions of special security.

Stages of change. A number of stages are involved in behavioural change according to Prochaska and DiClimente. In the precontemplation stage, no changes are planned in the near future. The contemplation stage covers that period when costs, benefits, and ability to cope are being reappraised. In the action stage positive steps are being taken. During the maintenance stage vigilance is still relatively high, in an attempt to prevent relapse. (See also **processes of change**).

Statistical analysis. The process of subjecting a number of figures to a particular manipulation (which may include correlation, analysis of variance, calculation of means) essentially to condense the figures to show some central characteristics and measures of spread of the data. The *statistical significance* of the results is the probability that the result could have been achieved by chance, or by random allocation, and is conventionally expressed at probability levels of 5, 1, or 0.1 per cent (or as 0.05, 0.01, or 0.001).

Stimulus control. Stimulus control is the extent to which an antecedent event influences the subsequent occurrence of a particular behaviour. It is measured as a change in response probability that results from a change in stimulus value. The greater the change in response probability the greater the degree of stimulus control with respect to the continuum being studied.

Stress. *Either* unpleasant aspects of the external social and physical environment *or* the subjective response of the individual to threats and challenges arising from that environment.

Stroke. A rupture or disruption in the blood supply to the brain, leading to a variety of symptoms depending on the area of the brain affected, and the extent of tissue damage.

Tests.
Attainment: sets of standard questions or items designed to measure specific achievements or attainments, such as reading, and distinguished from the measurement of more general abilities.
Intelligence: sets of standard problems and materials designed to measure maximum general mental ability, or power of learning and understanding, and typically yielding an intelligence quotient (IQ).
Personality: either sets of standard questions relating to a person's own distinctive character, or normal mode of functioning, scored to yield measures of different personality traits; or sets of *projective* materials which are essentially ambiguous or neutral in meaning, the responses to which are assumed to reveal underlying traits or characteristics.

Time out. Withdrawal of positive reinforcement for a particular behaviour (for example shouting, fighting) by taking the individual out of the environment where such behaviour is being reinforced. Often used in managing aggressive behaviour in children and adolescents.

Time-sampling. A behavioural assessment technique involving observation of the patient or setting for only a proportion of the total time possible, by observing according to a predetermined schedule of random or systematically chosen times, thus giving a representative sample of observations.

Transtheoretical model. Developed by Prochaska and DiClemente, it is a complex model of the change process, identifying three different dimensions of change: levels, stages, and processes. The stages of change are the most well known feature, and the model has proved extremely influential, initially in the field of addictions, but latterly in a variety of other areas, including health.

Validity. The extent to which a measurement procedure assesses what it is supposed to assess. This somewhat circular definition may be clarified by distinguishing between face or content validity—the extent to which inspection of the form or content of the procedure shows it is appropriate; and empirical validity—the extent to which the procedure is consistent with the scores derived from another totally independent measure of the same phenomenon.

Index

entries for tables and figures in italics